The Eurasian Way o

This book is a comparative study of military practice in Sui–Tang China and the Byzantine Empire between approximately 600 and 700 CE. It covers all aspects of the military art from weapons and battlefield tactics to logistics, campaign organization, military institutions, and the grand strategy of empire. Whilst not neglecting the many differences between the Chinese and Byzantines, this book highlights the striking similarities in their organizational structures, tactical deployments, and above all their extremely cautious approach to warfare. It shows that, contrary to the conventional wisdom positing a straightforward "Western Way of War" and an "Oriental" approach characterized by evasion and trickery, the specifics of Byzantine military practice in the seventh century differed very little from what was known in Tang China. It argues that these similarities cannot be explained by diffusion or shared cultural influences, which were limited, but instead by the need to deal with common problems and confront common enemies, in particular the nomadic peoples of the Eurasian steppes. Overall, this book provides compelling evidence that pragmatic needs may have more influence than deep cultural imperatives in determining a society's "Way of War."

David A. Graff is Associate Professor of History at Kansas State University, USA. He is the author of *Medieval Chinese Warfare, 300–900* (Routledge, 2002) and co-editor of the *Journal of Chinese Military History*.

Asian States and Empires
Edited by Peter Lorge
Vanderbilt University

The importance of Asia will continue to grow in the twenty-first century, but remarkably little is available in English on the history of the polities that constitute this critical area. Most current work on Asia is hindered by the extremely limited state of knowledge of the Asian past in general, and the history of Asian states and empires in particular. *Asian States and Empires* is a book series that will provide detailed accounts of the history of states and empires across Asia from earliest times until the present. It aims to explain and describe the formation, maintenance and collapse of Asian states and empires, and the means by which this was accomplished, making available the history of more than half the world's population at a level of detail comparable to the history of Western polities. In so doing, it will demonstrate that Asian peoples and civilizations had their own histories apart from the West, and provide the basis for understanding contemporary Asia in terms of its actual histories, rather than broad generalizations informed by Western categories of knowledge.

The Eurasian Way of War

Military practice in seventh-century
China and Byzantium

David A. Graff

LONDON AND NEW YORK

First published 2016 by Routledge

2 Park Square, Milton Park, Abingdon, Oxfordshire OX14 4RN

711 Third Avenue, New York, NY 10017

Routledge is an imprint of the Taylor & Francis Group, an informa business

First issued in paperback 2017

British Library Cataloguing in Publication Data
A catalogue record for this book is available from the British Library

Library of Congress Cataloging in Publication Data
Names: Graff, David Andrew, 1962- author.
Title: The Eurasian way of war : military practice in seventh-century China and
    Byzantium / David A. Graff.
Other titles: Military practice in seventh-century China and Byzantium
Description: New York, NY : Routledge, [2016] | Series: Asian states and empires ; 11 |
    Includes bibliographical references and index.
Identifiers: LCCN 2015040244| ISBN 9780415460347 (hardback) |
    ISBN 9781315627120 (ebook)
Subjects: LCSH: China—History, Military—221 B.C.-960 A.D. | China—History—Tang
    dynasty, 618-907. | Military art and science—China—History—To 1500. | Military art
    and science—Byzantine Empire—History. | Strategic culture—Case studies. |
    Byzantine Empire—History, Military. | Byzantine Empire—Military policy. |
    Byzantine Empire—Foreign relations. | China—Foreign relations—Asia, Central. |
    Asia, Central—Foreign relations.
Classification: LCC DS747.43 .G72 2016 | DDC 335.009495/09021—dc23
LC record available at http://lccn.loc.gov/2015040244

ISBN: 978-0-415-46034-7 (hbk)
ISBN: 978-1-138-47720-9 (pbk)

Typeset in Times New Roman
by Swales & Willis Ltd, Exeter, Devon, UK

Contents

Preface

This history has a rather long history of its own. It was back in 1990, during the early stages of my Ph.D. program at Princeton University, that I first became aware of the parallels between Chinese and Byzantine military writings thanks to a tangential comment in Peter A. Boodberg's much earlier doctoral dissertation (University of California, 1930) dealing with the *Questions and Replies between Tang Taizong and Li, Duke of Wei* (*Tang Taizong Li Weigong wen dui*), a revered Chinese military classic that is probably a forgery dating from the Five Dynasties or early Northern Song. Intrigued by Boodberg's observations about the similarity between the Byzantine *cursores* and *defensores* and the offensive and defensive tactical roles described by Li Jing (571–649) in the surviving fragments of his authentic writings preserved in the late eighth-century *Tong dian*, I began to read the few Byzantine military texts then available in translation and to devote more and more attention to the Li Jing materials. The original nucleus that would eventually grow into this book took the form of a paper I presented at a graduate student "coffee hour" in Princeton's Department of East Asian Studies during the academic year 1991–1992.

Although I set the Byzantine comparison aside to focus on other problems in my doctoral dissertation, I was drawn back to it again in the early 2000s after the publication of my first book, *Medieval Chinese Warfare, 300–900*. Professor Jeremy Black, the series editor for that volume, encouraged me to highlight military comparisons between China and the early medieval West (including Byzantium), and in a book review published in the *Journal of Asian Studies* Professor Kenneth M. Swope challenged me to further develop the comparative angle. Also encouraging in this regard were my contacts with Professor Tsang Shui-lung (Zeng Ruilong) of the Chinese University of Hong Kong, who had been drawn to Song–Byzantine military parallels just as I had been attracted by the similarities between the Tang military and its Byzantine counterpart. I first met Professor Tsang at a conference at Academia Sinica in Taipei in December 2000, and we were both scheduled to present papers at the 2003 conference of the Chinese Military History Society at Marist College in Poughkeepsie, New York. My paper compared the Li Jing fragments with the *Strategikon*, a military manual of the same era conventionally attributed to the Byzantine emperor Maurikios (or Maurice), and I was looking forward to receiving comments and suggestions from Professor Tsang. That was not to be, alas, due to his sudden and untimely death only a few days before the conference.

By that time, I had already chosen an examination and explication of Tang–Byzantine military similarities as the focus of my second book project. This was due not only to the influences already mentioned, but also to my experience as a relatively new faculty member at Kansas State University, in one of the very few history departments in North America with a strong emphasis in military history. One of the topics of animated discussion among junior faculty and graduate students was the notion of a "Western Way of War" that had been put forward by Victor Davis Hanson and others, and it was not long before I realized the significance of my own research as a partial test of Hanson's thesis. Some of the main ideas and arguments of this book were first sharpened in conversations with friends and colleagues, most prominently Professor Michael A. Ramsay, over mugs of stout at the only brew pub in Manhattan, Kansas. I accomplished most of the initial research during a sabbatical leave during the academic year of 2004–2005, but I did not manage to finish the book in a couple of years as I had originally planned. Others, such as George T. Dennis and Edward N. Luttwak, kept publishing books that I had to read and, in addition to the daily grind of teaching and administrative responsibilities, life has also had a way of intervening. I began this project a year before I met my wife, Guizhen Luo, and was already four years into it when our son William—now eight—was born.

As is all but inevitable with a work this long in gestation, there have already been numerous previews in conference papers and published articles. The list of presentations begins with the 2003 conference of the Chinese Military History Society (May 10) and goes on to include the Second Annual Agnes Chen Memorial Lecture at Haverford College (November 3, 2003), the 2005 annual meeting of the Association for Asian Studies (Chicago, March 31–April 3), a presentation to members of the History Department of Peking University during a brief stint as a visiting scholar in April 2005, a Phi Alpha Theta lecture at Hastings College in Nebraska (February 13, 2006), the New York Military Affairs Symposium (May 4, 2007), the 2010 Dumbarton Oaks spring symposium on "War in the Byzantine World" (April 30–May 2), the 2011 annual conference of the Society for Military History (Lisle, Illinois, June 10), and the 2014 annual conference of the Chinese Military History Society (Kansas City, April 4). Along the way, my thinking about this project has benefited from the questions and comments of many listeners, with those from Rob Babcock, Paul Jefferson, Edward N. Luttwak, Jonathan Karam Skaff, and You Zhanhong being especially worthy of mention. Any problems that remain are, of course, entirely my own responsibility.

Portions of this book, especially Chapters 3 and 4, build upon my 1995 doctoral dissertation and update it on the basis of more recent scholarship. My dissertation research was conducted largely at the National Central Library in Taipei, and I would like to take this opportunity to again express my gratitude for the grant from the National Central Library's Center for Chinese Studies that made it possible. Additional research specifically for this book was conducted at Princeton University's East Asian Library and Gest Collection and the libraries of the University of Kansas, Kansas State University, and Peking University, and I am grateful for the assistance provided by librarians at all these locations.

As a historian of China who is proficient in Chinese but has never studied the Greek language, I would not have been able to approach this subject at all were it not for the earlier contributions of dedicated translators such as R.C. Blockley, F.B. Dewing, Eric McGeer, Denis F. Sullivan, Michael and Mary Whitby, David Whitehead, and—above all—George T. Dennis, whose translation of the *Strategikon* was my single most important source for the Byzantine side of this study. I have also benefited enormously from the substantial secondary literature on the Byzantine military produced by these and other scholars. Among the modern authorities, I am especially grateful for the support and encouragement I have received from Professor John Haldon of Princeton University. It was Professor Haldon who invited me to present a comparative paper at the 2010 Dumbarton Oaks symposium devoted to "War in the Byzantine World." This paper, which previewed some of the main arguments presented in this book, was subsequently published in *Dumbarton Oaks Papers* 65/66, edited by Margaret Mullett (2012). I would like to thank the Dumbarton Oaks Research Library and Collection, and the Trustees for Harvard University, for permission to adapt portions of that article into the present book.

Finally, I must also thank Peter Sowden at Routledge and Peter Lorge, the series editor, for their patience in the face of one delay after another.

1   War and culture

In the spring of 630 two great military powers, the Eastern Türk empire and the Tang dynastic state in China, were locked in an armed confrontation to determine which of them would dominate the mainland of East Asia. During the years when the newly proclaimed Tang dynasty (618–907) was consolidating its hold over China, the qaghan of the Eastern Türks had given his backing to various regional powers and rival claimants to the imperial throne in a bid to divide—if not to rule—the vast realm to the south. When those contenders had been eliminated, the Türks took the field themselves. In the autumn of 626, their qaghan Illig (or Xieli, in the Chinese sources) raided to within a few miles of the northern gates of the Tang capital Chang'an, withdrawing only after the second Tang emperor, who had taken the throne only days before, agreed to the payment of a substantial tribute. By the autumn of 629, however, the tables had turned. Not only had the Tang empire built up its forces, but Illig had been greatly weakened by severe winter weather that had caused the die off of much of his people's livestock and encouraged the defection of many of their vassal tribes. The Tang emperor appointed his highly capable minister of war, the fifty-nine-year-old Li Jing, as commander-in-chief of several field armies totaling some 100,000 men, and sent him against the border town of Dingxiang, near which Illig had established his headquarters. A bold advance by Li Jing, culminating in a night attack on the walls of the town, persuaded Illig to quit Dingxiang and pull back to a place called Iron Mountain (Tieshan), in the Yinshan mountain range to the north of the great Ordos bend of the Yellow River. Li Jing and his colleague Li Shiji advanced to Baidao, south of Iron Mountain, and contemplated their next move.

In the meantime, an envoy sent by the emperor had arrived in the qaghan's camp and begun discussion of peace terms. His presence there inspired the two Tang generals to plan a surprise attack on the Türks at Iron Mountain in the expectation that their opponents would have been lulled into a false sense of security by the ongoing negotiations. Starting from his camp at Baidao, several days south of Iron Mountain, Li Jing set out northward with a column of 10,000 horsemen carrying twenty days' rations for each soldier. At the same time, Li Shiji led a second column by another route to a place called Qikou, "the mouth of desert," cutting off the Türks' most obvious escape route, one of the major tracks across the Gobi. The blow fell on March 27, 630. Benefiting from the cover of mist as well as their opponents' lax security, Li Jing's army stormed into the qaghan's encampment. What followed was an utter rout. It seems that the Tang vanguard of 200 mounted archers alone was sufficient to throw the unprepared Türks into panic; there was little left for the main body of the attackers to do except loot and slaughter. Illig was able to make his getaway on a fast horse, but tens of thousands of his followers surrendered when they found their escape blocked by Li Shiji's force. Chinese sources claim that 10,000 Türks were killed in the raid on Iron Mountain and more than 100,000 men and women fell into the hands of the victors. These figures may well be exaggerated, but the magnitude of the victory is beyond question. Illig was soon handed over to Chinese troops by one of his own kinsmen, and the subjugation of the Eastern Türks provided the basis for nearly half a century of Tang hegemony over the nomadic peoples of the North Asian steppelands.[1]

Li Jing himself is supposed to have cited an earlier Chinese precedent for his strategy at Iron Mountain: In 204 BCE, during the civil wars that attended the establishment of the Han dynasty, the Han general Han Xin was preparing to attack Tian Guang, the king of Qi, when he learned that a Han envoy was already negotiating a peace settlement with Qi. The general was persuaded to take advantage of this situation to launch an immediate offensive that resulted in the rapid conquest of Qi, though it cost the life of the Han envoy. This story is found in the *Shiji* (*Historical Records*), written by the great Han historian Sima Qian around 100 BCE and well known to the educated elites of the Tang court.[2] Yet the playbook for the victory at Iron Mountain might just as well have been provided by a contemporary of Li Jing, writing in Greek rather than Chinese and living at the opposite end of the Asian landmass.

The *Strategikon*, dating from about 600 CE and of unknown authorship (though conventionally attributed to the Eastern Roman emperor Maurikios, who reigned from 582 to 602), is a concrete, practical handbook of military tactics and techniques. Among its many observations and recommendations are the following:

> Some commanders have welcomed embassies from the enemy and replied in gentle and flattering terms, sent them on their way with honors, and then immediately followed along and attacked them unexpectedly. Some have themselves sent embassies with favorable proposals and then launched an attack. Some have gone after the enemy in their camps by getting information about how securely they set up camp, and then on a moonlit night two or three hours before daybreak they would make their attack. Archers are essential for an operation of this sort.[3]

> The conduct of night attacks has varied among commanders. Some have pitched camp about a day's march from the enemy, and have sent a deputation or two to offer proposals for peace. When the enemy have reason to hope that an agreement is being reached, and they become careless, then these generals march their army at night and attack unexpectedly before dawn.[4]

> Night attacks are best made by archers or javelin throwers, both mounted and dismounted. . . . The army should always move on the alert and ready

for action, carrying only what is necessary. They should regulate their march according to the distance between the two camps so as to arrive two hours before dawn someplace about one or two miles from the enemy's camp, marching easily so they will not be exhausted. There the army should stay in hiding and rest, and then attack the enemy just before dawn.[5]

Not all the details of Li Jing's operation accord with the advice of the *Strategikon*; his attack was launched over a greater distance, involved the opportunistic exploitation of his ruler's peace effort rather than a deceptive demarche of his own devising, and hit the Türks' camp at an uncertain hour (although the presence of mist is certainly suggestive of late night or very early morning). Nor is there any mention in the Chinese sources of Li Jing's pausing to rest or regroup just prior to the assault. Nevertheless, the basic outline—the exploitation of negotiations to achieve complete surprise in a raid on the enemy camp, and the key role of archers in the operation—is remarkably similar.

In only one important respect did Li Jing's plan diverge significantly from the *Strategikon*. The Byzantine text advised attacking the enemy camp from no more than three sides, leaving a clear line of retreat as surety that a defeated foe would not "be forced to close ranks and fight."[6] Our sources do not tell us from how many directions Li Jing's troopers attacked the qaghan's camp at Iron Mountain, but his dispatch of Li Shiji's column to block the Türks' escape route at Qikou suggests that he had no intention of letting them get away. This move not only contravened the advice that Li Jing would have found in the *Strategikon*, had it been available to him, but also ran counter to the wisdom of *Sunzi bingfa* and other ancient Chinese military treatises that were well known to him, which cautioned against trapping one's opponents lest they be galvanized to fight with the desperation that might turn defeat into victory.[7]

Renowned for his mastery of the earlier literature on the art of war, Li Jing was also the author of a military text of his own. Although the *Li Jing bingfa* (Li Jing's "Military Methods") survives in only fragmentary form today, the topics covered in those fragments—army organization, basic tactics, military law, the training of individual soldiers, group drills, military signals, formations for battle and march, arrangements for scouting and patrolling, the layout of the camp, the treatment of sick and wounded soldiers, the burial of the dead—are basically the same as those treated in the *Strategikon*.[8] A careful comparison of the contents of the two books, to be presented at length in the chapters that follow, reveals that the similarities between Chinese and Eastern Roman military methods of the early seventh century CE run much broader and deeper than the single instance of Li Jing's raid on Iron Mountain would indicate; it is only the tip of the proverbial iceberg. Given the vast differences between the landforms, material resources, historical experiences, belief systems, and other cultural inheritances of these two early medieval empires, the similarities in their approaches to the conduct of war cry out for explanation.

For an earlier generation of military historians and theorists, writing for the most part in the early and middle years of the twentieth century, the reason for the overlap between Li Jing and the *Strategikon* would have been obvious and, indeed, unproblematic. In their view, war—or to be more precise, the *successful* conduct of war—is governed by certain immutable, universal principles, as objective as the laws of chemistry or physics and no less valid for all times and places. Writing in the 1920s, Colonel J.F.C. Fuller identified nine principles of war: direction, concentration, distribution, determination, surprise, endurance, mobility, offensive action, and security.[9] There were many variations on the theme. The other great British military theorist of the interwar period, B.H. Liddell Hart, once managed to reduce the "essence of war" to six fundamental, universal axioms (and would no doubt have analyzed the battle of Iron Mountain, had he known of it, as an instance of his first axiom, "*Always try to choose the line (or course) of least probable expectation—by the enemy*").[10] A distinguished recent proponent of the notion of a universal science of war was the late Michael Handel, who sought to demonstrate the essential congruence of the teachings of Sunzi with those of the early nineteenth-century Prussian Carl von Clausewitz—the preeminent Western theorist of war, despite the two authors' vast separation in time and space—and asserted that neither "states anything that cannot be understood intuitively by an intelligent, rational political or military leader who has never read their writings."[11] The principles of war, to be sure, have not always been observed in actual practice, but to flout them is to either invite defeat or offer a clear demonstration that a society is "primitive," that is, not yet sophisticated enough to be able to wage "true" war along rational lines.[12] Astute practitioners facing similar conditions of geography, technology, and so forth would make the same rational choices. In the view of Alfred H. Burne, an experienced British officer and military historian writing in 1950, "When in doubt on some ancient battlefield, it is a sound practice to place oneself in the shoes of the commander, stand where he stood, and issue the orders that seem most natural under the circumstances."[13]

However, since the 1970s, and especially in the last twenty years, our understanding of military practice has taken a different turn. Universalizing theories have fallen out of favor as researchers have increasingly devoted their attention to the investigation of local differences and particularities, for which the preferred terms are "ways of war" (among historians) and "strategic cultures" (among political scientists). Russell Weigley's now classic 1973 study *The American Way of War* has been joined by Richard Harrison's *The Russian Way of War* and Robert Citino's *The German Way of War*; studies have appeared addressing the strategic cultures of (inter alia) Austria, Denmark, Finland, Sweden, and Taiwan, and several books and articles debate the existence and specific content of a Chinese strategic culture.[14] So much has been written that a thorough survey of the existing literature as of 2005 required a book-length work.[15] Much of this literature is descriptive rather than explanatory, but when explanation is needed the general tendency has been to rely heavily on the concept of culture: different states and peoples have made war in different ways because their cultures are different. Three authors—John Keegan, Victor Davis Hanson, and John Lynn—have used culture as the touchstone for broader, synoptic studies of world military history that highlight the differences between war making in major world regions and civilizations.[16] War, Keegan proclaimed in 1993, "is always an expression of culture, often a determinant of cultural forms, in some societies the culture itself."[17] It is in the context of this cultural turn that any similarity between Tang China and Byzantium becomes problematic. How could two cultures as different as Orthodox Byzantium with its Greco-Roman inheritance and a China shaped by Confucianism and Buddhism ever give rise to similar ways of war?

The Sino-Byzantine parallel is even more problematic when juxtaposed against a particularly influential subset of the culturally oriented scholarship, those works that promote the idea of a distinctive and culturally rooted Western approach to war. First put forward by the classicist Victor Davis Hanson in *The Western Way of War: Infantry Battle in Classical Greece* (1989), this thesis was accepted by John Keegan in his *History of Warfare* (1993) and exerted a strong influence on *The Cambridge Illustrated History of Warfare* (1995), written by a team of scholars (including Hanson) under the editorship of Geoffrey Parker. In *Carnage and Culture: Landmark Battles in the Rise of Western Power* (2001), Hanson further adumbrated the concept and attempted to demonstrate its continuity from the fifth century BCE to the present. His original argument, presented in a work concerned primarily with the experience of hoplite combat in classical Greece, held that Greek warfare was characterized by the direct, frontal collision of masses of spear-armed foot soldiers, with armies seeking the quickest possible resolution of the conflict by means of decisive battle leading directly to the destruction of the enemy; there was no use for evasion or trickery, and missile weapons such as bows were scorned in favor of the "hammer blows" of "shock combat" with edged weapons. Hanson went on to assert (not demonstrate) that, although weapons technology and tactical systems would change over time, these same characteristics have remained true of European and Euro-American war making ever since.

Keegan's contribution was to develop the idea of a non-Western or "Oriental" way of war, implicit in Hanson's work but unexplored. Treating the ways of the Chinese, the steppe nomads such as the Huns and Mongols, and even "primitive warfare" as more or less interchangeable, Keegan held that

> Oriental warmaking, if we may so identify and denominate it as something apart and different from European warfare, is characterised by traits peculiar to itself. Foremost among these are evasion, delay and indirectness. . . . The horse warriors chose to fight at a distance, to use missiles rather than edged weapons, to withdraw when confronted with determination and to count upon wearing down an enemy to defeat rather than by overthrowing him in a single test of arms.[18]

Sunzi bingfa, the most important early Chinese text dealing with "the art of war," with its emphasis on deception and risk avoidance, could be presented as the quintessential formulation of this Oriental approach to warfare.[19]

In *Carnage and Culture*, Hanson directed his attention beyond the battlefield to identify a set of cultural characteristics that have provided the basis for the success

of Western arms, and cast his chronological net more widely to examine a set of
battles between Western and non-Western forces ranging from Salamis (480 BCE)
to the Tet Offensive of 1968. His list of cultural traits, in part echoing a similar list
in Parker's introduction to *The Cambridge Illustrated History of Warfare*, includes
individualism, rationalism, capitalism, willingness to adopt new technology, civilian audit of the military, and civic militarism—"the notion that those who vote must
also fight to protect the commonwealth, which in the exchange had granted them
rights."[20] It is these characteristics, appearing in varying permutations, that have
given Western armies and navies an edge over all adversaries for the last 2,500
years.[21] Although Hanson does not include any Byzantine examples among the
"landmark battles," he nevertheless makes it amply clear that Byzantium belongs
on the Western side of his great divide.[22] In light of the many direct institutional,
intellectual, and cultural continuities from Greece and Rome to Constantinople, it
would be difficult to do otherwise.

The "Western Way of War" thesis, if such it may be called, has already generated a great deal of criticism. Scholars working in Hanson's home field of classical
Greece have reminded us of the important roles played by cavalry, archers, and
light-armed troops (peltasts) in Hellenic warfare. The hoplite phalanx itself was
always a work in progress rather than a fixed point, and deception and trickery
were far from absent in the warfare of a people who counted the wily Odysseus
among their heroes.[23] The Peloponnesian War, the epic struggle between Athens
and Sparta that lasted from 431 to 404 BCE, saw few major land battles but much
evasion and delay.[24] Other critics have targeted Hanson's claim that there is an
essential continuity in Western war making from antiquity to the present, pointing
especially to the widespread avoidance of battle in medieval and early modern
Europe. In the view of John Lynn,

> Hanson's mature theory, with its complex of elements, works best when one
> jumps from the late Roman republic to the nineteenth century. From Marius
> to Robespierre is a gap of nearly 1,900 years in a claimed continuity of 2,500
> years, making it no continuity at all.[25]

Lynn, author of the most thorough and sustained critique of the "Western Way of
War" to appear thus far, faults Hanson (and Keegan) on a number of other points
as well. Not only have cultural differences leading to differences in war making
been quite pronounced in different periods of Western history, but comparison of
the early Chinese and South Asian discourses on war indicates that non-Western
approaches have also been quite diverse.[26] Nor was the West always superior;
it was peoples such as the Mongols and Türks, horse archers, who "represented
the most successful military tradition in history, measured by the span of the
globe that they dominated before the modern era."[27] In addition, Lynn offered a
tentative comparison of ancient Chinese with Western discourses and practices
suggesting that the differences have been overdrawn. "Put in proper context,"
he concluded, "a stark contrast between Western battle seeking and Asian battle
avoidance evaporates."[28]

While Lynn's *Battle: A History of Combat and Culture* (2003) was painted with a very broad brush, more modestly focused studies illuminating the war making of particular times and places have tended to confirm his assertion of great diversity within both the West and the non-West, and also highlight discontinuities in the "Western Way of War." A case in point is John Grenier's *The First Way of War: American War Making on the Frontier, 1607–1814* (2005). Although framed as a corrective to Weigley's inadequate treatment of the colonial, revolutionary, and early national periods in *The American Way of War* (1973), Grenier's picture of English colonists driven by necessity to adopt a "skulking" mode of warfare involving raid, ambush, and massacre could just as well be construed as an affront to the Hanson-Keegan vision of properly Western war making.[29]

Other critics of the "Western Way of War" thesis, most notably Jeremy Black and Harry Sidebottom, have tended to echo Lynn's major points while adding a few new twists. For Sidebottom, the Western way of war is

> not so much an objective reality, a genuine continuity of practices, but more . . . a strong ideology which since its creation by the Greeks has been, and still is, frequently reinvented, and changed with each reinvention. Those who subscribe to the ideology do not necessarily fight in a very different way to others, it is just that they genuinely think they do.[30]

This may help to explain the concept's popularity in the U.S. military, and would make Hanson himself a part of the phenomenon rather than simply its chronicler. Black, for his part, has maintained that European superiority is a relatively recent development, a product of the nineteenth century rather than the stuff of the *longue durée*, and, more importantly, has pointed out Hanson's "tendency to reify cultural factors and too readily give them explanatory force."[31] The inadequate conceptualization of "culture" and its improper use as an analytical construct is a serious problem not just for Hanson's argument, but for much of the wider literature on strategic culture and ways of war—a subject to which we shall be returning in due course.

Insofar as it argues the essential similarity of Tang Chinese and Byzantine methods of warfare, the book you are reading now reinforces one of the main criticisms of the "Western Way of War" thesis already offered by Lynn, Black, and Sidebottom, namely that the distinction between Western and non-Western military behavior is not nearly as clear as Hanson (and Keegan) would have it. On the Byzantine side of the equation, it offers yet another example, actually a quite detailed case study, of a time and place when "Westerners" did not behave as they should. It is from the Chinese side, however, that the largest contribution is to be made. Earlier critiques of the "Western Way of War," especially Lynn's, have suggested that the military tactics of China, for most of recorded history the greatest power to be found in the non-Western world, may have been quite similar to those of the West, with disciplined infantry units drilled to maneuver on command and execute direct, frontal attacks should the need arise. Yet the wording of the proposition is often highly tentative, even speculative, reflecting the severely limited body of evidence available to military historians who do not read Chinese.[32] Drawing upon Li Jing's "Military Methods" and the records of military events found in Tang histories, sources that have hitherto been largely inaccessible to non-Sinologues, this study will offer ample evidence that, in the seventh century at least, Chinese soldiers were indeed capable of fighting in a "Western" fashion. The picture that emerges is of Eastern Roman soldiers far too Oriental, and Chinese soldiers far too Western, for the Hanson-Keegan thesis to contain. They meet in the middle, on common ground that I have chosen to call "the Eurasian Way of War."

On one level, then, this book is intended as a refutation of the idea of a "Western Way of War." If that were its only purpose, there are some who might argue that it is not worth the time and ink that have been poured into it.[33] But there are other purposes, and other levels. By the same token that it challenges the Hanson-Keegan thesis, it is no less a challenge to its Chinese counterpart, the notion that there is a unique, distinctive Chinese approach to warfare with *Sunzi bingfa* as its fountainhead, a sort of negative image of the "Western Way of War," always defensively oriented rather than aggressive in nature, and favoring deception, cunning, and indirection over the straightforward frontal assault. If the "Western Way of War" is, as Sidebottom would have it, a "strong ideology," the same can certainly be said of its Chinese counterpart. The uniqueness—and superiority—of China's culturally specific approach to conflict is a virtual orthodoxy in today's Chinese military, which has seen it as offsetting the technological superiority of hypothetical opponents, and an article of faith among the general public.[34] Yet it will become apparent, as we examine military practices and the conduct of war in the Eastern Roman Empire, that the Byzantines would have found little that was new or surprising in either *Sunzi bingfa* or the military techniques of the Tang empire.

This book's elaboration of seventh-century Chinese military practice, too, fills a gap in the existing scholarship that goes well beyond the tentative, uncertain treatment of China by earlier critics of Hanson. In broad syntheses and surveys by both military historians and world historians, the extreme paucity of accessible source materials in Western languages has led to either neglect or misrepresentation of China's martial past. To consider only one example, William H. McNeill, the founding father of world history as a sub-discipline in the United States, could not be accused of neglecting China, nor has he been a proponent of the "Western Way of War" thesis. His book *Keeping Together in Time: Dance and Drill in Human History* (1995), which argues that rhythmic group exercises, such as dance and close-order military drill, build social cohesion through "muscular bonding" and contribute to military effectiveness, contains plenty of non-Western examples; in McNeill's view, the phalanx of well-drilled spearmen begins not with the Greeks, but with the Sumerians of *c*.2450 BCE.[35] Yet his treatment of Chinese military history, guided by the limited sources at his disposal, is seriously flawed. Accepting the presence of well-drilled foot soldiers in ancient China, he goes on to claim that the introduction of cavalry and the crossbow put an end to real drill and banished effective infantry from the battlefield – until close-order drill was reinvented in the sixteenth century by the Ming general Qi Jiguang, a Chinese Maurice of Nassau.[36] This construction is at odds with the testimony of Li Jing's "Military Methods" and other Chinese sources, which show that disciplined, well-drilled infantry was still alive and well in the middle period of Chinese history. The present study, it is hoped, will make it easier for future synthesizers to avoid mistakes of this sort.

In addition to offering descriptions that may contribute to a more accurate understanding of Chinese military practice while confounding the proponents of Chinese and Western uniqueness, this book has the more ambitious aim of accounting for the observed similarities between Tang China and the Eastern Roman Empire. What factor or combination of factors—perhaps technological or environmental, perhaps the result of earlier lessons learned or even influence and diffusion across the length of Asia—gave rise to this Eurasian way of war? Whatever explanation is offered will necessarily have to downplay cultural factors without, however, reviving the now discredited notion of immutable, universal principles of war. And herein lies a third, even more ambitious aim of this work: to promote, as an alternative to the "cultural turn," a process-oriented and fully historicized explanation of military variation that may be found applicable to many times and places other than seventh-century Eurasia.

Culture, Jeremy Black has observed, "is a term so widely and loosely used as to have its analytical value at least in part compromised."[37] Historians and political scientists seeking to explain diversity in military practice with reference to cultural influences have encountered difficulties in defining culture, accounting for variation within particular cultures, and dealing with change over time. All of these have tended to vitiate whatever conclusions might be derived through the use of culture as an analytical tool. In general, historians and political scientists have adopted quite opposite approaches such that the vices of each mirror the virtues of the other. Military historians writing in English have bandied the term "culture" about quite freely, attaching enormous causal weight to it without bothering to offer much in the way of definition; meanwhile political scientists, or at least the better ones, have been constrained by the construction of overly cautious definitions. Let us look more closely at one outstanding example of each approach, Victor Davis Hanson's *Carnage and Culture* and Alastair Iain Johnston's *Cultural Realism: Strategic Culture and Grand Strategy in Chinese History* (1995).

In a book of 455 pages that identifies Western culture as the source of Western military power, Victor Davis Hanson nowhere provides any definition of his central term. The closest he comes is to say that it embraces government, science, law, and religion. This is indicative rather than exhaustive or exclusive, and what it seems to indicate is that everything that is not strictly dictated by genes or geography, the entire realm of nurture as opposed to nature, is subsumed under the capacious rubric of culture.[38] Anthropologists, the academic tribe that has given the most thought to the concept of culture, have come up with numerous conflicting definitions; as Clifford Geertz once pointed out, Clyde Kluckhohn's general introduction to the subject offered no less than eleven different definitions in a twenty-seven-page chapter.[39] In particular, there has been considerable disagreement among anthropologists as to whether culture should be defined in terms of behavior and practice, or viewed as a matter of knowledge, understanding, and conceptualization—in other words, the ways that people are taught to make sense of the world around them and comport themselves within it—and various attempts have been made to bridge this gap, with Geertz's work standing as a particularly distinguished example.[40] To deal with this conceptual minefield by pretending it doesn't exist is no guarantee that one will come through unscathed. If the main purpose of *Carnage and Culture* were to argue that culture, as opposed to other causal factors, has been responsible for a peculiarly Western approach to war making (rather than simply trumpeting the West's difference and superiority), it would be open to the same sort of criticism that Alastair Iain Johnston leveled at what he called the "first generation" of strategic culture theorists. With analytically separable variables such as beliefs and institutions, attitudes and behavior, etc. all lumped together in a single package pointing in a single direction, the outcome is said to be "overdetermined," and can even become tautological; when everything is culture, the concept actually loses most of its explanatory power. In addition, variation from the putative cultural norm becomes difficult to explain— if culture trumps all and battle seeking is the Western way, how are we to account for such notable Westerners as Pericles and Fabius Cunctator?[41]

In his own work on China's strategic culture, Johnston strove mightily to avoid these pitfalls. Defining strategic culture as "an ideational milieu that limits behavioral choices," or more precisely, "an integrated system of symbols (i.e. argumentation structures, languages, analogies, metaphors, etc.) that acts to establish pervasive and long-lasting grand strategic preferences by formulating concepts of the role and efficacy of military force in interstate political affairs," he posited that this system consists of a "central paradigm" answering three fundamental questions about "the role of war in human affairs," the "nature of the adversary," and "the efficacy of the use of force," plus a limited, ranked menu of options (or "grand strategic preferences") generated on the basis of those assumptions.[42] Although delivering the clarity and simplicity needed to achieve his goal of conducting, for the benefit of fellow political scientists, a rigorous, empirically "falsifiable" test of the explanatory value of strategic culture as an independent variable bearing on strategic choice or strategic behavior, Johnston's definition seems far too constraining to have much utility for military historians. In particular, the system has a binary, yes–no character precluding the sort of nuanced, textured understanding of the past that historians generally prefer; there are only two possible answers to each of the three questions that make up the "central paradigm" (leading, in effect, to only two paradigms inasmuch as answers are likely to be consistent across all three questions), and even the menu of grand strategic options is limited to only three terms: aggression, passive defense, and accommodation. Although there may be a certain rough-and-ready applicability to certain basic questions, such as whether to seek battle or avoid it, this scheme is not easily extended to cover the manifold complexities of decision making at the operational and tactical levels, nor does it offer much help with regard to the more subtle and qualitative (as opposed to one-and-zero) dimensions of strategy: what goals are (and are not) worth fighting for? What means are (and are not) acceptable in the conduct of war? What costs are (and are not) acceptable on the way to victory? And how is "victory" defined, anyway? Culture surely has an influence on the way all of these questions are answered, and there would seem to be as many possible answers (or permutations of answers) as there are different cultures.

This brings us to the second problem, that of variation. How many strategic cultures (or ways of war) are there, and what level of difference is sufficient to distinguish one from another? Here, Hanson and Johnston appear to have arrived at rather similar answers by quite different routes. Hanson, as we have seen, presents us with what are in effect two ways of war, the Western way and a non-Western way that is everything the Western way is not; the West, in this scheme, refers to societies sharing a common cultural tradition

> that arose in Greece and Rome; survived the collapse of the Roman Empire; spread to western and northern Europe; then during the great periods of exploration and colonization of the fifteenth through nineteenth centuries expanded to the Americas, Australia, and areas of Asia and Africa.[43]

Although he concedes that not all elements of the Western cultural package have been present in all eras, the distinctions are not really significant. As for Johnston, his methodological rigor with its preference for binaries also seems geared to distinguish, at best, between two strategic cultures, an aggressive, *Realpolitik* pattern and a much more passive culture emphasizing conflict avoidance. Hence, it is not a great surprise when he does indeed find two strategic cultures; the interesting twist is that the *Realpolitik* model has apparently been operative in both China and the West, while China has at the same time asserted a second strategic culture, one Johnston calls "the Confucian–Mencian paradigm," which has had little or no discernable influence on actual behavior. The schemata devised by Hanson and Johnston both appear far too simple to embrace all of the diverse and varied behaviors to be observed in the history of warfare; moreover, they are also at odds with most of the rest of the literature on strategic cultures and ways of war, which appears to take as a starting assumption that every nation-state must have an approach to conflict distinctive enough to warrant a book or at least an article. Johnston's work also raises the important possibility that multiple ways of war may exist within a single polity. If a number of cultures or subcultures may coexist based on differences in ethnicity, class, occupation, and religious faith etc., it seems reasonable to suppose that attitudes toward war and war making are equally diverse. Although it also stands to reason that in normal times only the culture of the ruling elite shapes the state's strategic culture, other viewpoints may come into play during times of civil war or social upheaval. The sort of black-and-white logic proposed by Johnston and Hanson (each in his own way) is clearly unsatisfactory, but the alternative—a vast proliferation of only very subtly distinguished cultures and subcultures of war—also seems inherently problematic.

A third problem area is change over time. For both Hanson and Johnston, a culture of war making has its origin in early formative experiences and a set of conditions that obtained at some point in the past; in Hanson's case, the Western penchant for aggressive, decisive war is found to be rooted in the pressing need of the citizen-soldiers of ancient Greece to resolve conflicts quickly in order to get back to their shops and farms.[44] Once the preferences stemming from such conditions are crystallized, valorized, and encoded as "culture," however, they acquire enormous staying power, enduring for thousands of years essentially impervious to changes in technology or even quite fundamental transformations of the underlying social structures, belief systems, and ways of life (such as, for example, the replacement of Greco-Roman paganism by Christianity, or the introduction of Buddhism into China). To be sure, Hanson recognizes that not all of his Western characteristics are present in all periods of the West's history, while Johnston leaves open the possibility that more subtle and less long-lived cultural influences on strategy may be identified (although his agenda of persuading fellow political scientists of the value of strategic culture as an explanatory variable drives him to focus on phenomena persisting over very long periods of time).[45] Nevertheless, the emphasis in both cases is overwhelmingly on continuity rather than change. This puts them somewhat at odds with much anthropological thought that sees culture as fluid and malleable rather than something set in concrete at some formative point in the distant past, and sits uncomfortably with most historians' preference for tracing change over time and attributing great significance to more rapidly occurring developments. In the hands of some practitioners, moreover, the cultural approach to military history, with its nebulous conception of "culture" and inattention to change, could be taken as a more politically correct stand-in for the sort of crude, old-fashioned national character argument that (in the United States, at least) made all Japanese out to be fanatically loyal, Italians militarily ineffectual, and Frenchmen prone to surrender.

For all of these reasons, I am inclined to think that culture should be a last resort rather than the first stop of historians seeking to explain the differentiation of military practice across different societies. The present study will not entirely eschew the use of this ever so useful term, but will employ it sparingly and define it so as to avoid making it a catch-all on the one hand or imposing an unduly rigid, narrow, or idiosyncratic interpretation on the other. While recognizing that it has been defined in many different ways and may have rather different connotations for different audiences, I will take as a starting point Geertz's concept of culture as "an historically transmitted pattern of meanings embodied in symbols, a system of inherited conceptions expressed in symbolic forms by means of which men communicate, perpetuate, and develop their knowledge ·about and attitudes toward life."[46] (A symbol can be anything—an "object, event, act, quality, or relation"— that serves as a vehicle for significance beyond itself.[47]) Culture thus encompasses shared, socially established understandings of how the world works, what sorts of actions are and are not effective, and what is invested with value. Since actions can themselves be symbols and meaning must often be inferred from observed behavior, culture does not pertain solely to the realm of thought or that of action, but bridges the two.[48] Similarly, since objects also serve as symbols—and are the material reflection of notions of efficacy and value—I accept "material culture" as a legitimate component of the larger concept. Social and institutional structures are a more complicated case. Though permeated with culture as the loci of so much of cultural activity and often themselves freighted with symbolic value, their own persistence through time and sheer complexity are sufficient to warrant treating them as analytically separable from culture itself. In general, anthropologists have seen culture and social reality as exerting a reciprocal influence on one another, with changes in society—though perhaps only after a very considerable time lag—producing changes in culture.[49] Moreover, anthropologists have tended to regard culture as responsive to historical experience; Kluckhohn, for example, once described culture as "a precipitate of history," and for M.J. Herskovitz ideas of beauty and truth were "products of the particular historical experience of the societies that manifest them."[50] Culture is, in short, the created as well as the creator. Responsive to material conditions, social relations, technology, and historical experience, it is constantly being reworked and refashioned. Not everything changes quickly, of course, but everything—or almost everything—does change eventually. I would even suggest that, when taken as an entire package, the set of symbols and significances that makes up a culture does not remain *absolutely identical* from one day to the next. Rather than treating culture as an independent variable that generates specific behavior (something anthropologists themselves seem reluctant to do),[51] it might make more sense to refocus our attention directly on the material, social, and historical forces that shape culture.

This is the approach that will be taken with regard to the central problem of this study, the explanation of the convergence of Chinese and Byzantine military practice that culminated near the beginning of the seventh century in the remarkably similar teachings of the *Strategikon* and Li Jing's "Military Methods." The chapters that follow will explore a wide range of potential influences bearing on the methods and techniques described in these two texts, with an eye to identifying key similarities and differences. We will begin, in Chapter 2, with an overview of the political–military fortunes of the Chinese and Eastern Roman realms, highlighting the strategic challenges facing the two empires in the first half of the seventh century. This chapter will consider the geographical situation of the two empires and the resources, both human and material, available to each; it will also compare their organization and institutions, including military finance, the recruitment of soldiers and officers, the terms and conditions under which they served, the structure of the military establishment, the command hierarchy, and civil–military relations at both the elite and popular levels. A particular focus of the chapter will be how the two empires sought to reconcile the desideratum of military effectiveness with the need to prevent an over-powerful military from becoming a threat to the state and its ruler.

Chapter 3 will take material culture as its starting point, examining and comparing the weapons, armor, and other military equipment used by the Chinese and the Byzantines *c*.600 CE. It will go on to consider the ways that men were trained to use those weapons effectively in battle, in coordination with one another and in response to command signals, and the standard formations and deployments that were employed on the battlefield. Special attention will be devoted to the various roles of infantry and cavalry, and the ways in which their efforts were coordinated. It is in this chapter that many of the most important similarities between Chinese and Byzantine military practice will be spelled out in detail.

In the next chapter I move on to consider the operational level of warfare, which in this period involved the conduct of campaigns of limited duration often culminating in a major battle or siege. Some attention will be given to the logistical methods of the Chinese and Byzantines, since the ability to supply armies in the field was often a determining factor in the success or failure of a military campaign, and the chapter will also examine fortification, siegecraft, and the role that the attack and defense of fortified places played in larger campaign strategies. Above all, however, this chapter will focus on the critical decision of when, where, and under what conditions to engage in a potentially decisive battle with the enemy. In this connection, further similarities in the military practice of the two empires will be identified and adumbrated. Both the Chinese and Byzantines had various means of avoiding combat when they considered it disadvantageous; these included reliance on walled cities, fortified camps, and of course, adroit maneuvering and exploitation of the advantages of terrain. In general, both militaries were extremely risk-averse and preferred to avoid battle when the odds were not tilted heavily in their favor.

Whereas the major focus of Chapters 2 through 4 is the identification of key areas of similarity and difference in the military practice of the Chinese and Eastern Roman empires, the three chapters that follow will turn to consider possible explanations—especially for the similarities, which are the most in need of explanation. Chapter 5 is devoted to the cultural heritages of Tang China and early medieval Byzantium, both of which were governed by literate elites who were heirs to very substantial bodies of writing about the ordering of the military and the conduct of war. The Byzantines had at their disposal a corpus of Greek military writing dating back to the fourth century BCE that included the works by Aineias the Tactician, Asclepiodotus, Onasander, and Polyaenus, as well as Latin authors such as Frontinus and Vegetius and all of the classical historians beginning with Herodotus and Thucydides. Their Chinese contemporaries had Sunzi's "Art of War" and several other ancient military treatises, along with a very substantial corpus of philosophical and historical writing that frequently touched on military matters. Examination of this body of evidence reveals important similarities between the Chinese and the Byzantines. It will be seen that many of the stratagems described by Western authors had exact equivalents in the Chinese literature, but the most important point to emerge from this chapter is that the two empires had much the same attitude toward war. Long before the beginning of the seventh century, the dominant approach to warfare in both civilizations could be characterized as mature, sophisticated, and highly rational. War was not to be undertaken lightly; it was not just a trial of strength and courage, but rather a dangerous business requiring the application of intellect and cunning to gain every possible advantage.

Chapter 6 explores cultural borrowing, the direct diffusion of ideas and practices from one empire to the other, as a possible explanation for similarity between China and Byzantium. It examines the range of contacts between the two empires, including the movement of goods over the Silk Road, the Byzantine acquisition of silkworms from China in the sixth century, the diffusion of military technology such as the stirrup and the traction trebuchet from East to West, and indirect dealings through intermediary powers such as Sasanian Persia and the Türk qaghanate. Particular attention is given to the role in these developments of the nomadic Avars, tentatively identified with the Rouran of the eastern steppe, whose migration westward to the Danubian frontier of the Eastern Roman Empire in the middle of the sixth century offered a promising vector for the spread of technology and ideas from China to the Mediterranean world. This chapter reaches the conclusion that while there is ample evidence of the diffusion of tools and techniques associated with the cavalry warfare of the Eurasian steppes, the transference of higher-order military concepts—and specific practices not associated primarily with the steppe nomads—was not only unlikely but also all but impossible to substantiate, even if it did indeed take place.

A third explanation for the military similarities between China and Byzantium will be considered in Chapter 7, one already hinted at in the preceding chapter. This is the threat that both empires faced from nomadic peoples of the Eurasian steppe zone, and the need to develop an effective mix of symmetric and asymmetric responses in order to cope with it. This chapter traces the interactions of the Byzantines (and their Roman precursors) with peoples such as the Alans, Huns, and Avars, and China's dealings with the steppe from the time of King Wuling of Zhao's adoption of nomad dress and mounted archery in the late fourth century BCE. Many of the weapons, tactics, practices, and outlooks detailed in the earlier chapters are shown to be the legacy of these interactions, including the importance of mounted archers in both armies, their obsession with intelligence and scouting, their frequent use of feigned flights and ambushes, their wariness in pursuit, and their cautious approach to potentially decisive engagements. As a way of gauging the importance of the steppe factor, this chapter also includes a brief comparative look at the military practices of other states of the early medieval period, including Sasanian Persia and the Kievan Rus.

With regard to the central problem of explaining the military similarity between Tang China and seventh-century Byzantium, this book argues that it was above all the military challenge from the nomads of the Eurasian steppe that pushed the two powers toward convergence with one another. Facing the same sort of opponent, an opponent with a particular set of highly effective tactical and operational techniques that in many ways constituted the dominant military paradigm throughout most of medieval Eurasia, in the long run the two empires had little choice but to adjust their own approach to war making in such a way as to effectively counter the challenge. This should not be taken as either an appeal to technological determinism or the assertion of a simple diffusionist model. There were certain key areas (such as siegecraft) where the nomads were usually far inferior to their sedentary opponents, and given the resources of the sedentary powers and the skills found among their populations, a fully symmetrical response to the mounted archer was out of the question. What happened instead was that the Chinese and the Romans were driven gradually toward composite responses that incorporated the same basic elements, because those responses were found to be effective. Culture was by no means irrelevant to the outcome, but it functioned more to define the context and conditions under which essentially rational choices were made than as a causal power in its own right. It was, moreover, also quite capable of pointing in more than one direction and recommending contradictory courses of action, greatly limiting its explanatory and predictive power. The striking similarities between China and Byzantium indicate that culture is not the whole explanation or even the most important part of it. When seeking to account for similarities and differences between military practice in diverse historical contexts, it may be more fruitful to direct our attention to expedient, contingent, and malleable responses to specific, historically grounded problems and conditions rather than putative long-term continuities dictated by cultural imperatives.

Since this argument relies very heavily on evidence drawn from two sources, Li Jing's "Military Methods" and the *Strategikon* that has been conventionally attributed to the emperor Maurikios, a somewhat closer examination of these texts is desirable at the outset. Although the *Strategikon* is more than three times as long as what survives of Li Jing's work, both books address the same sorts of topics within the general subject area of military organization and tactics. It is worth bearing in mind that Li Jing's book, unlike the *Strategikon*, has not been passed down to us as an integral work. Lost during the Song period (960–1279) or possibly even before the end of the Tang dynasty in 907, the "Military Methods" survived in the form of substantial extracts quoted in the *Comprehensive Canons* (*Tong dian*), an encyclopedic work compiled by the prominent scholar-official Du You in the second half of the eighth century and presented to the throne in 801.[52] We have no way of knowing how much of the "Military Methods" did not survive and what topics might have been covered in any lost material, nor is it possible for us to recover the structure and organization of the original seventh-century work.[53] The best we can do is to avoid *ex silentio* assertions (for example, that Li Jing was uninterested in logistics because what is left of his book does not mention the provisioning of armies) while recognizing that there are some aspects of the two texts that must necessarily elude comparison.

When assessing the value of the *Strategikon* and what is left of the "Military Methods" as sources for the study of early seventh-century military practice, there are several questions that must be asked. The first is whether these two texts are indeed what they purport to be, authentic descriptions of military practice dating from that time and preserved without significant emendation or interpolation in later periods. A related question concerns their authorship: how confident can we be that these materials were written by the men whose names have become attached to them, or that they are the work of authors with deep, practical experience of armies and war rather than the fantasies of armchair generals? How can we be sure that their contents are descriptive rather than prescriptive in nature? And how can we be sure that these authors have not engaged in an act of mimesis, relying upon and recycling contents from earlier military writings that are irrelevant to the actual military practice of their own time?

Although most surviving manuscript copies of the *Strategikon* bear the name of the emperor Maurikios (or Maurice) and some modern scholars have seen no reason to challenge that attribution, current opinion generally holds that the evidence for his imperial authorship is insufficient.[54] Other names have been proposed. One authority, John Wiita, has argued that the author was actually Maurikios' brother-in-law Philippicus, who commanded troops both against the Persians and in the Balkans and then lived in monastic seclusion from 603 to 610, with ample time to write a summary of "lessons learned."[55] Another, Eugène Darkó, once speculated that the author might have been none other than the emperor Herakleios (or Heraclius, r. 610–641), who beat back the Persian invaders in a desperate war lasting nearly two decades.[56] None of these suggestions has gained widespread acceptance, however. What would seem to be the current consensus view is concisely stated by Mark Whittow: the *Strategikon* was "associated with the emperor Maurice" and reflected "military thinking at the imperial court."[57] Although he began his career as a notary and rose through the empire's civil bureaucracy, Maurikios was placed in command of the army on the Persian frontier in 577 and, after ascending to the throne in 582, campaigned successfully against both the Persians in the east and the Slavs and Avars in the Balkans. He also promoted reforms aimed at increasing the effectiveness of the empire's armies, reforms whose specific content may well be reflected in the pages of the *Strategikon*.[58] The book's recommendations for fighting the Slavs are more precise and detailed than those for fighting the Persians, suggesting that it may have been written by one of the participants in Maurikios' Balkan campaigns with no personal experience of warfare in the east, and its specific proposal that imperial forces winter in Slav territory north of the Danube gives reason to believe that it could not have been written after 602—when Maurikios' decision to do precisely that provoked a mutiny that led to his deposition and murder.[59] Recent, datable events mentioned in the *Strategikon* point to the 590s, and there is general agreement that the book could not have been composed before the arrival of the Avars in the 550s or after the Arab onslaught of the 630s (since the Avars figure prominently in its pages, while the Arabs are not mentioned at all).[60] There is also nearly universal agreement that, in view of the practical, nuts-and-bolts character of its contents, it must be the work of an experienced military man.[61]

The text of the *Strategikon* has been handed down in several manuscript versions, the best of which is now housed in the Laurentian Library in Florence. Copied around the middle of the tenth century as part of a larger compendium of military writings, it contains fewer errors, omissions, and interpolations than other versions and is thought to be "the closest to the original work, separated from it by no more than three or four copies."[62] This manuscript provided the basis for the English translation by George T. Dennis published in 1984, which will be cited and quoted in this book.[63]

Reflecting China's quite different history of textual transmission and publishing, what remains of the "Military Methods" of Li Jing has survived not in manuscript form but rather in the printed text of Du You's *Tong dian*, whose earliest surviving copies represent woodblock editions of the Northern Song period (960–1127). The earlier transmission of the *Tong dian* is murky, but it was reportedly well received by scholars in the ninth century and presumably existed in numerous manuscript copies; its presence is certainly well attested in early bibliographies and library catalogues.[64] In contrast to other works attributed to the same author, the authenticity of the Li Jing quotations incorporated in the *Tong dian* has never been seriously challenged. This is due in part to the authority of Du You, who was usually careful to identify his sources and began compiling the *Tong dian* only about 110 years after the death of Li Jing, and in part to the close fit between the quotations and Li Jing's biography. Although Li began his career as a civil official and did not hold his first military command until near the age of fifty, he was the nephew of a prominent general of the Sui dynasty and as a youth was already noted for his mastery of the ancient Chinese military classics such as *Sunzi bingfa*.[65] Scoring his first military successes in the civil wars that brought the Tang dynasty to power, Li Jing gained fame in 621 when he led a fleet downstream from Sichuan to bring the middle and lower Yangzi regions under Tang control. Later in life, he commanded the armies that defeated the Eastern Türks in 629–630 and another steppe people, the Tuyuhun inhabiting the region around Kokonor (today's Qinghai province), in 634–635. Li was renowned for embodying a combination of martial and literary abilities that enabled him to hold civil and military posts interchangeably, and there is anecdotal evidence that he was once assigned by the emperor to teach another officer what might today be called "military science."[66] The materials attributed to Li Jing in the *Tong dian* frequently quote the ancient military classics, and they assume a highly mobile nomadic foe such as the Türks or Tuyuhun; their character is also consistent with what Li Jing is supposed to have taught at the emperor's behest. The date of composition is uncertain, but it seems most likely that it was some time between Li's defeat of the Eastern Türks in 630 and his death in 649.

Since only a few small snippets of the "Military Methods" have been published in English or other Western languages, all translations from it appearing in this study are my own. The text cited here, and quoted in translation, is the typeset, punctuated edition of Du You's *Tong dian* issued by the Chinese publisher Zhonghua shuju in 1988, which is based on careful collation of the best early printed editions.

In both the Chinese and Greek textual traditions it was commonplace for military writers to borrow extensively from earlier works in the same genre, often without any sort of attribution. The *Taktika* (or "Tactical Constitutions") composed by the emperor Leo VI near the beginning of the tenth century, for example, borrowed heavily from the *Strategikon*, while much material from Li Jing's "Military Methods" was copied, without attribution, into the *Wujing zongyao* ("Essentials of the Military Classics"), a military encyclopedia compiled at imperial command in the Northern Song and presented to the throne in 1044.[67] Under these circumstances, it is essential to distinguish between material that was original at the time of composition and earlier—in some cases much earlier—writings incorporated into the later work. With regard to the *Strategikon*, expert opinion holds that most of its content does indeed date from the late sixth century, the main exception being the section of Book XII dealing with infantry, which includes anachronisms more appropriate to the early sixth century CE (such as "Gothic shoes" and "Herulian swords") and probably represents "an earlier work adapted, perhaps somewhat revised, by the author and incorporated into the *Strategikon*."[68] The "Military Methods" also contains a fair amount of older material; much of this consists of easily identifiable quotations from the ancient military classics, but there are also some passages that contain obvious anachronisms such as the mention of chariots as a tactical element (when they had already fallen out of use well before the end of the Han dynasty).[69]

In addition to checking our texts against earlier military works and keeping an eye out for anachronisms, there are other means of assessing their value as guides to military practice. One is to compare them with other texts produced by the same society at roughly the same time. Although far from a certain indicator that what was written down was also being practiced, this may at least enable us to distinguish the idiosyncratic prescriptions of individual authors from the mainstream of military thought and practice. Thus some attention will be given to the anonymous Byzantine text known as the *Peri Strategikes*, now thought to date from the ninth century, with a particular focus on the common ground it shares with the *Strategikon*.[70] On the Chinese side, reference will occasionally be made to Li Quan's *Taibai yinjing*, probably dating from the middle of the eighth century, and to a variety of other military materials worked into the *Tong dian* alongside the passages from the "Military Methods." Of course, all of the caveats that have already been stated with regard to the *Strategikon* and the "Military Methods" apply to these other texts as well, and great care must be taken to distinguish common ground from the sort of direct copying disclosed by identical or near identical wording.

A more reliable check on the military texts is to look for parallels between their recommendations and whatever information can be gleaned from the accounts of actual military operations in roughly contemporaneous histories. For the Byzantines, these would include such works as the *Histories* of Procopius which describe the wars waged under the emperor Justinian in the first half of the sixth century, the work of Theophylact Simocatta on the reign of Maurikios, and accounts of Herakleios' campaigns against the Persians and Arabs by authors such as George of Pisidia. On the Chinese side there are numerous historical works covering this period, including not only the histories of the Sui dynasty and its northern precursors compiled under government auspices in the early years of the Tang dynasty, but also books composed as late as the Five Dynasties (907–960) and Northern Song (960–1127) on the basis of Tang or even earlier materials, such as the *Old Tang History* (*Jiu Tangshu*, dating from the 940s) and Sima Guang's magisterial *Comprehensive Mirror for Aid in Government* (*Zizhi tongjian*, completed in the mid-eleventh century). Modern scholars who have compared these histories with the military texts have generally been impressed by the extent to which they corroborate one another. Whitby, for example, notes that Philippicus' deployment against the Persians at Solachon in 586 was very similar to a battle plan recommended in the *Strategikon*, while Kaegi has detected the influence of the same book in Herakleios' campaigns against the Persians and in the Byzantine deployment against the Arabs at the Yarmuk in 635.[71] My own preliminary investigation of the "Military Methods" found quite precise agreement with certain techniques for scouting, reconnaissance, and camp security mentioned in the histories of the Northern Dynasties in connection with events that occurred in the sixth century, suggesting that Li Jing's recommendations were a codification of preexisting military practice rather than an exercise of the imagination.[72] Further parallels can be found between the "Military Methods" and techniques employed in military campaigns described in the histories of the Sui and Tang dynasties, and the authenticity and reliability of the Li Jing materials preserved in the *Tong dian* is also supported by a very special body of primary evidence: the documents of Tang military administration that have been recovered in modern times from Dunhuang, Turfan, and other sites in China's arid northwest. These parallels will be spelled out in the chapters that follow.

Notes

1 For a more detailed account of the defeat of Illig (Xieli), with references to the Chinese sources on which it is based, see David A. Graff, "Strategy and Contingency in the Tang Defeat of the Eastern Turks, 629–630," in Nicola Di Cosmo (ed.), *Warfare in Inner Asian History (500–1800)* (Leiden: Brill, 2002), especially pp. 48–56.

2 There is some disagreement in the sources as to which Tang general first proposed the plan to surprise Illig's camp. Li Jing's biographies in the Tang dynastic histories give full credit to him (*JTS* 67, p. 2479; *XTS* 93, p. 3814). The biographies of Li Shiji, however, identify their subject as the author of the strategy, but go on to say it was Li Jing who recognized the classical precedent and agreed to implement it (*JTS* 67, p. 2485; *XTS* 93, p. 3818). My reasons for preferring the latter version are laid out in David A. Graff, "Early T'ang Generalship and the Textual Tradition" (Ph.D. diss., Princeton University, 1995), pp. 494–97. The account of Han Xin's conquest of Qi can be found in *SJ* 92, p. 2620.

3 *Maurice's Strategikon: Handbook of Byzantine Military Strategy*, trans. George T. Dennis (Philadelphia: University of Pennsylvania Press, 1984) [hereafter cited as *Strategikon*], p. 93.

4 *Strategikon*, p. 94.

5 *Strategikon*, p. 95.

6 *Strategikon*, p. 96.

7 See *Sunzi jiaoshi*, ed. Wu Jiulong et al. (Beijing: Junshi kexue chubanshe, 1990), chapter 7, "Jun zheng pian," p. 126.

8 As will be explained in more detail later, what is left of Li Jing's book survives in the form of extracts quoted at length in chapters 148–59 of the *Tong dian*, an encyclopedic work dating from the late eighth century. It should not be confused with the *Questions and Replies of Tang Taizong and Li Duke of Wei* (*Tang Taizong Li Weigong wendui*), conventionally attributed to Li Jing and designated in the eleventh century as one of the "Seven Military Classics" (*Wu jing qi shu*); the *Questions and Replies* is a forgery, albeit a brilliant one, dating from the Five Dynasties (907–960) or early Northern Song (960–1127).

9 J.F.C. Fuller, *The Foundations of the Science of War* (London: Hutchinson and Co., 1926), p. 221.

10 B.H. Liddell Hart, "The Concentrated Essence of War," *Infantry Journal* 27 (1930), pp. 607–8; the quotations are from page 607 (italics in the original). Harry Holbert Turney-High, drawing on a US cavalry manual of the 1930s, listed fourteen principles overlapping somewhat with those of Fuller; see his *Primitive War: Its Practice and Concepts*, 2nd ed. (Columbia: University of South Carolina Press, 1991), pp. 25–6.

11 Michael I. Handel, *Masters of War: Classical Strategic Thought*, 2nd, revised ed. (London: Frank Cass, 1996), p. 16.

12 Turney-High, *Primitive War*, especially chapter 2.

13 Alfred H. Burne, *Battlefields of England* (London: Methuen and Co., 1950), p. 39.

14 Russell F. Weigley, *The American Way of War: A History of United States Military Strategy and Policy* (Bloomington: Indiana University Press, 1973); Richard W. Harrison, *The Russian Way of War: Operational Art, 1904–1940* (Lawrence: University Press of Kansas, 2001); Robert M. Citino, *The German Way of War: From the Thirty Years' War to the Third Reich* (Lawrence: University Press of Kansas, 2005). With regard to Chinese strategic culture, the most important books have been Alastair Iain Johnston, *Cultural Realism: Strategic Culture and Grand Strategy in Chinese History* (Princeton, NJ: Princeton University Press, 1995), Andrew Scobell, *China's Use of Military Force: Beyond the Great Wall and the Long March* (Cambridge: Cambridge University Press, 2003), and Huiyun Feng, *Chinese Strategic Culture and Foreign Policy Decision-Making: Confucianism, Leadership and War* (London and New York: Routledge, 2007). For a sense of the rest of the literature, see the bibliography in Lawrence Sondhaus, *Strategic Culture and Ways of War* (London and New York: Routledge, 2006).

15 Sondhaus, *Strategic Culture and Ways of War*, already outdated by the continuing torrent of scholarly production.

16 John Keegan, *A History of Warfare* (New York: Alfred A. Knopf, 1993); Victor Davis Hanson, *Carnage and Culture: Landmark Battles in the Rise of Western Power* (New York: Random House, 2001); John A. Lynn, *Battle: A History of Combat and Culture* (Boulder, CO: Westview Press, 2003). Hanson's book was published in the United Kingdom under the title, *Why the West Has Won*.

17 Keegan, *A History of Warfare*, p. 12.

18 Keegan, *A History of Warfare*, pp. 387–8. Also see pages 221, 244, and 332–3.

19 Keegan, *A History of Warfare*, p. 202.

20 Hanson, *Carnage and Culture*, p. 123; the list is presented most succinctly on pages 21–2. For Parker's list, see Geoffrey Parker (ed.), *The Cambridge Illustrated History of Warfare* (Cambridge: Cambridge University Press, 1995), pp. 2–8.

21 Hanson, *Carnage and Culture*, pp. 12, 20, and *passim*. Parker makes much the same point but in a more nuanced way; see his mention of Asiatic horse archers, *The Cambridge Illustrated History of Warfare*, p. 2.

22 Hanson, *Carnage and Culture*, pp. 96, 129–30, 154, and 162.

23 See Hans van Wees, "The Development of the Hoplite Phalanx: Iconography and Reality in the Seventh Century," in Hans van Wees (ed.), *War and Violence in Ancient Greece* (London and Swansea: Duckworth and The Classical Press of Wales, 2000), pp. 125–66, and Peter Krentz, "Deception in Archaic and Classical Greek Warfare," pp. 167–200 in the same volume. Krentz lists more than 140 examples of deception ranging from the eighth century to the fourth century BCE, including the battle of Sepeia in 494 BCE, when the Spartans caught an Argive army off guard by pretending to disband for breakfast (p. 184). For cavalry and peltasts, see Leslie J. Worley, *Hippeis: The Cavalry of Ancient Greece* (Boulder, CO: Westview Press, 1994), p. 1; Worley does not mention Hanson by name, however. A response by Hanson that might be interpreted as a grudging concession that these critics may not be entirely wrong can also be found in the van Wees volume: "Hoplite Battle as Ancient Greek Warfare: When, Where, and Why?" in *War and Violence in Ancient Greece*, pp. 201–32.

24 Harry Sidebottom, *Ancient Warfare: A Very Short Introduction* (Oxford: Oxford University Press, 2004), p. xi.

25 Lynn, *Battle*, pp. 18–19; the quotation is from page 19. Sidebottom makes the same point, and in almost the same words; *Ancient Warfare*, p. 126.
26 Lynn, *Battle*, pp. xvi, xxiii, 20, and 70.
27 Lynn, *Battle*, p. 23.
28 Lynn, *Battle*, p. 71, also see pp. 23–25 and 70.
29 John Grenier, *The First Way of War: American War Making on the Frontier, 1607–1814* (Cambridge: Cambridge University Press, 2005), pp. 10, 32–4, and *passim*.
30 Sidebottom, *Ancient Warfare*, p. x. Other shots at Hanson can be found on pp. xi, xiii, and 124–6. Interestingly, Hanson himself chose to emphasize the normative and ideological aspect of his subject in "Hoplite Battle as Ancient Greek Warfare: When, Where, and Why?" See p. 206 in particular.
31 Jeremy Black, *Rethinking Military History* (London and New York: Routledge, 2004), p. 55; other criticisms of the "Western Way of War" can be found on pp. 1–2, 57–8, 84, and 95.
32 One example from Lynn will suffice: "It is impossible to establish the level of training and coordination in Chinese forces with certainty, so the question remains as to whether Chinese troops constituted disciplined armies or something less." Lynn, *Battle*, p. 38; another, similar statement can be found on p. 40.
33 In recent years, bashing the "Western Way of War" thesis has become something of an academic cottage industry. In addition to the examples already cited, two other books that criticize Hanson are Ian Morris, *War! What Is It Good For? – Conflict and the Progress of Civilization from Primates to Robots* (New York: Farrar, Straus and Giroux, 2014), especially chapters 2 and 3, and Beatrice Heuser, *The Evolution of Strategy: Thinking War from Antiquity to the Present* (Cambridge: Cambridge University Press, 2010), pp. 43–4, 89, and 96. Heuser points specifically to the Byzantine experience as a contradiction of Hanson's thesis (pp. 43–4). The cultural approach exemplified by "the Western Way of War" is also subjected to critical scrutiny in Patrick Porter, *Military Orientalism: Eastern War Through Western Eyes* (New York: Columbia University Press, 2009), with specific mention of Hanson on pp. 5 and 17.
34 Perhaps because it is so ubiquitous, this phenomenon has received relatively little attention from researchers. Scobell has examined what he calls "The Chinese Cult of Defense" – really just one aspect of the larger whole (see *China's Use of Military Force*, especially pp. 26–38). Another Western work that remarks on the phenomenon is Ralph D. Sawyer, *The Tao of Deception: Unorthodox Warfare in Historic and Modern China* (New York: Basic Books, 2007), pp. 328–31. For a Chinese perspective, see Peng Guangqian and Yao Youzhi (eds.), *The Science of Military Strategy* (Beijing: Military Science Publishing House, 2005), pp. 87–93 and 128. At the personal and anecdotal level, a Chinese academic well connected with military circles in the PRC once told me that the Gulf War of 1991 had caused consternation within the PLA leadership not only because of its demonstration of U.S. technological prowess, but also because it showed a level of mastery of Sunzi's teachings that had been thought unattainable by Westerners.
35 William H. McNeill, *Keeping Together in Time: Dance and Drill in Human History* (Cambridge, MA: Harvard University Press, 1995), pp. viii, 2–4, 10, and 106.
36 McNeill, *Keeping Together in Time*, pp. 110–12, 122–4, and 127.
37 Black, *Rethinking Military History*, p. 57.
38 Hanson, *Carnage and Culture*, p. 8.
39 Clifford Geertz, *The Interpretation of Cultures* (New York: Basic Books, 1973), pp. 4–5.
40 Geertz, "Thick Description: Toward an Interpretive Theory of Culture," in *The Interpretation of Cultures*, pp. 3–30.
41 Johnston discusses these problems, without reference to Hanson of course, in *Cultural Realism*, pp. 5–15.
42 Johnston, *Cultural Realism*, pp. 36–8.
43 Hanson, *Carnage and Culture*, p. xv.

44 Hanson, *The Western Way of War*, pp. 35, 38, 224–25; also see Hanson's contribution in Parker, *The Cambridge Illustrated History of Warfare*, pp. 15–16.
45 Johnston, *Cultural Realism*, p. 38 (especially note 5).
46 Geertz, "Religion as a Cultural System," in *The Interpretation of Cultures*, p. 89.
47 Geertz, "Religion as a Cultural System," p. 91.
48 Geertz, "Thick Description," pp. 10, 12, and 17–18.
49 Unlike genes and other nonsymbolic information sources, which are only models *for*, not models *of*, culture patterns have an intrinsic double aspect: they give meaning, that is, objective conceptual form, to social and psychological reality both by shaping themselves to it and by shaping it to themselves.
  (Geertz, "Religion as a Cultural System," p. 93)
50 Geertz, "Thick Description," p. 5 (Kluckhohn); Geertz, "The Impact of the Concept of Culture on the Concept of Man," in *The Interpretation of Cultures*, pp. 41 (Herskovitz 1955) and 52.
51 As interworked systems of construable signs (what, ignoring provincial usages, I would call symbols), culture is not a power, something to which social events, behaviors, institutions, or processes can be causally attributed; it is a context, something within which they can be intelligibly – that is, thickly – described.
  (Geertz, "Thick Description," p. 14)
52 For more on the *Tong dian*, see Denis Twitchett, *The Writing of Official History Under the T'ang* (Cambridge: Cambridge University Press, 1992), pp. 104–7.
53 An attempt to reconstruct the original text from the fragments in the *Tong dian* was made by Wang Zongyi (1837–1906). But his *Li Weigong bingfa jiben* rests on far too many unwarranted assumptions regarding the organization and contents of Li Jing's work. Wang's reconstruction was reprinted in 1988 in the second volume of the massive *Zhongguo bingshu jicheng* collection issued by the PLA publishing house (Jiefangjun chubanshe), and there is also an annotated, punctuated edition with a translation into modern Chinese: Deng Zezong, *Li Jing bingfa jiben zhuyi* (Beijing: Jiefangjun chubanshe, 1990).
54 *Strategikon*, pp. xvi–xvii.
55 John E. Wiita, "The Ethnika in Byzantine Military Treatises" (Ph.D. diss., University of Minnesota, 1977), p. 29 ff.
56 Eugène Darkó, "Influences Touraniennes sur l'évolution de l'art militaire des Grecs, des Romains et des Byzantins," *Byzantion* 12 (1937), pp. 122–3.
57 Mark Whittow, *The Making of Orthodox Byzantium, 600–1025* (Basingstoke, Hampshire: Macmillan, 1996), p. 69. Also see Michael Whitby, *The Emperor Maurice and His Historian: Theophylact Simocatta on Persian and Balkan Warfare* (Oxford: Clarendon Press, 1988), p. 132, especially note 63, and Walter E. Kaegi, *Heraclius: Emperor of Byzantium* (Cambridge: Cambridge University Press, 2003), p. 14.
58 Whitby, *The Emperor Maurice*, pp. 6–7, 13; *Strategikon*, p. xii.
59 Whitby, *The Emperor Maurice*, pp. 131–2, 179, and 242. One opinion holds that the *Strategikon* was written for Roman commanders in the Balkans at the end of the sixth century; see James Howard-Johnston, "Heraclius' Persian Campaigns and the Revival of the East Roman Empire, 622–630," *War in History* 6.1 (January 1999), p. 31.
60 *Strategikon*, p. xvi; Whitby, *The Emperor Maurice*, p. 130; Kaegi, *Heraclius*, p. 96; Wiita, "The Ethnika," p. 15.
61 "The author, it is clear, was an experienced soldier who had commanded troops on at least two fronts." Dennis in *Strategikon*, p. xv.
62 *Strategikon*, p. xix.
63 Dennis was building in part on the earlier, unpublished work of Oliver I. Spaulding, Jr., and others. A new translation of the *Strategikon* by Philip Rance was said to be underway at the time of writing, but was not yet available for reference.
64 *JTS* 147, p. 982; *THY* 36, p. 660; *XTS* 59, p. 1563; Wang Yaochen et al., *Chongwen zongmu* (Taipei: Taiwan shangwu yinshuguan, 1965) 3, p. 176; Chao Gongwu, *Junzhai*

dushu zhi (Taipei: Guangwen shuju, 1967) 14, p. 18a. Also see Wang Wenjin's preface to the 1988 Zhonghua edition of the *Tong dian*, pp. vi–vii.

65 Li's biographies can be found in *JTS* 67, p. 2475 and *XTS* 93, p. 3811; there is also a modern biography by Lei Jiaji, *Li Jing* (Yonghe, Taiwan: Lianming wenhua youxian gongsi, 1980).

66 Wu Jing, *Zhenguan zhengyao* (Taipei: Hongye shuju, 1990) 2, p. 60; *XTS* 94, p. 3828.

67 For Leo VI, see *Strategikon*, p. xiii. Of the Byzantine authors, Alphonse Dain has observed, "Au lieu de tenir compte des faits, les écrivains militaires n'ont eu d'autre souci que de reproduire les renseignements et les recettes qu'ils tenaient de leurs prédécesseurs." See "Les Stratégistes byzantins," *Travaux et mémoires* 2 (1967), p. 318.

68 *Strategikon*, p. xviii.

69 For example, *TD* 148, p. 3789.

70 Translated by George T. Dennis in *Three Byzantine Military Treatises* (Washington, DC: Dumbarton Oaks, 1985). Experts, including Dennis, long thought the work dated from the sixth century. More recently, however, Salvatore Cosentino has argued convincingly that it is really a product of the mid-ninth century; see S. Cosentino, "The Syrianos' Strategikon: A Ninth Century Source?" *Bizantinistica: Rivista di studi bizantini e slavi*, n.s. 2 (2000), 243–80.

71 Whitby, *The Emperor Maurice*, pp. 281–2; Walter E. Kaegi, *Byzantium and the Early Islamic Conquests* (Cambridge: Cambridge University Press, 1992), p. 123; Kaegi, *Heraclius*, pp. 108–9, 115, 117, 129–30, 161, 168, and 308–9.

72 David A. Graff, "Li Jing's Antecedents: Continuity and Change in the Pragmatics of Medieval Chinese Warfare," *Early Medieval China*, vol. 13–14, part 1 (2007), pp. 81–97.

2 Resources and institutions

Parallels between the Roman Empire and Han China once fueled the historian Arnold Toynbee's speculations about the life cycles of civilizations; more recently, the Rome–Han comparison has become one of the staple subjects treated in world history textbooks.[1] Both empires arose at roughly the same time, around 200 BCE, when Rome overcame its major rivals in the Mediterranean world and the Han dynasty founder Liu Bang rebuilt the shattered and short-lived Qin empire on a more lasting foundation. Both controlled territories and populations of comparable size.[2] Although they did not fall at exactly the same time—the collapse of Han's political heir, the Western Jin dynasty, at the beginning of the fourth century CE anticipating the dissolution of the Roman Empire in the west by more than a century—the pattern of their demise was remarkably similar. In both cases a large part of the old empire was lost to "barbarian" interlopers; the western half of the Roman Empire, including Gaul, Spain, Britain, Italy (with the city of Rome itself), and much of North Africa, fell under the control of Germanic invaders, while northern China—the ancient heartland of Chinese civilization in the watershed of the Yellow River—was overrun by various peoples of steppe origin. In both cases, a portion of the empire was able to survive. The Eastern Roman emperors, with their capital at Constantinople on the Bosporus, the waterway linking the Black Sea and the Aegean, maintained their grip on the richer and more urbanized half of the old empire, including Greece, the Balkans, Anatolia, Syria, and Egypt. In China, the Jin ruling house retained control of vast territories in the south, from the Yangzi River valley to the area around today's Hanoi. In their time of decline, moreover, both empires saw the spread of new "salvationist" religions, Buddhism in China and Christianity in the late Roman world.

Thereafter, however, east and west parted company. Repeated efforts by Eastern Roman emperors to recover the western half of the old empire ultimately ended in failure. The seaborne expedition to Carthage launched by Leo I in 468 was a costly fiasco, and even the more famous and geographically far-reaching efforts undertaken by Justinian and his general Belisarius in the middle decades of the sixth century resulted in no more than the temporary recovery of portions of Italy, Spain, and North Africa. An especially disastrous chain of events began in 602 with the emperor Maurikios' decision to have his Balkan army winter north of the Danube, which led to the mutiny of that army and the murder of Maurikios, which in turn provided the Sasanid Persian ruler Khusro with a pretext for attacking the Eastern Roman Empire. In the long, desperate struggle that ensued the emperor Herakleios eventually prevailed over Khusro in 628, but only after the temporary loss of Syria, Palestine, and Egypt and a siege of Constantinople by the Persians and their Avar allies in the summer of 626. Weakened as it was by this ordeal, the empire was ill prepared to confront its next major challenge, the Arab onslaught that began in the 630s. Inspired and united by their new religion of Islam, the Arabs overran Palestine, Syria, Egypt, and eventually North Africa and Spain as well. From that time onward, the empire essentially consisted of Anatolia and the lower Balkan Peninsula, plus a mix of scattered outposts that varied over time. Although there were periods of limited revival and expansion, most notably between the early ninth century and the mid-eleventh century, the empire was never again in a position to entertain the recovery of the formerly Roman lands around the western Mediterranean. Dwindling gradually over time until it consisted of little more than the city of Constantinople itself, the empire finally fell to the Ottoman Turks in 1453. Although its rulers and people continued to call themselves "Romans" down to the very end, by the mid-seventh century at the latest Greek had completely supplanted Latin as the language of administration and the lingua franca of the empire's still quite diverse peoples. In recognition of this, scholarly convention generally affixes the label "Byzantine" to this diminished, Greek-speaking realm (after Byzantium, the original name of the city that became Constantinople in the first half of the fourth century).

East Asia followed a different trajectory. The failure of the legitimist Eastern Jin dynasty and its successor states in the south to muster the necessary resources and political will to recover the lost north would at first appear to parallel the Eastern Roman experience, but from there the pattern diverged dramatically. By the early 380s, the (temporarily) dominant warlord in the north was attempting (unsuccessfully) to conquer the south, an effort that would be repeated by the Toba Wei rulers who united the north under their control in the middle of the fifth century. Although they, too, were unsuccessful, their period of dominance in the north saw the beginning of the emergence of a new, mixed-blood elite that combined the martial prowess of the steppe warrior with Han Chinese traditions of literacy and statecraft. When rebellion and civil war split the Northern Wei into two rival regimes in the 530s, Western Wei (later Northern Zhou) in the Wei River valley around the old Han capital of Chang'an and Eastern Wei (later Northern Qi) in the North China Plain, the leaders of the western regime pioneered the creation of new military institutions that enabled them to augment their initially meager resources by drawing soldiers from the indigenous (mainly Han) farming population. With the new armies thus created, the Northern Zhou was able to overcome its eastern competitor and reunify the northern part of China in the late 570s. Then, after a coup d'état within the ruling circle had brought a new family to power with the new dynastic name of Sui, the now united north finally succeeded in conquering the south in a massive campaign undertaken in 588–589.[3] Virtually all of the territories once ruled by the Han dynasty were now reunited under a single monarch, but he came from the barbarian north rather than the legitimist south. In Western terms, it was as if Charlemagne had not simply been crowned emperor at Rome in 800, but had gone on to take Greece, Syria, Egypt, North Africa, and Constantinople itself, eliminating the eastern emperor and reconstructing the old Roman Empire—in its entirety—under Frankish rule.

Although the reunified Chinese empire dissolved again into rebellion and civil war in the early 610s under the combined impact of natural disasters and the second Sui emperor's foolhardy persistence in massive and costly campaigns to subdue the northern Korean kingdom of Koguryŏ, another family soon emerged from within the same northwestern leadership circle to overcome the various centrifugal forces and reunite the empire under new management. In 617 Li Yuan, a high-ranking officer of the Sui dynasty and first cousin of the reigning emperor, occupied the capital; the following year he proclaimed himself the founding emperor of the new Tang dynasty, and by the end of 623 had crushed all serious rivals within China. His son and successor, Li Shimin (Tang Taizong), went on to defeat the Eastern Türks in 630, bringing the dynasty close to the peak of its military power. Although considerably weakened in its later years, the Tang dynasty lasted until 907. After an interregnum of several decades, the so-called "Five Dynasties and Ten Kingdoms," it was succeeded by another unified dynastic regime, the Northern Song (960–1127). Despite occasional and often lengthy periods of disunity and civil war thereafter, China's unity has been restored repeatedly and for much longer periods of time—in marked contrast to the fragmentation that prevailed and persisted in Europe and the Mediterranean world.

The juxtaposition of these histories with the peculiar geographies of East Asia and the Mediterranean had quite different implications for the security of early Tang China and the Eastern Roman Empire. Once imperial unity had been restored within China, all serious security threats came to be situated along an arc running from the mountain fringe of Sichuan in the west to southern Manchuria and the approaches to the Korean Peninsula in the northeast. Directly to the north and northwest were vast grasslands and deserts; too arid for Chinese-style agriculture, these territories were the home of a variety of nomadic peoples including Türks, Qidan, Qay (also called Tatabï and Xi), and the Turkic Tiele tribes of whom the most powerful and significant were the Uighurs. During the Sui and early Tang up to 630 the dominant power in this region was the Eastern Türk qaghanate, and after its elimination by the Tang other contenders such as the Xueyantuo attempted to take its place. A narrow sliver of Chinese settlement ran northwestward along the so-called Gansu Corridor as far as the neighborhood of Dunhuang. The network of trade routes known today as the Silk Road followed this path, continuing westward through the scattered Indo-Iranian oasis communities of the Western Regions (today's Xinjiang), into Sogdiana with its trading cities of Samarkand, Ferghana, and Tashkent, and eventually reaching the shores of the Black Sea and the Mediterranean. Although the inhabitants of these regions did not themselves pose a serious threat to the security of the Tang empire, control of the trade routes through Gansu and the Western Regions did present a military challenge for China's rulers given the presence of hostile powers on both their northern and southern flanks. Immediately to the south, in the

Kokonor region (today's Qinghai province), were the Tuyuhun, a pastoral people of mixed Turkic and Tibetan origin, and to their south, with its core territory in the Yarlung Tsangbo valley, was the vast Tibetan empire, a newly arisen power that was well positioned to threaten not only the northwestern trade routes but also the western edge of the Sichuan Basin. In the far northeast, the other end of the frontier arc was less obviously threatened but still problematic. The Liao River marked the boundary of the strong northern Korean kingdom of Koguryŏ, which had connections with the steppe nomads and was also frequently embroiled in conflicts with the other two Korean states, Paekche in the southwest and Silla in the southeast. The reunified Chinese empire was easily drawn into the power politics of the Korean Peninsula, which had once been a part of the Han empire. This involvement carried the potential for conflict with another, more distant power with strong interests and alliances in Korea, the emerging Yamato state in the Japanese islands.

The southern and eastern arc of Tang China's periphery, in contrast, confronted no major powers. Although the far south—today's provinces of Guangdong, Guangxi, and Guizhou, plus northern Vietnam—was by no means placid, conflicts there tended to be offensive "wars of choice" against lesser states (such as the 605 Sui campaign against Linyi in central Vietnam) or police actions against restive indigenous tribes. No real threat came from this quarter, and the eastern and southeastern coasts were even quieter; with no maritime power looming beyond the eastern horizon, there were no disturbances above the level of small-scale piracy. The Chinese empire in this period thus had no need for a standing navy and did not bother to maintain one. Huge flotillas of warships and transports might be constructed on an ad hoc basis, as when Sui and Tang forces swept down the Yangzi River from Sichuan to conquer the south (in 588–589 and 621, respectively), or when Sui and Tang launched seaborne expeditions to the Korean Peninsula (in 612 and 660, respectively), but these forces were promptly disbanded as soon as the immediate need for them had passed. This configuration also meant that there was a vast, secure, and relatively peaceful hinterland that could supply manpower and provisions to sustain imperial forces along the lines of confrontation in the north and west. The distance from the entrepôt of Guangzhou in the far south to the eastern capital of Luoyang near the Yellow River was 1,300 kilometers as the crow flies; from Chengdu in the Sichuan Basin to the metropolis of Yangzhou near the mouth of the Yangzi the distance was 1,420 kilometers. A canal network built by the Sui emperors and maintained by their Tang successors greatly facilitated the transfer of resources from south to north. The Tongji Canal crossed the Henan plains to connect the Yellow River with the rich rice basket of the Lower Yangzi region, then extended westward along the Yellow River and the Wei River (as far as Chang'an) as a supplement to those silt-laden and not easily navigable natural waterways. Another extension, the Yongji Canal, ran from Liyang on the Yellow River across the Hebei plain to the vicinity of today's Beijing to provision the armies on the northeastern frontier. Although military efforts in one sector of the northern arc might be undercut by developments in another sector, as when challenges from the Türks and Tibetans necessitated the withdrawal of Chinese forces from the Korean Peninsula in the late 670s, the early Tang empire never had to deal with simultaneous, potentially mortal threats arising from opposite points of the compass.

The position of the Eastern Roman empire was far more precarious. For Sui and Tang China, the sea was remote and peripheral; for Byzantium it was central and ever-present. The main imperial territories were coastlands or rocky peninsulas, such as Greece and Anatolia, jutting into the Mediterranean. With Upper Egypt as the only major exception, there were few places in the empire where one could be more than a hundred miles from salt water. Given this geographical configuration, the deterioration of the old Roman roads (such as the Via Egnatia, running from Dyrrachium on the Adriatic across Thrace to Constantinople), and the superior cost-effectiveness of water transport in premodern times, the defense of the empire was heavily reliant upon seaborne lines of communication. Maritime forces were essential, and a navy was always maintained as a regular part of the military establishment. Naval forces and water transport were all the more essential insofar as the Eastern Roman Empire (again in contrast to Tang China) frequently faced major threats in more than one sector, the largest problems being the Sasanian Persian empire confronting the Byzantines on the upper Euphrates and migrating tribes pressing upon the Danube frontier. The latter included peoples of steppe origin—first the Huns, then the Avars, and later the Bulgars—as well as the less organized Slav tribes that were often under their domination. The empire lacked the wherewithal to be strong everywhere at once. Peace with the Persians after 591 freed the emperor Maurikios to campaign against the Slavs and Avars in the Balkans, but the outbreak of full-scale war with the Sasanians after Maurikios' overthrow in 602 necessitated the transfer of substantial forces from west to east and the virtual abandonment of the lower Balkans to Slav and Avar inroads. The loss of Egypt and Syria to the Arabs opened a third front from the 640s onward: the eastern Mediterranean and the Aegean, formerly a logistical asset, became a new line of attack as Arab fleets menaced the empire's coastlands and even the capital itself. On the landward side, the line of the Taurus and Anti-Taurus Mountains in southeastern Anatolia proved an effective barrier to permanent Arab occupation but never afforded absolute protection against raiding parties and invading armies. On more than one occasion, as in 673–678 and 717–718, the survival of the empire depended upon the massive walls of Constantinople itself, and the ability of the Byzantine navy to keep the capital supplied by sea. The Chinese capitals, Chang'an and Luoyang, had no such strategic role; although surrounded by a wall totaling twenty-two miles in length, Chang'an was never successfully defended against attack during the Sui and Tang dynasties.

The population of the Roman Empire in the second century CE was probably larger than that of late Han China, but the shape of the Byzantine realm, its military institutions, and the peculiar circumstances it faced dictated that its rulers would usually not be able to mobilize human and material resources on the same scale as their Chinese counterparts. Figures from the year 609, when the Sui dynasty was at the height of its power, indicate that the Chinese population registered by the state was approximately forty-six million. (The actual population was surely somewhat larger. The bias in the official reporting system was always downward: households sought to avoid registration by the authorities in order to evade taxation, and local officials were not likely to inflate the figures since they would be expected to come up with larger tax revenues if they did so.[4]) Figures from the 740s, when the Tang empire was at its height, are at roughly the same level, showing an empire-wide total of 48,909,800 registered individuals.[5] In between these two peaks, however, is a trough, and it lies in precisely the period of greatest interest for the present study. Figures thought to date from 639 show a total of less than three million households, not even one-third of the comparable figure for 609.[6] This dip is generally interpreted as a consequence of the decade of civil war that gripped the country from the beginning of the Sui collapse in 613 to the Tang consolidation in the early 620s, and seen as less a matter of deaths due to warfare (although there were surely a great many) than of the inability or unwillingness of the nascent Tang regime to fully reregister the population, especially in the populous but politically sensitive and potentially unstable region of the North China Plain where many local powerholders had submitted to the new rulers in exchange for their tacit acceptance of a modicum of local autonomy.[7] In spite of these straitened circumstances, the early Tang rulers were not short of soldiers. One authority has estimated that in 626 the part-time soldiers (*fubing*) who formed the backbone of the empire's military establishment numbered about 260,000; once standing guard units in the capital and various other components are figured in, the regular military establishment—exclusive of short-term conscripts—must have been well in excess of 300,000.[8] In 630 Tang Taizong sent a total of 100,000 men against the Eastern Türks, divided among several widely separated field armies, and 100,000 were likewise mobilized for the 645 campaign against Koguryŏ, with 60,000 marching overland and 40,000 going by sea.[9] The mobilizational capability of the Tang dynasty's Sui predecessor was apparently far greater. In 588 the Sui, then a regional regime controlling only the north, deployed 518,000 men (also divided among several field armies) to conquer the Chen state in the south.[10] And for his gargantuan effort against Koguryŏ in 612, the second Sui emperor reportedly called up 1,133,800 soldiers and twice that many men to serve in logistical support roles. Of these, only 305,000 managed to cross the Liao River into Koguryŏ.[11] An "army" of this size—if indeed it really *was* this size—would only have been possible if it consisted of a number of smaller contingents marching separately (ideally by different routes), and occupying their own camps. In fact, we are told that this Sui army was divided into marching columns of 20,000 men each, roughly comparable to the Napoleonic *corps d'armée*.[12] The early Tang general and military writer Li Jing took 20,000 men as the standard size for an expeditionary army, and what we know of early Tang army sizes suggests that this was not an arbitrary choice.[13]

Estimates of the population of the Roman Empire between the reconquests of Justinian and the fall of Maurikios vary widely, from a conservative figure of seventeen million to high-end guesses of thirty or even forty million, and have a much weaker documentary basis than the corresponding numbers for Sui and Tang China.[14] As A.H.M. Jones lamented, our information is so vague, and facts and figures are so sparse that it is impossible to calculate what the population of the empire was at any date, or how much it declined, if, as is very probable if not certain, it did decline.[15]

More recent scholarship indicates that the famous "plague of Justinian" which first broke out in 541 and returned in several waves later in the sixth century, may have eliminated 30 percent or more of the empire's population.[16] The territorial losses suffered in the first half of the seventh century—first temporary losses to the Persians, followed by the permanent loss of essentially the same territories to the Arabs—further reduced the human and material resources available to the Byzantine state, whose population fell to perhaps seven million inhabitants of the remaining core territories (Asia Minor, Greece and the southern Balkans, and parts of Italy).[17] The loss was material and financial as well as demographic, a point that is especially obvious in the case of Egypt, the imperial grain basket that had provisioned Constantinople.

The overall size of the Roman military establishment in the sixth and seventh centuries is another matter of considerable uncertainty. The starting point for most estimates is the figure of 150,000 given by the historian Agathias, a contemporary of Justinian. This number is likely both too low and too high—too low, because it evidently covers only the mobile field armies (the *comitatenses*) without making any allowance for the more numerous second-tier frontier and garrison troops (the *limitanei*) who may have numbered as many as 300,000 or 350,000; too high, because if it has any basis at all it is necessarily derived from the paper strength of the *comitatenses* and does not account for such things as officers keeping non-existent soldiers on the rolls in order to collect their ration allowances and other emoluments, a practice that was commonplace at the time but whose precise impact on unit strengths is simply impossible to gauge.[18] Several modern estimates have placed the paper strength of Justinian's military establishment at between 250,000 and 500,000 men, while recognizing that not all of the *limitanei* were militarily effective and that some allowance must be made for padding of the rolls in both the field armies and the second-tier units.[19] We may be on firmer ground with the reported strengths of Byzantine expeditionary and campaign armies. Very large deployments, such as the 52,000 that Anastasius is supposed to have fielded against the Persians in 503, are extremely rare in the sources. The sixth-century campaign armies whose sizes are mentioned in the histories of Procopius and Agathias range from 7,500 up to 30,000; Belisarius reportedly commanded 25,000 at the battle of Dara in 530 and led only 15,000 regular troops to Africa in 533. The impression given by the histories is confirmed by the technical military writings. The late Roman military author Vegetius, probably writing in the fifth century, recommends a force of 12,000 men for an ordinary campaign and up to 24,000 for a larger effort, while the *Strategikon* considers an army of 15,000 to 20,000 to be "large" and armies in the 5,000 to 15,000-man range as more the usual case.[20] There is no reason to believe that armies became any larger in the first half of the seventh century; by then, according to Walter Kaegi, "It was extremely difficult for the government to support more than about 15,000 expeditionary troops of reasonable quality in the field."[21] After the loss of the better half of the empire to the Arabs, campaign forces became smaller still, often no more than 3,000 men, and the total military establishment may have shrunk to less than 80,000 men.[22]

As "soft" as they are, these numbers nevertheless permit us to draw a few tentative generalizations when the Chinese and Byzantine figures are juxtaposed. The first is that at almost every point from the Sui conquest of the south in 589 to the end of the seventh century and beyond, the population from which the Sui and Tang emperors were able to extract resources exceeded that controlled by their Roman counterparts *at the same time*. (The obvious exception would be the decade from 613 to 623, a period of civil war that saw the collapse of the Sui dynasty and its eventual replacement by the Tang, though this was also a time when the Eastern Roman Empire had to deal with a Persian invasion and the temporary loss of important territories such as Syria and Egypt.) Once it had consolidated its power, the Tang empire faced nothing comparable to the permanent losses that the Byzantines suffered at the hands of the Arabs beginning in the mid-630s, at least not until the rebellion of An Lushan erupted in 755. From the founding of the dynasty to that cataclysmic event, the secular trend of the empire's population registration was upward, with a total of 52,880,488 individuals recorded on the eve of the rebellion.[23] However, the population of the Eastern Roman empire in the second half of the sixth century, from Justinian to Maurikios, was larger—perhaps even twice as large— as the *registered* population of China under Tang Taizong in the second quarter of the seventh century. This ratio is to some extent reflected in the relative size of the regular military establishments of the two empires; if the *limitanei* are included, the late sixth-century Roman manpower total is higher than the Chinese total under Taizong, though probably not by a factor of two. On the other hand, the campaign armies that Chinese rulers put into the field in the sixth and seventh centuries were usually larger than those fielded by the Eastern Roman emperors. The straitened circumstances faced by Tang Taizong did not prevent him from raising and deploying forces that exceeded those of the Eastern Roman Empire at its height in the second half of the sixth century, and his reign was in fact a period of vigorous expansion.

If this pattern is anything more than a mistaken impression resulting from poor data, it may be in part explained by the differing spatial configurations that have already been described: facing more and more serious threats from more points of the compass, and with a less favorable ratio of secure hinterland to threatened perimeter, the Byzantines had more that needed to be protected and less leeway to concentrate forces in great quantity for offensive (or defensive) purposes. A more complete explanation, however, requires that the military institutions of the two empires be taken into account.

As the inheritor of the military traditions of the Principate, the Eastern Roman army of the sixth and seventh centuries was made up largely of men who were in theory, and to a considerable extent in practice as well, professional soldiers— professional in the sense that they enlisted for long periods of time, served for pay, and relied on soldiering as their main or even their sole source of income.[24] Men entered the service through both conscription (with landowners required to furnish quotas of recruits) and voluntary enlistment, though over the course of the sixth century the latter element became increasingly predominant.[25] Military service also had a hereditary aspect. Although sons of soldiers were no longer required to join the army as had been the case during the fourth century, recruiters looked favorably on military parentage and soldiers were often eager to secure the advantages of military status for their sons.[26] Thus, the emperor Maurikios's decision to grant his soldiers the right to have their sons succeed them in the army was a highly popular move.[27] Once enlisted, men typically remained in the army for decades, even the whole of their working life. In the fourth century soldiers were expected to serve for a minimum of twenty years, and could not receive full benefits (such as grants of cash or land, and exemptions from taxes and corvée) until they had completed twenty-four years. There was no upper age limit, with the result that men of sixty years of age, or more, could still be found in the ranks.[28] Compensation took several forms that included substantial cash gifts (donatives) once every five years and also whenever a new emperor came to the throne, ration allowances (called *annonae*) that came to be commuted from payment in kind to cash payments, and allowances, also paid in cash, for the purchase of clothing, weapons, and horses.[29] The ration allowances were far from lavish, with the lowest ranking soldiers in the mid-sixth century receiving somewhat less in a year than an Egyptian day laborer could expect to make over the same period, but pay increased with rank and time in service, and it was possible, by economizing, to make a profit off the various other allowances. In addition, soldiers were exempted from a variety of taxes and enjoyed certain legal privileges as well.[30]

This professional model of service was more fully reflected in the mobile field armies, the *comitatenses*, than in the second-tier units that made up the *limitanei*. Organizationally descended from the legions and other formations that had been positioned to guard the empire's frontiers during the Principate, and usually continuing to bear the same unit names and designations, the *limitanei* had tended to devolve over time into static garrisons that performed frontier defense and gendarmerie roles. In general, they had a stronger local identity than the units of the *comitatenses*; they were less likely to be transferred outside of their home areas, and were more deeply rooted in the local economy and society, as illustrated by the Upper Egyptian soldiers documented in the late sixth-century Syene papyri, many of whom doubled as boatmen.[31] At some point in the fifth century, the *limitanei* of the East appear to have received grants of land from the government to aid in their support, which, of course, would have furthered this trend.[32] For a while, during a financial crisis under Justinian, they were asked to go without pay, something that would not have been possible unless these men had had alternative or supplementary sources of income. The other advantages of military service, such as tax exemptions and legal privileges, were such that even after a period without regular pay it would seem that the *limitanei* continued to exist as effective forces.[33]

The expedient adopted by Justinian with regard to his second-tier troops is suggestive of the extent to which a large army serving for pay had become a burden on the empire's finances. Although attempts to calculate what percentage of state revenue was expended on the military in a particular year may be more precise than the available evidence will bear, there is widespread agreement that the support of the armies was the largest single item of expenditure and accounted for well over half of the empire's total expenditures.[34] Justinian, according to Treadgold, "had to struggle meet his military payrolls, and in the process he often delayed payments and tolerated other abuses."[35] In the hope of reducing expenses Maurikios sought to replace cash allowances with the actual issue of clothing and weapons, and the same emperor's decision to have his Balkan army winter north of the Danube in 602, whose disastrous consequences have already been seen, was in part motivated by a desire to economize by feeding off of enemy territory.[36] The already serious problem of paying the army was vastly magnified by the troubles of the early seventh century, culminating in the permanent loss of Syria and Egypt to the Arabs. At that point, the *limitanei* disappear from the scene, and it seems that the remnants of the eastern field armies were withdrawn into Asia Minor where they were eventually settled in military districts that became known as *themata*. Although some paid, mobile forces continued to exist in each of these districts, the pay of many soldiers was cut to such a low level as to become purely nominal; these men had to support themselves by farming or other non-military activities and performed military service only part of the year or in times of emergency. There is also some evidence of a return to conscription and hereditary military obligations. Even under these new conditions, however, military service was not entirely without advantages: soldiers and their families still received tax exemption and the pay, low as it was, was one of the few reliable sources of gold coin in an increasingly cash-poor economy.[37]

Both before and after the Heraclean debacle, however, soldiers—that is men with a regular, ongoing military obligation—were always clearly distinguished from the civilians who made up the vast majority of the population and, under all but the most unusual circumstances, had no military obligation whatsoever. Justinian had made the production and distribution of weapons a state monopoly; soldiers purchased their arms from government manufactures, and civilians were, in the interest of public order, not allowed to own weapons. "More important than this legal prohibition was the attitude of mind which it reflected. Citizens were not expected to fight, and for the most part they never envisaged the idea of fighting."[38] Some weapons were stored in city armories so that the populace might assist in the defense in the event of a siege, but apart from this sort of special situation the Eastern Roman state appears never to have contemplated the short-term conscription of large numbers of civilians to meet even its most pressing military needs.[39]

The professional character of the Eastern Roman military and the clear line drawn between soldier and civilian, together with certain dysfunctional tendencies within the professional military, gave rise to both high costs and a high degree of rigidity. The system was, as we have seen, expensive, and a portion of the funds spent on it were paid for men who were simply not there, or for soldiers who were drawn into the civilian economy and lost their effectiveness as fighting men. The latter were most prevalent among the *limitanei*, but could also be found in many units of the field armies. Added to this was the localization of the military, which came to characterize the *comitatenses* almost as much as the *limitanei*. There was a tendency to distribute even field army units into local garrisons and assign them to internal security duties, and from the early sixth century onward, the government tended to refrain from transferring men outside of the areas where they were originally enlisted, which were usually their home communities.[40] Although of some assistance in recruitment, this policy made it difficult to move troops from where they happened to be to where they were most needed. When substantial numbers of fighting men were needed in a hurry, the usual expedients were to enlist contingents of foreign allies or to turn to traditional recruiting grounds such as the western Balkans or the mountains of southeastern Anatolia in search of short-term volunteers; depending on the period, Illyrian and Isaurian subjects of the emperor and foreign contingents of Armenians, Huns, Gepids, Goths, Heruls, and Arabs all played prominent roles in the empire's armies.[41] When heavy losses were sustained or entire armies destroyed, as happened with distressing frequency in the first half of the seventh century, their replacement was necessarily a slow and costly process.[42]

The professional character of the military and the clear separation of soldier and civilian so pronounced in the late Roman world are not without parallels in Chinese history. In the first two centuries CE, the Eastern Han dynasty relied mainly on full-time, long-service fighting men who were mostly either of barbarian origin or convicts sentenced to military service at the frontier.[43] And during the centuries of division that followed the Han collapse, armies tended to be made up of semi-servile dependents, non-Chinese tribesmen (especially those of North Asian nomadic origin), and other hereditary status groups that were clearly demarcated from the general population. The institution of universal military service developed during the Warring States and continued into the early Han, remarkably similar to the "cadre-conscript" system instituted by the major powers of continental Europe prior to World War I, was long gone by Sui and Tang times and would never be recreated by any of China's later imperial regimes.[44] Nevertheless, there are two important elements of the inherited tradition of Chinese statecraft that served to vitiate the professional aspect of the military while facilitating the raising and maintenance of large armies. One was the expectation that the military establishment should be largely self-supporting, with soldiers responsible for their own sustenance when not on active duty in the field. The other was the notion that military service was no more than a specialized form of the corvée labor duty that was incumbent on most of the adult male taxpayers, which meant that the Chinese imperial state was not at all squeamish about conscripting its subjects for short-term military service when the need arose. These ideas distinguished the military establishments of Sui and Tang China from their late Roman counterpart, and both had their roots in the Warring States' identification of the farming population as essentially coterminous with the state's reservoir of military manpower.[45] Rather than tracing the origin and development of these views and their associated policies, a potentially lengthy exercise, this discussion will focus on the ways they were realized on a practical level in the military institutions of Sui and early Tang.

The best trained, most highly skilled and "professional" Chinese fighting men of this period were the *fubing*, a term that may be translated as "soldiers of the headquarters" or "regimental soldiery." This particular military institution had taken shape under the Northern Zhou, reached maturity in the Sui period, and was quickly restored by the Tang founders in the 620s and 630s. It owed its name to the fact that men were enrolled under locally based regimental headquarters, which eventually came to number more than 600 when the system was at its maximum extent shortly after 700 CE. In the early Tang there were large regiments whose regulation strength was 1,000 men, intermediate regiments of 800 men, and small regiments of 600.[46] Men became eligible to be selected for service as *fubing* when they reached the age of twenty. During the seventh century selections were made once every three years, with the actual choice being made by the civilian authorities at the local level. The selection criteria were household wealth, physical strength, and the number of males in the household: "When wealth is equal take the strong; when strength is equal take the rich; when wealth and strength are both equal, take from the household with the greater number of adult males."[47] Once chosen, men were expected to serve until the age of sixty. During their period of service they were considered to have military status (*jun ming*), though they and their families continued to be listed in the household registers kept by the local civil authorities. Like other registered adult males, they were supposed to receive allotments of state-owned farmland under the "equal field" (*jun tian*) system. In return for their military service, however, they were excused from taxes and corvée labor. Another material advantage of service as a *fubing* was that it gave a man the opportunity to acquire honorific rank through exploits on the battlefield, which in turn entitled him to hold far more "land in perpetuity" (*yong ye tian*) than would otherwise gave been allowed under the equal field system. For this reason alone, relatively well-to-do families seeking to build up their holdings may have found military service an attractive option.[48]

It has often been suggested that the *fubing* were a sort of militia of farmer-soldiers. Although the government required them to perform guard duty in the capital according to a complicated schedule of rotation that typically claimed two months of service from a man each year, and also made them eligible to be called up for three-year tours of duty in frontier garrisons and indeterminate periods of service in ad hoc campaign armies, these men did not spend the majority of their time on active duty during the years or decades the state classified them as soldiers.[49] The fact that they were provided with land allotments makes it quite clear that they were supposed to be self-supporting when not on active service, and it also seems that soldiers were expected to provide their own provisions for at least part of each period when they were assigned to campaign, garrison, or guard duty.[50] On the other hand, this does not mean that every man was necessarily himself a farmer; land could be cultivated by other family members, or, in the case of the better off among the *fubing*, by servants or slaves.

The fact that *fubing* remained in service for almost the whole of their adult lives meant that it was possible for them to acquire considerable military experience and attain a high level of proficiency at arms, even though the state did not require that they devote their time exclusively to soldiering. The individual soldier was supposed to practice archery and other martial skills on a daily basis while dwelling at home, and each year, in the last month of winter, the entire regiment assembled for a period of group drill, mock combats, and hunting (which was considered another form of military training). Further opportunities for training arose when the soldiers of many regiments were brought together for a great imperial inspection.[51] Due to their extensive training and long-term organizational affiliation, the *fubing* were almost certainly the toughest and most reliable troops at the disposal of the court under the Sui dynasty and during the first century of Tang rule.

Despite the central role of the regimental soldiery in Sui and early Tang, the empire's military establishment was always an extremely complicated structure with many different but complementary components. Expeditionary armies usually included short-term conscripts (*bingmu*), tribal auxiliaries, and sometimes even gentleman volunteers (*yizheng*, literally "righteous campaigners") as well as soldiers from the regiments, and in the frontier garrisons *fubing* served alongside *fangding*, "defense conscripts" drafted for a one-year term with no continuing military obligation thereafter.[52] Even the primary task of guarding court and capital was shared with permanent, full-time guard units. Under the Tang these formed the so-called "palace army" (*jin jun*), a force that had its origin in the army the Tang founder Li Yuan led from Taiyüan to Chang'an in 617. The palace army fluctuated greatly in both size and military effectiveness; its members were rarely sent into the field, but sometimes played a Praetorian-like role in the internecine political struggles of the Tang court.

The multiplicity of the empire's military institutions can in part be explained by the numerical insufficiency of the regimental soldiery: there were simply not enough *fubing* to provide for all aspects of imperial defense. The need to maintain the rotation schedules and ensure that sufficient men were always available for service in the capital, together with the expectation that the *fubing* were to support themselves by farming most of the year, meant that even a manpower pool of 600,000 was inadequate. Regimental soldiers returning from prolonged service in the field were excused from two consecutive tours of guard duty, creating a further disincentive for sending out large armies composed mainly of *fubing*.[53] The numerical insufficiency of the *fubing* was rooted in the fact that the vast majority of the empire's males were not eligible for recruitment; of the approximately 320 prefectures that made up the Tang empire, only about ninety contained regimental headquarters (*zhechongfu*) enrolling local men for service as *fubing*. The majority of these were located in the northwestern part of the empire, with the capital and its immediate environs being especially favored. Various explanations have been offered for this lopsided distribution, but the major factor seems to have been that the Sui and Tang rulers, whose regime originated in the northwest, lacked confidence in the loyalty of the other parts of their empire.[54]

Military manpower was extracted from the east and south not through the regimental headquarters, but by means of a separate conscription system administered by the local civil authorities. Soldiers raised in this way were designated as "conscript-recruits" (*bingmu*). They were chosen from among the general population to serve in an expeditionary army for the duration of its campaign, at the end of which they were demobilized and sent home. The court could assign troop quotas to any of the empire's prefectures, and the number of men demanded could be tailored to fit the requirements of a particular campaign. The numbers could be quite large, as in 661 when more than 44,000 men were raised from sixty-seven prefectures to take part in military operations against the northern Korean state of Koguryŏ. Conscript-recruits were supposed to be chosen in accordance with the same criteria of wealth, strength, and number of males in the household that governed the selection of *fubing*, but there was a strong preference for men holding honorific rank (*xun guan*, usually won on the battlefield) or those with some other previous experience of military service. Unlike *fubing*, they were not expected to bring their own provisions. Issued weapons and clothing by their prefecture of origin, during their time in the field they ate government grain that was either sent along with them or drawn from prefectures on their line of march. Before the 660s, it seems that *bingmu* quotas were at least partly filled through voluntary enlistment, with local officials then having recourse to conscription to make up the difference. As time passed and military service became more onerous (for reasons to be explained shortly), the voluntary element largely disappeared.[55]

Just as the Sui and Tang empires drew their fighting men from a variety of different sources under different conditions and terms of service, the imperial defense system into which this manpower was channeled was also an elaborate, multilayered structure. The capital, Chang'an, was the site of a major concentration of military force, which included both permanent imperial guard formations (the palace army) and more than 50,000 *fubing* doing rotational service in the capital at any given time.[56] Some stood guard at the southern gate of the imperial palace, while others manned the gates of the imperial city (*huang cheng*), which housed the offices of the central government. Still others were detailed to guard the residences of imperial princes or to serve as bodyguards for military officials. They performed escort duty whenever the emperor ventured outside the palace, and some acted as a sort of metropolitan gendarmerie, manning police posts at major intersections and patrolling the avenues of the capital at night. Although not intended as an "army in being" capable of undertaking military campaigns, this strong garrison certainly provided effective security for the capital city and the imperial court.

When a campaign army was needed, an ad hoc force consisting mostly of temporary or part-time fighting men was assembled from diverse sources and sent into the field under the command of a general drawn from one of the imperial guard headquarters in the capital. Once it had achieved its objective, the army was disbanded; its soldiers were sent home and their general returned to his peacetime billet in the capital.[57] After the subjugation of the Eastern Türks in 630, contingents of steppe cavalry commanded by their own chieftains became an extremely important component of many of the Tang expeditionary armies alongside the regimental soldiers and conscript-recruits. Submitted tribal groupings, some of them "settled" on suitable pasture lands along the frontier, were incorporated into the empire as "bridle prefectures" (*jimi zhou*): their chiefs received bureaucratic rank and offices in the Tang system of territorial administration, but these posts tended to be held on a hereditary basis with government generally following tribal custom rather than the Tang legal code.[58]

At most times, the frontiers were guarded by only a thin screen of small garrisons (*zhen*) and even smaller outposts (*shu*). Manning these positions was a mixture of regimental soldiers and "defense conscripts" drawn directly from the civilian population, with both groups serving limited tours of duty at the frontier.[59] This configuration was best suited to the conditions under which it had originally emerged—a divided China in which nearby enemies could be defeated quickly, allowing the soldiers of an expeditionary army to return to their homes and farms. When the empire encountered foes such as the Tibetans, who could not be destroyed in a single campaign and continued to threaten the borders year after year, change became necessary. From the 670s onward expeditionary armies began to settle in position, becoming what were in effect permanent garrisons far more powerful than the earlier thin screen of frontier guards. As conditions worsened and tours of duty were extended, military service became less attractive to those who had homes, farms, and families in the interior of the empire, and the burden of military service imposed on the poor must surely have become heavier as the well to do used their influence and connections to avoid selection.[60] Gradually, the part-time and temporary fighting men of the early Tang were transformed into (or replaced by) full-time, professional soldiers more closely resembling their Eastern Roman counterparts of the period before the Arab conquests.

During its heyday, however, the expeditionary army system yielded tangible benefits for the empire's rulers. The first and most obvious was financial. The most expensive items in the military inventory, including armor, most weapons, cavalry mounts, and possibly also the horses or donkeys used as pack animals, were provided out of state funds and regarded as state property.[61] In addition, the government assumed some responsibility for feeding and clothing soldiers serving in border garrisons and expeditionary armies. Nevertheless, the basic principle was that men who were not on active duty (and even some who were, such as *fubing* performing guard duty in the capital) were responsible for their own upkeep, and even the most "professional" of the empire's soldiery were compensated with tax exemptions rather than cash payments. This made it possible for the Sui and early Tang emperors to field large armies without assuming the crushing burden of supporting soldiers on an ongoing basis when their services were not immediately needed, and spared them the payroll worries of their late Roman counterparts. The institution of conscript-recruits in particular made for maximum flexibility at minimal cost, permitting rapid and substantial—albeit temporary—increases in military manpower.

A second benefit of the system was that it minimized the danger that the military (or elements within it) might pose to the ruler. Not only was there no powerful standing army, but in addition almost every structural feature made military authority either fragmented or temporary. As we have seen, expeditionary armies, frontier guards, and the forces responsible for the security of the capital were all assembled from multiple, diverse sources; expeditionary armies were formed on a temporary, ad hoc basis, and the composition of guard and garrison forces was always in flux thanks to the rotational principle. Generals did not hold permanent or long-term commands. When a campaign army completed its mission, its commander returned to his sinecure position in one of the guard headquarters in Chang'an. These agencies (of which there were twelve in the early Tang) had a supervisory role with regard to the territorial regiments. Each regiment was formally affiliated with one of them, so that each of the guard commands had several dozen local regiments (the exact number varied over time) within its purview. The guard headquarters did not have direct operational, line-of-command authority over any of those local units, but was merely responsible for providing leadership and assigning tasks to the thousands of soldiers from its regiments who came up to the capital each month for guard duty. The personnel serving in the capital changed from month to month as duty shifts dispatched by the regiments came and went, and the shifts themselves were not organized units but drafts of manpower that varied in size based on the parent regiment's distance from the capital.

The local regiments had an elaborate table of organization. Each was headed by a colonel (*zhechong duwei*), who was assisted by two lieutenant-colonels (*guoyi duwei*). Lower organizational echelons were the administrative battalion (*tuan*) of 200 men, the administrative double company (*lü*) of 100 men, and the company (*dui*) of fifty men headed by a company commander (*dui zheng*). When an expeditionary army was formed, it was possible for a regiment to be called up for service *in toto*, with all of its officers and men from the colonel on down.[62] The usual practice, however, was to create a field army by bringing together contingents, often quite small, from a number of different regiments. Thus, the regiments and most of their subunits were actually administrative agencies that were concerned with personnel management and training rather than tactical command. The expeditionary army had a quite different structure, with divisions (*jun*) of several thousand men, subdivided into encampments (*ying*) of about 1,000 men each, battalions (*tong*) of 300, and companies of fifty; of these units, all except the encampment had a tactical role. A division might include both *fubing* and conscript-recruits, and an encampment could be made up of contingents from many different regiments. Even the company, an organizational element common to both the regiment and the expeditionary army, was not necessarily carried over intact from one to the other. Tang administrative documents recovered from northwestern China make it clear that soldiers were drawn from regiments as individuals and assigned to new, temporary companies that were formed within the framework of the expeditionary army.[63] Although the newly formed combat company did consist entirely of men from the same regiment who were almost certainly led by one of that regiment's junior officers, comrades and leaders might no longer be the same as back home (or on the last deployment, for that matter). The result, no doubt intentional, of all of these divisions, rotations, and reorganizations was to ensure that soldiers never spent enough time under the operational control of any particular general (or even mid-level officer) to form lasting bonds of affection and loyalty. That this assurance of intramural security was purchased at the cost of a certain amount of unit cohesion and hence military effectiveness either did not trouble the empire's rulers or was a price they were willing to pay. As if these devices were not enough, there were further institutional safeguards against the autonomous exercise of military power. The regimental commanders, who *did* have long-lasting relationships with the troops under their supervision, were forbidden by law from mobilizing more than ten men without authorization from the center. Under the Tang Code, the penalty for unauthorized movement of an entire regiment of 1,000 men was death by strangulation.[64] The commanders of armies on campaign were sometimes accompanied by "army supervisors" (*jianjun*), civil officials responsible for observing their conduct and reporting it to the throne. From the mid-eighth century onward, this job was given to trusted court eunuchs who were assigned to nearly all of the empire's field armies; their authority has sometimes been likened to that of political commissars in the Leninist armies of the twentieth century.[65]

Like their Eastern Roman counterparts, Chinese rulers of this period restricted civilians' access to weaponry. Under Sui and Tang law, ordinary people were permitted to possess sabers (*dao*), bows, and short spears for self-defense and hunting, but private ownership of strictly military equipment such as crossbows, long lances, and horse armor was prohibited.[66] When such articles were discovered in the possession of persons of high status (such as imperial princes), it was taken as evidence of treasonable intent. Even within the military itself, the prohibited classes of weaponry were considered state property, held in government armories, and issued to soldiers only when needed for training, campaign, or guard duty. Military headquarters kept careful records of what had been issued to whom and even the condition of the items when they were returned.[67]

The defense system of the Eastern Roman Empire was no less complex than that of Tang China, but its complexity was more the product of evolution over time in response to strategic needs rather than a mechanism deliberately crafted and set in place to prevent the military from posing a threat to the ruler. As we have already seen in the discussion of enlistment and conditions of service, the armed forces controlled by Byzantium were divided into several categories with different historical origins and different strategic roles. Descended from the legions and auxiliary formations of the Principate that had long ago been set in place to guard the perimeter of the empire, the *limitanei* were distributed in relatively static garrisons that remained responsible for either frontier defense or the local security of certain areas in the interior of the empire; in the late sixth century they were controlled through approximately twenty-five provincial-level commands under the leadership of *duces* (singular: *dux*).[68] Beginning under the emperor Constantine in the early fourth century CE, the twin threats of civil war within the empire and barbarian incursions capable of breaching its perimeter defense necessitated the creation of mobile field armies, the *comitatenses*. These were formed from a combination of sources, including both entirely new formations and contingents (vexillations) skimmed from the perimeter forces. In the late sixth century there were six of these armies, each commanded by a *magister miletum* ("master of soldiers") and each responsible for the security of a major region of the empire:

the army of Illyria on the middle Danube (roughly today's Serbia and Croatia), the army of Thrace on the lower Danube (Bulgaria), the army of Armenia (eastern Turkey), the army of the East (Syria), the army of Africa (Tunisia), and the army of Italy (with its headquarters at Ravenna). In addition to these regional forces there were two other mobile field armies stationed close to Constantinople, one in northwestern Anatolia and the other in southeastern Thrace.[69] These were the Praesental forces, soldiers who literally served "in the presence" of the emperor and constituted the ultimate strategic reserve of the late Roman state. The capital itself was secured by several palace guard forces of whom the most numerous where the Scholae: 3,500 men organized into seven regiments of cavalry. Although theoretically available for field service in the Praesental armies, by the sixth century the Scholae had long been ceremonial guard units with little or no military effectiveness—much like their equivalents in Tang China, the soldiers of the northern palace armies.[70]

Arrangements were not always clear-cut, and there was tendency toward blurring of lines between the various categories of troops. Units could be called up from the *limitanei* for service in the field armies, often for long periods of time, in which case they were designated *Pseudocomitanses* as a reminder of their humble origin and lower status. And as we have already seen, there was a countervailing tendency for units of the mobile field armies (including Praesental troops) to be assigned to static garrison duties; they might even be placed under the command of the *duces*. As one authority (Haldon) has observed, "the practical differences in military terms between field troops and *limitanei* were not always very clear."[71] The military pressures and disasters of the early seventh century also caused considerable disruption in the system as garrisons were overrun and entire field armies transferred or even destroyed; in the early 630s, however, the emperor Herakleios was apparently in the process of restoring the defense structure to something resembling the status quo ante of 602, at which point the Arab onslaught necessitated the introduction of an entirely different set of arrangements.[72]

The major units that made up the Eastern Roman army were known by a great variety of different designations, depending upon when and how they had been formed and whether they were made up of infantry or cavalry. These included old and new legions (*legiones*) of native "Roman" infantry, cohorts (*cohortes*) of infantry or cavalry, *Alae* of "barbarian" auxiliary cavalry, vexillations of cavalry, and newer formations such as *auxilia* and *cunei equitem*. By the sixth century, this rather confusing picture had been greatly simplified through use of the generic term *numeri* (singular: *numerus*), usually translated as "regiments," to refer to all of these units. Each regiment was commanded by a tribune, assisted by a small administrative staff. In most cases, it seems that the usual paper or regulation strength of a regiment was either 500 or 1,000 men—although it is not impossible that some units of 3,000 or even 6,000 were still to be found among the older legions of the *limitanei*. Its subdivisions included units that in theory were supposed to be made up of 200, 100, fifty, and ten men, though the actual numbers seem to have differed greatly in practice.[73] In the late sixth- or early seventh-century *Strategikon*, the basic tactical unit of maneuver is the *tagma* (or *bandon*) made up of between

200 and 400 cavalrymen.[74] It has been plausibly suggested that a *tagma* was what a cavalry regiment with a paper strength of 500 men could actually put into the field, once allowance had been made for soldiers remaining behind in garrison or otherwise unable to participate.[75] On campaign and on the battlefield, the *tagma* were brigaded into larger, ad hoc formations (*moira* or chiliarchies) of 2,000 or 3,000 men, and in larger armies the *moira* might be further grouped into three divisions (*meros*) of 6,000–7,000 men each.[76]

With the exception of a few territories with special security problems, notably the two distant "exarchates" of Africa and Ravenna established by the reconquests of Justinian, the late Roman system distinguished, in theory, between civil and military authorities and their respective chains of command. Military leadership rested with the *magistri miletum* and the *duces*, while civil administration was the responsibility of provincial governors.[77] Apart from this, however, the Byzantine system lacked the arrangements for checks and balances, bifurcated authority, and temporary or rotational service that were so marked a feature of the military institutions of Sui and early Tang China.[78] Under the Byzantine system soldiers went into battle beside the same men who had been their comrades in peacetime garrisons, and generals could command the same troop units for years on end. While this no doubt contributed to military effectiveness, the implications for the empire's internal political stability were mostly negative.

The late fifth century saw emperors challenged or dominated by a string of powerful military commanders such as Aspar and Zeno (who eventually made himself emperor), and in the second decade of the sixth century the uprising of Vitalian in Thrace could only be quelled by granting the unruly general a promotion—though he remained a potential threat to the throne until his assassination was arranged in 520.[79] The rest of the century saw a great deal of unrest, sedition, and mutiny among the common soldiery but, perhaps because of rivalries between generals and the fortuitous absence of large troop concentrations near the capital, there were no outbreaks that seriously threatened the incumbent emperor.[80] This run of luck came to a spectacular end in the autumn of 602 when the army that had been gathered in Thrace to confront the Avars and Slavs rose in revolt. The immediate cause of the mutiny was the Emperor Maurikios' order for the army to cross to the north bank of the Danube to winter in dangerous and inhospitable territory, but behind it lay long-simmering grievances over military pay, conditions of service, and poor leadership. Putting forward a low-ranking officer, the centurion Phokas, as their leader, the soldiers marched on Constantinople. By the end of November, Maurikios and his family had been put to death and Phokas elevated to the imperial purple. In 608 Phokas was himself confronted with the revolt of Herakleios, the exarch (or viceroy) of Africa; two years later, a seaborne expedition led by the exarch's son, also named Herakleios, took Constantinople, killed Phokas, and put the younger Herakleios on the throne.[81] Later in the century emperors were unseated by military revolt in 641, 695, and 698, and this would remain a recurring pattern of Byzantine political history for several centuries thereafter.[82]

The resolution of political disputes through the application of armed force was not unknown in Sui and Tang China. The patterns, however, were somewhat different.

In the early Tang, they involved conflicts within the ruling family that were decided by the violent action of small units of privileged guardsmen; field armies and their commanders were not an important part of the picture. The military revolts that contributed to the demise of the Sui dynasty—including the rising of the Tang founder at Taiyuan and his march on Chang'an in 617—bear a superficial resemblance to the events of 602 and 608–610 in the Byzantine world, but there were significant differences: instead of initiating a crisis of the regime, as Phokas and his supporters did in 602, the local governors and military commanders who turned against the Sui in its final days were practicing a form of self-help when imperial institutions were already in a state of near collapse due to years of floods, famine, peasant rebellion, and the Sui emperor Yang's foolhardy persistence in his costly campaigns against Koguryŏ. The unsuccessful revolts of Yuchi Jiong (against the Sui founder's coup at the Northern Zhou court) in 580 and Yang Liang, Prince of Han (against his elder brother Yang Guang's accession to the throne) in 604 come closest to the Byzantine model, yet both were political insiders challenging the legitimacy of an imperial succession. At no time prior to the mid-eighth century was the voice of the common soldiery, so central in the rising against Maurikios in 602, a factor in Chinese revolts.

To conclude this survey of the structures of Chinese and Byzantine defense with a brief summary, before the loss of Syria and Egypt both empires could draw upon human and material resources that were of roughly the same order of magnitude (though not exactly equal). Landforms and human geography, however, conspired to advantage the Sui–Tang empire insofar as it was threatened from fewer points of the compass and commanded a larger, more secure hinterland—all of which meant that more manpower could be concentrated against a particular threat at a given time. This advantage was compounded by Chinese military institutions, which emphasized various forms of part-time and temporary military service with the result that the state was able to field large numbers of soldiers when needed, without putting too much pressure on the imperial fisc. The professional Romano-Byzantine model was more costly and less flexible, making it difficult to create large new armies in a hurry—but probably also making for a higher average level of unit cohesion and combat effectiveness than was usually seen in Chinese armies of this period. This cohesion and effectiveness carried yet another cost, however. A final difference between Chinese and Eastern Roman military institutions was that the latter allowed soldiers to pose more of a threat to their political masters.

Notes

1 For a recent comparative study that is less superficial than the usual treatments of this subject, see Walter Scheidel (ed.), *Rome and China: Comparative Perspectives on Ancient World Empires* (New York: Oxford University Press, 2009).

2 Both empires controlled about four million square kilometers of territory. The Roman Empire attained a larger population (perhaps seventy-four million) than the Han at its height (about sixty million). Scheidel, *Rome and China*, p. 11, note 4.

3 These events are examined in greater detail in David A. Graff, *Medieval Chinese Warfare, 300–900* (London and New York: Routledge, 2002).

4 Edwin G. Pulleyblank, "Registration of Population in China in the Sui and T'ang Periods," *Journal of the Economic and Social History of the Orient* 4 (1961), pp. 292–3 and 299.

5 *JTS* 9, p. 216.

6 Weng Junxiong, *Tang chu zhengqu yu renkou* (Beijing: Beijing shifan xueyuan chubanshe, 1990), pp. 36 and 56.

7 See Robert M. Somers, "Time, Space, and Structure in the Consolidation of the T'ang Dynasty (A.D. 617–700)," *Journal of Asian Studies* 45.5 (November 1986), pp. 971–94.

8 Swee Fo Lai, "The Military and Defense System under the T'ang Dynasty" (Ph.D. diss., Princeton University, 1986), p. 12, citing *Yu hai*, chapter 138, p. 13b.

9 *ZZTJ* 193, p. 6066; *ZZTJ* 197, p. 6214.

10 *ZZTJ* 176, p. 5498.

11 *SS* 4, p. 81; *SS* 29, p. 808; *ZZTJ* 181, p. 5666.

12 *ZZTJ* 181, pp. 5659–60. Asami Naoichirō argues that the columns were more than 30,000 men each; see his "Yōdai no dai ichi ji Kokuri enseigun: sono kibo to heishu," *Tōyōshi kenkyū* 44.1 (June 1985), pp. 23–44.

13 *TD* 148, p. 3792. For Tang army sizes, see David A. Graff, "Early T'ang Generalship and the Textual Tradition" (Ph.D. diss., Princeton University, 1995), pp. 49–53.

14 Walter E. Kaegi, *Byzantium and the Early Islamic Conquests* (Cambridge: Cambridge University Press, 1992), pp. 27 and 30; Warren Treadgold, *A History of the Byzantine State and Society* (Stanford, CA: Stanford University Press, 1997), pp. 137 and 278. The highest estimate comes from A. Fotiou, "Recruitment Shortages in Sixth-Century Byzantium," *Byzantion* 58 (1988), p. 73.

15 A.H.M. Jones, *The Later Roman Empire, 284–602: A Social, Economic, and Administrative Survey* (Norman: University of Oklahoma Press, 1964), vol. 2, p. 1040.

16 See Edward N. Luttwak, *The Grand Strategy of the Byzantine Empire* (Cambridge, MA: The Belknap Press of Harvard University Press, 2009), pp. 89–91, and the essays collected in Lester K. Little (ed.), *Plague and the End of Late Antiquity: The Pandemic of 541–750* (New York: Cambridge University Press, 2007).

17 Kaegi, *Byzantium and the Early Islamic Conquests*, p. 30; Treadgold, *History of the Byzantine State and Society*, p. 403.

18 The number of *limitanei* comes from John Haldon, *Warfare, State and Society in the Byzantine World, 565–1204* (London: UCL Press, 1999), p. 100. One scholar who accepts Agathias without demur is Warren Treadgold; see *Byzantium and Its Army, 284–1081* (Stanford, CA: Stanford University Press, 1995), p. 60, and *History of the Byzantine State and Society*, p. 255. Those who consider Agathias' figure too high include Kaegi (*Byzantium and the Early Islamic Conquests*, p. 39) and Whittow (*The Making of Orthodox Byzantium, 600–1025* (Basingstoke, Hampshire: Macmillan, 1996) pp. 182–3; among those who think he errs on the low side are the authors of two of the essays in Averil Cameron (ed.), *The Byzantine and Early Islamic Near East*, vol. 3: *State, Resources and Armies*, ed. (Princeton, NJ: The Darwin Press, 1995), Michael Whitby ("Recruitment in Roman Armies from Justinian to Heraclius [*ca.* 565–615]," pp. 73–4) and James Howard-Johnston ("The Two Great Powers in Late Antiquity: A Comparison," p. 168), as well as A.H.M. Jones (*The Later Roman Empire*, vol. 1, p. 684). Jones (vol. 2, p. 1055) also discusses the problem of missing soldiers.

19 Jones, *The Later Roman Empire*, vol. 1, p. 682; Whitby, "Recruitment," pp. 73–4, Howard-Johnston, "The Two Great Powers," p. 168; Haldon, *Warfare, State and Society*, pp. 100–1.

20 Haldon, *Warfare, State and Society*, p. 100. For Anastasius' army in 503, see Howard-Johnston, "The Two Great Powers," p. 166; Geoffrey Greatrex, *Rome and Persia at War, 502–532* (Leeds: Francis Cairns, 1998), p. 33, holds that this force was more likely in the range of 30–40,000.

21 Walter E. Kaegi, "Byzantine Logistics: Problems and Perspectives," in John A. Lynn (ed.), *Feeding Mars: Logistics in Western Warfare from the Middle Ages to the Present* (Boulder, CO: Westview Press, 1993), p. 43. In *Byzantium and the Early Islamic*

Conquests, Kaegi estimates that the Byzantine army defeated at the battle of the Yarmuk in (maybe) 636 did not exceed 20,000 men all told (p. 131).

22 Haldon, *Warfare, State and Society*, pp. 101 and 103; Treadgold, *A History of the Byzantine State and Society*, pp. 307 and 374; Whittow, *The Making of Orthodox Byzantium*, pp. 191–2.

23 *ZZTJ* 217, p. 6929.

24 Hélène Ahrweiler, "L'organisation des campagnes militaires à Byzance," in V.J. Parry and M.E. Yapp (eds.), *War, Technology and Society in the Middle East* (London: Oxford University Press, 1975), p. 89.

25 Haldon, *Warfare, State and Society*, p. 120; Jones, *Later Roman Empire*, vol. 1, p. 615.

26 Jones, *Later Roman Empire*, vol. 1, pp. 650 and 653; there is evidence that service in the *limitanei* in the late sixth century was a privilege limited to the offspring of soldiers (p. 669).

27 Treadgold, *Byzantium and Its Army*, p. 154.

28 Jones, *Later Roman Empire*, vol. 1, pp. 635–6. It appears that in the sixth century retired soldiers no longer received discharge bounties or grants of land (p. 675).

29 Jones, *Later Roman Empire*, vol. 1, pp. 670–1.

30 Haldon, *Warfare, State and Society*, p. 121; Jones, *Later Roman Empire*, vol. 1, p. 675. The exact pay rates are greatly debated and need not detain us here; for more on this subject see Haldon, *Warfare, State and Society*, p. 318, note 46, Treadgold, *Byzantium and Its Army*, pp. 145–9 and 154, and Jean-Michel Carrié and Sylvain Janniard, "L'armée romaine tardive dans quelques travaux récents: 1re Partie, L'institution militaire et les modes de combat," *L'Antiquité Tardive* 8 (2000), pp. 334–6.

31 Jones, *Later Roman Empire*, vol. 1, 662–3, 669, and 670.

32 Jones, *Later Roman Empire*, vol. 1, pp. 649 and 653.

33 Haldon, *Warfare, State and Society*, pp. 318–19, note 46. Treadgold (*Byzantium and Its Army*, p. 16) believes that the *limitanei* went entirely without pay after 545.

34 Treadgold, *Byzantium and Its Army*, pp. 141, 166–7, and 194; Haldon, *Warfare, State and Society*, p. 36.

35 Treadgold, *A History of the Byzantine State and Society*, p. 255.

36 Jones, *Later Roman Empire*, vol. 1, pp. 670–1 and 678; Haldon, *Warfare, State and Society*, p. 145.

37 The situation of soldiers in the early *themata* is very poorly documented; the tentative sketch here is based on Haldon, *Warfare, State and Society*, p. 122; Whittow, *Making of Orthodox Byzantium*, pp. 117 and 119; and Carrié and Janniard, "L'armée romaine tardive," p. 337. Treadgold's claim that the soldiers of the *themata* were granted lands from imperial estates to support themselves (see *A History of the Byzantine State and Society*, p. 316) has met with considerable skepticism.

38 Jones, *Later Roman Empire*, vol. 2, p. 1062.

39 Jones, *Later Roman Empire*, vol. 1, p. 671; Kaegi, *Byzantium and the Early Islamic Conquests*, pp. 37, 50, 52, and 259–60.

40 Jones, *Later Roman Empire*, vol. 1, pp. 670 and 686; vol. 2, p. 1037.

41 Jones, *Later Roman Empire*, vol. 1, pp. 203 and 660. For the Heruls, a Hunnic tribe settled in Pannonia by Anastasius, see Greatrex, *Rome and Persia at War*, p. 31; for the Arabs, see Kaegi, *Byzantium and the Early Islamic Conquests*, p. 43.

42 Whitby, "Recruitment," pp. 83–4 and 120.

43 Mark Edward Lewis, *The Early Chinese Empires: Qin and Han* (Cambridge, MA: The Belknap Press of Harvard University Press, 2007), pp. 138–9 and 248–50; and for greater detail, Mark Edward Lewis, "The Han Abolition of Universal Military Service," in Hans van de Ven (ed.), *Warfare in Chinese History* (Leiden: E.J. Brill, 2000), pp. 33–76.

44 On universal military service, see Lewis, "The Han Abolition of Universal Military Service." For the cadre-conscript system, see Eliot A. Cohen, *Citizens and Soldiers: The Dilemmas of Military Service* (Ithaca and London: Cornell University Press, 1985), pp. 28–29. Kegasawa Yasunori, *Fuheisei no kenkyū* (Tokyo: Dohosha, 1999), p. 230, has claimed that Emperor Yang of the Sui dynasty was taking concrete steps toward the

revival of the early Han system, but does not provide enough evidence for his argument to be persuasive.

45 See Mark Edward Lewis, *Sanctioned Violence in Early China* (Albany: SUNY Press, 1990), p. 54 and *passim*.

46 Around 685 these quotas were raised by 200 to produce regiments of 1,200, 1,000, and 800 men. Hamaguchi Shigekuni, "Fuhei seido yori shin heisei e," *Shigaku zasshi* 41 (1930), pp. 1266–70.

47 Liu Junwen, *Tang lü shuyi qian jie* (Beijing: Zhonghua shuju, 1996), chapter 16, p. 1173.

48 For status, land allotments, and the advantages of military service, see: *XTS* 50, pp. 1324–5; *THY* 72, p. 1298; Tang Zhangru, *Tangshu bingzhi jianzheng* (Beijing: Kexue chubanshe, 1957), p. 6; Nunome Chōfū, "Tōdai eji banjo no futan," in *Yamamoto hakushi kanreki kinen tōyōshi ronsō* (Tokyo: Yamakawa shuppansha, 1972), p. 377; Gu Jiguang, *Fubing zhidu kaoshi* (Shanghai: Shanghai renmin chubanshe, 1962), p. 203.

49 Hamaguchi, "Fuhei seido yori," p. 1462; Niida Noboru, *Tōryo shui* (Tokyo: Toho bunka gakuin Tokyo kenkyujo, 1933), p. 369; Tang Zhangru, *Tangshu bingzhi jianzheng*, pp. 22–3.

50 Gu Jiguang, *Fubing zhidu kaoshi*, pp. 192–6; Hamaguchi, "Fuhei seido yori," p. 1290. On the other hand, Zhang Guogang, *Tangdai zhengzhi zhidu yanjiu lunji* (Taipei: Wenjin chubanshe, 1994), holds that during most of their time on duty *fubing* were fed by the state (pp. 18–20).

51 Gu Jiguang, *Fubing zhidu kaoshi*, pp. 177–8; Hamaguchi, "Fuhei seido yori," p. 1281; *XTS* 50, pp. 1325–6.

52 Kang Le, *Tangdai qianqi de bianfang* (Taipei: National Taiwan University, 1979), pp. 171–4; Zhang Guogang, *Tangdai zhengzhi*, p. 84; Sun Jimin, *Tangdai xingjun zhidu yanjiu* (Taipei: Wenjin chubanshe 1995), p. 83; *XTS* 50, p. 1328.

53 Cen Zhongmian, *Fubing zhidu yanjiu* (Shanghai: Renmin chubanshe, 1957), p. 52; Hamaguchi, "Fuhei seido yori," p. 1282; *TLD* 5, p. 156.

54 Edwin G. Pulleyblank, *The Background of the Rebellion of An Lu-shan* (London: Oxford University Press, 1955), pp. 75–81; Kikuchi Hideo, "Tō setsushōfu no bunpu mondai ni kansuru ichi kaishaku," *Tōyōshi kenkyū* 27.2 (September 1968), pp. 11–16; Gu Yiqing, *Tangdai fubing zhidu xingshuai: cong weishi fudan tanqi* (Taipei: Xin wenfeng chuban gufen youxian gongsi, 2002), pp. 29, 32–3, 35, and 37–9.

55 This outline of the *bingmu* system is based on the following studies: Kikuchi Hideo, "Tōdai heibo no seikaku to meishō to ni tsuite," *Shien* 67–68 (May 1956), pp. 75–98; Tang Geng'ou, "Tangdai qianqi de bingmu," *Lishi yanjiu* 1981, no. 4, pp. 159–72; Zhang Guogang, *Tangdai zhengzhi*, pp. 29–53.

56 Zhang Guogang, *Tangdai zhengzhi*, pp. 23–24.

57 *XTS* 50, p. 1328.

58 Sun Jimin, *Tangdai xingjun zhidu*, pp. 114 and 115; Zhang Guogang, *Tangdai zhengzhi*, pp. 97–8 and 100–1; Zhang Qun, *Tangdai fanjiang yanjiu* (Taipei: Lianjing, 1986), p. 96. I follow Jonathan Skaff in translating *jimi zhou* as "bridle prefecture" rather than the more usual "loose rein prefecture." See Jonathan Karam Skaff, *Sui-Tang China and Its Turko-Mongol Neighbors: Culture, Power, and Connections, 580–800* (New York: Oxford University Press, 2012) pp. 61–2.

59 Kikuchi Hideo, "Setsudoshisei kakuritsu izen ni okeru gunseido no tenkai," *Tōyō gakuhō* 44.2 (September 1961), p. 55, and *THY* 70, p. 1233; Hamaguchi ("Fuhei seido yori," p. 1462) argues the term for *fubing* was three years; Zhang Guogang (*Tangdai zhengzhi*, p. 84) holds that conscripts served for only one year.

60 In fragmentary early eighth-century household registers from Dunhuang in the far northwest, we find that *fubing* are most likely to come from those occupying the lowest tier in the government's nine-level classification of household wealth and status. See Gu Yiqing, *Fubing zhidu xingshuai yanjiu*, pp. 171–3.

61 Hamaguchi, "Fuhei seido yori," pp. 1286–9. For horses in particular, see Gu Yiqing, *Tangdai fubing zhidu xingshuai yanjiu*, p. 232; Sun Jimin, *Dunhuang Tulufan suo chu Tangdai junshi wenshu chutan* (Beijing: Zhongguo shehui kexue chubanshe, 2000),

pp. 4, 10; and Wang Yongxing, *Tangdai qianqi xibei junshi yanjiu* (Beijing: Zhongguo shehui kexue chubanshe, 1994), p. 411.

62 *XTS* 50, p. 1325.

63 Sun Jimin, *Tangdai xingjun zhidu*, pp. 91 and 95–9.

64 Liu Junwen, *Tang lü shuyi qian jie*, chapter 16, p. 1162.

65 For the army supervisors, see Zhang Guogang, "Tangdai jianjun zhidu kaolun," *Zhongguo shi yanjiu* 1981, no. 2, pp. 120–32. The twentieth-century parallel was suggested by Samuel B. Griffith in *Sun Tzu: The Art of War* (Oxford: Oxford University Press, 1963), p. 82, note 1.

66 Zhang Rongfang, "Tangdai zhongyang de wuqi guanzhi cuoshi," in *Di er jie guoji Tangdai xueshu huiyi lunwenji* (Taipei: Wenjin chubanshe, 1993), vol. 2, pp. 1351–66.

67 *TD* 149, p. 3820.

68 Haldon, *Warfare, State and Society*, p. 67.

69 Haldon, *Warfare, State and Society*, pp. 73–3.

70 Jones, *Later Roman Empire*, vol. 1, pp. 613–14.

71 Haldon, *Warfare, State and Society*, p. 67.

72 Haldon, *Warfare, State and Society*, p. 71.

73 Haldon, *Warfare, State and Society*, pp. 107–8; for the *numeri*, also see Jones, *Later Roman Empire*, vol. 1, pp. 640, 655, 659, and 680–1, and James Howard-Johnston, "Heraclius' Persian Campaigns and the Revival of the East Roman Empire, 622–630," *War in History* 6.1 (January 1999), p. 30.

74 *Strategikon*, pp. 16–17 and 35.

75 Treadgold, *Byzantium and Its Army*, p. 94.

76 *Strategikon*, pp. 16–17.

77 Jones, *Later Roman Empire*, vol. 1, p. 373 ff. Actual conditions were somewhat more complicated, especially at the local level; see Ramsay MacMullen, *Soldier and Civilian in the Later Roman Empire* (Cambridge, MA: Harvard University Press, 1963), pp. 72–6 and *passim*.

78 Walter Emil Kaegi, *Byzantine Military Unrest, 471–843: An Interpretation* (Amsterdam: Hakkert, 1981), pp. 103–4.

79 Kaegi, *Byzantine Military Unrest*, pp. 30, 62, and 92–3.

80 Kaegi, *Byzantine Military Unrest*, pp. 30, 34, 37, 39, and 56.

81 Kaegi, *Byzantine Military Unrest*, pp. 110–14 and 124–5.

82 Kaegi, *Byzantine Military Unrest*, pp. 120, 157, 188–9, and 201.

3   Weapons and tactics

Although separated by thousands of miles of mountains, deserts, and grasslands and shaped in distinctive ways by their own unique geographies and resource endowments, Tang China and Byzantium nevertheless had much in common with regard to the basic structures of material life. Both were "agrarianate" empires sustained by the extraction of taxes and tribute from the subsistence farmers who made up the great majority of the population and generated most of the society's resources. Thanks to millennia of contacts and exchanges among the originally scattered communities that made up the Eurasian ecumene, both empires enjoyed roughly comparable levels of pre-industrial technology. And in both realms "the limits of the possible" were essentially the same. Medieval Chinese armies, like those of Byzantium, moved on foot and on horseback with their supplies carried by some combination of human porters, beasts of burden, horse- or ox-drawn wagons, and wind- or oar-driven watercraft. On land, motive power was provided entirely by the muscles of men and animals. The length of a day's march was the same both east and west, as were the distances and speeds that messages and signals could travel. Soldiers fought either mounted or on foot, and—with only rare exceptions in this pre-gunpowder age—relied on their own muscle power to do violence to their enemies, either directly and at close range with swords and spears or at a greater distance with slings, bows, and crossbows. Thus, while the weaponry and other military equipment of early Tang China and seventh-century Byzantium displayed many fine distinctions of detail, there were few if any fundamental differences in kind. Both empires relied upon a cavalry composed of both mounted archers and armored lancers for their main strike force, supported by infantry armed with spears, swords, javelins, and bows.[1]

The most common of all the tools of war employed on medieval Chinese battlefields was almost certainly the spear or lance (*qiang*; *shuo*). Prompted by improvements in armor, the long, leaf-shaped blade favored *c.*300 CE and earlier had by Sui and Tang times evolved into a short, thick spearhead of iron or steel. Though less graceful in appearance than its predecessor, it was a much better design for punching through overlapping layers of iron lamellae or hardened leather.[2] Weapons of this sort were used by foot soldiers and horsemen alike. For infantrymen, especially, the spear required little training or skill to use, and this, together with its relatively low cost and ease of manufacture, goes far to explain its popularity. The spear (*qiang*) is the standard armament in the infantry drills described by Li Jing, and in the middle of the eighth century another military writer, Li Quan, chose to assign the same weapon to every soldier in his imagined model army of 12,500 men.[3] The lengths of spears and lances varied considerably. Probably near the upper end of the range, the cavalry lance used in the imperial military examinations in the early eighth century was eighteen feet, six inches in length.[4] At the other extreme, some foot soldiers carried short spears (*zuan*) that may have doubled as javelins.[5] On average, however, the typical infantry spear was probably longer than the typical cavalry lance.

Another common weapon used by both infantry and cavalry was the *dao*, perhaps better translated as "saber" rather than "sword." This was a straight or very slightly curved blade with a single cutting edge that had begun to supplant the straight, two-edged sword of Chinese antiquity (the *jian*) during the Han dynasty. The new weapon was much better suited to the cavalry's need for a heavy instrument for chopping and slashing: for this purpose one cutting edge was as good as two, besides which the one-edged blade was sturdier and less likely to shatter on impact.[6] Under the Tang dynasty, the saber—called *pei dao*, "saber worn at the waist," or *heng dao*, "horizontal saber"—was a standard item of military equipment issued to infantry and cavalry alike, though in most cases it seems to have been carried as a secondary weapon or sidearm by men who placed their principal reliance on bow or spear.[7] Rather less frequently, it appears as the main weapon used by bodies of troops who are sometimes also equipped with shields (*dun*).[8]

A more elaborate variant of the humble saber and one that attracted considerably more attention on the battlefield was the *chang dao*, a saber-staff or long-handled saber. This weapon, essentially the blade of a saber affixed to a wooden shaft, bore a strong resemblance to the Japanese *naginata* and the glaive of medieval Europe.[9] Unlike the spear and the saber, it required considerable skill to wield effectively—but in the hands of an expert could do terrible damage. It was said that one famous warrior of the first Tang reign carried a great saber more than ten feet long and could kill several men with a single sweeping blow.[10] On early Tang battlefields, this fearsome weapon was carried by relatively small units of elite infantry that were often used to spearhead attacks on the enemy's formation.[11]

The blade of the *chang dao*, together with almost all the saber-blades, spearheads, arrowheads, and other assorted edged and pointed weapons of the Sui–Tang period, was made of iron or steel, with the bronze weapons that dominated the battlefields of antiquity having long been relegated to ritual and ceremonial uses.[12] The transition from bronze to iron was already far advanced by the Western Han period, but the centuries of division that preceded the reunification of China under Sui rule in 589 saw the development of a new and more efficient method of converting iron into steel, which made it possible for the first time to equip very large numbers of troops with high-quality steel weapons.[13] And during this same period, the adoption of more sophisticated techniques of quenching (calling for the immersion of newly forged blades in urine or fat rather than water) provided the average weapon with a sharper cutting edge than ever before.[14]

No matter how strong and sharp their blades, however, troops wishing to harm an enemy standing more than a few paces away had to have recourse to missile weapons. Hence, the bow (*gong*) was one of the most common items in the Tang armory. Accounts of Sui and Tang battles are filled with arrows. One of the horses that Li Shimin rode into battle in the summer of 621 took five arrows in the chest; in the same fight, Shimin's young cousin Li Daoxuan had so many arrows stuck in his armor after forcing his way through the enemy line that he looked like a porcupine.[15] Every one of the Tang *fubing* was supposed to carry a bow and thirty arrows, and Li Jing specified that 22 percent of the combat infantry in an expeditionary army should be archers.[16] Bows were of two basic types. The foot archers carried bows made of mulberry wood (*sangzhe*), and in battle were not supposed to shoot until the enemy came within sixty paces (or about ninety meters) of their position.[17] Mounted archers were equipped with the *jiao gong* or "horn bow" made from overlapping layers of wood, horn, and sinew; in basic design, this was the powerful composite bow that had been used by pastoral peoples of the Eurasian steppes since ancient times. Bows of this type can send a war arrow to a distance of 280 yards, but as both velocity (penetrating power) and accuracy fall off rapidly with distance, the range within which they became militarily effective against troops protected by armor must have been considerably less, perhaps only 75–100 yards.[18] Nor does shooting from a moving horse improve the accuracy of one's aim, with the result that some horse archers of the early Tang period actually dismounted in the midst of battle in order to use their bows to greater effect.[19]

The training of even a foot archer was a long and arduous process, as indicated by the advice of an eighth-century Chinese treatise on archery:

> The target must first be placed at a distance of one *zhang* [about 3 meters]. When one hits the target one hundred times with one hundred shots, one *cun* [about 2.5 centimeters] is added to the distance. Gradually, one arrives at one hundred paces [about 150 meters], and if he still hits one hundred times with one hundred shots, his skill is considered complete.[20]

While steppe tribesmen raised in the saddle and aristocratic warriors like Li Shimin—who is supposed to have shot down three charging lancers in quick succession—may have been trained to this standard, most soldiers probably were not.[21]

The other important missile weapon used by Chinese armies, the crossbow (*nu*), had the distinct advantage that it could be quite effective in the hands of men who had very little skill or training.[22] For the archer, drawing, aiming, and loosing the bow required a single smooth, coordinated motion. For the crossbowman, on the other hand, these were separate operations. The bow was drawn with the full strength of both arms and secured to a catch, so that its operator could aim at leisure and release the bolt simply by pulling a trigger. And the crossbow had other advantages as well, since it could send a heavier missile to a greater distance with more penetrating power and greater accuracy.[23] The standard for shooting with the basic infantry crossbow (*bi zhang nu*), a weapon that could be drawn with the strength of the arms, was to hit the target at least half the time at a range of 230 paces (345 meters).[24] While foot archers were not supposed to shoot until the enemy had come within sixty paces, crossbowmen were expected to release their bolts when the enemy were still 150 paces (225 meters) away.[25]

The crossbow also had its disadvantages, however. Although some Tang crossbows were intended for use by mounted men, the bow was so cumbersome and difficult to draw on horseback that it never became an important cavalry weapon.[26] A more serious consequence of the difficulty of drawing the crossbow was its slow rate of fire, which left its users terribly vulnerable in battle. According to a later (Northern Song) military encyclopedia,

> because drawing [the crossbow] is slow, it is difficult to respond to sudden surprises; when facing the enemy there is no time for more than three or four shots before the blades come together. Hence, some hold that battle is inconvenient for crossbows.[27]

Various solutions were attempted. Li Jing recommended that crossbowmen throw aside their bows and defend themselves with sabers and cudgels whenever the enemy came within twenty paces of their position, while there is some evidence that the best trained and disciplined crossbow units were able to hold even cavalry at bay by keeping up a continuous volley fire, with the rear ranks reloading as those in front let fly at the enemy.[28] The crossbowmen were never completely secure, however, unless they were protected by fortifications or fieldworks.[29] Perhaps for this reason, the crossbow seems to have been confined to relatively small units of specialists. According to Li Jing, only 20 percent of the infantry in an early Tang expeditionary force should be armed with the crossbow, the same proportion given by Li Quan in the middle of the eighth century.[30]

Although with some differences in detail, the Byzantines of *c*.600 CE employed essentially the same range of weapons as the early Tang military. These included a twelve-foot cavalry lance and a slightly longer (12–14-foot) iron-tipped spear for the infantry, as well as shorter throwing spears and javelins. The bow used by both horsemen and foot soldiers was the recurved composite bow of wood, horn, and sinew whose basic pattern would have been familiar to Chinese fighting men. It is only when we come to the sword, the *spatha* or *spathion*, that we encounter a non-trivial difference, for in contrast to the Chinese saber it had a double-edged blade, straight and usually somewhat less than a meter in length. The Byzantines had no equivalent to the Chinese long-handled saber, but continued to make some use of an ancient missile weapon of the Mediterranean world not attested in Tang China, the sling. Finally, the *Strategikon* also lists lead-pointed darts among the infantry weapons.[31]

Whether the Byzantines had the crossbow or not is a question that has generated much disagreement and debate. The basic concept of mounting a bow on a tiller had been known in the Mediterranean world since the invention of the *gastraphetes* ("belly bow") in 399 BCE. Hand-held crossbows were used as hunting weapons in Gaul in the late Roman period, and large, crew-served crossbows continued to be used by the Byzantines in naval combat and siege warfare. What is uncertain is whether Eastern Roman armies of the sixth and seventh centuries employed the hand-held crossbow as an infantry weapon. Much of the debate has revolved around the meaning of the term *solenarion*, which appears in the *Strategikon*. One view holds this to refer to the crossbow, while another interprets the device in question as an arrow guide—"a hollow piece of wood that enabled short arrows to be shot from a fully drawn bow" and with greater range and speed than ordinary arrows.[32] Regardless of which view is correct, two points stand out when the problem is viewed from a comparative perspective: the Chinese made much more extensive use of the crossbow as an infantry weapon than the Byzantines did, and the Chinese crossbow was a more sophisticated device than its Western counterpart. European crossbows used a revolving nut and one-lever trigger, while Chinese crossbows had a precisely engineered, three-piece bronze mechanism including "an intermediate lever that enabled the bowman to fire a heavy bow with a short, crisp and light pull on the trigger."[33]

For partial protection against missiles and edged weapons on the battlefield, both Chinese and Byzantine soldiers might carry shields of rather similar design and construction. Chinese shields were made from wood and leather, and in some instances may have been coated with lacquer. There were two basic patterns. The *peng pai*, a large shield in the shape of a rectangle or oval, was carried by foot soldiers, while a smaller circular shield, the *tuan pai*, was issued to the cavalry.[34] Shields were not used by all soldiers; in Sui and Tang battle accounts, they usually appear in combination with sabers or relatively short spears—probably because they would have interfered with the use of weapons such as bows, long spears, and long-handled sabers.[35] Like their Chinese contemporaries, Eastern Roman soldiers of *c*.600 CE used two basic models: a small, circular shield for cavalry and light infantry, and a larger round or oval shield for heavy infantry. These shields were made of wood with metal bosses (which might be conical, domed, or spiked), and sometimes had a covering of cloth or leather attached with rivets. Shields were often painted, with the colors serving as unit identifiers.[36]

Byzantine armor varied considerably, not only by troop type but also based on a soldier's position within his formation. At the end of the sixth century the best heavy cavalrymen, fighting at the front of the formation, were supposed to wear hooded mail coats, reaching down to their ankles, over padded robes (*zabai*); they are also credited with metal helmets complete with plumes and cheek pieces and possibly arm protectors as well. Men farther back in the formation may have had little more than the *zabai*, however. The same sort of distinction could also be found in the heavy infantry, where soldiers in the front ranks might wear a mail shirt over padded jerkin, a helmet, and splinted greaves of iron or wood, while their comrades in the rear ranks wore only the *zabai*, alone or supplemented with a chest protector of leather scales. The light infantrymen, with only quilted jerkins, had even less protection.[37]

Chinese armor could be of either iron or hide. There is no evidence that large sheets or plates of iron armor (in the fashion of late medieval Europe) were ever used in medieval China, but many Tang tomb figurines appear to be wearing armor made of smooth sheets of leather, often with two round metal plaques protecting the chest and sometimes with additional plaques for the back and the abdomen.[38] Another very common type of armor was lamellar, made up of many small rectangular plates (or lamellae) laced together horizontally and vertically. The lamellae could be of either iron or leather. The largest of the 322 iron lamellae of Tang date unearthed near Xi'an in 1976 are 9.6 centimeters long, 2.6 centimeters wide, and 0.28 centimeters in thickness; the smallest are 9 centimeters long, 1.3 centimeters wide, and 0.22 centimeters thick.[39] Whether iron or leather, lamellar or not, a full suit of armor was composed of the same basic elements. These included a helmet, a corselet protecting the front and back of the torso, épaulières covering the shoulder and upper arm, and long flaps or skirts hanging down from the left and right sides of the corselet to shield the legs.[40] There was, of course, considerable variation between individual suits of armor, and not all of these elements were present in all cases. The stone carving of a warrior named Qiu Xinggong removing an arrow from one of Li Shimin's chargers, which once adorned the emperor's mortuary complex at Zhaoling, has Qiu wearing what is apparently a soft cap rather than a helmet, and while the upper portion of his armor is covered by a heavy robe or surcoat, it is drawn aside to reveal a lamellar skirt reaching almost to the ankles.[41]

In the early Tang, well-equipped troops such as the *fubing* were issued helmets, armor, and war robes (*zhan pao*). There is some evidence that, in theory, sixty percent of the soldiers were supposed to have real armor (normally of lamellar construction), while the remaining forty percent wore only the *zhan pao*.[42] According to one authority on early Chinese costume, the *zhan pao* was not really armor at all, but a streamlined version of the civil official's robe, with a shorter, tighter body and narrow sleeves so as not to hinder the wearer's movements in combat.[43] This medieval battledress probably did have some protective value, however, since Li Jing tells us that each robe was supposed to be weighed when it was issued to a soldier and then again when it was returned to the armory, suggesting that it was made from a heavy, thick material (perhaps comparable to the Byzantine *zabai*).[44] One protective material that the Chinese, in sharp contrast to the Byzantines, did not wear during this period was chain mail. It came into use only much later in the Tang period, having been introduced into China from Central Asia or Tibet.[45] The Byzantines, for their part, were well aware of lamellar armor but made relatively little use of it before the seventh century.[46]

As a rule, the Chinese cavalry of Sui and Tang times was better armed and equipped than the infantry. While the foot soldiers had to make do with little or no armor, the typical Sui heavy cavalryman not only had a full suit of armor for himself but was also mounted on an armored horse. The horse's armor, made of iron or leather lamellae, covered almost the whole of its body with the exception of the lower legs.[47] Riders were normally armed with lance and saber, and often carried a shield for additional protection. Almost certainly encouraged by the invention of the stirrup, which was known in China by 322 CE, this type of heavy cavalry made its debut during the fourth century and soon came to occupy the most prominent place in the military establishments of both the northern and southern regimes.[48] Heavy cavalry formed the backbone of the Sui armies, too; it played an important role in the conquest of the southern Chen state in 588–589, and forty squadrons of armored soldiers on armored horses, a total of 4,000 men, reportedly formed the fighting core of each of the thirty Sui "armies" that invaded the northern Korean kingdom of Koguryŏ in 612.[49]

Within a few years of the Korean debacle, however, this heavy cavalry had been largely if not completely supplanted by "light cavalry" (*qing ji*) made up of armored riders on unarmored horses.[50] The reason for this change is not entirely clear, though it was likely related to the origin of the army of the newly risen Tang dynasty as a frontier force engaged in fighting the highly mobile Eastern Türks before it was plunged into the vortex of China's internal conflict. In 616, long before his march on the Sui capital, the Tang founder Li Yuan selected 2,000 of his cavalrymen, equipped them in Turkish fashion, and trained them to fight in the manner of the Türks.[51] After the Tang consolidation of power, when there were no more sedentary Chinese opponents to be dealt with, light cavalry no doubt continued to prove more useful than heavy in the empire's repeated confrontations with highly mobile steppe peoples.[52]

In the Sui armies, there had been a clear distinction between units of heavy cavalry with a "shock" mission, and units composed of mounted archers. This distinction continued into the Tang period, with the cavalry of the *fubing* being divided into two categories: the *yue ji* (who were mounted archers) and the *wu ji* (who were cavalrymen but not archers).[53] Accounts of early Tang battles, however, suggest that the distinction was not always clear-cut, with quite a few horsemen able to perform in either combat role as necessary.[54] In this respect, they resembled steppe warriors such as the Türks, their sometime opponents and sometime allies. According to Chinese reports, the Türks fought primarily as mounted archers – but they also carried sabers and lances, and some of them had helmets and armor as well.[55] The descriptions of combat left by the Eastern Türks in their runic inscriptions make it clear that their battles were more than just archery contests, and were often decided with the lance.[56]

Regardless of whether they were armed with bow or lance, whether their mounts were armored or unarmored, horsemen were a distinct minority in most Sui and Tang armies. Except for small, picked strike forces or auxiliary contingents recruited from steppe clients and allies, Chinese armies of this period were seldom able to put more than one-third of their soldiers on horseback. The 20,000-man expeditionary army described by Li Jing includes 4,000 cavalry (who account for 29 percent of its 14,000 combat troops), and there is some evidence that only about ten percent of the Tang *fubing* were trained to fight on horseback.[57]

Despite their relatively small numbers, mounted troops usually played the decisive role on Sui and Tang battlefields. Their superior mobility enabled them to maneuver against the enemy flank or rear, or exploit openings in the opposing battle line, and their charges could throw poorly trained infantry into panic-stricken flight. At the battle of Huoyi in 617, Li Yuan ensured the destruction of the opposing Sui army by sending two detachments of horsemen to cut off its retreat, and his son Li Shimin went on to win almost all of his victories with cavalry charges that carried through the enemy line. In the view of one authority on early Chinese warfare, the relationship between infantry and cavalry is summed up on a painted brick of Sui date unearthed near Liuan, Anhui, which shows an unarmored foot soldier who has thrown away his saber and shield and is kneeling in supplication beneath an armored horseman.[58]

It would be a mistake, however, to assume that cavalry always prevailed over infantry. Tang military history affords many examples of foot soldiers holding their own or even putting horsemen to flight. In 657, Tang infantry, formed in a dense array with "their spears pointing outward," beat back three charges by Western Türk cavalry.[59] Earlier, at the battle of the Nuozhen River in 641, the Xueyantuo archers dismounted and fought on foot in order to improve their aim; the Tang commander, Li Shiji, won the fight by dismounting a portion of his own cavalry who then attacked on foot with long lances.[60] A one-sided emphasis on the tactical superiority of cavalry not only fails to account for cases such as these, but also obscures the fact that in most armies of the period each of these arms was a necessary component of the whole. The two functioned best when used in coordination, as part of a larger system. In the 657 battle, for example, the Türks' unsuccessful assaults on the infantry square exposed them to a devastating counter-attack by the Tang cavalry. According to Li Jing, the cavalry were the army's "eyes and ears" and could also be used to pursue fugitives, exploit openings, and ride down dispersed enemy troops, while the infantry formed the stable core around which the cavalry could maneuver.[61]

The Roman cavalry had also evolved over time, with the result that by turn of the seventh century its role was quite similar to that of the early Tang cavalry in China. Horsemen had had only a minor place in the Roman armies of the Republic and Principate, but in order to cope better with mounted opponents such as Alans, Sarmatians, and Persians, new cavalry units began to be created as early as the second century CE. In the centuries that followed, there was no sudden transformation, but rather a gradual and continuing long-term trend toward more cavalry units with greater striking power. These units included heavily-armored *clibanarii* and *cataphracti*, horse archers (*sagittarii*), and lightly-armored lancers. At the beginning of the fifth century the infantry was still dominant, but the balance had clearly tipped in favor of cavalry by the first half of the sixth century when we have Procopius' accounts of battles decided by the actions of versatile, rather lightly-armored horsemen, equally adept with lance and bow, riding unarmored horses. A half-century farther on, the *Strategikon* prescribes face, neck, and chest armor (of iron, felt, or possibly also lamellar) for at least some of the horses, and states that a well-proportioned army should consist of between one-quarter and one-third cavalry. By this time, the infantry seems to be performing a supporting role in battle as a defensive screen or secure base behind which the cavalry can rally and regroup. Like their Chinese counterparts, Byzantine horsemen sometimes found it to their advantage to dismount and fight on foot. Fighting against the Persians at Solachon in 586, a Roman commander ordered the cavalry of his center to "form a wall of shields with spears projecting hedgehog-like to the front, in order to resist the enemy cavalry on foot."[62]

The basic organizational building blocks of late Roman and Byzantine armies were the *numeri*, or "regiments," with a paper strength of 500 men each for the cavalry.

The *bandon* or *tagma*, the fundamental tactical unit of between 200 and 400 men described in the *Strategikon*, probably represents the actual strength of a regiment on the battlefield. Although there is reason to believe that at one time each regiment was supposed to be more or less homogeneous with regard to weaponry and troop type, with regiments of heavy infantry, regiments of foot archers, regiments of slingers, regiments of armored cavalry, regiments of lancers, regiments of horse archers etc., by the beginning of the seventh century the distinction had broken down somewhat, with the result that a *bandon* of cavalry might include both armored lancers (in the front ranks) and unarmored archers (in the interior of the formation).[63] In combat, regiments might be brigaded together into larger formations; these might also be homogeneous in weapon-type—like the 8,000 foot archers stationed on the wings of the Roman army at Taginae in 552—but were not necessarily so. In creating such tactical group-ings, the most basic distinction was surely that between infantry and cavalry. Typical deployments, recorded in accounts of historical battles and in manuals such as the *Strategikon*, tend to place infantry formations in the center, with cavalry formations on the flanks and perhaps also in reserve positions to the rear; an additional refinement might see units of mounted archers deployed on the outer flanks beyond the lancers and heavy cavalry.[64]

The *Strategikon* mentions the presence of subordinate groupings within the *bandon*, including, in the cavalry, units of 100 men, further subdivided into units of approximately ten men, themselves dividing into groups of either five or four. These smaller units, however, do not seem to have a clear tactical function—except insofar as they constitute files of seven to ten men within the larger formation of the *bandon*. In a heavy infantry regiment (*tagma*), the main subordinate group-ings are sixteen-man files that are further subdivided into two eight-man squads.[65] Curiously, the *Strategikon* does not mention any units of fifty men even though, as Edward Luttwak has pointed out, "Fifty . . . is just about the biggest number that can achieve familial sentiments and maximum cohesion – in all modern armies the basic combat unit is the platoon of thirty men or so."[66] This deficiency was, however, rectified later in the seventh century, and the unit (*bandon*) of fifty men appears as the basic tactical "building block" in the late ninth-century *Praecepta Militaria* of Nikephoros II Phokas.[67]

The early Tang tactical organization appears to have been more finely articu-lated and flexible than what is described in the *Strategikon* because of the role of the fifty-man company (*dui*) as a tactical unit capable of independent maneuver. According to Li Jing, this is the fundamental, irreducible unit for all deployment and maneuver on the battlefield. It has a full complement of five officers, includ-ing a captain (*duitou*), his lieutenant or deputy (*fu duitou*), a standard bearer (*qitou*, *zhiqi*), and two color guards (*qianqi*); it is also the smallest unit to be provided with a flag. The company has a fixed battle formation five ranks deep in which each man has his assigned place. Led by the flag, which is borne by the captain himself, the company is expected to advance, retreat, and maneuver as a single body.[68] The importance of the *dui* has been independently confirmed by the archaeological dis-covery, in China's arid northwest, of a late seventh-century formation diagram in which each soldier is identified by name.[69] (It is interesting, too, that this company formation includes only twenty-six men, suggesting that Chinese units, like their Byzantine counterparts, were usually well below their regulation strength.) Minus its officers, the company broke down into five squads of nine men, with each of these in turn subdividing into three-man "buddy" groups. These were, however, groupings whose significance was administrative rather than tactical.[70]

Though capable of independent maneuver, a single *dui* was clearly too small to operate very effectively by itself. With its flanks and rear vulnerable to attack, it had to be brought together with other companies to create a larger formation. Hence, Li Jing provides instructions for joining varying numbers of *dui* tightly together to form larger blocs (*da dui*) of 150, 250, 450, and 500 men.[71] Six companies combine to form a unit called a *tong* (battalion), commanded by an officer with the title of *tongtou*; with one *dui* told off to guard the baggage, the remaining five could be deployed in several configurations and assigned different combat roles on an ad hoc basis. Battalions of this sort—about the same size as the Byzantine *bandon* or *tagma*—may have been the most important level of tactical organization in the early Tang.[72] In surviving Sui and Tang battle narratives we find detachments sent off to perform specific missions on the battlefield ranging in strength from 100 to 200 men up to 5,000 or more, though for the most part the degree of articulation is rather less than we might expect from reading Li Jing. When Li Yuan fought Wang Mantian in 616, his army was divided into a formation of "weak" troops in the center and two smaller cavalry formations placed in ambush on the flanks; in his next major battle, fought at Huoyi in 617, the Tang founder organized his army into three corps of infantry and two much smaller bodies of cavalry.[73] At the battle of Shizihe, fought earlier that same year, the rebel leaders Li Mi and Zhai Rang divided their troops into ten "companies" (*dui*) of unknown strength, six of which faced the opposing Sui army head-on while the other four were sent to block a separate Sui column.[74]

The relationship between tactical organization and weaponry is, unfortunately, not presented very clearly in what survives of Li Jing's military writings. We are told that *dui* might be assigned to half a dozen different tactical roles such as cavalry, archers, assault troops, or maneuver troops, but we are usually not told what weapons the soldiers assigned to each of these functions are supposed to be carrying. A significant exception is the crossbow, which was used by special companies of crossbowmen.[75] On this basis, we may speculate that other *dui* may have been armed primarily with bow, spear, lance, or long-handled saber. This interpretation also gets some support from battle narratives in which the users of specialist weapons appear to be organized into discrete units of some size. In a battle fought in 620, for example, the rebel leader Fu Gongshi spearheaded his attack with 1,000 men armed with long-handled sabers.[76]

In the Tang army, as in the Byzantine, the most fundamental distinction was between infantry and cavalry. According to Li Jing, each of the subordinate divisions (*jun*) of an expeditionary army should include at least 500 cavalry organized as a discrete unit, but when the army deployed into its battle formation all of these horsemen were to be brigaded together on the flanks.[77] The separation of soldiers on foot from those on horseback is even more pronounced in the historical battle narratives. When Li Shimin was fighting Wang Shichong near Luoyang in the spring of 621, he ordered his infantry into battle first and did not send in the cavalry until the infantry were already heavily engaged; when Su Dingfang was fighting the Western Türks in 657, he, too, deployed his infantry and cavalry in separate formations some distance apart and let the foot soldiers bear the brunt of the enemy's attack.[78] Given the very different strengths and capabilities of infantry and cavalry, and the different missions they were expected to perform, it should not be surprising that many Chinese armies of the early seventh century drew a clear distinction between the two arms at a very high level in their organizational hierarchy, with some of their top leaders explicitly designated as cavalry commanders.[79]

In order to coordinate the movements and activities of the subordinate units into which a field army was divided, there had to be an effective system of communications to connect the different levels of the command hierarchy. However, the communications tools available to the premodern commander were strictly limited, and did not extend beyond direct visual and acoustic signals and messengers on foot and on horseback.[80] Tang military and administrative works record various types of drums, gongs, and bells, together with flags of various colors and shapes that were intended for use in signaling commands. In ancient times, the beating of drums was supposed to signal an advance, while the gong or other metallic instrument was struck to signal a halt or withdrawal; in Tang times, drums still signaled the advance, but the gong or bell had been largely supplanted by the horn (*jiao*).[81] All of these instruments had multiple uses. Drums could be used to raise the alarm or send a distress signal, and in Li Jing's drills we find horns blown several times in succession to order the execution of each step in a fixed sequence of actions.[82] The commander of a Tang expeditionary army had five flags, one in the color of each of the five directions, to direct the movements of his troops. When two flags were crossed, for example, the companies were supposed to respond by combining into larger formations.[83]

One drill described by Li Jing calls for the commanding general to position himself on a height with twelve drums, twelve horns, and one set of five colored flags arrayed on each side of him. The troops draw up facing him in the plain below. They are enjoined to "watch the flags with their eyes, listen for the drums and horns with their ears, and hold the commands in their minds."[84] Even if the general were able to find himself a suitable eminence, communication would have been more challenging under combat conditions. The soldiers would be facing the enemy, not their own general, and many might be out of both sight and earshot of his command post. Battle accounts speak of the choking clouds of dust and the terrific din that arose on all sides when two armies collided.[85] And when closely engaged with the enemy, most soldiers would have been in no position to look over their shoulders for flag signals. Once the commander of a premodern army had committed all of his troops to combat, there was very little he could do to influence the outcome—which may help to explain why Tang commanders were reluctant to have the majority of their troops close with the enemy until victory seemed assured.

Although there were elaborate systems of signals to make the commander's will known to his subordinates, there does not seem to have been any corresponding system for sending reports upward; for the most part, Tang commanders seem to have gained their knowledge of what was happening on the battlefield from their own direct observation.[86] This method could leave much to be desired. In the autumn of 617, Tang troops assaulting the commandery city of Hedong had succeeded in gaining control of a portion of the wall when a storm came up. Li Yuan, not realizing how close they were to victory, had the horn blown to recall the troops until the weather had cleared—losing his chance to capture the city.[87] A few months later, the Sui general Wang Shichong made a similar mistake in a battle against Li Mi, and on this occasion the result was not merely a lost opportunity but a disastrous defeat with many thousands of casualties.[88]

The quickest and most reliable way Tang commanders could be apprised of what was transpiring at a distance from their headquarters was through the use of fire- and smoke-signals. Battle accounts indicate that such signals were often used by beleaguered outposts to summon help from the main army, and prearranged smoke signals could also be used to coordinate the movements of troops over distances beyond the range of flags or acoustic signals.[89] When Li Shimin fought Wang Shichong outside the west gates of Luoyang in the spring of 621, he opened the battle with 5,000 infantry; once they were heavily engaged, their commander sent up a smoke-signal, which was Shimin's cue to charge down from the heights with his elite cavalry.[90]

Although there were differences in detail, the range of communications devices used by the Byzantines was essentially the same as in China. The *Strategikon* mentions trumpets, horns, bugles, flag signals, voice commands, and the banging of lance against shield; the only element of the Chinese repertory that is missing is the drum.[91] Among the Byzantines, as in China, the flag

> was meant to be a rallying point for the troops. It was also used to convey signals and commands. This was done by holding it high steadily, inclining it to the right or the left, waving it or dipping it.[92]

Both the Tang and Byzantine systems used flags with different colors, symbols, shapes, and sizes to distinguish between different units and different levels of the command hierarchy, with the Chinese also taking the number of flags as an indicator of command authority.[93] The basic shape of flags in both armies was also very much the same: a square or rectangular base or head attached at one end to the flagpole, with a variable number of streamers added at the other end.[94] The Byzantines, however, seem to have been especially careful to avoid the confusion that might arise from a superabundance of signals in the heat of battle. Flags were distributed only down to the level of the *bandon* or *tagma*, and each battle line was supposed to have no more than three trumpets—and ideally, only one.[95]

If soldiers are to recognize such signals and respond to them effectively, they must be thoroughly trained. Hence, the *Strategikon* contains instructions for a number of different drills. Some focus on the weapon-handling skills of individual soldiers, but the majority are designed to teach men to maneuver in formation in response to preset signals. In the cavalry drill called "African," for example, the center remains in position while the two wings charge forward to attack. Then, one wing falls back toward the center while the other wing either halts or falls back more slowly on the outside:

> The wing which had halted then starts moving back to the main line; the other wing moves quickly out to meet it, riding off to one side, and in this way the two wings come face to face, but without colliding.[96]

In general, both cavalrymen and infantrymen were taught to move into battle in open order and then, when within two to four bowshots of the enemy, to close up into a denser formation. For the infantry, close order meant that "the shields of the men in the front rank are touching each other and those lined up behind them are almost glued to one another."[97] It was easier to march and maneuver in open order, but the tighter formation was much harder for the enemy to penetrate. Some large-scale, army-level drills involved mock combats between two opposing battle lines. The "enemy" line

> should sometimes move in formation against our battle line, sometimes raising dust, shouting, and in disorder, sometimes from behind, or attacking our flanks or rear. In this way, our soldiers, foot and horse, will become accustomed to all kinds of conditions and not be disturbed by them, and the merarchs will gain facility in meeting attacks.[98]

Perhaps because of their fragmentary state, Li Jing's military writings do not contain as many drills as the *Strategikon*. An infantry drill involving mock combat between two opposing lines is, however, described at length and in considerable detail:

> In all cases when teaching combat formations, fifty men make up a company (*dui*). Coming from the camp, they keep their spear pennons furled. Arriving at the left or right side of the training ground, each company unfurls its pennons and deploys in sequence. The companies are positioned ten paces apart, and each company [occupies a space] ten paces square, [with the soldiers] distributed evenly [in that space]. The support companies (*zhu dui*) block the gaps, standing twenty paces behind the forward companies. Once the deployment has been completed, the various officers of the several encampments go at the same time to the commanding general's position to receive instructions. Every second company is designated as a combat company (*zhan dui*) and goes out toward the front, each advancing fifty paces. When they hear the sound of the first horn call cease, the several companies simultaneously [open out to] stand in open order. When the sound of the second horn call ceases, the several companies simultaneously plant their spears and furl the pennons, string their bows and draw their sabers. When the sound of the third horn

call ceases, the several companies simultaneously raise their spears. When the sound of the fourth horn call ceases, the several companies simultaneously draw in their spears and kneel. Their eyes observe the large yellow flag at the commander-in-chief's position, their ears listen for the sound of the drum. The yellow flag inclines toward the front, the drum begins to beat. In unison they shout, "Wuhu! Wuhu!" and in unison they move forward. Upon reaching the center line, they begin to fight at the same time and in unison; shouting "Kill!" they charge in together. After the "enemy" have retreated in defeat, they may be pursued for thirty paces. When it is determined through investigation that the "enemy" really have been defeated, the cavalry corps (*ma jun*) comes from the rear to pursue the fugitives. When they hear the metallic gong struck, they must cease their shouting and fall back, resting their spears on their shoulders. They turn about by first facing to the side, and return to stand in open order at their original positions. When the sound of the first horn calls ceases, they simultaneously plant their spears and unfurl the pennons. When the sound of the second horn call ceases, they simultaneously raise their spears. When the sound of the third horn call ceases, they simultaneously adopt a dense formation. As soon as they see two flags cross at the commander-in-chief's position, five companies combine to form a single company – that is, with 250 men forming one unit (*dui*). Its unit drill and movements such as furling pennons, raising spears, compressing the formation, and engaging in combat all follow the methods previously described.[99]

In this drill, the companies are initially arrayed in a loose checkerboard formation. Within each *dui*, the individual soldiers have ample room to maneuver since each "pace" here actually represents a Chinese double-pace (*bu*) of approximately five feet. Each soldier should be five feet away from the men on each side of him and ten feet from those to front and rear. As the drill continues, however, this loose and no doubt easily maneuverable formation is compressed into a closer order and *dui* are joined into larger groupings to better meet the demands of combat. Like their Byzantine counterparts, Chinese commanders well understood the advantages and disadvantages of close and open order and envisioned a tightening of the formation as battle was joined.

The common ground in military training and practice extended to some quite specific matters of detail. In both the Tang and Byzantine armies, spears and lances were supposed to be furnished with pennons. In the drill described by Li Jing there is much furling and unfurling of these pennons, but at the point of contact with the "enemy"—the moment in a real battle when spears would be thrust home—they are to be in the furled position. The author of the *Strategikon* insists that pennons should be completely removed before combat, explaining that they present a fine appearance but interfere with the practical use of the lance and obstruct "the fire of the archers in the rear ranks."[100]

As we have already seen, both Tang and Byzantine armies were articulated into a number of units capable of maneuvering independently on the battlefield; these training exercises and drills prepared them to operate smoothly in coordination with one another. In the Byzantine army, an infantry battle line might be divided into three or four blocs of maneuver, with additional formations of cavalry on the wings—some acting as flank guards for one's own army, and others as "out-flankers" to operate against the flanks of the enemy line.[101] Byzantine deployments of the early seventh century were characterized not only by this kind of lateral segmentation or articulation, but also by a "vertical" articulation into a series of discrete lines or echelons. At the very least this meant the formation of two strong battle lines. A somewhat weaker rear guard or reserve line could be created by holding back a few *bandons* from the second line, and before battle was joined one or two *bandons* might be sent forward to screen the main formation. During the approach to battle the second line was supposed to follow more than a mile behind the first, but then close up to within four bowshots when nearing the enemy.[102] Division into multiple echelons meant that a part of the army would be ready to respond to sudden contingencies or reversals while others were already engaged, and made it possible to feed in fresh troops gradually as required by the tempo of battle. This was of particular value when fighting against a more numerous enemy, and it also offered the prospect of surprising a disordered opponent with fresh and well-ordered troops of one's own—if that opponent was not also organized into multiple echelons.[103] These deployments, so prominent in the *Strategikon*, were actually a quite new development in the Byzantine military at the time that work was written. Earlier Roman armies had made do with a single battle line plus a small reserve.[104]

What survives of his military writings makes it clear that Li Jing also favored a formation of multiple echelons. In the drill instructions quoted above, we see an initial deployment into two lines of companies (*dui*), each five ranks deep, with the support line positioned twenty paces behind the main line. As the drill progresses, half the companies in the main line advance fifty paces to the front to form a third line that may be tentatively labeled as the "spearhead" line.[105] Other passages from Li Jing indicate that cavalry formations should be positioned to the right and left of the support line, and that in battle other companies may be placed even farther back to guard the baggage train.[106] There is some evidence from the Tang histories that Li Jing's multiple-echelon deployment is a faithful reflection of actual military practice. At the battle of Raoyang in 621, we are told, the anti-Tang warlord Liu Heita had so few troops that he was forced to form his army in only a single line—implying that common and accepted military practice of the time called for deployment in two or more echelons.[107]

In both the Chinese and the Byzantine cases, there is a clear functional distinction between the various echelons. Under normal circumstances the first line will be the first to engage in combat, while the second line and any other reserve lines hold back to exploit opportunities, provide assistance as needed, and form a secure base behind which the first line may fall back and rally if necessary. There is, however, an additional layer of tactical complexity. Both the Li Jing fragments and the *Strategikon* describe the assignment of units to specific tactical roles that do not necessarily depend on the echelon to which they have been assigned. In the Byzantine army, the key distinction was between the "assault troops" (*cursores*) and the "defenders" (*defensores*). The author of the *Strategikon* offers the following definitions of these tactical roles:

> Assault troops is the term used for those who move out ahead of the main line and rush upon the retreating enemy. Defenders are those who follow them, not charging out or breaking ranks, but marching in good order as a support for the assault troops if they should happen to fall back.[108]

In the *meros*—the largest cavalry formation, consisting of as many as 6,000–7,000 men—one-third of the riders, mainly archers, were to be assault troops positioned on the flanks, while the remaining two-thirds were to be defenders stationed in the center:

> If the enemy be driven back by the charge, then the assault troops should quickly chase after them continuing their pursuit right up to the enemy camp. The defenders should follow without halting and maintaining their formation. Then, in case the enemy wheels around and the assault troops cannot handle the fighting at close quarters, they can take refuge among the defenders and rally.[109]

A single echelon could include both *cursores* and *defensores*, thus providing the same sort of insurance against sudden reversals as afforded by a deployment in multiple lines or echelons.[110]

The system of tactical roles described by Li Jing is rather more complicated. After an initial differentiation has been made between the companies of combat troops (*zhan bing*) and the baggage guards, the former are sorted into five categories: crossbowmen, archers, cavalry, assault troops (*tiaodang bing*), and maneuver troops (*qi bing*). With the exception of the cavalry, which has its own position on the flanks, these companies are then assigned to any one of three tactical roles: spearhead company (*zhanfeng dui*), combat company (*zhan dui*), and support company (*zhu dui*).[111] In the drill we have already seen, these correspond to the three lines of the formation; excluding the cavalry and the baggage guards, one-quarter of the companies are in the spearhead line, one-quarter in the combat line, and one-half in the support line. Other passages, however, describe an alternative arrangement with one spearhead company, two combat companies, and two support companies organized into a *tong* or battalion (whose sixth and weakest company has already been told off to guard the baggage).[112] This gives us not simply a "horizontal" organization in each of the three battle lines, but also a "vertical" command structure integrating elements from all three lines. It is not entirely clear whether there is supposed to be a fixed relationship between troop categories and tactical roles, but one passage suggests that the archers and crossbowmen are to be found among the combat companies: when the enemy comes to within twenty paces of their position, they are to drop their bows and crossbows, take up sabers and cudgels, and engage in mêlée combat alongside the spearhead troops; their discarded missile weapons, meanwhile, are to be retrieved by men from the support line. Li Jing continues:

The cavalry, assault troops, and maneuver troops may not move on their own initiative. Should the infantry be pushed back by the enemy, the assault troops, maneuver troops, and cavalry go forward to meet the enemy with a spirited attack; the infantry must fall back and reform to assist the troops in front. Should the assault troops, maneuver troops, and cavalry be repulsed by the enemy, the spearhead and other companies must advance together to attack vigorously. If the enemy fall back, the maneuver troops and cavalry may not exploit over a distance. Only after it has been learned through careful examination that the enemy are panicked and in disorder are they permitted to mount their horses to pursue and exploit. The support companies may not move on their own initiative.[113]

Close reading of this passage suggests that the spearhead companies, archers, and crossbowmen are infantry, whereas the support companies are none other than the assault troops and maneuver troops, dismounted horsemen who mount up and ride out only when higher headquarters have determined the moment to be propitious for a vigorous pursuit. As in the *Strategikon*, we are presented with a system where some soldiers fight while others hold back and try to maintain the best order they can. When one group runs into trouble it falls back to take refuge behind the other; once it has rallied, it returns to the fray, allowing the other group to fall back and rally in its turn. Indeed, we find a similar alternating motion suggested in the *Strategikon*, where a hard-pressed first line of cavalry may regroup behind the second line before joining it in returning to the attack.[114] In Li Jing's system, there is usually a close correlation between a company's position in echelon and its tactical role, but as in the *Strategikon*, this is not always and necessarily the case. In one passage, we are told that each of the five troop categories (here, these are assault companies, cavalry companies, maneuver companies, spearhead companies, and support companies) is assigned its own commander. "When going into battle, one first uses a particular category of soldiers in the combat. If more soldiers are needed, take them one category at a time until all have been used."[115]

We have already encountered two passages in which Li Jing makes it clear that pursuits are to be carefully controlled. They are to be undertaken only after investigation, under orders from higher commanders; they may not be carried out by units charged with other tasks, and (at least in the initial stage) may cover only a limited distance. Here is yet another example:

In all cases when the spearhead companies and the other companies have defeated the enemy, each of the support companies selects twenty brave and sturdy men to pursue the enemy. The baggage-guard companies shout from a distance to provide moral support, but are not allowed to move. In exploiting the enemy's retreat, the assault companies and the companies of maneuver troops are not allowed to go beyond one hundred paces. If it is determined through investigation that the enemy troops have scattered in defeat, then we must seize the opportunity to pursue the fugitives.[116]

Insofar as some men of the support companies have been assigned to a pursuit role while their fellows are presumably expected to remain in place, what is described here is rather similar to the *cursores* and *defensores* of the Byzantines.[117]

Throughout Li Jing's writings, there is a strong emphasis on the integrity of formations and the imperative of acting only in response to proper commands. Soldiers are not to leave their assigned positions in the ranks for any reason. Since the lure of plunder might lead men to engage in unauthorized pursuits or advances with the result that their formation might be disrupted, endangered, or even destroyed, the Tang general decreed, "When the enemy is defeated, the first to engage in plundering will be executed." He also made it clear that, once the formation is set, "if someone advances or retreats, or goes forward first to take the enemy causing the ranks to become disordered, the affected ranks in front and behind and to the right and left of him are to cut him down."[118] To deal summarily with men who might try to hang back or escape toward the rear, the deputy commander of each company was stationed to the rear of its formation holding a long-handled blade (*modao*). But as an added disincentive for bad behavior, anyone could visit summary justice upon the malefactor:

> Should a combat company or other company have a man who does not rush in together with the others, a man of the same company who is able to cut off his head will be rewarded with fifty lengths of fabric. If a different company sees a man who does not rush in, the one who is able to cut off his head will be rewarded with fabric according to the aforementioned standard.[119]

The Byzantine attitude was the same. Pursuits were to be cautious, controlled, and over limited distances. The *Strategikon* advises the general to "avoid disordered and uncoordinated pursuits."[120] Cavalry are instructed to pursue for a distance of only three to five bowshots, and are not supposed to get too far away from their supporting infantry. In their drills, meanwhile, the foot soldiers are told, "Keep your position. Follow the standard. Do not leave the standard and pursue the enemy."[121] The Byzantine military manual contains repeated injunctions against looting, especially before a battle is entirely over, and soldiers who leave their position in the ranks for any reason are to be severely punished:

> If during the time when the battle lines are being formed and during combat a soldier shall abandon his post or his standard and flee, or if he charges out ahead of the place where he has been stationed, or if he plunders the dead, or races off to pursue the enemy, or attacks the baggage train or camp of the enemy, we order that he be executed, and that all the loot he may have taken be confiscated and given in to the common fund of his tagma, inasmuch as he has broken ranks and has betrayed his comrades.[122]

In the event that an entire *tagma* turns and flees, it may be shot at and decimated by the other *tagmas*.[123]

The concerns expressed by the Chinese and Byzantine military theorists may be attributed in part to the overriding need of virtually all premodern armies to keep their men in formation and under control lest tactical cohesion—and with it, all military effectiveness—be lost. Yet the Byzantine material in particular points repeatedly to a more specific fear, reflecting a keen awareness of the battlefield as a place of traps, surprises, ambushes, and sudden reversals of fortune. Again and again, the injunction against breaking ranks at the moment of apparent victory to engage in looting or reckless pursuit is justified on the grounds that the soldiers may fall into an enemy ambush or be overwhelmed by the counterattack of a seemingly beaten foe who has managed to rally. Here are two examples from the *Strategikon*:

> If the enemy is put to flight, our soldiers must be restrained from plundering. Otherwise while they are scattered about doing this, the enemy army might reform and attack them.[124]

> The cavalry should not be ordered to race after the enemy or to get too far away from the infantry line, even if the enemy turns in flight. They might run into an ambush and, by themselves, few in numbers, far from any assistance, they may be badly beaten.[125]

The same text recommends the deployment of flank guards to protect one's own flank and "outflankers" to attack the enemy's flank. It recommends the use of a concealed second echelon, positioned some distance behind the first and beyond the enemy's range of observation. And it also calls for some troops to be placed in ambush positions, concealed by the terrain or other friendly units, in order to take the enemy by surprise at a critical moment in the battle.[126] The author of the *Strategikon* shows a keen awareness that the enemy may be capable of using any or all of these devices against the Roman army, and therefore advises extensive use of scouts and patrols on the battlefield to guard against the unexpected:

> Stationed at intervals, depending on the nature of the terrain, before the battle and until it is all over, they should keep both the enemy and their own units under observation to prevent any attack from ambush or any other hostile trick.[127]

A particular danger was the feigned flight:

> Instead of a large number of troops, some commanders draw up the smaller part of the army. When the charge is made and the lines clash, those soldiers quickly turn to flight; the enemy starts chasing them and becomes disordered. They ride past the place where the ambush is laid, and the units in ambush then charge out and strike the enemy in the rear. Those fleeing then turn around, and the enemy force is caught in the middle.[128]

The author of the *Strategikon* labels this the "Scythian ambush," and goes on to say that the "Scythian peoples," that is, the nomads of the vast Eurasian steppelands, "do this all the time." But what is a danger in one context may be an opportunity in another; the same ploy may be used with every expectation of success by Byzantine commanders facing Slavs or other "undisciplined peoples."[129] In fact, there is much evidence that Byzantine commanders used the feigned flight against quite a variety of opponents, not all of them undisciplined.[130]

Perhaps because of the fragmentary nature of what survives of his work, Li Jing appears to be much less concerned with flank attacks and ambushes on the battlefield—though he is not entirely unaware of the possibility: " . . . [I]f there is ground that both we and they consider advantageous, then yield it and set an ambush; as [they] rush toward that which they cherish we will surprise them from the side."[131] He mentions feigned flight by the enemy as a risk to be guarded against—"if maneuver troops have been concealed in ambush, they will purposely entice us with fleeing troops"—but does not go so far as to recommend its use against the enemy.[132] The historical sources, however, contain battle accounts making it clear that ploys such as ambushes and attacks against the flank or rear were used by Chinese armies on numerous occasions during Li Jing's lifetime and were an accepted and even expected element in the conduct of military operations.[133] During his march against the Sui capital in 617, the Tang founder Li Yuan overcame one Sui army when a detachment of his "roving cavalry" fell upon the enemy rear.[134] In the autumn of the preceding year, another Sui army commanded by Zhang Xutuo had been smashed by the rebel forces of Zhai Rang and Li Mi. Acting in accordance with Li Mi's advice, Zhai Rang had led his main body of troops out to confront the Sui forces. Meanwhile,

> Mi concealed a detachment of more than a thousand men in the woods north of the Great Sea Temple. Xutuo, who had never taken Rang seriously, advanced in a square formation. Rang joined battle, and it did not go in his favor. Xutuo exploited it and pursued the fugitives more than ten *li*; Mi sprang the ambush to surprise them, and Xutuo's troops were defeated. Mi and Rang, together with Xu Shiji and Wang Bodang joined forces to surround them. Xutuo broke out of the encirclement but not all of his entourage were able to get out, so he spurred his horse and went in again to rescue them, going back and forth several or even four times until he died fighting.[135]

In the summer of 580, when Li Jing was still a young child, a general serving the Sui founder Yang Jian, who had just recently seized power from the Northern Zhou dynasty in a palace coup, faced off against an army of several tens of thousands of Zhou loyalists near Liangjun in today's Henan province. The Sui general Yu Zhongwen pretended to flee after provoking battle with his weakest troops. The Zhou commander took no precautions, with the result that Yu Zhongwen was able to counterattack and smash his army, taking more than 5,000 men alive and cutting off more than 700 heads.[136]

A better substantiated difference between Chinese and Byzantine tactics than the use of the feigned flight and other such ploys is the differing emphasis that each military culture placed on the tactical employment of elite troops. Following up on a theme that was already well developed in the ancient Chinese military classics, Li Jing declared that "those whose formations are without a picked spearhead . . . will be defeated."[137] As we have already seen, the drills and deployments he describes call for setting out a front line of "spearhead companies" (*zhanfeng dui*), or for a battalion (*tong*) to advance in a wedge-shaped formation led by its spearhead company. The practice of imposing a disproportionate tactical burden upon relatively small contingents of elite troops is even more pronounced in Sui and Tang battle narratives. Li Shimin won almost all of his victories by charging a critical weak point in the enemy line at the head of his elite cavalry after the enemy had been pinned down, softened up, or distracted by other elements of his army, and by the beginning of 621 he had organized a special squadron of 1,000 horsemen, clothed in black and wearing black armor, to perform in this role.[138] The creation of such *corps d'élite* was a common practice of the Chinese military leaders of the period. The rebel leader Li Mi formed an "Inner Army" (*nei jun*) of 8,000 men, and once said of them, "These eight thousand are a match for a million."[139] Another anti-Sui rebel, the Huainan bandit chieftain Du Fuwei, created a picked force of 5,000 warriors "who dared to face death." He called them his "superior recruits" (*shang mu*), offered them generous material rewards, and used them to spearhead his army's attacks. The men were inspected after each battle, and those found to have been wounded in the back were immediately put to death.[140]

The preferred battle tactics of the time aimed to exploit the differential between such bands of high-quality fighters and the indifferent mass of the ordinary soldiery. Instead of having his entire army advance against the enemy line as a body to make a single, concerted attack, the Chinese general would often send out a relatively small detachment to attack a selected portion of the line in the hope of breaking through, creating a panic, or otherwise causing the hostile formation to come undone. Yang Su, one of the most ruthless and successful of the generals who served the first Sui emperor, was in the habit of sending out a force of 100–200 men to accomplish this task. If they failed to overcome the enemy formation, he had them all executed and sent forward a slightly larger force to repeat the operation.[141] Fu Gongshi, a lieutenant of Du Fuwei, used a spearhead (*qianfeng*) of 1,000 elite armored troops (*jing jia*) brandishing long-handled sabers in much the same fashion during a battle fought at the end of 620.[142] These tactics were still in use more than a century later, when the Tang general Gao Xianzhi, fighting the Tibetans at Lesser Balûr in 747, sent forward a small party of crack troops wielding long-handled blades (*modao*) to break the enemy line.[143]

Since generals preferred to direct their attacks against the weakest part of an enemy force, countermeasures were tailored accordingly. As we have seen, one of the most common stratagems in early Tang warfare was to deploy a force of obviously weak or decrepit troops in plain view of the enemy as a decoy while better quality troops were placed in ambush positions nearby. When Li Yuan confronted the bandit army of Wang Mantian in Shanxi in 616, he deployed his "weak" troops—who seem to have accounted for the majority of his army of 5,000–6,000 men—in the center with the baggage train and all of the army's banners, drums, and horns. When the bandits charged this tempting target, they exposed themselves to a decisive counterstroke by the much smaller bodies of elite cavalry that the Tang founder had concealed on both flanks.[144]

On the Byzantine side, there was certainly an awareness that not all troops were of equal quality. Procopius' account of the wars of Justinian accords great prominence to the *bucellarii* or private retainers of Belisarius, and to the cavalry more generally, while occasionally expressing concerns about the reliability of the infantry.[145] The author of the *Strategikon* recommends that the general should always keep a body of chosen troops with him to deal with sudden crises.[146] Much later, in the tenth century, Byzantine armies did include small, elite units of very heavily armored horsemen that performed in a spearhead or line-cracking role quite similar to that of Chinese elite units in the Sui–Tang period.[147] Such units, however, are not found in the *Strategikon* and other sixth- and seventh-century sources where, for the most part, qualitative differences do not loom large—certainly not as large as in the contemporary Chinese materials—and do not shape the tactical system. This difference may perhaps be explained by the fact that whereas the late Roman army was an almost entirely professional force, Chinese recruitment methods yielded a much more uneven mix of short-term conscripts, part-time soldiers, and truly elite warriors.

For the most part, however, Chinese and Byzantine commanders of the early seventh century operated on shared tactical ground that was defined above all by prudence and caution, by sensitivity to risk, and by a set of quite similar measures aimed at risk avoidance and force protection on the battlefield. In the next chapter, we will find that their approach to leading armies on campaign, over longer time periods and greater distances, was driven by very much the same concerns.

Notes

1 This paragraph is informed by the ideas of prominent world historians such as Marshall Hodgson, Fernand Braudel, William H. McNeill, and David Christian.

2 Wei Zhenfu et al., *Bingqi*, vol. 1 of *Zhongguo junshi shi* (Beijing: Jiefangjun chubanshe, 1983), pp. 20 and 23; Yang Hong, *Gudai bingqi shihua* (Shanghai: Shanghai kexue jishu chubanshe, 1988), pp. 151–2; Zhou Wei, *Zhongguo bingqi shigao* (Taipei: Mingwen shuju, 1981), pp. 207 and 212.

3 For Li Jing, see *TD* 149, p. 3813; for Li Quan, see *Taibai yinjing*, in *Zhongguo bingshu jicheng*, vol. 2 (Beijing and Shenyang: Jiefangjun chubanshe and Liao-Shen shushe, 1988), p. 537.

4 *TD* 15, p. 355, and Terrence Douglas O'Byrne, "Civil-Military Relations During the Middle T'ang: The Career of Kuo Tzu-i" (Ph.D. diss., University of Illinois at Urbana-Champaign, 1982), p. 24.

5 *TD* 158, p. 4052; *XTS* 84, p. 3682; Wen Daya, *Da Tang chuang ye qi ju zhu* (Shanghai: Shanghai guji chubanshe, 1983), p. 24.

6 Yang Hong, *Zhongguo gu bingqi luncong*, 2nd ed. (Beijing: Wenwu chubanshe, 1985), pp. 123–4.

7 *TLD* 16, p. 461; Yang Hong, *Gudai bingqi shihua*, p. 150; Zhou Wei, *Zhongguo bingqi shigao*, p. 221; *XTS* 50, p. 1325; Li Quan, *Taibai yinjing*, p. 538.

8 *ZZTJ* 182, pp. 5674–5; 186, p. 5832.
9 A new variant, the *modao*, became widespread beginning in the late seventh century. It differed from the *chang dao* in that it had two cutting edges rather than one; see Wei Zhenfu, *Bingqi*, pp. 23–4, and Guo Dehe, *Gudai bingqi* (Beijing: Zhongguo da baike quanshu chubanshe, 2006), p. 31. Because no identifiable specimens of these weapons have been found, much remains uncertain. It is possible that *chang dao* and *mo dao* are simply different names for the same weapon, as assumed by Lorge and argued at greater length by Li Jinxiu. Lorge describes the weapon as single-edged, with a three-foot blade, four-foot handle, and steel butt spike, while Li is largely silent with regard to its construction and appearance. See Peter A. Lorge, *Chinese Martial Arts: From Antiquity to the Twenty-first Century* (New York: Cambridge University Press, 2012), p. 103; and Li Jinxiu, "Modao yu da Tang diguo de junshi," in *idem*, *Tangdai zhidu shi lue lun gao* (Beijing: Zhongguo zhengfa daxue chubanshe, 1998), pp. 295–308. For a description of the *naginata* and its use in combat, see Karl F. Friday, *Samurai, Warfare and the State in Early Medieval Japan* (New York and London: Routledge, 2004), p. 86.
10 *CFYG* 396, p. 3a.
11 *ZZTJ* 188, pp. 5898–9; 215, p. 6885; 220, p. 7033. In Li Quan's model army, only 20 percent of the troops are equipped with any such weapon (the *modao*); see Li Quan, *Taibai yinjing*, p. 538). This type of weapon would have been impossible to use effectively from horseback, and one text (*TLD* 16, p. 461) specifically states that the *modao* is for infantry use. Also see Li Jinxiu, "Modao yu Tang diguo de junshi," pp. 301–2. From the mid-eighth century there are reports of formations of as many as 5,000 men armed with *modao*, but Li Jinxiu's argument that it was the main weapon used by the infantry from very early in the Tang dynasty is unconvincing.
12 Zhou Wei, *Zhongguo bingqi shigao*, pp. 206, 208, 210, 212, and 221; Yang Hong, *Zhongguo gu bingqi luncong*, pp. 125 and 127–8.
13 Albert E. Dien, *Six Dynasties Civilization* (New Haven and London: Yale University Press, 2007), pp. 258–9; Yang Hong, *Gudai bingqi shihua*, pp. 142–3. The technique involved the mixing of wrought iron (low carbon content) with pig iron (high carbon content) in a furnace to produce steel (intermediate carbon content), and is described in detail in Joseph Needham, *The Development of Iron and Steel Technology in China* (London: The Newcomen Society, 1958), pp. 27–8, 30, and 38; as well as Yang Kuan, *Zhongguo gudai yetie jishu fazhan shi* (Shanghai: Shanghai renmin chubanshe, 1982), pp. 447–50. This process required less time and skill than the old method of producing blades by repeated forging.
14 Yang Kuan, *Zhongguo gudai yetie jishu fazhan shi*, pp. 282 and 284; Yang Hong, *Gudai bingqi shihua*, p. 143.
15 *QTW* 10, 20b-21a; *ZZTJ* 189, p. 5914.
16 *XTS* 50, p. 1325; *TD* 148, pp. 3792–3.
17 *TLD* 16, pp. 460–1; *TD* 157, p. 4033. For bow materials, also see Yang Hong, *Weapons in Ancient China*, trans. Zhang Lijing (Rego Park, NY: Science Press, 1992), p. 246, and Charles Benn, *Daily Life in Traditional China: The Tang Dynasty* (Westport, CT: Greenwood Press, 2002), p. 170.
18 For the figure of 280 yards, see W.F. Paterson, "The Archers of Islam," *Journal of the Economic and Social History of the Orient* 9 (1966), p. 83; Saxton T. Pope, "A Study of Bows and Arrows," *University of California Publications in American Archaeology and Ethnology* 13.9 (August 10, 1923), p. 373; Ralph Payne-Gallwey, *A Treatise on the Construction, Power and Management of Turkish and Other Oriental Bows of Mediaeval and Later Times* (London: Longmans, Green, and Co., 1907), p. 20; A.D.H. Bivar, "Cavalry Equipment and Tactics on the Euphrates Frontier," *Dumbarton Oaks Papers* 26 (1972), p. 283. On velocity and penetrating power, see Wallace McLeod, "The Range of the Ancient Bow," *Phoenix: The Journal of the Classical Association of Canada* 19 (1965), pp. 7–8; and Paterson, "The Archers

of Islam," p. 86. For a careful and detailed study of the characteristics of composite bows, including variation over time and among different peoples, see Christopher A. Bergman and Edward McEwen, "Sinew-Reinforced and Composite Bows: Technology, Function, and Social Implications," in Heidi Knecht (ed.), *Projectile Technology* (New York and London: Plenum Press, 1997), pp. 143–60.

19 *ZZTJ* 196, pp. 6171–2. For comparisons of mounted and foot archery, see John Masson Smith, Jr., "Äyn Jālūt: Mamlūk Success or Mongol Failure?" *HJAS* 44.2 (December 1984), pp. 316, 324; and Paterson, "The Archers of Islam," p. 84.

20 Wang Ju, *She jing*, in *Zhongguo bingshu jicheng*, vol. 2, pp. 1033–4.

21 For Li Shimin's skill as an archer, see *CFYG* 44, p. 12a.

22 Stephen Selby, *Chinese* Archery (Hong Kong: Hong Kong University Press, 2000), pp. 154 and 162; Wei Zhenfu, *Bingqi*, p. 37.

23 With regard to the various advantages of the crossbow, see Joseph Needham and Robin D.S. Yates, *Science and Civilisation in China*, vol. 5: *Chemistry and Chemical Technology*, part 6: *Military Technology: Missiles and Sieges* (Cambridge: Cambridge University Press, 1994), pp. 120 and 155–6; Alfred W. Crosby, *Throwing Fire: Projectile Technology Through History* (Cambridge: Cambridge University Press, 2002), pp. 78 and 80; C. Martin Wilbur, "The History of the Crossbow," *Annual Report, 1936* (Washington, DC: Smithsonian Institution, 1937), p. 434; Yang Hong, *Zhongguo gu bingqi luncong*, pp. 209–10.

24 *TLD* 16, p. 461; *XTS* 50, p. 1327. The longest-range crossbow that could be drawn by the strength of a single man had a range of more than 450 meters but was probably too cumbersome for battlefield use.

25 *TD* 157, pp. 4033, 4036.

26 *TLD* 16, p. 461. I have found no mention of the actual employment of the cavalry crossbow in battle in any Tang historical source. For the difficulty of using the cross-bow on horseback, see Wilbur, "The History of the Crossbow," p. 433, and Yang Hong, *Zhongguo gu bingqi luncong*, p. 210. For Chinese methods of drawing the crossbow, see Yang Hong, *Gudai bingqi shihua*, pp. 105 and 140–1.

27 Zeng Gongliang, *Wujing zongyao*, in *Zhongguo bingshu jicheng*, vol. 3 (Beijing and Shenyang: Jiefangjun chubanshe and Liao-Shen shushe, 1988), p. 103.

28 For Li Jing, see *TD* 157, pp. 4033 and 4036; for an example of volley fire from 756, see *ZZTJ* 217, pp. 6954–5.

29 Yang Hong, *Zhongguo gu bingqi luncong*, p. 226.

30 *TD* 148, pp. 3792–3; Li Quan, *Taibai yinjing*, p. 537.

31 Byzantine weaponry of this period is discussed in three works by John Haldon: "Some Aspects of Byzantine Military Technology from the Sixth to Tenth Centuries," *Byzantine and Modern Greek Studies* 1 (1975), especially pp. 20, 23, 31–2, and 39; *Warfare, State and Society in the Byzantine World, 565–1204* (London: UCL Press, 1999), pp. 129–32; and "Some Aspects of Early Byzantine Arms and Armour," in D. Nicolle (ed.), *A Companion to Medieval Arms and Armour* (Woodbridge, UK: The Boydell Press, 2002), p. 71. Also see *Strategikon*, pp. 12 and 139; and Jon Coulston, "Arms and Armour of the Late Roman Army," in D. Nicolle (ed.), *Companion*, pp. 12–14. The *Strategikon* also mentions the "Herul sword" as an infantry weapon, but no source actually describes it. According to Geoffrey Greatrex, the Heruls were a Hunnic tribe settled in Pannonia who furnished troops to the Eastern Roman Empire in the early sixth century; see *Rome and Persia at War, 502–532* (Leeds: Francis Cairns, 1998), p. 31. Although it does not appear in the *Strategikon*, the four-foot sling-staff was mentioned by Vegetius and may have continued in use; see Coulston, "Arms and Armour," p. 13, and Pat Southern and Karen Ramsey Dixon, *The Late Roman Army* (New Haven and London: Yale University Press, 1996), p. 166.

32 David Nishimura, "Crossbows, Arrow Guides, and the *Solenarion*," *Byzantion* 58 (1988), pp. 423–4. The identification of the *solenarion* with the crossbow was originally proposed by John Haldon in his article "*Solenarion* – The Byzantine

Crossbow?" *Historical Journal of the University of Birmingham* 12 (1970), pp. 155–7, and endorsed by George Dennis in "Flies, Mice and the Byzantine Crossbow," *Byzantine and Modern Greek Studies* 7 (1981), pp. 1–5. In "Crossbows and Crosswords," *Isis* 64 (1973), pp. 527–33, Bert S. Hall questioned whether the crossbow survived except as a hunting weapon between the second century BCE and its reappearance in the tenth century CE. The identification of the *solenarion* with the arrow guide was put forward by Nishimura in 1988 and subsequently accepted by Haldon (see "Some Aspects of Early Byzantine Arms and Armour," p. 78). The crossbow interpretation still has its defenders, most notably Bernard Bachrach; see his *Early Carolingian Warfare: Prelude to Empire* (Philadelphia: University of Pennsylvania Press, 2001), p. 112.

33 Vernard Foley et al., "The Crossbow," *Scientific American*, vol. 252, no. 1 (January 1985), p. 107. The Chinese trigger mechanism is described and diagramed in Needham and Yates, *Science and Civilisation in* China, vol. 5, part. 6, p. 128.

34 Yang Hong, *Gudai bingqi shihua*, p. 153; Zhou Wei, *Zhongguo bingqi shigao*, p. 230; Wei Zhenfu, *Bingqi*, p. 46; *TLD* 16, p. 462.

35 For an example of the shield-and-saber used together, see *ZZTJ* 186, p. 5832. Yang Hong believes this combination was the most common panoply during the Northern and Southern Dynasties period (*Gudai bingqi shihua*, p. 137).

36 For Byzantine shields, see Haldon, *Warfare, State and Society*, pp. 129–32; Haldon, "Some Aspects of Early Byzantine Arms and Armour," pp. 71–2; Coulston, "Arms and Armour," p. 10; and *Strategikon*, p. 139.

37 For Byzantine armor, see Haldon, "Some Aspects of Early Byzantine Arms and Armour," pp. 68–71; Haldon, *Warfare, State and Society*, pp. 129–31; and *Strategikon*, pp. 12, 139.

38 Albert E. Dien, "A Study of Early Chinese Armor," *Artibus Asiae* 43 (1982), pp. 31–2; Yang Hong, *Gudai bingqi shihua*, p. 153.

39 Yang Hong, *Zhongguo gu bingqi luncong*, pp. 57–8. Leather lamellae could be some-what larger; see Zhou Wei, *Zhongguo bingqi shigao*, p. 217. For a general description of lamellar armor, see H. Russell Robinson, *Oriental Armour* (London: Herbert Jenkins, 1967), p. 7. For Sui and Tang lamellar, see Dien, "Early Chinese Armor," p. 24 and *passim*.

40 Descriptions of full armor can be found in Zhou Xibao, *Zhongguo gudai fushi shi* (Beijing: Zongguo xiju chubanshe, 1984), p. 231, and Yang Hong, *Gudai bingqi shihua*, pp. 153, 155.

41 This description is based on my own inspection of the relief carving, which is in the collection of the University Museum of Archaeology/Anthropology at the University of Pennsylvania and appears on the cover of this book.

42 For the issuing of armor to the troops, see *XTS* 50, p. 1325, and *TD* 149, p. 3820 (where it is clear that the armor is made up of lamellae). The 60/40 division can be found in Li Quan, *Taibai yinjing*, p. 536, and *TD* 148, p. 3794.

43 Zhou Xibao, *Zhongguo gudai fushi shi*, p. 159.

44 *TD* 149, p. 3820.

45 With regard to the introduction of chain mail into China, see Paul Demiéville, *Le Concile de Lhasa: Une controverse sur le quiétisme entre Bouddhistes de l'Inde et de la Chine au VIIIe siècle de l'ère chrétienne* (1952; rpt. Paris: Collège de France, Institut des Hautes Études Chinoises, 1987), note on pages 373–6.

46 Haldon, "Some Aspects of Early Byzantine Arms and Armour," pp. 70 and 73.

47 Yang Hong, *Zhongguo gu bingqi luncong*, p. 48; Dien, "Early Chinese Armor," p. 38.

48 Albert E. Dien, "The Stirrup and Its Effect on Chinese Military History," *Ars Orientalis* 16 (1986), pp. 36–8; Dien, "Early Chinese Armor," pp. 5 and 40; Yang Hong, *Gudai bingqi shihua*, pp. 122 and 140.

49 Yang Hong, *Zhongguo gu bingqi luncong*, p. 50; *ZZTJ* 176, p. 5499; and 181, p. 5660; and Asami Naoichirō, "Yōdai no dai ichiji Kōkurei enseigun: sono kibo to heishu," *Tōyōshi kenkyū* 44.1 (June 1985), p. 28 and *passim*.

50 Yang Hong, *Gudai bingqi shihua*, pp. 144–5 and 153–5, and *Zhongguo gu bingqi luncong*, pp. 51–2.
51 Wen Daya, *Da Tang chuang ye qi ju zhu*, p. 2; *ZZTJ* 181, p. 5638.
52 Dien, "Early Chinese Armor," p. 41.
53 For the Sui army, see *SS* 8, pp. 160–1; for the Tang *fubing*, see *XTS* 50, p. 1325.
54 See, for example, *ZZTJ* 188, pp. 5902–3.
55 Chen Qinglong, "Tujue xizu de bingqi," *Dalu zazhi* 68.5 (May 15, 1984), pp. 234–8.
56 The Orkhon inscriptions, dating from the first half of the eighth century, are translated in Talat Tekin, *A Grammar of Orkhon Turkic* (Bloomington: Indiana University, 1968); a typical description of combat can be found on p. 270.
57 For Li Jing, see *TD* 148, pp. 3792–3. It should be noted, however, that some of Li Jing's passages seem to describe an expeditionary army composed mainly of mounted infantry, that is, soldiers who ride to the battlefield but fight dismounted. This problem will be addressed in Chapter 4 below. Another source, *XTS* 50, p. 1325, describes a drill involving ten companies of infantry and only one company of cavalry.
58 Yang Hong, *Gudai bingqi shihua*, p. 140.
59 *ZZTJ* 200, p. 6306.
60 *ZZTJ* 196, pp. 6171–2.
61 *TD* 148, p. 3789.
62 The paragraph condenses material from several sources, especially Philip Rance, "Narses and the Battle of Taginae (Busta Gallorum) 552: Procopius and Sixth-Century Warfare," *Historia* 54 (2005), pp. 427–8, 431–2, 435–6, 438, and 459–60. Also see Procopius, *History of the Wars*, trans. H.B. Dewing (London: William Heinemann Ltd., 1954), vol. 1, pp. 7–9; and *Strategikon*, pp. 13, 133, and 144. For Solachon, see John Haldon, *The Byzantine Wars* (Stroud, Gloucestershire: Tempus, 2001), p. 56.
63 The *Notitia Dignitatum* in A.H.M. Jones, *The Later Roman Empire, 284–602: A Social, Economic, and Administrative Survey* (Norman: University of Oklahoma Press, 1964), vol. 2, pp. 1417–50; vs. *Strategikon*, p. 29; there is also evidence that an infantry *bandon* might include both heavy infantry and lightly armed archers (*Strategikon*, p. 141).
64 Positioning of cavalry: *Strategikon*, p. 144; additional refinement: *Strategikon*, p. 26.
65 *Strategikon*, pp. 17, 27–8, and 140–2.
66 Edward N. Luttwak, *The Grand Strategy of the Byzantine Empire* (Cambridge, MA: The Belknap Press of Harvard University Press, 2009), p. 373.
67 Luttwak, *Grand Strategy of the Byzantine Empire*, p. 373; also see Michael J. Decker, *The Byzantine Art of War* (Yardley, PA: Westholme Publishing, 2013), p. 76, and Eric McGeer, *Sowing the Dragon's Teeth: Byzantine Warfare in the Tenth Century* (Washington, DC: Dumbarton Oaks, 1995), p. 39.
68 *TD* 148, p. 3794; 149, p. 3812; 157, pp. 4026 and 4035.
69 Sun Jimin, *Tangdai xingjun zhidu yanjiu* (Taipei: Wenjin chubanshe, 1995), p. 170.
70 For the administrative role of the squad (*huo*) see *TD* 149, p. 3822, and the more complete discussion in Chapter 4 below. For the buddy system, see *TD* 148, p. 3794.
71 *TD* 149, pp. 3813–14; 157, p. 4033.
72 *TD* 149, p. 3812; 157, p. 4026; and Gu Jiguang, *Fubing zhidu kaoshi* (rpt. Taipei: Hongwenguan chubanshe, 1985), p. 166.
73 Wen Daya, *Da Tang chuang ye qi ju zhu*, pp. 3, 27–8; David A. Graff, "The Battle of Huo-i," *Asia Major*, 3rd Series, 5.1 (1992), pp. 44–6.
74 *ZZTJ* 183, p. 5721.
75 *TD* 157, p. 4036.
76 *ZZTJ* 188, pp. 5898–9.
77 *TD* 148, pp. 3792–3; 157, pp. 4027–8, and 4033–4.
78 *ZZTJ* 188, pp. 5902–3; 200, p. 6306.
79 For examples, see *ZZTJ* 186, p. 5810; 188, p. 5886; and Graff, "The Battle of Huo-i," pp. 42–3.

80 See Martin van Creveld, *Command in War* (Cambridge, MA: Harvard University Press, 1985), p. 17 and *passim*.

81 *TLD* 16, p. 460. The gong is still mentioned in some of Li Jing's drill instructions (e.g. *TD* 149, p. 3813), but the horn looms much larger in battle accounts (such as *ZZTJ* 184, p. 3813). Li Quan, *Taibai yinjing*, p. 536, states explicitly that horns are used to replace metallic instruments.

82 *TD* 149, p. 3813; 157, p. 4027.

83 *TD* 149, pp. 3812, 3814.

84 *TD* 149, p. 3815.

85 See for example, Wen Daya, *Da Tang chuang ye qi ju zhu*, p. 28.

86 One example is Li Shimin's observation of the enemy army from an elevated vantage point at Hulao in 621; see *JTS* 2, p. 27.

87 *ZZTJ* 184, p. 5754.

88 *ZZTJ* 185, p. 5772.

89 *ZZTJ* 184, p. 5761; 188, p. 5901.

90 *ZZTJ* 188, pp. 5902–3. For additional examples of the use of fire and smoke signals in a coordinating role, see *ZZTJ* 185, p. 5797; and 263, p. 8585.

91 *Strategikon*, pp. 32, 37, 38, 141–3, 145, 159, and 163. Fire and smoke signals are not included in the *Strategikon*, but were earlier mentioned by Vegetius. See *Vegetius: Epitome of Military Science*, trans. N.P. Milner (Liverpool: Liverpool University Press, 1993), p. 71.

92 George T. Dennis, "Byzantine Battle Flags," *Byzantinische Forschungen* 8 (1982), p. 56.

93 Dennis, "Byzantine Battle Flags," *passim*; *TD* 149, pp. 3812–13.

94 Dennis, "Byzantine Battle Flags," pp. 53–4; Chinese military flags are very nicely illustrated in the Dunhuang painting of the procession of General Zhang Yichao, dating from the mid-ninth century. A sketch can be found on p. 189 of Valerie Hansen, *The Silk Road: A New History* (New York: Oxford University Press, 2012).

95 *Strategikon*, pp. 32, 33, 141, and 143.

96 *Strategikon*, p. 61.

97 *Strategikon*, pp. 35–7 and 146.

98 *Strategikon*, p. 149; also see p. 41.

99 *TD* 149, p. 3813.

100 *Strategikon*, pp. 30 and 77. This explanation was repeated by Leo VI in the ninth century; see *The Taktika of Leo VI*, trans. George T. Dennis (Washington, DC: Dumbarton Oaks, 2010), p. 269.

101 *Strategikon*, pp. 27 and 141; when necessary, once engaged in combat individual *tagmas* could maneuver independently (p. 151).

102 *Strategikon*, pp. 23–4, 26, 31, 50–1, 62, and 144.

103 This can be inferred from *Strategikon*, pp. 27, 51, and 55.

104 Haldon, *Warfare, State and Society*, pp. 205–7.

105 *TD* 149, p. 3813.

106 *TD* 154, p. 3948; 157, pp. 4033–4 and 4035.

107 *ZZTJ* 189, pp. 5930–1.

108 *Strategikon*, p. 15.

109 *Strategikon*, p. 48; for the division of the *meros* into thirds, see pp. 26 and 76.

110 *Strategikon*, p. 62.

111 *TD* 148, pp. 3792–3.

112 *TD* 157, pp. 4025–6 and 4034–5.

113 *TD* 157, pp. 4033–4.

114 *Strategikon*, pp. 48–9.

115 *TD* 157, p. 4035.

116 *TD* 154, p. 3948. And for a *further* example, see *TD* 157, pp. 4035–6.

117 The similarity between Li Jing's tactical system and that of the Byzantine use of *cursores* and *defensores* was first pointed out by Peter A. Boodberg in "The Art of War

in Ancient China: A Study Based upon the Dialogues of Li Duke of Wei" (Ph.D. diss., University of California, 1930).

118 *TD* 149, pp. 3823–4.
119 *TD* 157, p. 4035–6.
120 *Strategikon*, p. 64.
121 *Strategikon*, p. 145. For the cavalry, see pp. 133 and 144.
122 *Strategikon*, pp. 19–20; further injunctions against breaking ranks to plunder may be found on pp. 68, 78, and 86–7.
123 *Strategikon*, p. 20.
124 *Strategikon*, pp. 86–7. For an example of the same concern expressed in a battle narrative, see Procopius, *History of the Wars*, vol. 1, p. 129 [Book I, ch. xiv, 52–4].
125 *Strategikon*, p. 144; for additional examples, see pages 68, 82, and 84.
126 *Strategikon*, pp. 16, 27, and 49 (flanks and rear); pp. 70, 75, and 135 (concealed echelon); pp. 27, 40, 51, 52, and 56 (ambushes).
127 *Strategikon*, p. 30. For more examples of scouting and patrolling on the battlefield, see pp. 16, 51, 55, 74–5, and 162; for awareness of what the enemy can do, see also pages 81 and 117.
128 *Strategikon*, pp. 52–3.
129 *Strategikon*, pp. 52 and 123.
130 Greatrex, *Rome and Persia at War*, pp. 177, 188, and 209; *The* History *of Theophylact Simocatta*, trans. Michael and Mary Whitby (Oxford: The Clarendon Press, 1986), p. 68; Walter E. Kaegi, *Heraclius: Emperor of Byzantium* (Cambridge: Cambridge University Press, 2003), pp. 115 and 309.
131 *TD* 159, p. 4088. Also see 149, pp. 3823–4; 157, p. 4034; and 158, pp. 4061–2.
132 *TD* 150, pp. 3840–1.
133 For examples of attacks to flanks and rear, see *ZZTJ* 183, p. 5721; 184, p. 5763; 186, pp. 5810–11; 187, pp. 5860–1. For ambushes, see *ZZTJ* 186, pp. 5828 and 5832; 189, p. 5938; and 198, pp. 6225–6.
134 *ZZTJ* 184, p. 5753.
135 *ZZTJ* 183, p. 5711; versions of the story can also be found in *SS* 71, p. 1647, and *TD* 152, p. 3889.
136 This is a paraphrase of *ZZTJ* 174, pp. 5425–6; also see *SS* 60, p. 1452.
137 *TD* 150, p. 3840.
138 *ZZTJ* 188, p. 5901; *CFYG* 44, p. 12a.
139 *ZZTJ* 183, p. 5726.
140 *ZZTJ* 183, p. 5718; Cen Zhongmian, *Sui Tang shi* (Beijing: Gaodeng jiaoyu chubanshe, 1957), p. 86.
141 *ZZTJ* 177, p. 5532. In 599, Yang Su defeated the Türk leader Tardu with an attack spearheaded by elite cavalry (*jing ji*); see *ZZTJ* 178, p. 5564.
142 *ZZTJ* 188, pp. 5898–9.
143 *ZZTJ* 215, p. 6885.
144 Wen Daya, *Da Tang chuang ye qi ju zhu*, pp. 2–3.
145 Rance, however, has suggested that the qualitative distinction between infantry and cavalry is more an artifact of Procopius' bias than a reflection of historical reality; "Narses and the Battle of Taginae," pp. 428–9 and 434.
146 *Strategikon*, p. 92.
147 See McGeer, *Sowing the Dragon's Teeth*, especially pp. 37, 47, and 277; and Haldon, *The Byzantine Wars*, pp. 96 and 111.

4   The army on campaign

Overcoming the enemy on the field of battle, an action of perhaps a few hours' duration in an arena of no more than a few square miles, was surely the most spectacular achievement of generalship in the premodern age, and indeed all ages prior to the twentieth century. To arrive at that pinnacle, however, a general had to maneuver across much greater distances, often through challenging terrain and in the face of determined opposition, for days, weeks, or months in order to bring his army, intact and ready for battle, to the decisive point. He had to concern himself with scouting and reconnaissance, and with the security of the marching column, the layout and security of the army's camps, the capture (or bypassing) of fortified places, and the fraught, potentially fatal decision to give battle or avoid it. Above all, he had to ensure that his men, along with their horses and other livestock, did not perish from thirst or starvation before they were ever in a position to confront the enemy in battle. For both Chinese and Byzantine commanders, these were matters of the utmost concern.

No matter how numerous they may be, no matter how well trained and well equipped, soldiers who are not adequately supplied with provisions for themselves and their horses are unlikely to be very effective on the field of battle—if, indeed, they are able to get there at all. In the seventh century, a miscalculation with regard to supply could destroy an army without any action on the part of the enemy. In 662 the Tang general Zheng Rentai led a light column of 14,000 cavalry to raid the wagons and pastured livestock of the Tiele tribes. Failing to make contact with the enemy, the Tang horsemen turned back—but only after they had consumed all the grain they had brought with them. Unfortunately, their return route passed through a desert region where the troopers were reduced to eating first their horses and then one another. By the time they reached the border forts only 800 men were left alive, and Zheng Rentai, who had somehow survived the ordeal, was impeached for having failed to calculate the logistical requirements of his army.[1]

The surviving portions of Li Jing's "Military Methods" have little to say about how soldiers were fed, but we may tentatively fill the gap by turning to a military treatise of the mid-eighth century: Li Quan's *Taibai yinjing*. According to Li Quan, the standard daily ration was two *sheng* (approximately 1.2 liters) of hulled grain (*mi*) per man.[2] Assuming that this grain was millet—the most likely possibility—the daily ration would have weighed around 1.2 kilograms and yielded a potential nutritive value of more than 4,000 calories, an amount more than adequate to meet the basic nutritional requirements of the soldiers.[3] Of course, millet was by no means the only foodstuff provided. A variety of cereals and pulses could be substituted for the millet ration in varying proportions. Ten measures of wheat, for example, were considered equivalent to eight measures of hulled millet. Among the other foodstuffs listed are buckwheat, barley, soybeans, and green peas.[4] The *fubing* of early Tang is supposed to have taken nine *dou* (fifty-four liters) of milled wheat with him when he set out on campaign, along with two *dou* (twelve liters) of hulled millet.[5] Rice would have been the principal grain ration for troops serving in the south, while soldiers campaigning in the grasslands beyond the northern frontier could supplement their grain ration by slaughtering livestock. Although grain was usually milled and polished before it was stored, the troops might sometimes be supplied with unhulled grain instead. It was no doubt against this contingency that each squad of *fubing* was supposed to carry a foot-worked pestle.[6]

When soldiers' rations fell below their minimum daily nutritional requirements, the consequences were rarely as dire as in Zheng Rentai's case. But from the perspective of military effectiveness, malnourishment exacts an immediate price in terms of physical weakness, the need for long periods of rest, and a general "lack of drive and initiative" on the part of the troops.[7] All other things being equal, well-nourished troops will outperform those who have not been adequately fed—there are even stories of medieval Chinese armies being defeated because they were forced to fight before their morning meal.[8]

If the soldiers were still able to function even when inadequately nourished, the same was not true of their cavalry mounts and transport animals:

> Unlike men, the physical condition of cavalry and transport animals cannot be restored by rest and proper diet after they have been worn out by several days of excessive work and inadequate rations; such treatment renders them unfit for further use.[9]

A medium-size horse doing "moderate" work requires at least nine kilograms of foodstuffs each day; modern veterinary sources recommend that half the weight of this ration should be in grain and the other half in fodder (hay and straw).[10] The Tang standard was a little different. According to Li Quan, a horse received a daily ration of one *dou* (six liters) of unhulled grain (*su*), which probably weighed about five kilograms, plus two bundles (*wei*) of hay.[11]

Conditions permitting, horses could be allowed to graze on pasture instead of being fed grain and dry fodder. Ecological necessity dictated that this would be how the steppe nomads fed their herds, and the Chinese also adopted it for the sake of economy.[12] Li Quan tells us that the daily ration of grain and hay was issued only during the six-month period beginning on the first day of the tenth lunar month; after the first day of the fourth month, the horses were apparently expected to subsist entirely by grazing.[13] But grazing also had its drawbacks. Horses fed entirely on fresh grass have less strength and endurance than those fed with grain, and grazing is a time-consuming activity. A 600-pound pony, for example, has to consume 31.3 pounds of fresh bromegrass per day, and requires 10.5 hours in which to so—enough time to impose serious limitations on the speed and pace of cavalry operations.[14]

The choice between grazing and grain feeding of horses is indicative of the range of supply options available to premodern armies. Stated in simplest terms, an army could either live off the land, obtaining all of its supplies from the countryside through which it passed, or it could carry its provisions from a distance by various means. Each method had its drawbacks. A large army could easily exhaust the resources of even a rich and populous agricultural district if it stayed there long enough. In less fortunate regions, armies had to move about frequently if they were not to starve.[15] On the other hand, a force that carried all its supplies with it could also expect to encounter serious difficulties. The load-bearing capacity of a premodern army was strictly limited; after a certain number of days without resupply, it would have consumed all of the provisions it was carrying. The marching range of such a force was limited in much the same way that the range of a modern aircraft is limited by its fuel supply. In the most extreme case, that of an army passing through a desert region and forced to carry not only food but also water, that range could be as little as two days' march.[16] Although the army might be resupplied by convoys from base, the same constraints would also apply to the supply columns—meaning that provisions could only be transported a limited distance if there was to be any "payload" left at the end. It has been estimated, for example, that it took a team of oxen in early modern Europe only eight days to eat up the entire load of the wagon they were pulling.[17]

In practice, military commanders seldom placed their sole reliance on either of these approaches to logistics, but employed varying combinations of the two. Chinese armies of the Sui–Tang period normally carried at least some of their supplies with them, and were usually accompanied by a considerable baggage train. Each squad of *fubing* was supposed to have six packhorses (*tuoma*); although some of these animals must have been fully laden with arms, cooking pots, tents, heavy tools, and other items of equipment, it seems likely that some would also have been used for carrying the grain that each man was required to bring with him on campaign.[18] In the mid-eighth century, Li Quan provided his imaginary model army of 12,500 men with 7,500 donkeys and 25,000 horses, and each soldier was supposed to carry twelve *sheng* of dried grain, enough for at least six days.[19]

Whenever an army had to remain in the same location for any length of time, resupply by convoy soon became necessary. When Li Yuan's army was halted by heavy rains north of the Sui stronghold of Huoyi in the summer of 617, men had to be sent back to the Tang base at Taiyuan to bring up additional supplies.[20] In the spring of 621, when Li Shimin and Dou Jiande faced off at the strategic pass of Hulao on the south bank of the Yellow River, both armies were in a position to receive food supplies by boat from the territories under their control. And in the following year, when Li Shimin confronted Dou's former lieutenant Liu

Heita along the line of the Ming River, Liu was drawing his provisions from the prefectures of central Hebei by wagon train and by boat.[21] Supply lines and convoys played a significant role not only in military operations within China proper, but also in many expeditions beyond the borders. When the Tang general Pei Xingjian was campaigning against the Türks in 680, for example, his army was resupplied by columns that included as many as 300 carts loaded with grain.[22]

Chinese armies employed many different modes of transport to carry their supplies: human porters, pack animals, wheelbarrows, carts, and boats are all mentioned in the sources. For pack animals, Chinese armies had horses, donkeys, and (occasionally) camels. Horses were preferred to donkeys as they can carry heavier loads and move faster, but they were not always available in sufficient numbers.[23] The Chinese wheelbarrow, unlike its Western counterpart, had a centrally positioned wheel that made it possible for one man to transport nearly 120 kilograms of grain.[24] More frequently encountered in the sources are two-wheeled supply carts. Tang pictorial representations from Dunhuang show a box-like vehicle with a semi-cylindrical roof cover. The carts in these paintings are each drawn by a single ox, yoked between shafts, but horses, donkeys, and even camels could also be used.[25] Since the collar-harness was already in common use in China by Tang times, a horse could be made to yield the same tractive power as an ox and was potentially capable of pulling as much as 1,500 kilograms. Fragmentary evidence suggests that the usual payload of a military supply cart may have been around 500 kilograms.[26]

By far the most efficient means of long-distance supply in Sui–Tang China, as in other premodern societies, was waterborne transport. The standard-size grain boat that plied the Tang canal system had a capacity of 1,000 *hu*—that is, approximately 39,000 kilograms of rice or 60,000 kilograms of millet—and boats with twice that capacity were to be found on the major rivers. Even with a crew of thirty-five men, a boat of the 1,000-*hu* class could travel for 1,428 days before its payload was entirely consumed.[27] When a large army was forced to stay in a single location for an extended period, the shipment of supplies by boat was usually the only feasible option. The superiority of water transport was well known to Chinese generals and military planners. In 446, for example, the Northern Wei commander Diao Yong submitted a memorial asserting that 200 large riverboats of 2,000-*hu* capacity could transport 500,000 *hu* of grain to the frontier post of Woye in the space of only six months, whereas 5,000 oxcarts would need three years to do the same job, and at much higher cost.[28] In 648, when the Tang court was debating the possibility of launching another expedition against Koguryŏ in the following year, it was pointed out that supplies would have to be transported by water since the proposed operations would require over one year's supply of grain, more than carts and pack animals were capable of carrying.[29]

Although water transport was generally more efficient than wheeled vehicles, which in turn were more efficient than pack animals (with human porterage the least efficient), generals did not always make their choices on the basis of efficiency alone.[30] Military operations often had to be conducted in areas far from navigable waterways, and pack animals and porters could negotiate rugged mountain tracks that were off-limits to carts and wheelbarrows. When the Korean state of Silla sent a convoy of 2,000 carts to carry grain to the Tang army besieging Pyongyang at the beginning of 662, winter storms and ice-covered roads left no solution except to unhitch the draft animals, load them with grain, and send them on again as pack animals.[31] Since the maximum speed of wagons and carts, even on good roads, was considerably less than the rates that could be attained by infantry and especially by cavalry, generals who wished to move more quickly than usual hastened to disencumber themselves of their baggage trains. Tang generals campaigning against the Tibetans in the second half of the seventh century left their carts behind in fortified camps while they led cavalry and light troops forward to seek out the enemy.[32]

During periods of administrative breakdown, as in North China during the Sui–Tang transition, armies often had no choice but to attempt to live off the land, as in 616 when the rebel leader Zhai Rang brought his army into Xingyang because he could not find enough food for his men in neighboring Dong commandery.[33] In general, however, an army that survived by seizing whatever it needed from the locale in which it was operating was perceived to be in a position of weakness rather than strength. In 619, for example, Li Shimin pointed out that his opponent, Song Jin'gang, had no accumulated stores but was supporting himself by plundering the countryside of southern Shanxi, and went on to predict that Song would have to retreat when there was nothing left to eat—as was eventually the case.[34]

When they could, most Sui and Tang commanders preferred to support their armies by convoys moving provisions forward from a secure resource base. Once this logistical choice had been made, however, it necessarily circumscribed their strategic options. Movements were most conveniently channeled along rivers, canals, and established roads, and armies were seldom willing to bypass fortresses and walled cities held by strong enemy garrisons. In 645, for example, the principal Tang field commander in the expedition against Koguryŏ, Li Shiji, refused to march on Jian'an until he had subdued the fortress of Anshicheng: "Jian'an is in the south and Anshi is in the north, and our army's provisions are all at Liaodong [north of Anshi]; if we skip over Anshi to attack Jian'an, the enemy might cut our supply line, and then what would we do?"[35] The emperor approved Li's plan without question, and the Koreans' successful defense of Anshi ultimately spelled the failure of the 645 expedition. The unwillingness to bypass major fortified places in the path of an advance had already played a role in the failure of the Sui emperor Yang's campaign against Koguryŏ in 612, and similar considerations would later be credited with preventing the followers of the rebel general An Lushan from penetrating the Yangzi valley in 756 and 757.[36]

Not surprisingly, one of Li Shimin's favorite maneuvers was to disrupt the supply lines of his adversaries. In 620 he sent cavalry detachments to raid the supply convoys of Song Jin'gang in Hedong, and he did the same against Dou Jiande in Henan in 621 and Liu Heita in Hebei in 622.[37] The Tang prince was not the only military leader of his time to recognize the effectiveness of this technique. When Li Shimin was operating in the vicinity of Luoyang in 620, his opponent Wang Shichong sent troops to cut his supply line at Shanzhou, and in the summer of

645 when he was besieging Koguryŏ's stronghold of Baiyancheng, the leader of the Korean relief column was advised to send cavalry to disrupt the transport of provisions to the Tang army before challenging it in open battle.[38]

When an army found itself unsupplied in the face of the enemy, whether because its supply line had been cut or because it had used up all the provisions to be found in the vicinity of its camp, the usual response was to retreat. When his troops ran out of food in the fourth month of 620, for example, Song Jin'gang immediately began to withdraw northward toward his base at Taiyuan.[39] On the other hand, supply crises could inspire other commanders to launch sudden, desperate attacks. This was the course chosen by Liu Heita in 622, and by the Sui general Wang Shichong when the rebel Li Mi had him cornered in Luoyang in the autumn of 618.[40] The conventional military wisdom of the time held that it was in the interest of a general who was running out of supplies to seek a decision by battle as quickly as possible, whereas the commander whose army was amply provisioned had everything to gain by postponing the showdown.[41]

The basic material realities of logistics—including daily march rates, the nutritional needs and carrying capacities of men and animals, and the resulting consumption rates— were essentially the same in both China and the Eastern Roman world. There were, of course, also many differences shaped by the environment, inherited infrastructures, and cultural preferences. Where the Chinese soldier's usual meal was most likely to be millet porridge or (couscous-like) boiled millet, his Byzantine counterpart subsisted on a basic daily ration of between 654 and 981 grams of bread (usually made from wheat, though barley or millet could be substituted) or double-baked hardtack, supplemented with dried or salted meat and perhaps cheese.[42] And Byzantine soldiers also expected rations of wine and sour wine, whereas beverages are not mentioned at all in the Chinese sources. Eastern Roman armies carried their supplies in ox-drawn wagons and on pack animals (horses, mules, and donkeys); by the sixth and seventh centuries, thanks to the deterioration of the old Roman roads, it would seem that pack animals had largely prevailed over wheeled transport.[43] Water transport, too, loomed less large in Byzantine campaigning than it did in China, probably because there was no real equivalent to Sui–Tang China's network of navigable rivers linked by extensive canal systems. Byzantine armies were apparently less concerned about supply lines and regular resupply from a secure base. When operating in friendly territory they could resupply from stockpiles provided by the local authorities, and when carrying the war into hostile territory they could subsist by foraging; campaigns were carefully timed to coincide with the seasonal availability of grain and fodder in the lands to be fought over.[44]

There was also some common ground, however. Byzantine military writers recognized that it might be necessary to leave wagons behind and move forward with pack animals, and they recommended leaving the baggage train behind in a secure location—just as the Chinese did against the Tibetans—to permit greater mobility and flexibility in the field.[45] And great emphasis was placed on damaging the enemy by depriving them of supplies; according to the *Strategikon*, "The general achieves the most who tries to destroy the enemy's army more by hunger than by force of arms."[46] On the other hand, it seems that the Byzantines were less likely to be deterred by the presence of unreduced fortresses in their rear—as suggested by Herakleios' daring incursion into northwestern Iran and the Sasanian heartland in 627.

Nevertheless, sieges were frequent events in both Sui–Tang China and the Byzantine world. Walled cities did not just block transportation routes and lines of supply, but they were also significant concentrations of wealth and other resources, administrative centers that dominated the surrounding districts, and—in some cases, such as Constantinople, Jerusalem, and Chang'an—sites invested with enormous political and cultural value. The great sieges of Constantinople by the Avars and Persians in 626 and the Arabs in 717–718 were among the most spectacular military events of the early Middle Ages, and in Byzantium's various wars against the Ostrogoths, Persians, Avars, and Arabs in the sixth and seventh centuries, a great many other cities were subjected to siege, including Palermo, Naples, Rome, Ravenna, Pavia, Verona, Amida, Dara, Antioch, Petra, Damascus, Jerusalem, Tiflis, Chalcedon, and Thessalonica. Whether a city was captured or successfully defended was influenced by many factors, among them the sizes of the garrison and the besieging army, the determination of both sides, the condition of the defenses, and the presence (or absence) of a friendly field army capable of breaking the siege. A passage included in Du You's *Tong dian* offers the following summary:

> Cities that cannot be defended are those which are large but have few people, those which are small but contain numerous masses, those in which grain is scarce and firewood and water cannot be supplied, those where the ramparts are thin and there are insufficient weapons, those where the earth of the walls is loose and they are in a low-lying position such that the city can be flooded by diverting a watercourse, and those where the walls have gaps but the people are too weary to complete the work of repair. In all of these situations, the city should be speedily evacuated. When the ramparts are high and the earth thick, the walls hard and the ditches deep, the grain plentiful and the masses numerous, and the topography is narrow and obstructed, this is what is called a position that can be held even if it is not defended.[47]

Supply was often a key consideration, with the outcome hinging on whether the attackers or the defenders would be the first to use up all of their provisions. According to Du You, there was a real possibility that the besiegers would exhaust the resources of the surrounding countryside before the defenders had eaten through their own stores.[48] This notion was not at all alien to the author of the *Strategikon*, who advised that essential supplies be gathered into the fortress, the countryside denuded of provisions, and ambushers sent out to discourage foraging so as to "make it very tight for the enemy."[49] In 756, the Tang general Li Guangbi had to give up his siege of Boling after only ten days because his army had run out of food.[50] This was a common scenario in medieval warfare, both east and west. As a tenth-century Byzantine military writer observed, "it is extremely difficult to have any success in besieging strong cities, well stocked with supplies and with a multitude of fighting men."[51]

Yet cities and fortresses did fall. To consider only the Chinese cases, in 645 the Tang army succeeded in storming Koguryŏ's great border fortress of Liaodongcheng, and in 696 the Qidan, a pastoral people with little experience of siegecraft, took Jizhou by assault during their invasion of Hebei. When Dou Jiande assailed Yuwen Huaji at Liaocheng in 619, the place fell because one of Huaji's officers opened the gates to admit the attackers. Among the many walled cities and fortresses that were starved into surrender were the Luokou Granary (617), Puban (620), Mayi (623), and Shuofang (628).[52] Other strongholds were taken by means of a range of poliorcetic techniques that enabled the attackers to fight their way over, under, or through the walls.

The typical Sui–Tang city—especially in North China, the imperial heartland—was built on a quadrilateral plan and had thick walls of pounded earth (*hangtu*), made by pouring a layer of earth into a wooden frame, pounding it until it was hard, and repeating the process layer after layer until the wall had attained the desired height.[53] Sometimes brick was used as an outer facing, especially at vulnerable points such as gates and corners. One of the most impressive specimens, the inner or "imperial" city at Luoyang, had brick walls that were eleven meters thick at the base and eleven meters high.[54] Many other town walls were within the range of 3–10 meters in both thickness and height, and the walls were often supplemented with ditches or moats, shallow projecting bastions (*mamian*) that exposed attackers at the foot of the wall to flanking fire, and a variety of outerworks such as barbicans (*wengcheng*), lunettes (*yuecheng*), and low outer walls (*yangmacheng*). For last-ditch resistance, some cities also had a citadel (*zicheng*) inside the main wall.[55]

A considerable range of poliorcetic devices had been known in China since ancient times.[56] These included lever-operated traction trebuchets that could hurl twenty-five-pound stones against city walls from a distances of a hundred yards or more, massive crew-served crossbows for use against defenders on top of the walls, and battering rams and covered approach vehicles that might enable attackers to break down gates or chip away at the foot of the wall. Tunnels were dug to undermine city walls, and earthen mounds, wooden towers, and overlook vehicles were used to permit archers to shoot down on the defenders. Ramps of earth might be piled up to give assault troops access to the battlements, or the attackers might employ "cloud ladders" (*yunti*)—wheeled vehicles carrying long, two-sectioned ladders that could be extended by means of counterweights—for an escalade of the walls. And since many Chinese cities were built on low-lying ground near rivers, one of the oldest poliorcetic techniques was simply to divert the water into a new channel in order to inundate the city and its defenses.

Defenders did not have to wait passively until these measures had produced their intended effect. Long before Tang times, a range of ingenious countermeasures had been devised to thwart every one of the techniques mentioned.[57] The most direct and brutal attempts to storm the walls with unprotected infantry could be met not only with arrows, sabers, and spears, but also with stones, ashes (to blind the attackers), boiling oil, molten iron, and heated feces, while ladders could be pushed away from the wall with forked poles.[58] If the attackers neared the foot of the wall protected by an approach vehicle whose ox-hide roof somehow withstood the rain of molten metal and incendiary materials, their cover might still be caught and overturned by a hook lowered from the top of the wall; a battering ram, likewise, could be caught and lifted up by a loop made of wood or iron.[59] The trebuchets of the attackers were vulnerable to stones thrown by the trebuchets of the defenders, and the impact of projectiles launched against the walls could be softened by mats of cloth or bamboo lowered from the parapet.[60] When a wall collapsed as a consequence of battery or undermining, the breach could be filled with improvised palisades or earthworks; when a mound threatened to overlook the top of a wall, the wall could be built higher.[61] Wooden towers and large approach vehicles such as cloud ladders could be destroyed by trebuchets, by fire, or even by tunneling underneath them. When, in the eleventh month of 783, the rebel forces of Zhu Ci tried to take the wall of Fengtian with an especially large cloud ladder, one of its wheels became stuck when it hit the tunnel that the defenders had dug beneath its approach path. Combustible materials were set alight in the tunnel while torches, pine pitch, and oil were thrown down from the walls. Before long the stricken vehicle and all of its occupants had been destroyed by fire, and the stench of burning flesh extended over a distance of several *li*.[62]

Although the principal building material for fortifications in the Mediterranean world was stone rather than earth, the range of poliorcetic techniques was roughly the same as in China. The *Strategikon* offers the following advice for defending a city against attack:

> Devices to defend against stone-throwing artillery should be procured. As protection against these, heavy mats can be hung over the wall along the battlements, or bundles, coils of rope, loose logs. Brick facing can also be built onto the ramparts. Against battering rams, cushions or sacks filled with grain husks and sand are effective. To ward off the swinging or beaked rams, use grappling irons, pitch, fire, or heavy, sharpened stones held by ropes or chains which can be suddenly dropped from machines and then hauled up again by other counterweights.[63]

During their siege of the Roman stronghold of Amida in 502–503 the Sasanians not only used battering rams protected by hide-covered roofs, but also raised a great approach mound to reach the top of the city wall. The repertory of Mediterranean and Near Eastern siegecraft also included tunneling to undermine or collapse sections of wall and the use of mobile siege towers to command the wall-top with archery or deliver an assault force directly to the parapet. Even the diversion of rivers to inundate fortresses, though much less common than in China, was not unheard of; during their siege of Tiflis in 627, the Türks and Byzantines used skins full of stones and sand to divert the River Kur "to rush and burst against the circuit wall."[64] Greeks and Romans, like the Chinese, used pitchforks to repel ladders, and both had methods of detecting tunnels so that they might be intercepted by countermines.[65]

Roman military engineers, like those in China, had long been acquainted with tension weapons, essentially large crossbows that could project heavy bolts or shafts at personnel and siege engines, and these devices probably continued in use into early Byzantine times.[66] With regard to stone-throwers, however, China and the Mediterranean world had followed quite different paths of development. Hellenistic and Roman stone-throwers were torsion machines that derived their propulsive power from twisted fibers or sinews, whereas in China, as we have seen, traction-based stone-throwers (or trebuchets) had been employed since ancient times and torsion-based devices are not attested. There has been much debate about whether even the simplest of the torsion machines, the one-armed "onager," remained in use into the early Byzantine period.[67] But the dominant trend was toward convergence, with the Byzantines adopting the traction trebuchet as their new stone-thrower (and possibly as early as 587).[68]

Although the Byzantines, thanks to their classical inheritance, were familiar with a very wide range of poliorcetic techniques, this does not mean that all of these were frequently encountered in actual practice. Modern authorities on Byzantine siegecraft have pointed out that there was a strong preference for solutions that were both simple and relatively cheap. Starvation was the favored method for subduing enemy strongholds, and when that was not practicable, the preference was for tunneling.[69]

One weapon in particular, the celebrated "Greek fire," may be quickly dismissed, as it looms much larger in the modern historical imagination than in the Byzantine military experience. First employed against the Arab fleet attacking Constantinople in the 670s, this probably petroleum-based substance was squirted from tubes in the bows of warships. Its use thereafter was quite infrequent, probably both for security reasons and because it posed almost as much of a threat to its users as it did to their intended targets.[70] The Chinese of the Sui–Tang period had no equivalent weapon; although gunpowder is thought to have been discovered by Chinese alchemists during the Tang dynasty, it was not "weaponized" before the tenth century at the very earliest.

Another aspect of the Byzantines' siegecraft that resonates more closely with their practices on the battlefield is their attention to scouts, outposts, and the avoidance of unpleasant surprises. When besieging an enemy fortress, the *Strategikon* advises, the siege camp

> must be very strongly fortified, and a large number of our sharpest scouts should be stationed around, covering even the most unlikely places, in order to prevent the besieged or forces outside the walls from suddenly attacking us, either by day or by night, and exposing the army to danger.[71]

At the same time, of course, the besiegers sought to surprise, deceive, or outwit the enemy. One common ploy was to make a show of weakness in order to lure the defenders out from their walls to fight in the open.[72] Chinese commanders, including Li Jing himself in 624, did exactly the same thing. On one memorable occasion in 617, when the Sui general Chen Leng was keeping to his fortifications and avoiding battle, the rebel leader Du Fuwei provoked him into marching out (to defeat) by sending him a gift of women's clothing and addressing him as "Granny Chen."[73] Sui and Tang commanders were also familiar with fortified siege camps and could throw up double lines of fortifications to hold off a relieving army while keeping the defenders penned up within their walls.[74]

When it came to moving the army from one place to another, especially in hostile territory, caution was again the watchword. Both the Chinese and Byzantine military texts recommended that marching columns be formed of substantial units—divisions (*jun*) for the Chinese and *moira* or *meros* for the Byzantines— kept distinct from one another and moving in proper sequence, each accompanied by its own baggage train.[75] When moving through dangerous country or facing the possibility of enemy attack, tighter formations were to be adopted. Li Jing advised placing the baggage train in the center, with a column of infantry marching twenty paces out on either of side of it and the cavalry columns another two *li* farther out to each flank.[76] The author of the *Strategikon* also called for the baggage to be placed at the middle of the column, and both Chinese and Byzantine texts described segmented columns of march that could quickly be converted into square formations capable of repulsing attacks from all directions.[77]

Scouts and patrols were to be sent out considerable distances to the front, sides, and rear of the column to uncover ambushes and provide early warning of the enemy's approach.

Evidently envisioning a campaign in the open spaces of the Eurasian steppe, Li Jing wrote that a force should be surrounded by a screen of outriders:

> to the front and rear and on the left and right flanks there should be two horsemen placed at a distance of five *li*, another two horsemen at ten *li*, and another two horsemen at fifteen *li*; out to a distance of thirty *li*, twelve horsemen will be used on a single path. If the troops are numerous and the column somewhat longer, add one or two more paths [of scouts] on the flanks in proportion, ordering them to stay within sight of one another. The riders [on a given path] are ordered to stay within observation distance of one another, so they normally keep to the high ground as they move along. Each grasps a different directional flag; when the enemy is not present the flag is normally kept furled, but when the enemy are sighted it must be rapidly unfurled.[78]

The *Strategikon* likewise calls for patrols to screen the front, rear, and flanks of a marching column; in open country these should be composed of cavalry, but in wooded or hilly terrain the job should be done mainly by light infantry with some cavalry support. An advance guard composed of both cavalry and light infantry was to march about one mile ahead of the main body. Although his focus is clearly on the more constricted landscape of the Balkans, the author of the *Strategikon* shares Li Jing's concern to occupy the high ground on both flanks with one's one men and provide advance warning of potential threats to the main column.[79]

In the event that the column actually did come under attack, there were set procedures to be followed. According to Li Jing,

> If, when the army is marching in an extended column, the lead division suddenly encounters the enemy, the lead division urgently beats its drums; the main body and the rear division, upon hearing the sound, must move forward urgently in order to rescue it. If the main body encounters the enemy, it must beat the drums; upon hearing the sound the vanguard division will stop and the rear division must move forward urgently to come to the rescue. If the rear encounters the enemy, it beats the drums; upon hearing the sound the van and the main body must stop and select a measured portion of their soldiers to rescue it.[80]

Under most circumstances, a portion of the army is to remain in place—in a defensive posture—while another portion is sent to assist the threatened segment of the column, thus guarding against the possibility of additional enemy attacks at other points. The author of the *Strategikon* recommends the same sort of measured response. If the alarm is sounded by one part of the column, the heavy-armed troops remain in place and in formation while the light infantry rushes to the threatened sector.[81]

In both the Chinese and Byzantine armies scouts, surveyors, and quartering parties moved well in advance of the marching column, not only to detect enemy activity but also to identify possible campsites and locate essential resources such as pastures and drinking water. In the Byzantine army, the surveyors were called *mensatoures*, and they and the quartering parties were supposed to move a full day's march ahead of the main column. The vanguard, meanwhile, was responsible for marking the road so that units following behind them would not take any wrong turns, and in rough, wooded, or otherwise difficult terrain some soldiers might also be sent ahead to clear and level the road. At especially difficult points such as river crossings, where the column was in danger of getting hung up, either the army commander himself or the various *meros* commanders were supposed to supervise the army's passage in person. A rear guard, finally, followed some fifteen to twenty miles behind the main body to gather in stragglers and guard against sudden enemy attacks.[82]

In the early Tang expeditionary army described by Li Jing, most of these functions were performed by the Left and Right Watch (*yuhou*), two of the seven divisions that made up the army of 20,000 men. At 2,800 men each, the two Watches were relatively large divisions that seem to have been considered especially reliable; they were assigned to the front and rear of the army's marching column, and also functioned as a sort of military police. They might be assisted in these duties by combat companies detached from the other divisions, or by "lesser watchmen" (*zi yuhou*) located within those divisions.[83] Functioning as the vanguard of the army, the Right Watch is responsible for scouting the road and finding water and grass—as well as widening narrow roads, repairing bridges, and making muddy spots more easily passable. The Left Watch defends the rear of the column and is responsible for gathering up lost or abandoned items. Assisted by the "lesser watchmen," it prevents different units from getting entangled with one another and makes sure the troops keep moving through narrow places where they might otherwise stop and clog the road.[84]

The Byzantine army was also concerned with gathering up lost items and returning them to their owners, though in contrast to the practices of the Chinese army this was the responsibility of designated men within each *tagma* rather than of dedicated units such as the Watches.[85] Both Li Jing and the author of the *Strategikon* make it clear that the army is to take care not to damage crops growing in the fields when it is campaigning in friendly territory, and both express reservations about hunting. The Chinese commander specifies that soldiers riding government horses and/or assigned to patrol or inspection will be punished if they take the opportunity to hunt, while his Byzantine counterpart forbids hunting while the army is on the march because "this causes noise and confusion and wears out the horses to no purpose." Both, however, recognize that at other times hunting may be an important and even essential part of military training.[86]

The construction, administration, and security of military camps were matters of no less concern than the protection of the army on the march. As part of their Roman military heritage, it was the standard procedure of the Byzantines to build a fortified camp wherever a campaign army stopped—even if only overnight, and even in friendly territory. Their camps were usually square or rectangular in shape.[87] The *Strategikon* describes the camp as a "four-sided oblong" protected by an outer ditch, a cordon of caltrops and pitfalls, and an inner trench 7–8 feet deep and 5–6 feet wide. The earth excavated to create the trench was piled up on the inner side to form an embankment, within which the army's baggage wagons were lined up to form the innermost defensive barrier. Variations were of course possible in accordance with local conditions. If the ground was too rocky or there was simply not enough time to dig in, caltrops alone might provide adequate protection. If the baggage train had been left behind, a wooden palisade could perform the same protective function. The camp had four main gates, one for each side, and a number of lesser entrances. Two broad streets 40–50 feet wide ran through the camp to connect the gates in a cruciform pattern; the soldiers' tents were set out in rows within the four quarters defined by the streets, and the army commander's tent was located near (but not in) the central intersection. The light infantry camped just inside the line of baggage wagons, separated from the tents of the other troops by empty space of between 300 and 400 paces so that archers shooting into the camp would be unlikely to inflict very many casualties. When the army was still some distance away from the enemy, cavalry units bedded down outside but nearby the main camp; as the distance closed, however, they were brought inside the camp, where sufficient space had been reserved for them.[88]

It was standard procedure for Chinese armies of the Sui–Tang period to construct fortified camps if they were operating in hostile territory. When Li Shimin marched against Koguryŏ in 645, it was considered quite remarkable that his forces were so confident they did not bother with this fundamental precaution—as if they were marching through the interior of the empire.[89] The design of the camp was variable, taking into account such considerations as the nature of the terrain and the probability of enemy attack. In open country a square configuration was preferred, but a rugged or mountainous landscape offered the possibility of a "half-moon" or semicircular camp with its rear secured by natural barriers rather than man-made fortifications. Li Jing also describes, in some detail, the layout of an apparently hexagonal camp. All of these camps were subdivided into "encampments" (*ying*), administrative units of variable size but mostly around 900 men if at full strength. In Li Jing's 20,000-man expeditionary army, all but one of the seven divisions (*jun*) break down into three encampments each. His hexagonal camp has the army's commander-in-chief and its Center Division positioned at the center as a single encampment of 4,000 men. Twelve avenues, each 22.5 meters wide, radiate outward from this core, and the other six divisions with their eighteen encampments are arranged around it like the petals of a flower. When the threat of attack was minimal, the encampments could be spread out more loosely in a checkerboard pattern with each separated from its neighbors by intervals of open space sufficient to accommodate another encampment. As the threat level rose, the encampments could be brought closer together and the open spaces filled in.[90]

The camp's defenses also varied in accordance with the environment and the threat level. Perhaps in recognition of this, Li Jing tells us rather vaguely that the perimeter is to be protected by "barriers."[91] If sufficient timber were available these could be wooden palisades, though it seems more likely that when campaigning on the open steppe the army's "barrier" would have been its baggage carts. During some seventh-century campaigns against the Tibetans and the Türks, the Tang armies reportedly protected their camps with no more than a simple ditch.[92] A more substantial option described in several Tang military texts called for palisades built of a double row of logs driven upright into the ground, with the logs in each row arranged to cover the gaps in the other. The outer face of the palisade was supposed to be covered with mud as a defense against fire, and, while no overall height is given, the inner side was supposed to be furnished with a walkway whose floor was 1.2 meters below the top of the rampart.[93] At the extreme, an army staying in one place for a long time might even erect thick, pounded-earth defenses similar to the city walls that have already been described.[94]

Just as when the army was on the march or on the battlefield, a great many precautions were also taken to protect it when it was in camp. According to Li Jing, whenever a camp was being made the mounted troops were to form an outward-facing cordon about a mile away from the camp while the foot soldiers were to deploy in battle formation twenty paces beyond the outermost line of tents. The same procedure was to be followed when the camp was being taken down as the army prepared to set out on the march.[95] In between, when the army was in camp, numerous other measures were to be taken to ensure its security. Just as when the army was on the march, cavalry scouts were to be sent out to a distance of ten miles in all directions.[96] But they were only the outermost layer of a much more elaborate system:

Outside the camp, at a distance of twenty paces from the tents, line up armed companies according to the same method as if they were facing the enemy and about to go into battle, to be on strict alert both day and night. Even if they meet with rain or snow, all the commanding officers of the companies may not leave their companies. Each encampment retains five horses which are all kept saddled and bridled even while they are being fed, to be prepared for an alarm or emergency when they are used to carry reports at the gallop. When night comes, place two listeners more than one hundred paces in front of each formation, and replace them with a new shift every two hours, in order to listen for the unexpected. In addition, order inspectors of the watch to check the alertness of the listeners so as not to allow them to fall asleep. During the daytime, the several divisions also place pickets (*chihou*) on high ground and at strategic points to their front, in order to observe [the enemy's] activity.[97]

Additional precautions were to be taken at night. Provided with one or two drums, three to five men from each division were sent out about a mile or more from the camp to establish outposts at locations that were "both secure and strategically situated." Farther out, at a distance of more than three miles from the camp, there were roving cavalry patrols, with each encampment responsible for providing four six-man patrols. If they encountered anything out of the ordinary, they were to gallop in to report it.[98] Great care was taken to ensure that men on guard duty remained alert throughout the night:

In all cases the troop units in a division's camp divide the night into two-hour watches, and men are ordered to make rounds of inspection. No one is allowed to call out the password in a loud voice. The one in motion taps his bow once, the one who is stationary raps his lance three times, and only then do they respond to one another by matching the army's passwords. Inspecting within the confines of a given encampment, as soon as a circuit is completed another one begins. If anyone makes a mistake in giving the password, he is to be judged and punished immediately. The colonels and lieutenant-colonels of the division control the troops both on guard duty and at rest. When one has completed a two-hour watch making the rounds and inspecting, he hands the responsibility over to another.[99]

If the army stopped in one place for three to five days or more, an additional early-warning system was required. Chains of fire beacons were to be set up at six- or seven- mile intervals beside the roads along which the enemy were likely to approach, out to a distance of thirty or even sixty miles. The beacon crews were to operate in concert with cavalry patrols and with listeners concealed in tall grass beside the road. The approach of the enemy was relayed to the camp by a prede-termined system of fire signals, with the number of torches indicating the size of the enemy force.[100]

Should the camp come under attack, there were again strict procedures to be followed. Each encampment was provided with one drum, and, in the event of a night attack, was to beat that drum to sound the alarm. Hearing the drum, the other encampments were to look to their own defense and were not permitted to move. If the threatened encampment were hard-pressed, the commander-in-chief himself would lead a relief force drawn from his Center Division:

> In all cases when the deranged enemy come by night to attack, the encampment that is under attack simply beats the drum and fights a defensive battle; the soldiers may not yell and shout. Once the several encampments have beaten the drum to spread the alarm, the sound of the drums ceases and they face the enemy, put on armor, and take defensive precautions. Since the encampment that is under attack beats the drum ceaselessly, the commander-in-chief himself leads soldiers to the rescue. Distinguishing markers having been discussed with the various leaders beforehand, the soldiers may be carrying small wooden bells with them as recognition signs; otherwise they beat the drums from inside to outside in order to assist and rescue them. The encampment that has been attacked by the enemy, hearing the sound of the drums and bells, will know that the commander-in-chief's soldiers have arrived.[101]

The outposts already mentioned could also help to thwart a night attack on the camp by beating their drums and shouting to give the enemy the impression that they were themselves under attack from the rear.[102]

Although Byzantine armies are not known to have set up networks of mobile fire beacons and do not seem to have achieved the baroque redundancy of systems advocated by Li Jing, both their threat awareness and many of their specific countermeasures are quite similar to what we find in the Chinese materials. In the words of one authority on the Byzantine military,

> Great stress was laid on camp security: passwords were issued for each watch, and watch-commanders were enjoined to allow no one past without the correct password (usually the name of a saint or similar symbol of Orthodoxy). Elaborate instructions were also issued – and apparently followed – on the circuits and patrols made by the watch at regular intervals."[103]

According to the *Strategikon*, some soldiers—normally the light infantry—were to be kept in formation and under arms while the camp was being set up. Outposts were to be maintained around the camp, especially if it was not fortified, and patrols sent out "in more than one direction." Patrols were to be sent out in strings, with those farthest out having the fewest men and those closer in having more; in addition, "[v]ery reliable officers should be sent to make unexpected visits to observe how things are going."[104]

A particular concern was the security and feeding of the horses while the army was encamped. When the Byzantine army was still some distance away from the enemy, the cavalry were supposed to bivouac outside of the camp and allow their the horses to graze—with the proviso that "double, even triple, patrols should be systematically sent out in all directions to a considerable distance and relieved at regular intervals." When the army was closer to the enemy, the cavalry were to move inside the camp—and fodder for the horses was to be cut outside, brought in, and stored.[105] The Chinese expeditionary army, as we have seen, had its own way of consolidating loosely spread out encampments into a single, more defensible camp in proximity to the enemy. It also sought to pasture its horses and donkeys outside of the main camp when conditions permitted. The animals belonging to different units were assigned to separate pastures, identified by a distinctive flag for each unit, and as a precaution against the possibility that livestock might be driven off by enemy raiders, the donkeys were to be positioned around the outside of the horse herd as a protective cordon. This was more than just a matter of placing the less valuable animals in the position of greatest risk, since donkeys (in contrast to horses) are more likely to stand their ground and fight rather than flee—with their braying serving as a very effective alarm system.[106] When threatened, and if circumstances permitted, the livestock were to be brought in and securely positioned at the rear of the camp.[107]

In addition to pasture, water was a major concern for both Chinese and Byzantine commanders. "In all cases when on the march or in camp," wrote Li Jing,

> in places where there is a lack of [sufficient] water even though there are springs and small, swift-flowing streams, assign men to oversee their proper use. Do not allow [the water] to become muddied or spoiled by the passage of many feet.[108]

The author of the *Strategikon*, meanwhile, advised that in "critical situations" a camp should be set up with a small river flowing through it "for the convenience of the troops." But care was to be taken that the water did not become fouled:

> If a good-sized river flows by the camp, the horses must not be watered above the camp. If they are, their trampling around will make the water muddy and useless. They should be watered downstream instead. If it is a small stream, water the horses from buckets; if brought to the stream, they will only stir it up.[109]

Another pressing concern when the army was in camp was the proper disposal of human waste. According to the author of the *Strategikon*, "It is very important that sanitary needs not be taken care of inside the camp, but outside because of the disagreeable odor, especially if there is some reason for the army to remain in one place." In general, and no doubt for health reasons, the army was not to "stay too long in one spot."[110] Chinese soldiers, unlike their Byzantine counterparts, apparently attended to necessary functions at dedicated facilities inside the camp, with every two companies being instructed to dig and presumably share a latrine.[111]

In both Chinese and Byzantine camps, the most basic and fundamental unit of organization was the group of men who cooked and ate together and shared a single large tent. In the Tang army a company's soldiers were divided among five tents, with each group probably consisting of a nine-man squad plus one of the company's five officers. Each squad was supposed to have six pack animals, a tent, a cooking pot, and various other items of equipment. The amount of space Li Jing allocated to each squad and its tent was four paces (six meters) or less, but more may have been allowed when armies camped in open terrain at a safe distance from the enemy.[112] The *Strategikon* does not mention the size of the Byzantine tent group or the space allotted to it, but extrapolating from earlier Roman and later Byzantine practice we may reasonably assume that it consisted of 8–10 men, about the same size as its Chinese equivalent.[113] Since every man had an assigned place in one of the tents and was known to his tent-mates, it was possible to apprehend spies and intruders by having every man go into his assigned tent in response to a prearranged trumpet signal.[114]

Driven by the need for security and order, other aspects of camp life were equally strict. The author of the *Strategikon* advises the general to prohibit dancing and handclapping in camp, "not only because they are disorderly and annoying, but they are a waste of energy for the soldiers."[115] Li Jing sought to enforce an evening lights-out in his camp; food was to be prepared as early as possible, and the fires were then extinguished. If officers wished to keep lights burning to read or copy documents after dark, it required prior approval from the leader of the encampment.[116] Both the Chinese and the Byzantines were keen to enforce noise discipline. Li Jing stipulated that in each encampment one officer was to have overall responsibility for keeping the troops quiet, with four more to take charge of the four sides of the encampment. And within each company as well, there was one man responsible for noise discipline.[117] In the Byzantine camp, according to the *Strategikon*, "Some of the general's own troops should be detailed to inspect the guards and to enforce silence throughout the camp, so that nobody would even dare call out the name of his comrade."[118]

One point on which the Chinese and Byzantine texts differ is who is permitted to accompany the army and enter the camp. The *Strategikon* frequently mentions servants, and at least one passage indicates that soldiers' children and other family members (presumably including wives) may be present in the camp.[119] The Li Jing fragments, in contrast, make no mention whatever of servants— except for soldiers, especially the weaker among them, who might be assigned to menial tasks rather than combat duty. An even sharper distinction is that Li Jing explicitly bans women from the camp, prescribing the death sentence for those who introduce them.[120] Prohibitions of this sort existed as early as the Former Han dynasty and appear to have been part of the deep structure of Chinese military management over a very long period. When Li Ling set out on his famous campaign against the Xiongnu nomads in 99 BCE, he ordered a search of the army's baggage carts and had all the women found hiding there immediately put to death.[121] It would seem that the Chinese had stricter rules than the Byzantines as to who could accompany the army into the field, but there is reason to believe that the rules were not always enforced. In a 623 battle against the Tuyuhun and Dangxiang peoples of the northwest, for example, the Tang general Chai Shao used two female dancers to distract the enemy while he sent a party of cavalry around to attack their rear.[122]

Chinese and Byzantine authorities were in complete agreement, however, when it came to regulating contact between the campaign army's personnel and the civilian population around them. The Byzantine general was responsible for seeing to it that civilians were not harmed, and taxpayers were to be compensated for injuries done to them by soldiers.[123] Li Jing went further. Soldiers were to camp at least ten *li* away from walled towns and markets:

> Should there be a need to enter the town the make purchases, an administrative assistant from among the encampment functionaries gives permission and dispatches a man to provide control and leadership; it is not permitted simply to enter the walled town. It is necessary to prevent drunkenness, brawling, theft, and sexual improprieties.[124]

In both military cultures, there was a starkly realistic awareness that soldiers were a dangerous, potentially predatory element that had to be restrained from doing harm to civilian populations, especially if those civilians happened to be one's own productive taxpayers.

Having moved his army from place to place safely, kept it supplied, besieged or bypassed hostile fortresses, protected his camp from surprise, and prevented his soldiers from harming friendly civilians, the general still faced the most momentous decision that was likely to arise during any premodern military campaign: whether or not to join battle with the enemy in the open field. Some circumstances might compel him to fight, such as a desperate supply situation or the approach of an enemy army to relieve a besieged city. Under most conditions, however, a general had considerable leeway to decide whether he would join battle or avoid it. And strategies of battle avoidance were facilitated by the prevalence of the fortified camps that have already been discussed. Field fortifications were used in this way by a great many Chinese commanders of the period, including the Sui general Yang Yichen in 616, the rebel Li Mi in 618, and the great Tang loyalist commander Guo Ziyi in 756. Li Shimin, the most consistently successful general of the Tang period, repeatedly made use of fortified camps to hold the enemy at bay until the odds had turned in his favor—against Xue Ren'gao in 618, Song Jin'gang in 619–620, and Liu Heita in 622.[125]

If the attackers did not outnumber the defenders by too great a margin, it was unusual for a fortified camp to be taken by siege or assault. The walls and ditches of the camp gave the defenders a significant advantage in combat, and, unlike city walls, the defenses of the camp could be knocked down or filled in very quickly to clear the way for large-scale, opportunistic counterattacks against a flagging or disorganized attacker.[126] If the camp was surrounded or attacked from more than one side, the defenders could concentrate most of their forces to strike a single segment of the attacking army before the others could come to its rescue. Generals were extremely reluctant to attack fortified camps, and when they did attack, they tended to place their hopes in some combination of surprise, advantageous natural conditions, treachery, and cunning. When the rebel leader Dou Jiande attacked the camp of the Sui general Xue Shixiong, for example, he moved under cover of darkness and was aided by a heavy mist, with the result that he was able to achieve complete surprise.[127] In general, however, the fortified camp seems to have been quite effective as a tool of defense, and there are numerous examples of offensives that were brought to a standstill by the ability of the defender to hold his ground while refusing battle. The result was that battles—if they were not surprise attacks or ambushes—rarely occurred without the consent of both parties.

And both Tang and Byzantine military authors were extremely chary of the resort to battle. It was well understood that a major battle in the open field involved enormous risks and was not to be entered into lightly. "With regard to arms," Li Jing tells his readers, "it would be better to go for a thousand days without using them than have a single day when one is not victorious."[128] Echoing the most influential of China's ancient military classics, the "Art of War" (*Bingfa*) attributed to Sunzi, on the need to prepare the conditions for success before one actually fights, he declares: "One is first victorious and only then does he give battle; one holds one's own ground but does not lose an opportunity. This is called the path to certain victory."[129] And he goes on to devote considerable attention to those conditions under which the enemy may be successfully attacked and those under which it would be better to avoid challenging him in battle. The former include the enemy's having covered a long distance without rest, marching in strong winds and bitter cold or under the heat of the blazing sun, or the enemy's not yet having formed his troops for battle or concentrated his forces.[130]

The author of the *Strategikon* is, if anything, even more cautious: "It is well to hurt the enemy by deceit, by raids, or by hunger," he advises, "and never be enticed into a pitched battle, which is a demonstration more of luck than of bravery."[131] Like Li Jing, he recommends the avoidance of battle when the odds are not in one's favor. One should not engage a numerically superior foe, and must always be ready to exploit opportunities that increase the likelihood of victory—such as when the enemy are not ready for battle or are facing into sun, wind, or dust.[132] Another Byzantine military treatise, probably written two centuries after the *Strategikon* but surely incorporating earlier material, also urges caution: "If conditions are equal on both sides and the victory could go either way, we should not advance into battle before the enemy have become inferior to us in some respect." The author then provides several examples of conditions under which the enemy has become inferior and may be engaged with less risk; some, such as the enemy having just completed an exhausting march, are nearly identical to conditions listed by Li Jing.[133] One authority, Walter Kaegi, has identified the avoidance of decisive battle as a key long-term feature of Byzantine military thought.[134]

Although it is certainly possible to find examples of battle-seeking and risky maneuvers, as in Herakleios' invasion of the Sasanian heartland in 627 or Wang Shichong's bold challenge to his rival Li Mi outside Luoyang in 618, what was accepted as military "best practice" in both China and Byzantium fell firmly within what some historians have identified as a premodern "Vegetian" consensus, in which battle was usually not the preferred option and battle-seeking was constrained by fortifications and logistics.[135] When generals did seek battle with inferior forces, they were often driven to it as a last resort—as Wang Shichong was by his desperate supply situation, and Herakleios by his need to reverse a desperately unfavorable strategic situation. And even then, they made every effort to tilt the odds in their favor: Herakleios by luring the Persians in pursuit and then turning to confront them on ground favorable to him; Wang Shichong by deploying his men with their backs to a river to stiffen their resolve and then sending a party of cavalry around to attack the enemy camp from the rear.[136] The labeling of their common ground as "Vegetian," after the late Roman military author Publius Flavius Vegetius Renatus who strongly advocated starving out the enemy while avoiding battle (and whose influence is visible in the *Strategikon*), points toward two possible explanations for the similarity between Chinese and Byzantine warfare in the seventh century.[137] One is the influence of parallel (though by no means identical) inherited traditions, and the other is the pervasive presence of a sort of basic military common sense rooted in shared material conditions. Both of these themes will be taken up in the next chapter.

Notes

1 *XTS* 111, p. 4141; *CFYG* 445, p. 6b; *ZZTJ* 200, p. 6328. The memorial impeaching Zheng is in *QTW* 168, pp. 17b–18b.

2 Li Quan, *Taibai yinjing*, in *Zhongguo bingshu jicheng*, vol. 2 (Beijing and Shenyang: Jiefangjun chubanshe and Liao-Shen shushe, 1988), pp. 556, 558. A Tang *sheng* was 0.6 liters; see Wu Chengluo, *Zhongguo du liang heng shi* (Shanghai: Commercial Press, 1957), p. 58, table 13.

3 The calculations are as follows: 2×0.6 liters $\times 1,000$ grams per liter $= 1.2$ kilograms. The figure for the bulk density of millet is based on the information in D.C. Twitchett, *Financial Administration Under the T'ang Dynasty* (Cambridge: Cambridge University Press, 1970), p. 25, that one *shi* of millet weighed 1.4 cwt. However, it should be noted that this figure is no more than a rough approximation, since the bulk density of any grain is highly variable, being influenced by such factors as moisture content, grain shape, compactness of packing, and the presence of impurities; see A.V. Myasnikova et al., *Handbook of Food Products: Grain and Its Products*, trans. by S. Nemchonok (Jerusalem: Israel Program for Scientific Translations, 1969), p. 94. The nutritive value of one kilogram of milled wheat is 3,500 calories, and the nutritive value of some varieties of millet is slightly higher than wheat; see Colin Clark and Margaret Haswell, *The Economics of Subsistence Agriculture*, 4th edition (London: Macmillan and St. Martin's Press, 1970), p. 58. Some modern interpretations of the relevant passages in Li Quan simply assume that *mi* means rice. My reasoning that this refers rather to millet is spelled out in detail in David A. Graff, "Early T'ang Generalship and the Textual Tradition" (Ph.D. diss., Princeton University, 1995), p. 91.

4 Li Quan, *Taibai yinjing*, pp. 558–9. The grains are presumably in their unhulled form since the list is headed by *su* (unhulled millet) in a ratio of 10:6 to *mi* (hulled millet). This is, incidentally, the same as the Tang government's official conversion rate between unhulled and hulled millet; see Éric Trombert et al., *Les Manuscrits chinois de Koutcha: Fonds Pelliot de la Bibliothèque Nationale de France* (Paris: Institut des Hautes Études Chinoises du Collège de France, 2000), pp. 94–5. For the terminology of millets, see Francesca Bray and Joseph Needham, *Science and Civilisation in China*, vol. 6, part 2: *Agriculture* (Cambridge: Cambridge University Press, 1984), p. 440.

5 *XTS* 50, p. 1325.

6 *XTS* 50, p. 1325. Although most grains keep better if stored in the husk, they were usually hulled and milled before storage in order to reduce their bulk; see Bray and Needham, *Science and Civilisation in China*, vol. 6, part 2, p. 382.

7 Clark and Haswell, *Economics of Subsistence* Agriculture, p. 21.

8 See, for example, *ZZTJ* 183, p. 5721.

9 Donald W. Engels, *Alexander the Great and the Logistics of the Macedonian Army* (Berkeley and Los Angeles: University of California Press, 1978), p. 129.

10 Engels, *Alexander the Great and the Logistics of the Macedonian Army*, pp. 126–7.

11 Li Quan, *Taibai yinjing*, p. 560. I assume that the unhulled grain mentioned here is millet. The Han data cited by Nancy Lee Swann, namely 16.5 *dou* of unhulled millet weighed one *shi*, indicate that the bulk density of unhulled millet is approximately 880 grams per liter; see Nancy Lee Swann, *Food and Money in Ancient China* (Princeton, NJ: Princeton University Press, 1950), p. 365. I have not found any reliable information on the exact value of the *wei* in Tang times. Fragmentary Tang administrative documents recovered from Kucha show that some horses were fed a mixture of millet and crushed soybeans, while others received bran and barley as well; see Trombert et al., *Les Manuscrits chinois de Koutcha*, pp. 71, 95–6.

12 Denis Sinor, "Horse and Pasture in Inner Asian History," *Oriens Extremus* 19 (1972), p. 177.

13 Li Quan, *Taibai yinjing*, p. 559.

14 John Masson Smith, Jr., "Äyn Jālūt: Mamlūk Success or Mongol Failure?" *HJAS* 44.2 (December 1984), pp. 331–3 (note 75) and 336–7.

15 These problems are explored in Martin van Creveld, *Supplying War: Logistics from Wallenstein to Patton* (Cambridge: Cambridge University Press, 1977), pp. 8–9 and 13–14, and in Engels, *Alexander the Great and the Logistics of the Macedonian Army*, pp. 45–6 and *passim*.

16 Engels, *Alexander the Great and the Logistics of the Macedonian Army*, p. 22.

17 John Keegan, *The Mask of Command* (New York: Viking, 1987), p. 64.

18 *XTS* 50, p. 1325; *TD* 149, p. 3822.

19 Li Quan, *Taibai yinjing*, pp. 539 and 559.

20 Wen Daya, *Da Tang chuang ye qi ju zhu* (Shanghai: Shanghai guji chubanshe, 1983), p. 27.

21 *ZZTJ* 199, p. 5947, and Graff, "Early Tang Generalship and the Textual Tradition," chapter 5.

22 *ZZTJ* 202, p. 6393.

23 Sui Yangdi began to acquire donkeys for his Korean expedition only after he ran out of horses (*SS* 24, p. 688). For the undesirable qualities of donkeys, see Engels, *Alexander the Great and the Logistics of the Macedonian Army*, pp. 15–16, note 15. Haldon, however, points out that donkeys "can survive on very mean rations as well as grazing thistles, poor grass, and other herbage." John Haldon, "Roads and Communications in the Byzantine Empire: Wagons, Horses, and Supplies," in John H. Pryor (ed.), *Logistics in the Age of the Crusades: Proceedings of a Workshop Held at the Centre for Medieval Studies, University of Sydney, 30 September to 4 October 2002* (Aldershot, Hampshire: Ashgate, 2006), p. 145.

24 For more on the Chinese wheelbarrow, see Joseph Needham, *Science and Civilisation in China*, vol. 4: *Physics and Physical Technology*, pt. 2: *Mechanical Engineering* (Cambridge: Cambridge University Press, 1965), pp. 270–4. In connection with Sui Yangdi's 612 campaign against Koguryŏ, *ZZTJ* 181, p. 5656, mentions two-man crews each pushing a load of three *shi* of hulled grain (*mi*). If this refers to millet, the weight should be about 180 kilograms; if rice, then closer to 120 kilograms.

25 Needham, *Science and Civilisation in China*, vol. 4, part 2, pp. 250, 319–20, and plate 213, figure 558. Plate 221, figure 569, shows a Dunhuang painting from about 600 of a camel-drawn cart.

26 For a detailed discussion of the history of effective harness in China, see Needham, *Science and Civilisation in China*, vol. 4, part 2, pp. 304–6, 313, and 325. The evidence for a 500 kilogram payload is presented in Graff, "Early T'ang Generalship and the Textual Tradition," p. 111, note 135.

27 Aoyama Sadao, *Tō Sō jidai no kōtsū to chishi chizu no kenkyū* (Tokyo: Yoshikawa kōbunkan, 1963), pp. 395–6. I take 660 grams per liter as the bulk density of rice, 1,000 grams per liter as the bulk density of hulled millet, and the daily ration as two *sheng* per man.

28 *WS* 38, pp. 868–9.

29 *ZZTJ* 199, p. 6258.

30 For relative efficiencies, see Clark and Haswell, *Economics of Subsistence Agriculture*, pp. 196–8, table 47.

31 John Charles Jamieson, "The *Samguk Sagi* and the Unification Wars" (Ph.D. diss., University of California at Berkeley, 1969), pp. 95–6. For other examples of supply convoys stopped by rain or snow, see *ZZTJ* 191, pp. 5991–2; 204, p. 6459; and 263, p. 8577.

32 *ZZTJ* 201, p. 6364.

33 *JTS* 53, p. 2210.

34 *ZZTJ* 188, p. 5874.

35 *ZZTJ* 198, p. 6228.

36 *ZZTJ* 197, p. 6213; and 220, p. 7038 (especially Sima Guang's *Kaoyi* comment).

37 *CFYG* 45, p. 15a; *JTS* 55, pp. 2259–60; *ZZTJ* 189, p. 5912; and 199, p. 5947.

38 *JTS* 61, p. 2367; *ZZTJ* 198, pp. 6223–5.

39 *ZZTJ* 188, p. 5880. For other instances of armies forced to retreat because of supply problems, see *ZZTJ* 188, p. 5899; and 257, pp. 8370–1.

40 *ZZTJ* 199, pp. 5948–9; *JTS* 55, pp. 2259–60; Graff, "Early T'ang Generalship and the Textual Tradition," chapter 4. An additional example can be found in *ZZTJ* 185, p. 5799.

41 See the statement by Li Miao (479–525), a Northern Wei general, in *WS* 71, p. 1595, and that by the Southern statesman and general Xiahou Xiang (433–507) in Yao Silian, *Liang shu* (Beijing: Zhonghua shuju, 1973), chapter 10, p. 192.

42 John Haldon, *Warfare, State and Society in the Byzantine World, 565–1204* (London: UCL Press, 1999), pp. 167–8. Haldon notes that because of the higher protein content of "ancient strains of wheat and barley," the bread ration alone "provided adequate nutrition for the duration of a campaign season even without meat."

43 John Haldon, "Roads and Communications in the Byzantine Empire: Wagons, Horses, and Supplies," p. 140; also see Walter E. Kaegi, "Byzantine Logistics: Problems and Perspectives," in John A. Lynn (ed.), *Feeding Mars: Logistics in Western Warfare from the Middle Ages to the Present* (Boulder, CO: Westview Press, 1993), p. 42. George T. Dennis (trans.), *Maurice's Strategikon: Handbook of Byzantine Military Strategy* (Philadelphia: University of Pennsylvania Press, 1984) [hereafter *Strategikon*] mentions both pack animals (pp. 14 and 17) and wagons (p. 97).

44 Haldon, *Warfare, State, and Society*, pp. 169–73; *Strategikon*, pp. 96–8.

45 *Strategikon*, pp. 59 and 161; John Haldon, *Byzantium at War, AD 600–1453* (rpt. New York and London: Routledge, 2003), p. 58.

46 *Strategikon*, p. 85; also see pp. 107–8 and 117.

47 *TD* 152, p. 3893.

48 *TD* 152, p. 3900.

49 *Strategikon*, p. 108.

50 *ZZTJ* 217, p. 6960.

51 "Campaign Organization and Tactics," in George T. Dennis (trans.), *Three Byzantine Military Treatises* (Washington, DC: Dumbarton Oaks, 1985), p. 303. Also see John Haldon, *The Byzantine Wars* (Stroud, Gloucestershire: Tempus, 2001), p. 50; Herbert Franke, "The Siege and Defense of Towns in Medieval China," in Frank A. Kierman,

Jr. and John K. Fairbank (eds.), *Chinese Ways in Warfare* (Cambridge, MA: Harvard University Press, 1974), pp. 193–4; Martin van Creveld, *Technology and War: From 2000 BC to the Present*, rev. ed. (New York: The Free Press, 1991), p. 34; John Beeler, *Warfare in Feudal Europe, 730–1200* (Ithaca and London: Cornell University Press, 1971), p. 44; J.F. Verbruggen, *The Art of Warfare in Western Europe during the Middle Ages* (Amsterdam and New York: North-Holland Publishing Company, 1977), p. 289; John Keegan, *A History of Warfare* (New York: Alfred A. Knopf, 1993), pp. 150–1; and H.G. Quaritch Wales, *Ancient South-East Asian Warfare* (London: Bernard Quaritch, 1952), p. 41.

52 *JTS* 54, p. 2238; *ZZTJ* 184, pp. 5755–6; 187, p. 5842; 188, p. 5875; 190, p. 5973; 192, p. 6050; 197, pp. 6220–1; 205, p. 6510.

53 Chinese town walls are treated in detail in Joseph Needham and Robin D.S. Yates, *Science and Civilisation in China*, vol. 5: *Chemistry and Chemical Technology*, part 6: *Military Technology: Missiles and Sieges* (Cambridge: Cambridge University Press, 1994), pp. 241–413.

54 Guo Rugui et al. (eds.), *Binglei*, vol. 6 of *Zhongguo junshi shi* (Beijing: Jiefangjun chubanshe, 1991), pp. 163–5.

55 Otagi Hajime, "Tōdai shū ken jōkaku no kibo to kōzō," in *Di yi jie guoji Tangdai xueshu huiyi lunwenji* (Taipei: Zhonghua minguo Tangdai xuezhe lianyihui, 1989), pp. 648–82; Huang K'uan-ch'ung, "Songdai cheng guo de fangyu sheshi ji cailiao," *Dalu zazhi* 81.2 (August 25, 1990), pp. 1–2.

56 These receive very thorough treatment in Needham and Yates, *Science and Civilisation in China*, vol. 5, part 6, pp. 184–240 and 413–85.

57 Also discussed in Needham and Yates, *Science and Civilisation in China*, vol. 5: part 6, pp. 413–85. For a fascinating look at the countermeasures adopted in a single medieval Chinese siege, see Benjamin E. Wallacker, "Studies in Medieval Chinese Siegecraft: The Siege of Yü-pi, A.D. 546," *Journal of Asian Studies* 28.4 (August 1969), pp. 789–802.

58 *TD* 152, p. 3897; Franke, "Siege and Defense of Towns," p. 178.

59 *TD* 152, pp. 3896–7, 3899; *ZZTJ* 252, p. 8156.

60 *TD* 152, pp. 3896, 3898.

61 *TD* 152, pp. 3899–3900; *ZZTJ* 198, p. 6229; 267, pp. 8715–16.

62 *ZZTJ* 229, pp. 7374–5; Benjamin E. Wallacker, "Studies in Medieval Chinese Siegecraft: The Siege of Fengtian, A.D. 783," *Journal of Asian History* 33.2 (1999), pp. 188–91.

63 *Strategikon*, p. 109.

64 For Amida and Tiflis, see Geoffrey Greatrex and Samuel N. C. Lieu, *The Roman Eastern Frontier and the Persian Wars*, Part II: *AD 363–630, A Narrative Sourcebook* (London and New York: Routledge, 2002), pp. 63–4 and 211. For Byzantine siege-craft and the classical traditions from which it derived, several studies may be helpful: Denis F. Sullivan (trans.), *Siegecraft: Two Tenth-Century Instructional Manuals by "Heron of Byzantium"* (Washington, DC: Dumbarton Oaks, 2000); Denis Sullivan, "Tenth Century Byzantine Offensive Siege Warfare: Instructional Prescriptions and Historical Practice," reprinted in John Haldon (ed.), *Byzantine Warfare* (Aldershot, Hampshire: Ashgate, 2007), pp. 497–518; Eric McGeer, "Byzantine Siege Warfare in Theory and Practice," in Ivy A. Corfis and Michael Wolfe (eds.), *The Medieval City under Siege* (Woodbridge: The Boydell Press, 1995), pp. 123–9; Paul Bentley Kern, *Ancient Siege Warfare* (Bloomington and Indianapolis: Indiana University Press, 1999); and Aineias the Tactician, *How to Survive Under Siege*, trans. David Whitehead, 2nd ed. (London: Bristol Classical Press, 2001).

65 The Chinese used earthenware jars as listening devices (geophones), while city defenders in the Late Roman world watched for the vibration of stones placed in metal bowls; see *TD* 152, p. 3897, and Hugh Elton, *Warfare in Roman Europe, AD 350–425* (Oxford: Clarendon Press, 1996), p. 262. For wooden pitchforks, see Aineias the Tactician, *How to Survive Under Siege*, pp. 92–3.

66 Paul E. Chevedden, "Artillery in Late Antiquity: Prelude to the Middle Ages," in Ivy
   A. Corfis and Michael Wolfe (eds.), *The Medieval City under Siege* (Woodbridge:
   The Boydell Press, 1995), pp. 163–4.
67 See, for example, Chevedden, "Artillery in Late Antiquity," pp. 131–73.
68 Stephen McCotter, "Byzantines, Avars and the Introduction of the Trebuchet"
   (2003). Paper posted at the *De Re Militari* web site: http://web.archive.org/
   web/20110720012051
   /http://www.deremilitari.org/resources/articles/mcotter1.htm (accessed May 7, 2013).
69 McGeer, "Byzantine Siege Warfare in Theory and Practice," p. 129; Haldon, *Warfare,
   State and Society*, pp. 184–5.
70 For Greek fire, see Alex Roland, "Secrecy, Technology, and War: Greek Fire and the
   Defense of Byzantium, 678–1204," *Technology and Culture* 33.4 (October 1992),
   pp. 655–79; John Haldon et al., "'Greek Fire' Revisited: Recent and Current Research,"
   in *Byzantine Style, Religion and Civilization: In Honour of Sir Steven Runciman*
   (Cambridge: Cambridge University Press, 2006), pp. 290–325; John H. Pryor and
   Elizabeth M. Jeffreys, *The Age of the Dromon: The Byzantine Navy ca 500–1204*
   (Leiden and Boston: Brill, 2006), pp. 607–30.
71 *Strategikon*, pp. 106 (quote) and 82; also see Haldon, *Warfare, State and Society*, p. 186.
72 Haldon, *Warfare, State and Society*, pp. 184–5.
73 *ZZTJ* 183, p. 5717. For Li Jing, see *ZZTJ* 190, 5980–1.
74 *ZZTJ* 188, p. 5893; 218, pp. 6988–9; 221, pp. 7068–9.
75 *TD* 157, pp. 4027–8; *Strategikon*, pp. 20–1 and 152.
76 *TD* 157, p. 4030.
77 *Strategikon*, pp. 60, 99, and 101; *TD* 157, pp. 4028–9; Haldon, *War, State and Society*,
   p. 156.
78 *TD* 157, p. 4029; also see pp. 4027–8.
79 *Strategikon*, pp. 152–3.
80 *TD* 157, p. 4027.
81 *Strategikon*, p. 154. In another passage, however, the same text offers rather contradictory advice that all must rush to the sector (p. 100). As with Li Jing, what exactly
   is done may depend upon quite specific conditions including the exact location of the
   attack.
82 *Strategikon*, pp. 21, 31, 100, and 101.
83 *TD* 148, 3792–3; 149, p. 3821; 157, pp. 4027–8. By the later years of the Tang dynasty,
   the Watch had evolved from a combat unit into a military police force; for that period,
   yuhou is better translated as "provost guard," and its commander (the *duyuhou*) as
   "provost marshal." See Charles Peterson, "The Autonomy of the Northeastern
   Provinces in the Period Following the An Lu-shan Rebellion," (Ph.D. diss., University
   of Washington, 1966).
84 *TD* 157, pp. 4027–8 and 4030.
85 *Strategikon*, p. 140.
86 *Strategikon*, pp. 21–2 and 165–9; *TD* 149, pp. 3822–3; 157, pp. 4030–1.
87 Haldon, *Warfare, State and Society*, p. 152; *Strategikon*, p. 81.
88 *Strategikon*, pp. 158–62, and the diagram on p. 164.
89 *ZZTJ* 198, p. 6227. For a few other mentions of fortified camps, see *ZZTJ* 201, p. 6364;
   202, p. 6394; 263, p. 8568; and *XTS* 221A, p. 6225.
90 *TD* 148, p. 3793; 157, p. 4025.
91 *TD* 148, p. 3793.
92 *ZZTJ* 202, pp. 6385 and 6394.
93 *TD* 152, pp. 3900–1; Li Quan, *Taibai yinjing*, pp. 523–4.
94 Guo Rugui et al., *Binglei*, pp. 66, 170–1, and 174.
95 *TD* 157, p. 4030.
96 *TD* 157, p. 4029.
97 *TD* 157, p. 4031.

 98 *TD* 157, p. 4032.
 99 *TD* 157, pp. 4031–2.
100 *TD* 157, pp. 4029–30.
101 *TD* 157, pp. 4032–3; also see p. 4027.
102 *TD* 157, p. 4032.
103 Haldon, *Warfare, State and Society*, p. 152.
104 *Strategikon*, p. 104; also see pp. 98–9, 103, and 155.
105 *Strategikon*, p. 99; also see pp. 68, 71–2, and 160–1.
106 *TD* 149, pp. 3821–2. I would like to thank Dr. Robert J. Smith, director of the muse-ums at Ft. Riley, Kansas, and his wife Karen, both experienced donkey owners, for the information presented here.
107 *TD* 157, p. 4025. This worked best when the army occupied a semicircular camp backed up against rough or impassible terrain.
108 *TD* 157, p. 4041.
109 *Strategikon*, p. 160.
110 *Strategikon*, p. 160.
111 *TD* 157, p. 4030.
112 *TD* 148, p. 3793; also see 157, p. 4025.
113 *Vegetius: Epitome of Military Science*, trans. N. P. Milner (Liverpool: Liverpool University Press, 1993), p. 45 (ten men); Graham Webster, *The Roman Imperial Army* (New York: Funk & Wagnalls, 1969), pp. 114 and 130–2 (eight men). In *Byzantium at War*, p. 67 Haldon says that in the tenth century soldiers "were organized in tent-groups of eight, called *kontoubernia*, sharing a hand-mill and basic cooking utensils as well as a small troop of pack-animals."
114 *Strategikon*, p. 105.
115 *Strategikon*, p. 159.
116 *TD* 149, p. 3821.
117 *TD* 157, pp. 4036–7.
118 *Strategikon*, p. 159.
119 *Strategikon*, p. 58.
120 *TD* 149, p. 3823.
121 Ban Gu, *Han shu* (Beijing: Zhonghua shuju, 1962), chapter 54, p. 2453, translated in Michael Loewe, "The Campaigns of Han Wu-ti," in Frank A. Kierman Jr. and John K. Fairbank, *Chinese Ways in Warfare* (Cambridge, MA: Harvard University Press, 1974) p. 120.
122 *JTS* 58, p. 2314; *ZZTJ* 190, p. 5969.
123 *Strategikon*, pp. 18–19 and 79.
124 *TD* 157, pp. 4030–1; also see 149, p. 3823 where the death penalty is to be imposed on those who loot civilian property.
125 *ZZTJ* 183, p. 5713; 185, p. 5797; 256, pp. 8327–8. For Li Shimin, see Graff, "Early T'ang Generalship and the Textual Tradition," pp. 429–34.
126 For examples, see *ZZTJ* 185, pp. 5772–3; 188, p. 5893; 263, p. 8582.
127 *SS* 65, p. 1534, and *ZZTJ* 184, p. 5747. For another example, see *ZZTJ* 186, p. 5819.
128 *TD* 150, p. 3840.
129 *TD* 150, p. 3839. This is a main point of Sunzi's chapter 4: Wu Jiulong et al., *Sunzi jiaoshi* (Beijing: Junshi kexue chubanshe, 1990), pp. 53–64; and Victor H. Mair (trans.), *The Art of War: Sun Zi's Military Methods* (New York: Columbia University Press, 2007), pp. 88–90.
130 *TD* 150, p. 3839. Also see *TD* 150, p. 3841; 154, pp. 3954–5; and 158, p. 4061.
131 *Strategikon*, p. 83; also see pp. 65, 80, and 87–8.
132 *Strategikon*, pp. 25, 86, and 107–8.
133 "The Anonymous Byzantine Treatise on Strategy" in Dennis, *Three Byzantine Military Treatises*, pp. 103–5.

134 Walter Emil Kaegi, Jr., *Some Thoughts on Byzantine Military Strategy* (Brookline, MA: Hellenic College Press, 1983).
135 See Stephen Morillo, "Battle Seeking: The Contexts and Limits of Vegetian Strategy," *Journal of Medieval Military History* 1 (2002), pp. 21–41, and John Gillingham, "'Up with Orthodoxy!' In Defense of Vegetian Warfare," *Journal of Medieval Military History* 2 (2004), pp. 149–58, as well the more critical view taken by Clifford J. Rogers, "The Vegetian 'Science of Warfare' in the Middle Ages," *Journal of Medieval Military History* 1 (2002), pp. 1–19.
136 For Wang Shichong, see Graff, "Early T'ang Generalship and the Textual Tradition," chapter 4, especially pp. 280–317. For Herakleios, see Kaegi, *Heraclius: Emperor of Byzantium*, pp. 161, 308–9, and *passim*.
137 With regard to avoidance of battle see, for example, *Vegetius: Epitome of Military Science*, p. 82.

5   The legacy of the past

It might be argued that most if not all of the military common ground shared by Sui–Tang China and seventh-century Byzantium is simply a matter of good military practice, showing only that both societies came close to conforming to a set of universal military norms based ultimately upon common sense. Marching with scouts in advance, a rear guard behind, patrols out to the flanks, and baggage train securely positioned in the center would seem to fall into this category, as would fortifying one's camp and guarding it with sentries and outposts, articulating the army into a number of well-trained and disciplined units capable of maneuvering separately in response to preset signals, and always remaining alert to the possibility of tricks and traps on the battlefield. The determination to avoid unnecessary risk, to fight a major battle only when the odds seem to be tilted in one's favor, would also appear to be common sense. Such principles have not only been followed by modern armies, but can also be glimpsed in the behavior of warriors in very early times. Translating information found in the Old Testament book of Numbers into modern military terms, the authors of a work on biblical warfare find that during the Exodus from Egypt the Israelites'

> headquarters and the staff moved after the first division, and the field sanctuary, presumably together with the train, moved between the second and third divisions. The main column was preceded by an advance guard that had among its duties the choice and marking out of the camp for the next night.[1]

Yet not all armies have acted so prudently. In the eleventh book of the *Strategikon*, detailing both the strengths and shortcomings of the peoples with whom the Byzantines had been in hostile military contact, we are told that Persians are vulnerable to night attacks "because they pitch their tents indiscriminately and without order inside their fortifications."[2] The "light-haired peoples," meaning the Franks and other Germanic groupings, come in for much sharper criticism. Disobedient to their leaders, they do not move in good order, pay no attention to security, and do not use scouts—and thus are easily surprised from the flank and rear. Their tactics consist mainly of rapid, impetuous charges, and "they consider any timidity and even a short retreat as a disgrace." Hence, they are vulnerable to ambush, stratagem, and delay.[3]

This particular portrait may tell as much about the Byzantines' self-image as about the actual military practices of their Germanic "other," but a great deal of additional evidence regarding warfare in early medieval Western Europe suggests that the representation is not entirely unfair. Among the peoples who threatened the Roman Empire from the north in the late fourth and early fifth century, scouting apparently left much to be desired as the Romans often managed to surprise their opponents. There is no evidence that the "barbarians" used rear guards or reserves, and their favored tactic was the mass infantry charge. "Though the tactics were simple," Hugh Elton has pointed out, "there was no realistic alternative. Barbarian command systems were not sufficiently sophisticated to be able to control more than a single body of soldiers."[4] Much of this continued to be seen in the warfare of the Latin West for the next few centuries. Formal command structures were generally lacking, and there were many instances of "indiscipline in the quest for distinction and its rewards."[5] Warriors' touchy sense of honor gave rise to behavior that offends the modern sense of military rationality. In an example from the early eighth century cited by Guy Halsall,

> as a result of one commander accusing another of cowardice, a Friulian Lombard army was destroyed in an insane charge up a steep hill against the fortified camp of a Slavic army. The troops followed their squabbling leaders because "they considered it base not to."[6]

The celebrated destruction of Charlemagne's rear guard in the Pass of Roncesvalles in 778, heroic though it may be, is also suggestive of inadequate scouting, poor march discipline, and inattention to the security of the marching column.[7] Rather than calculating the odds carefully before engaging, commanders in the early medieval West tended to be risk-takers "prepared to commit themselves and their armies to the lottery of battle with unusual frequency," notes Halsall. "Battles are common in this period."[8] Warfare was shaped not only by what might appear to us to be common sense, but also by social and political structures, cultural expectations, and the weight of historical experience.

One characteristic setting Byzantium and Sui–Tang China apart from many other powers of the early Middle Ages is that each was, to borrow Walter Kaegi's expression, "a very old bureaucratic empire."[9] This is not to suggest that they corresponded exactly to the ideal type of bureaucracy as defined by Max Weber; to consider only the Chinese side, a significant body of scholarship has already made it abundantly clear that Sui–Tang government included a very strong element of the informal, personalistic style of rule that the pioneer German sociologist labeled "patrimonialism."[10] Nevertheless, both empires did, to a considerable extent, practice a functional division of labor in their administration, considered merit to be a significant factor in their personnel management, collected information on a very large scale and consulted that material in their decision making, kept records compulsively, and generated impressive volumes of paperwork, much of which was stored away in administrative archives. In neither empire were these new developments. Despite the rise and fall of dynastic regimes, the

Chinese of Sui and Tang times were heirs to a literary tradition dating back at least as far as the Western Zhou period (1045–771 BCE) and administrative precedents and procedures formulated during the Warring States period (450–221 BCE) and further refined in the centuries that followed. At the other end of Asia, the Roman Empire had developed a strong administrative tradition of its own and had access to a corpus of literature in Greek and Latin reaching back at least to the epics of Homer. In both empires, the experiences and lessons of the past were recorded in writing, preserved and passed down to provide guidance for later generations. As we shall see, the military "lessons learned" in China and Byzantium were remarkably similar and pointed their learners in the direction of common solutions to security problems.

The bureaucratic aspect of the Tang military system is fully on display in Li Jing's "Military Methods." Each of the expeditionary army's encampments (*ying*) has four staff sections, each of which is responsible for a particular area of military administration. The Military Service Section (*si bing*) handles personnel matters; when the army encamps for the night, this section must determine which soldiers are present and which, if any, are missing. The director of the Mounts Section (*si qi*) and his assistants have the job of inspecting the horses and donkeys, identifying and treating injuries such as sores or welts, and bringing the men responsible for those injuries before the encampment master (*yingzhu*) for punishment. The director of the Equipment Section (*si chou*) is responsible for inspecting weapons, armor, and other sorts of equipment and arranging for the repair of damaged items. "If something has been discarded or lost," he is supposed to "report the reason for it, make a record of it, and deal with it under the appropriate category in accordance with the law." Finally, "the director of the Granary Section (*si cang*) and his assistants keep tight control of the soldiers' grain supply, storing it under seal and inspecting it so as to prevent waste."[11] Military administration required a considerable amount of writing and record keeping. Army staff kept detailed records of the armor and weapons issued to each soldier, for example the number of leather or metal plaques making up a suit of armor. If a deficiency was discovered when the items were returned, the soldier was required to make restitution.[12] Another measure to prevent theft required all soldiers to have written on their packs

> the number of articles of clothing, as well as other valuables, bows and arrows, saddles and bridles and weapons, and they should be made to write down the division (*jun*), encampment (*ying*), prefecture, county, regiment (*fu*), and guard (*wei*) to which they belong, along with their own names.

But this was not all. Li Jing continues:

> Furthermore, an encampment officer (*ying guan*) should be ordered the inspect [the list] and sign [the list with his endorsement]. The encampment functionaries (*ying si*) make a copy of each list to establish a written record. If something is ruined through use, the company commander (*duitou*) and the squad leader (*huozhang*) must apprise themselves of how it was being used, and copy it

down to make a written record which is reported to the encampment functionaries once every five days. If on inspection the valuables are found to be different from what is in the register, or there is a surplus of articles, then they have been obtained by theft.[13]

These and other passages indicate that quite a lot of writing and record keeping went on in the expeditionary army camp, and not all of this was done by men whose function was strictly clerical. Although most soldiers were probably illiterate, a certain rudimentary level of literacy seems to have been expected of the officers. For drilling soldiers to maneuver in response to flag signals, Li Jing's teaching method was "to have each officer from lesser commander (*zi zongguan*) on down make a copy, to teach the soldiers the same way they [themselves] were taught the flag methods."[14]

The pervasive documentation and record keeping found in Li Jing's text is corroborated by the documentary evidence of Tang military administration that has been recovered in modern times from Kucha, Turfan, and other sites in China's arid northwest. For example, the fragmentary documents that Paul Pelliot found at the site of the Douldour-âqour monastery in the Kucha oasis in 1907 include accounts of grain distributed to army personnel and of feed issued to horses, a register of beasts of burden, and an inventory of military materiel, as well as several reports praising the heroic deeds of individual soldiers.[15] The clerical meticulousness reflected in these materials was not a new development under the Tang. Documents of Han military administration, written on wooden and bamboo strips and dating mostly from the first century CE, recovered from the ruins of forts and watchtowers along the Han border limes in the Edsen Gol region of Inner Mongolia about the same time that Pelliot was working at Kucha, give exactly the same impression. Among the documents studied and translated by Michael Loewe are a "record of the monthly amounts of pay received by officers, either in cash or in textiles"; a "[r]ecord of barley issued to individual soldiers"; a "[r]ecord of civilians admitted in and out a pass at the frontier," including distinguishing features of each individual "together with notes of the weapons carried and vehicles or horses used in transport"; a "[r]egister of cattle, with details of age, height, colouring, and other distinctive features"; and even a "[r]egister of outgoing correspondence" whose "entries include a short summary of the subjects of the communication, and the dates on which they were sealed."[16]

The author of the *Strategikon* says less about the army's administrative staff and paperwork than Li Jing does, but several of his passages hint at their presence. The text repeatedly states that things are to be done in accordance with regulations that have presumably already been set down in writing, and there is clear evidence of written communication within the command hierarchy. Just as in Li Jing's expeditionary army, drill instructions are to be handed down the chain of command in written form.[17] Higher levels of administration linked the local garrisons and field armies with the capital. Soldiers paid by the imperial government had their names recorded in official rolls, with copies held by both their local headquarters and the relevant administrative department in Constantinople.[18] These Byzantine practices were, of course, heavily influenced by well-established late Roman procedures and precedents for military administration. The commanders of field armies and frontier ducates as of 395 had significant administrative staffs that included a chief of staff (*princeps*), a disciplinary officer (*commentariensis*), two head account-ants (*numerarii*), clerks (*scrinarii*), and secretaries (*exceptores*).[19] At a lower level, "regimental staff would have kept the voluminous amounts of paperwork the army produced. We know that individual soldiers had enrolment papers (*probatoriae*) and dogtags (*bullae*) and that units had troop rosters and theoretically produced daily ration indents."[20] As in the Chinese case, documents recovered by modern archaeologists have provided striking confirmation. Wooden tablets dating from around 100 CE found at the Roman fort of Vindolanda in northern England "include unit-strength reports of various kinds, records of casualties and promotions, notes from the governor assigning new recruits and animals to individual units, and let-ters to and from the governor."[21] The archives of the *cohors XX Palmyrenorum* found at Dura Europos (Syria) in 1931–1932 include a complete working roster of the cohort's personnel in 219 CE and a list of troopers and their mounts from 251 CE with the age, sex, color, and brand of each horse duly noted. Receipts for hay allowances and grain rations generated by other Roman units during the second century CE, along with many other administrative documents, have also survived.[22]

Continuities in paperwork and record keeping were just one aspect of a broader continuity in imperial military practice seen in both China and the Mediterranean world. For the most part, neither Li Jing nor the author of the *Strategikon* advocated new or original systems, but instead detailed what were already well-established procedures. In both Sui–Tang China and Byzantium, the art of fortification was already many centuries old and was inherited without a break, as were a great many techniques of siegecraft.[23] Many of the measures recommended by Li Jing, includ-ing methods of scouting, patrolling, and guarding the camp, were already being used in northern China during the wars of the sixth century CE. On the eve of the battle of Shayuan in 537, for example, the Western Wei leader Yuwen Tai sent four horsemen to reconnoiter the Eastern Wei camp. At sunset, at a distance of a hun-dred paces from the camp, they dismounted and listened from hiding, thus learning the Eastern Wei passwords. They then mounted again and made the rounds of the enemy camp just as if they were officers making a night inspection of the sentries, even beating men whose behavior was not in accordance with regulations.[24] The system they were able to exploit sounds very much like that described by Li Jing, with night sentries divided into two-hour watches and officers making regular cir-cuits of inspection, exchanging password and countersign with the sentries, and promptly punishing any who failed to respond correctly.[25] Reaching back half a millennium earlier, to the civil wars that attended the foundation of the Eastern Han dynasty in the first century CE, we find that Chinese armies were already building fortified camps, relying on long columns of supply carts for most of their provisions, and using cavalry for reconnaissance and to disrupt enemy supply lines. Generals routinely tried to mislead their opponents by feigning weakness, concealing troops in ambush, and launching "sudden attacks on the flanks or the rear." The importance of maintaining a reserve in battle was also well understood by that time.[26]

Many of the Byzantine practices recounted in the *Strategikon* are also attested in Roman works dating from centuries earlier, and so too are some techniques quite similar to those mentioned by Li Jing. We find the use of reconnaissance troops and scouts, the formation of a marching column with its baggage train positioned in the center and flank guards off to the sides, and the practice of constructing fortified camps, with sentries, watchwords, and regular procedures for checking on the vigilance of the sentries. In battle deployments, we find the cavalry positioned on the wings and a reserve of picked troops retained behind the main formation.[27] The still extant military manual written by the late Roman official Publius Flavius Vegetius Renatus, who was probably active in the last quarter of the fourth century CE, mentions almost all of these features, and it also speaks of the need to assign experienced drillmasters and other officers to keep a troop column moving at an even pace to prevent gaps from opening up that might be exploited by the enemy. When a camp is being made and there is danger of attack by the enemy, all the cavalry and half the infantry are to remain drawn up in a defensive line until the work is completed.[28] Well aware of the possibility that a defeated army may turn on its pursuers if they are themselves in disarray, Vegetius recommends that the heavy-armed soldiers remain in formation while only the light troops pursue the enemy—anticipating in rudimentary form the *defensores* and *cursores* of the *Strategikon*. In another passage he tells us

> that whereas the front two lines hold their ground, the third and fourth lines always go out to challenge the enemy with missiles and arrows, in the forward position. If they can put the enemy to rout, they set off in pursuit themselves plus the cavalry. But if they are driven back by the enemy, they return to the first and second lines and retire between them to their own stations.[29]

The influence of Vegetius' earlier work is clearly visible in the *Strategikon*, not only in its repetition of specific measures and techniques but also occasionally in its phrasing; in a passage that has already been quoted, for example, it offers an unattributed Greek paraphrase of one of Vegetius's observations: "It is preferable to subdue an enemy by famine, raids, and terror, than in battle where fortune tends to have more influence than bravery."[30]

Textual parallels such as this indicate that the contents of the *Strategikon* should not simply be taken as evidence of a high degree of continuity in military practice, for they also alert us to the book's significance as part of an ongoing textual tradition of military thought. Governed by literate elites, and with more than a few "ardent bibliophiles" among its military commanders,[31] the Byzantine Empire inherited a very substantial corpus of classical literature dealing with the conduct of war. This was a dual heritage inscribed in both Latin and Greek. From the Latin side came writings such as Vegetius' *De re militari* and the collection of stratagems compiled by Sextus Julius Frontinus in the first century CE, as well as a great many works of history that gave privileged attention to military events. The Greek inheritance was even more important, given that it was older and more substantial—and that by the seventh century Greek had superseded

Latin as the common language of government administration and elite discourse. It reached back to the seminal fifth-century BCE histories written by Herodotus and Thucydides, and included a number of military handbooks beginning with the work of "Aineias the Tactician" on how to defend a city against siege, probably written by an Arkadian general in the mid-fourth century BCE.[32] Later works included those of Asclepiodotus (first century BCE), Aelian the Tactician (first century CE), and Arrian of Nicomedia (second century CE), and there were also collections of stratagems and military anecdotes by Onasander (first century CE) and Polyaenus (second century CE). As one authority has pointed out, there is "an absolute continuity between the Byzantine tradition and the ancient tradition," with the words of the early Greek writers frequently reappearing in later Byzantine texts.[33] Within this tradition, the *Strategikon* is actually one of the more original (or less imitative) works, in contrast to, for example, the *De re strategica*, now thought to have been composed in the ninth century by an author known as Syrianos Magister, which draws heavily from Aelian, Asclepiodotus, and Arrian to describe rigid phalanx formations.[34] The *Strategikon* itself became tremendously influential in its turn and has been called "the bible of Byzantine military theory."[35] The late ninth-century *Taktika* of Leo VI, for example, incorporates much material from the *Strategikon*, as well as borrowing from earlier authors such as Onasander and Aelian.[36]

Clearly, not all of the material found in the Greco-Byzantine military corpus would have been of equally great value to military practitioners. Some passages, such as Aineias the Tactician's advice that patrols should inspect the sentries to make sure they are not asleep, remained no less relevant a thousand years after they had been written.[37] Other material, such as that dealing with the ancient hoplite phalanx, would have been of no more than antiquarian interest. As Eric McGeer has pointed out, "The majority of classical and Byzantine military writers were not soldiers and did not write for specialists. They were instead rhetoricians and philosophers who explained *tactics* and *strategy* in literary/rhetorical rather than practical terms." Yet, the same author goes on to conclude that:

> the military handbooks were certainly used for the training of prospective commanders and for the continuing instruction of active soldiers. A soldierly upbringing combined mastery of martial skills, acquired through military exercises and the related pursuits of hunting and athletics, with knowledge of tactical procedures gleaned from the military handbooks.[38]

In a tenth-century text of Constantine Porphyrogenitus on imperial expeditions, we find military manuals specifically mentioned among the baggage to be taken on campaign by the imperial headquarters, and some scholars have found resonances between the historical accounts of Byzantine military operations and the contents of the handbooks. Walter Kaegi has, for example, characterized Herakleios' campaign of 625 as "a text-book execution of the advice of the Maurikios *Strategikon* on how to fight the Persian," complete with a surprise attack on the Sasanian camp.[39] In general, Byzantinists have concluded that the corpus of military manuals was not entirely antiquarian in nature and was never divorced from the actual practice of warfare. On the contrary, Byzantine military effectiveness owed a great deal to consciousness of this written tradition— especially in the emphasis placed on discipline, training, tactical cohesion, and logistics—and, more generally, to awareness of historical precedents handed down in writing.[40]

Like the Byzantines, literate Chinese of the Sui–Tang period were heirs to a rich textual tradition of strategic thought, and one that was already of considerable antiquity. By the time of the Sui dynasty, the corpus of military writings was quite large; the bibliographic monograph of the early-seventh century *Sui History* (based on the catalogue of the imperial library) lists no less than 133 works under the heading of "military books" (*bing shu*), a total of 512 chapters (*juan*).[41] Not all of these books were of equal importance, however, nor were all of them accorded the same degree of respect. While most are known to us only as titles listed in the *Sui History*'s monograph and other bibliographies, a select few are quoted again and again in Tang literature. The *Qun shu zhi yao*, a collection of "condensed books" brought together and edited by the early Tang statesman Wei Zheng (580–643), incorporates sections from seven military works: *Liu tao* and *Taigong yinmou* (both conventionally attributed to the ancient strategist Qi Taigong, an associate of the founders of the Zhou dynasty in the eleventh century BCE), *Sima fa*, *Wuzi*, *Wei Liaozi*, *San lüe*, and *Sunzi bingfa*.[42] The *Yiwen leiju*, an encyclopedia of literary models assembled by Ouyang Xun (567–641), includes passages from *San lüe*, *Liu tao*, and several other works attributed to the Taigong, while the military chapters of Du You's great eighth-century administrative encyclopedia, the *Tong dian*, quote from *Sima fa*, *Wuzi*, various works attributed to the Taigong, and above all *Sunzi bingfa*, which is accorded near-canonical status.[43] The extracts from Li Jing's "Military Methods" included in the *Tong dian* contain several quotations from *Sunzi bingfa* and *Wei Liaozi*.[44]

At a time when most military texts claimed to be of great antiquity, these books really were. Though probably not the work of the legendary figures to which they were traditionally attributed, all had been handed down to the people of Tang times from the very distant past. Most of them are now thought to date from the Warring States period (450–221 BCE); one, the *San lüe*, is probably of somewhat later vintage, while another, *Sunzi bingfa*, may have been written as early as the fifth century BCE.[45] Whatever its exact age, it is *Sunzi bingfa* that was the most respected of all of these military texts during the Tang period. In the Sui and Tang bibliographies, it is listed in more editions and has received more commentarial attention than any other military text, and when the histories of the period portray statesmen or generals as quoting from "military science" (*bingfa*), their words are found more often than not to have been borrowed from *Sunzi bingfa*.[46]

The many long quotations from *Sunzi bingfa* that are found in the *Tong dian* and other Tang works—together with the several Tang commentaries on it which have survived to the present day—afford ample evidence that the text known to the people of Tang times was almost exactly the same as that which is still in circulation today.[47] The same cannot be said of the other early military texts. A partial manuscript copy of the *Liu tao*, recovered from Dunhuang and probably dating from the reign of Tang Taizong (626–649) contains a large amount of material not found in the currently circulating Northern Song redaction, and the order of the sections is also different.[48] On the other hand, while the extracts from the *Liu tao* in the *Qun shu zhi yao* also include additional material, the order of the sections there is exactly the same as in the later version. It seems that as of the first half of the seventh century the text of the *Liu tao* had not yet stabilized, that there were several (or many) different versions in circulation, and it is possible that the book did not attain its present form until the eleventh century when it was edited for inclusion in the *Seven Military Classics* (*Wu jing qi shu*). Judging from the Song editors' treatment of the *Liu tao*, there is reason to believe that their intervention consisted mainly of discarding some material and reorganizing or reordering what was left. If this was indeed the case, the essential contents of today's editions of *Liu tao*, *Wuzi*, *Wei Liaozi*, *Sima fa*, and *San lüe* would have been available to people of Tang times, even if the texts they held in their hands were not exactly the same as ours.

Although quite a few scholars have pointed out subtle differences between these six ancient military books (often with the aim of establishing their intellectual affinities with the different philosophical traditions of the Warring States period),[49] they share enough ground with one another and with later works—such as the "Military Methods" of Li Jing—for us to regard them as belonging to a single, coherent tradition of military thought comparable to that of the Greco-Roman-Byzantine world. The Chinese military texts borrow freely from one another, with the same expressions and concepts often turning up in two or more of them. Much of the *San lüe*, for example, consists of quotations from the *Liu tao*.[50] While each book has its own unique emphases, all of them cover much the same range of problems and offer much the same solutions.[51] All or most of them devote considerable attention to such matters as the importance of calculation before battle, the uses of stratagem, surprise, and trickery, the employment of psychological devices to manipulate the soldiery, the importance of rewards and punishments, and the need for the ruler to give his general a free hand in the conduct of military operations.

The ancient military classics were not, however, the only texts available to provide Tang readers with martial wisdom. China had a long tradition of historical writing reaching back at least as far as the *Zuo zhuan*, a chronicle dealing with the events of the Spring and Autumn period (722–481 BCE), and continuing through the *Historical Records* (*Shiji*) completed by Sima Qian early in the first century BCE and the dynastic histories of the Western Han (*Han shu*, first century CE), Eastern Han (*Hou Han shu*, 445 CE), and Three Kingdoms (*San Guo zhi*, 297 CE). These works contained a great deal of material dealing with military events, with considerable attention given to strategic plans and clever stratagems. To choose only one from among thousands of possible examples, the *Zuo zhuan* tells us that in 511 BCE the strategist Wu Zixu advised King Helü of Wu on how to defeat the more powerful neighboring state of Chu: "When they come forth, then [we should] withdraw; when they withdraw, [we should] then go forth." This advice continued to influence Chinese guerilla warriors in the twentieth century.[52] In Tang times, according to David McMullen, "Historical records, especially those of the Han period, were 'second to the canons,' and were immediately familiar to educated men."[53] Li Jing is said to have been thoroughly familiar with the histories and, as we have seen, found a Han-dynasty precedent for his surprise attack on the camp of Illig Qaghan in 630. Li Shimin is known to have studied the *Han shu*, and quoted from its account of the battle of Jingxing (205 BCE) after his victory over Dou Jiande at the Hulao Pass in 621.[54] Insofar as they contain explicit and concrete descriptions of a large number of tried-and-true stratagems, the histories may well have provided the most literate military commanders with a more useful and practical guide to action than the teachings of the military treatises. In this connection, it is worth noting that in 731 a Tang official objected to the presentation of a copy of the *Zuo zhuan* to the rulers of Tibet on the grounds that this record of ancient history would provide China's foreign enemies with new insights into military strategy.[55]

Just how many Chinese commanders of the Sui–Tang period were able to draw on these textual traditions, and in what way, is a difficult question to answer. Literate, well-educated leaders from aristocratic backgrounds, such as Li Shimin and Li Jing, were clearly familiar with the contents of both the histories and the most important of the military treatises; Li Shimin is reported to have quoted the military classics several times, and in almost all of his campaigns he followed a standard formula of avoiding combat and waiting for the right moment to strike after the enemy had weakened (often due to logistical difficulties)—a formula that adheres closely to precepts found in *Sunzi bingfa*.[56] A good case can be made that some other educated commanders also studied and applied the histories and military treatises, among them the Sui official Wang Shichong in the early seventh century and the Tang general Li Su two centuries later.[57] Yet in the Tang officer corps, if such it may be called, it would seem that book learning and high levels of literacy were the exception rather than the rule. A great many senior military men were of humble origin, even former bandits, and others, such as the Türk Ashina She'er, had been steppe chieftains before they entered the imperial service. Even the northwestern aristocracy that produced Li Shimin and Li Jing was, in the view of one authority, marked by "a robust anti-intellectualism, a disdain of book-learning and those whose lives were devoted to it."[58] When regular examinations were introduced as a route to military office in 702, neither the qualification examination (*wuju*) nor the selection examination (*wuxuan*) included a written component, and both stressed physical skills such as archery, horsemanship, and even weight-lifting rather than cerebral qualities.[59] Even for those who might have been more intellectually inclined, there was the additional complication that under both the Sui and Tang dynasties private possession of military treatises was illegal and regarded as ipso facto proof of rebellious intentions.[60]

It is possible and even likely, however, that knowledge of the classical military texts and the military precedents found in the histories circulated among both literate and non-literate officers in the form of aphorisms, maxims, and anecdotes learned and transmitted by word of mouth. When the Tang histories have military men citing textual authority, their citations usually take the form of short, pithy maxims which are assigned the generic label of *bingfa* ("military methods" or "military science") rather than attributed to a particular treatise or author—a mode of presentation which suggests that the ancient wisdom on the "art of war" was transmitted mainly by word of mouth rather than direct textual study.[61]

If there remained a certain distance between military men and textual traditions in China (and Byzantium), however, it was not nearly as great as the yawning chasm found in early medieval Western Europe. Although Vegetius and some other military writings (such as the *Stratagems* of Frontinus) survived and were copied in the West, they did not circulate very widely and their actual influence on the behavior of warriors appears to have been minimal. As Halsall puts it,

> There is no evidence at all that Vegetius's detailed tactical and organisa-
> tional recommendations were ever put into practice, and it seems unlikely
> that his advice on campaigning was followed closely either. In many cases it
> is abundantly clear that it was not.[62]

We have already seen that Western armies were careless about security and often quick to give battle, and in this respect were something of an outlier in the early medieval Eurasian context. The textual traditions and actual practices of the Chinese and Byzantines, in contrast, were alike in emphasizing security and caution. They also prized cunning, advocated deception whenever possible, and held a distinctly un-heroic attitude toward war. For both Tang and Byzantine soldiers, Roland's refusal to summon assistance at Roncesvalles by blowing his horn would have been incomprehensible.[63]

Their approach to warfare may be characterized as mature, pragmatic, and for the most part highly rational. For the soldiers of both Byzantium and Sui–Tang China, war was not just a trial of strength and courage, but rather an activity requiring the application of intellect, cunning, and trickery to gain every possible advantage. It was seen as a serious and dangerous business, not to be undertaken lightly, for it could easily lead to disaster. *Sunzi bingfa* opens with the observation, "Warfare is the greatest affair of state, the basis of life and death, the Way to survival or extinction."[64] The famous admonition of Laozi's *Daodejing* (in existence by about 300 BCE) that "arms are instruments of ill omen" was borrowed and repeated by the authors of several other Chinese military texts, both ancient and medieval.[65] In Byzantium, meanwhile, we find one author expressing the opinion that "war is a great evil and the worst of all evils."[66]

By the seventh century CE, both the Chinese and Byzantines had long traditions of employing diplomacy, subsidies, marriage alliances, subversion, and assassination to deal with potential foes without resort to armed conflict, and both were well versed in the art of fighting wars by proxy and "using barbarians to control barbarians."[67] When war was found to be necessary, both powers approached it just as they approached battle, in a methodical, calculating manner—weighing the odds, stacking the deck in their favor, and trying to minimize risk. The author of the *Strategikon* repeatedly advises generals to avoid risk and think matters through before taking action: "Long and careful deliberation promises great safety in war, whereas hasty and impetuous generals usually commit serious blunders."[68] The wise general studies the enemy before going to war and then is able to exploit their weaknesses, but the one "who does not carefully compare his own forces with those of the enemy will come to a disastrous end."[69]

The author (or authors) of *Sunzi bingfa* could not have agreed more. The first chapter of the ancient Chinese military treatise is devoted to calculations of the relative strength of oneself and one's opponent, and makes it abundantly clear that one should not go to war unless the results are in one's own favor, while the last chapter deals with the espionage and intelligence-gathering that must be performed if these calculations are to have any validity. The text confidently proclaims that if this task is performed properly, victory and defeat may be predicted with certainty.[70] Writing in the early Tang, Li Jing also devotes considerable attention to espionage, intelligence analysis, and "estimating the enemy," echoing Sunzi with a rhetorical question: "Estimating on the basis of these calculations, how could I not guarantee our victory?"[71] Although the Byzantines were perhaps less completely confident of victory even when the indications were favorable, the bottom line is that in both traditions success in war was understood to be, ultimately, a matter of mental acumen rather than physical strength. The *Strategikon* likens warfare to hunting:

> Wild animals are taken by scouting, by nets, by lying in wait, by stalking, by circling around, and by other such stratagems rather than by sheer force. In waging war we should proceed in the same way, whether the enemy be many or few. To try simply to overpower the enemy in the open, hand to hand and face to face, even though you might appear to win, is an enterprise which is very risky and can result in serious harm. Apart from extreme emergency, it is ridiculous to try to gain a victory which is so costly and brings only empty glory.[72]

The idea of using one's wits to defeat the enemy without actually having to fight a battle loomed large in the inherited traditions of both the Chinese and the Byzantines. *Sunzi bingfa*'s famous claim that the highest skill produces not victory in battle but rather subjugation of the enemy without combat is paralleled in the *Strategikon*: "Strategy makes use of times and places, surprises and various tricks to outwit the enemy with the idea of achieving its objectives even without actual fighting."[73] This aspect of the Byzantine text is consistent with the earlier Greek military literature, which sought "to avoid the risks of battle except under the most favorable circumstances, and to use every conceivable nonmilitary device to improve the likelihood of accomplishing one's purposes with the minimum of losses."[74]

This celebration of cleverness had a venerable pedigree in the Greek cultural traditions inherited by the Byzantines, stretching back as far as the wily Odysseus in the *Illiad* and the *Odyssey*. The ancient Greeks called the form of cunning intelligence exemplified by the inventor of the Trojan horse *metis*. According to Lisa Raphals,

This mode of intelligence embraces a set of skills and mental attitudes that range from wisdom, forethought, keen attention, and resourcefulness to subtle indirection, craft, deception, and cunning. It relies on skill, strategy, and a general knack for handling whatever comes along.[75]

Raphals' "metic intelligence" was often employed in Greek warfare. One modern scholar of ancient Greece, Peter Krentz, has cataloged no fewer than 140 examples of trickery ranging from the eighth century to the fourth century BCE. In one of these cases, at the battle of Sepeia in the early fifth century BCE, Kleomenes of Sparta surprised and defeated the men of Argos after pretending to have his own troops stand down for breakfast—with the result that 6,000 of the Argives were reported to have been killed.[76] In his book *The Cavalry Commander*, Xenophon (*c.*430–354 BCE), who was not only an eminent historian but also an experienced soldier, declared that "in war nothing is more profitable than deceit."[77] Despite their self-representation as a more straightforward people than the devious Greeks, the Romans' actual behavior in war tended to conform to Greek precedents.[78] And the tradition continued among the Byzantines. The *Strategikon* maintains that deception "is often helpful in warfare" and offers numerous means of misleading an opponent; in order to retreat in safety, for example, one should "build a fire in one place and go off to another; the enemy will head for the fire." And one should not allow oneself to be deceived by the enemy's humane acts, by his pretending to retreat, or by false reports brought by his deserters.[79]

On the Chinese side, *Sunzi bingfa* pronounces warfare to be "a way of deception" and offers quite a few specific recommendations for deceiving an enemy.[80] Other classical military texts also place a great emphasis on deceit. The *Liu tao*, for example, offers a list of twelve duplicitous measures to prepare for the overthrow of a ruler; the first of these is to "accord with what he likes in order to accommodate his wishes. He will eventually grow arrogant and invariably mount some perverse affair. If you can appear to follow along, you will certainly be able to eliminate him."[81] In the historical literature from the *Zuo zhuan* and *Shiji* onward, battle accounts characteristically highlight elaborate stratagems while overlooking the more mundane aspects of combat and maneuver.[82] A typical example comes from the description of the battle of the Mang Hills found in Sima Guang's *Zizhi tongjian*, a late eleventh-century work. In the autumn of 618, during the chaos attending the collapse of the Sui dynasty, the rival warlords Li Mi and Wang Shichong faced off in hills northeast of Wang's base in the city of Luoyang. Sima Guang tells us that at the height of the action Wang had a soldier from his own army who happened to resemble Li Mi tied up and brought to the front line. He then raised the cry that his opponent had been captured, boosting the morale of his own army and undermining the determination of Li Mi's followers.[83] Incidents of this sort are standard fare in traditional Chinese battle narratives. Though we may doubt whether they are accurate representations of what transpired on the battlefield, these accounts surely tell us something about Chinese cultural ideals and what the educated men who wrote the histories thought war ought to be like.

The classicist Everett L. Wheeler has defined "stratagem" as

> a strategic or tactical act of trickery, deceit, or cunning in military affairs, especially war, whereby one attempts to gain psychological or material advantage over an opponent, to neutralize some part of an opponent's superiority, to minimize one's own expenditure of resources, or to restore the morale and physical state of one's own forces.[84]

The textual tradition stretching from Greece through Rome to Byzantium records many examples of such devices; some are gathered in collections of stratagems such as those of Frontinus and Polyaenus, while others appear in military manuals and histories. This literature not only shares the emphasis on deception and the exploitation of psychology with the Chinese strategic tradition, but it also includes some of the very same stratagems. The idea of distracting the enemy with a feint or demonstration, which could be done at either the strategic or tactical level, can be found in both Western and Chinese texts. In China the idea first appears in the *Zuo zhuan* and *Sunzi bingfa*, and in the eighth century CE was given the following formulation by the prominent scholar-offical Du You, compiler of the *Tong dian*: "Announce that you will strike in the east, but actually strike in the west."[85] In the Greco-Roman literature, Polyaenus recounts that Iphicrates, an Athenian general of the fourth century BCE, was once able to bypass an enemy position at night by having trumpets blown at one end of the enemy's line and then moving silently past at the opposite end.[86] He also tells the story of how another Athenian commander, Demosthenes, captured the Spartan stronghold of Pylos during the Peloponnesian War. When he found the place to be too strongly garrisoned for a direct attack, Demosthenes feinted in the direction of another Spartan strongpoint and, when many of the Spartans at Pylos marched off to reinforce that place, he returned to capture his original target.[87] His approach very much resembles the classic Chinese stratagem of "besieging Wei to rescue Zhao" (*wei Wei jiu Zhao*), defined as overcoming "the enemy indirectly by threatening one of his unprotected weak spots."[88] The *locus classicus* for this ploy is the biography of the legendary mid-fourth century BCE strategist Sun Bin in Sima Qian's *Shiji*, which describes a campaign wherein Sun Bin advised the army of the state of Qi to relieve the siege of the Zhao state's capital not by striking directly at the besieging forces from the state of Wei, but rather by marching on Wei's own capital city.[89]

Another stratagem attributed to Sun Bin in the Chinese tradition was the manipulation of campfires to deceive the enemy. During the Maling campaign of 341 BCE, the great strategist had the retreating Qi army diminish the number of its campfires each night, encouraging the opposing Wei general to race ahead in pursuit with a relatively small force and fall into a fatal ambush.[90] Later military writers both East and West, including Li Jing, Onasander, and the author of the *Strategikon*, were well aware that at night campfires could be used to mislead the enemy with regard to one's whereabouts and effective strength.[91]

Of course, those who were taught to employ such devices were also warned to be alert to the enemy's wiles. The literature even provides quite specific tips that might alert military men to their opponents' attempts at deception. Frontinus reports that when fighting the Etruscans around 280 BCE, the Roman general Q. Aemilius Paulus "saw afar off a flock of birds rise in somewhat startled flight from a forest, and realized that some treachery was lurking there, both because the birds had risen in alarm and at the same time in great numbers." As expected, his scouts found a large enemy force concealed in ambush where the birds had been.[92] All this would have been no surprise to readers of *Sunzi bingfa*, which warns that "when birds fly up, there is an ambush."[93]

Quite a few stratagems were built upon presumptions about human behavior and what is today called mass psychology: when confronted with a particular stimulus, men may be expected to respond in a predictable way. Again, the extent of the common ground that China shared with Greece, Rome, and Byzantium is striking. Wang Shichong's stratagem making use of the man who looked like Li Mi has a parallel in Onasander: " . . . when the leader of the enemy is some distance away either on one wing or holding the centre, [our general] should call out, 'The general of the enemy has been killed,' or 'the king,' or whoever it may be." This, it is assumed, will raise the spirits of one's own soldiers while at the same time demoralizing the enemy combatants and perhaps even triggering their general rout.[94] In the pages of Frontinus, we find the story of Valerius Laevinus, a Roman general who, in a battle against Pyrrhus of Epirus in 280 BCE, spread the rumor that his opponent had been killed. The soldiers of Pyrrhus were "panic-stricken at the falsehood, and thinking that they had been rendered helpless by the death of their commander, betook themselves in terror back to camp."[95] This trick would have been no less effective during the medieval period when, as the Byzantinist Eric McGeer has pointed out, personal bonds between leaders and followers were often the glue that held armies together.[96]

At both ends of Eurasia, soldiers' morale was understood to be situational; what men might and might not be expected to do was very much a function of the location and the context. In *Sunzi bingfa*, the skillful exploitation of "configuration" (*shi*) when sending soldiers into battle is likened to "turning over a round boulder at the top of a mountain ten thousand feet high."[97] Both the *Strategikon* and *Sunzi bingfa* point out that soldiers deep in enemy territory will fight with greater determination than in their home country, with the Byzantine text spelling out the psychological assumptions that are merely implicit in the Chinese work: men will take more risks in combat when their personal safety depends on a victorious outcome, and where there are no friendly strongholds to offer them refuge.[98] Armies were generally considered to be most vulnerable when they were returning home, their soldiers laden with booty and psychologically unprepared for renewed fighting.[99] And it was always considered advisable to face a worn-out enemy with troops who were fresh and well rested.[100]

Omens and auspices were treated with great seriousness by military writers in both China and the ancient Mediterranean world. According to Onasander,

> Before the general leads out his army he must see that it is purified, by such rites as either the laws or soothsayers direct, and must avert whatever taint there is in the state or in any citizen, by expiatory sacrifices.

Official "sacrificers and diviners" accompanied the army on campaign, and nothing was to be undertaken until the omens were favorable.[101] The idea that the mantic arts should be studied as a guide to action was also found in the Chinese tradition of military literature. Bibliographies from ancient and medieval China record the titles of numerous works of military prognostication in the cosmological traditions of yin-yang, the Five Agents, and "watching the ethers," and some of this content has survived to the present day (for example, in chapters 8–10 of Li Quan's eighth-century military compendium, the *Taibai yinjing*, and in *Li Weigong wang Jiangnan*, an anonymous work first attested in the eleventh century). The following passage is representative of the genre:

> On the cyclical days *bing* or *ding*, if you encounter a barrier of black clouds, do not rely on the number of your troops or the courage of the general. It is appropriate to defend firmly and lead the army back; an offensive campaign will certainly meet with disaster.[102]

In both China and the Greco-Roman world, such ideas were regarded as powerful— and potentially manipulable—influences on soldiers' morale. The approach recommended by *Sunzi bingfa* is to ban unofficial prognostication that might give rise to doubts among the troops. In one of its passages, this most influential of all Chinese military texts urges the general to "prohibit talk of omens and banish doubts," advice that was echoed by Li Jing in the Tang dynasty, who called for the execution of anyone who might "shake the morale of the masses" with talk of ghosts, spirits, and inauspicious omens.[103] Some military leaders in the West agreed. When campaigning in Spain in 134 BCE, the Roman general Scipio Aemilianus expelled all the soothsayers from his camp in order to restore discipline.[104]

In both the Chinese and the Greco-Roman traditions, we also find considerable evidence of a more positive approach making rather cynical use of favorable omens to improve morale. With evident approval, Frontinus and Polyaenus offer numerous historical instances of propitious omens deliberately contrived. To name only one example, the fourth-century BCE Theban general Epaminondas sent his soldiers to make vows at the temple of Herakles after he had surreptitiously arranged for the priests to polish some rusty weapons and place them beside the god's statue. Taken as a sign of supernatural assistance, this greatly improved the morale of the Thebans, who then went on to defeat the Spartans.[105] The East Asian historical sources make it quite clear that, whatever Sunzi had said to the contrary, there were also Chinese generals who saw the advantage of this approach. When a Xiongnu army was advancing on the city of Xingyang in 317 CE, the local Jin commander, Li Ju, had prayers offered to the spirit of Zichan, an ancient statesman associated with the Xingyang area, and arranged for a shaman to announce Zichan's will to the Jin troops: if they attacked, they would receive supernatural assistance from "spirit soldiers." With this encouragement, Li Ju's men made a surprise attack on the enemy camp and inflicted a severe defeat on the Xiongnu.[106] Three hundred years later, the Sui general Wang Shichong made use of essentially the same ploy. Before leading his troops out of Luoyang to do battle with his rival Li Mi in the autumn of 618, Wang claimed that the Duke of Zhou, the revered leader who had played a key role in establishing both the Zhou dynasty and the city of Luoyang more than 1500 years earlier, had appeared to him in a dream. On this pretext, he established a shrine by the bank of the Luo River and had shamans announce the Duke's intention: if the soldiers went out to fight Li Mi they would certainly win great merit, but if they refused they would all die of a pestilence.[107] In this regard, the Chinese—both ancient and medieval—had more in common with Mediterranean antiquity than with the Byzantines, in whose armies Christian prayers and liturgies had supplanted the ancient omens and auspices.[108]

A more mundane aspect of the psychological manipulation of the soldiery was the awareness of both Chinese and Byzantine commanders that solicitous treatment of the wounded and the dead might have a positive effect on the morale of the troops and their willingness to fight. The ancient Chinese literature includes an anecdote telling how Wu Qi, a renowned general of the fifth century BCE, went so far as to suck the pus from his men's abscesses in order to win their loyalty and affection.[109] By the early years of the Tang dynasty, this concern for the soldiers had been thoroughly bureaucratized. According to Li Jing,

> In all cases when there are invalids in the encampments, in each encampment designate one officer to inspect the thick soups and porridges being fed to them and to lead them when the army is on the march. A comprehensive report on those men who have just fallen ill and those who have been lost to sickness is made to the commander every morning, and a medical man is ordered to make the rounds of the encampment with medicine to cure the sick. If the army sets out, it is the responsibility of the encampment master to provide officers to inspect the invalids. Those of the invalids who are judged to have the energy and strength to walk are provided with one man as an escort. If the case is serious and the man is not able to walk, one donkey is provided in addition. If he is not able to ride an animal, he is provided with two donkeys and two men as escorts and is brought along secured to a stretcher. If invalids are abandoned, or if there are those who are not gathered in or those who are not fed, the officer responsible for inspecting the invalids and the men escorting the invalids are each to receive one hundred blows of the heavy stick. If there are those who are buried before they are dead, [the inspecting officer and the escorts] are executed.[110]

Although it might not be possible to provide an animal sacrifice and the ritually prescribed inner and outer coffins, the fallen were to receive at least a decent burial:

> If a man dies in enemy territory, the libation is made with a single cup of wine, the grave is four feet deep, and his commanding officer sends men to wail by the grave. For a man who dies in the interior and not in enemy territory, the sacrifice and wailing are as previously described but [the body] is sent to [the man's registered] place of origin.[111]

The connection between these arrangements and the mood of the troops, implicit in these passages from Li Jing, is spelled out in the *Strategikon*: "After the battle the general should give prompt attention to the wounded and see to burying the dead. Not only is this a religious duty, but it greatly helps the morale of the living."[112]

The Tang Chinese and the Byzantines did not always agree, however, nor did they interpret their inherited traditions in quite the same way. A particular area of divergence is the set of related problems that the Chinese military classics identified as "deadly ground" (*si di*) and "the desperate bandit" (*qiong kou*). The underlying psychological presumption is that troops who have been surrounded or cut off with no hope escape are especially dangerous foes because they will fight with a reckless courage born of desperation. Hence, the *Sunzi bingfa* insists that desperate bandits must not be pressed; encircled enemies must be allowed a way out so they may choose flight over fight.[113] Li Jing repeated the same logic in the early Tang:

> If the enemy is in deadly ground, with no place to rely on to make himself secure, where his provisions are already used up, and relieving troops cannot reach him, he is called a 'desperate bandit'. . . . Deploy but do not accept battle – this is the method for defeating the enemy's plan.[114]

The idea of giving a cornered enemy a path of retreat is no less prominent in the classical Western tradition than in the Chinese; it is mentioned, in some cases repeatedly, by Frontinus, Onasander, Polyaenus, and Vegetius. According to Polyaenus, the Athenian general Iphicrates made a point of never pressing enemy forces too closely against rivers or narrow mountain passes, lest they be forced to fight out of desperation.[115] Frontinus, meanwhile, devotes an entire chapter of his *Strategems* to "Letting the Enemy Escape, Lest, Brought to Bay, He Renew the Battle in Desperation," with examples drawn from the careers of Hannibal, Pyrrhus of Epirus, and Gaius Julius Caesar: "When certain Germans whom Gaius Caesar had penned in fought the more fiercely from desperation, he ordered them to be allowed to escape, and then attacked them as they fled."[116] The idea carried over seamlessly into the Byzantine tradition, appearing in the *Strategikon*, in the anonymous treatise now thought to have been written by Syrianos in the ninth century, and in the tenth-century treatise "On Skirmishing" written at the behest of Nikephoros Phokas.[117]

A closely related stratagem, built on the same understanding of military psychology, is the deliberate deployment of one's own army in a position of no escape in order to unlock the same sort of primal ferocity. This gambit is perhaps most fully articulated in *Sunzi bingfa*: "Throw your forces into positions from which there is no outlet; there they may die, but they will not be put to rout. Since they are ready for death, the officers and men will exert themselves to the utmost."[118] One should fight if occupying such "deadly ground," and may expect to do so with a psychological advantage.[119] The stratagem of placing one's soldiers in a desperate situation—especially attractive if they were relatively poor soldiers—was employed repeatedly in Chinese history, most famously by Han Xin at the Jingxing

Pass in 205 BCE, when he deployed his inferior force with its back to a river in order to defeat a superior opponent holding the heights above.[120] Centuries later, Yuwen Tai of the Western Wei deployed his much smaller army backed up against the Wei River and managed to defeat his Eastern Wei rival, Gao Huan, at the battle of Shayuan in 537.[121] Although Li Jing neither mentions nor recommends this ploy in what survives of his "Military Methods," it was used with success during his lifetime—most notably by Wang Shichong against Li Mi at the Mang Hills outside Luoyang in the autumn of 618.[122] If a river was not available the same effect could be contrived by artificial means, as demonstrated by the tactics of the Sui general Yang Su, who was in the habit of executing the surviving members of units that failed to break through the enemy's battle line.[123]

As with the cross-cultural wisdom about avoiding a "desperate bandit," there is nothing uniquely Chinese about this approach. Numerous historical examples of battle plans based on the same psychological assumptions can be found in the Greek and Roman literature; this one is from Polyaenus:

> Clitarchus upon the advance of an enemy, lest he should be blocked up in the town, marched out his forces; then ordered the gates to be locked, and the keys thrown over the walls: which he took, and showed to his soldiers; who, finding all hopes of a retreat cut off, fought bravely, and their courage was crowned with success.[124]

Onasander, however, was less enthusiastic, and recommended its use only under very special circumstances:

> Generals who destroy their own defenses or cross rivers or who post their armies with steep cliffs or yawning gulfs in their rear in order that the soldiers may either stand and conquer or in their desire to escape be killed, I am not wholly able to praise nor yet to blame, for everything that is ventured rashly is rather the part of recklessness than of wisdom, and has a greater share of luck than of good judgement.

However,

> If the destruction of one's army is evident, except through the use of some daring strategy, and if the destruction of the enemy by defeat is also evident, then I do not think a general would be at fault in cutting off the retreat of his own army.[125]

The available evidence suggests that the Byzantines were even less interested in the exploitation of "deadly ground." The deliberate placing of soldiers in desperate situations is recommended in none of their surviving military treatises, and when Byzantine armies fought from such positions it was not by choice. In the winter of 503–504, an Eastern Roman army deployed with its back to the River Nymphius and defeated its Persian pursuers, but it chose to fight only because the river blocked its retreat.[126] It would seem that in Byzantine eyes such ploys were associated with barbarians and were regarded as likely to do more harm to their users than to their intended target. According to the early seventh-century historian Theophylact Simocatta, before the battle of Solachon in 586 the Persian commander ordered his men to destroy the skins they had filled with water, to make clear to them that they would either die of thirst or fight their way through the Byzantine battle line to drink from the River Arzamon. "Nor indeed did his boldness stand him in good stead, commented Theophylact, "for it is foolish, by trusting the dice of Fortune, to be confident at the heights of peril, and to glean favourable outcomes from previous errors."[127] As it happened, the Persians were defeated and suffered terribly from lack of water during their subsequent retreat. The Byzantines' lack of interest in "deadly ground" stratagems was probably due to their limited reserves of trained manpower and an understandable reluctance to squander that precious resource in risky ventures. The Chinese, with their generally less "professional" armies, had access to vastly greater manpower resources from which to make good any losses, and may also have been attracted to such schemes as a means of compelling indifferently trained and poorly motivated conscripts to fight.

Such divergences and discrepancies notwithstanding, the Chinese and Byzantine traditions had much in common. In both societies, the hard-earned lessons acquired from past experience were recorded in writing, handed down to later generations, and applied to the conduct of warfare. For the most part, these lessons pointed in the same direction. War was not to be welcomed, and it had to be approached with the greatest care and caution. In the conduct of war, the emphasis was on rational planning and foresight rather than heroic bravado. Deception and trickery were prized rather than despised, as were any and all devices that might give one an advantage over the enemy.

Thus far, Sui–Tang China and the Byzantine Empire have been compared as if they existed in complete isolation from one another, like New Kingdom Egypt and the Olmec of ancient Mexico. Yet this was not the case. The two occupied different parts of a landmass across (and around) which travel was possible and indeed is known to have taken place. The question thus arises, to what extent were these very similar ways of war shaped by exchange of knowledge and technique across the length of Asia? This problem will be taken up in the next chapter.

Notes

1 Chaim Herzog and Mordechai Gichon, *Battles of the Bible* (Toronto: Stoddart Publishing Company, 1997), p. 243; also see pp. 244–5. For a more modern example, there is the following from a nineteenth-century British cavalry officer:

> Men cannot stand ready under arms day and night to resist an attack; the wants of men and horses must be satisfied; they must have rest, or they cannot fulfil their duties; thus every position, of whatever kind it may be, is surrounded by a chain of guards to protect it from surprise, and to give rest and security to the occupants.
>
> (Captain L.E. Nolan, *Cavalry: Its History and Tactics*, 2nd edition (London: Thomas Bosworth, 1854), p. 266)

2 George T. Dennis (trans.), *Maurice's Strategikon: Handbook of Byzantine Military Strategy* (Philadelphia: University of Pennsylvania Press, 1984), p. 115.

3 *Strategikon*, p. 119.

4 Hugh Elton, *Warfare in Roman Europe, AD 350–425* (Oxford: Clarendon Press, 1996), p. 82; also see pp. 78–81.

5 Karl Leyser, "Early Medieval Warfare," in Janet Cooper (ed.), *The Battle of Maldon: Fiction and Fact* (London: The Hambledon Press, 1993), pp. 94–5 and 102.

6 Guy Halsall, *Warfare and Society in the Barbarian West, 450–900* (London and New York: Routledge, 2003), p. 160.

7 This is pointed out in Helen Nicholson, *Medieval Warfare: Theory and Practice of War in Europe, 300–1500* (Basingstoke, Hampshire: Palgrave Macmillan, 2004), p. 127. For more on the lack of tactical sophistication in the early medieval West, see Halsall, *Warfare and Society in the Barbarian West*, pp. 147, 194, and 206; and Philip Rance, "Narses and the Battle of Taginae (Busta Gallorum) 552: Procopius and Sixth-Century Warfare," *Historia* 54 (2005), pp. 457–8. Despite his valiant effort to make a case to the contrary, Bernard Bachrach is very much an outlier in the recent literature. See his *Early Carolingian Warfare: Prelude to Empire* (Philadelphia: University of Pennsylvania Press, 2001), p. 246 and *passim*.

8 Halsall, *Warfare and Society in the Barbarian West*, p. 159.

9 Walter E. Kaegi, "Byzantine Logistics: Problems and Perspectives," in John A. Lynn (ed.), *Feeding Mars: Logistics in Western Warfare from the Middle Ages to the Present* (Boulder, CO: Westview Press, 1993), p. 47.

10 See Jonathan Karam Skaff, *Sui–Tang China and Its Turko-Mongol Neighbors: Culture, Power, and Connections, 580–800* (New York: Oxford University Press, 2012), and just about anything written by Andrew Eisenberg.

11 *TD* 157, p. 4031.

12 *TD* 149, p. 3820.

13 *TD* 149, pp. 3820–1.

14 *TD* 149, p. 3815. Also see *TD* 149, p. 3821, which mentions the copying of documents at night.

15 Éric Trombert et al., *Les Manuscrits chinois de Koutcha: Fonds Pelliot de la Bibliothèque Nationale de France* (Paris: Institut des Hautes Études Chinoises du Collège de France, 2000). For the Turfan documents, see the classic study by Hibino Takeo, "Tōdai Ho-shō-fu bunsho no kenkyū," *Tōhō gakuhō* 33 (1963), pp. 267–314.

16 Michael Loewe, *Records of Han Administration* (London: Cambridge University Press, 1967), vol. 1, pp. 19–21.

17 *Strategikon*, pp. 78, 164; for mention of regulations, see pp. 16–19.

18 John Haldon, *Warfare, State and Society in the Byzantine World, 565–1204* (London: UCL Press, 1999), p. 262.

19 Warren Treadgold, *Byzantium and Its Army, 284–1081* (Stanford, CA: Stanford University Press, 1995), p. 91. It is perhaps also worth mentioning that the historian Procopius of Caesarea was serving Belisarius in a secretarial role when he accompanied him on his campaigns against the Vandals, Goths, and Persians; George Ostrogorsky, *History of the Byzantine State*, trans. Joan Hussey, rev. ed. (New Brunswick, NJ: Rutgers University Press, 1969), pp. 24–5.

20 Elton, *Warfare in Roman Europe*, p. 90. Southern and Dixon believe that, given the volume of paperwork and variety of matters dealt with, "the administrative sections of all but the smallest units were probably divided into subsections." Pat Southern and Karen Ramsey Dixon, *The Late Roman Army* (New Haven and London: Yale University Press, 1996), p. 64.

21 N.J.E. Austin and N.B. Rankov, *Exploratio: Military and Political Intelligence in the Roman World from the Second Punic War to the Battle of Adrianople* (London and New York: Routledge, 1995), p. 155. Austin and Rankov also note that the "paperwork

generated by the Roman army was vast" (p. 155) and that a governor may well have had "a record of every individual soldier serving in his province" (p. 156).

22 Robert O. Fink, *Roman Military Records on Papyrus* (Cleveland, OH: Case Western Reserve University, 1971), pp. 1–2, 18, 304–5, 332–3, and 343–4.

23 For the continuity of the Romano-Byzantine tradition of fortification, see Haldon, *Warfare, State and Society*, p. 249; and for siegecraft, see Denis Sullivan, "Tenth Century Byzantine Offensive Siege Warfare: Instructional Prescriptions and Historical Practice," in N. Oikonomidès (ed.), *Byzantium at War (9th–12th Century)* (Athens: Institute of Byzantine Research, 1997), p. 179. For continuity on the Chinese side, see Joseph Needham and Robin D.S. Yates, *Science and Civilisation in China*, vol. 5: *Chemistry and Chemical Technology*, part 6: *Military Technology: Missiles and Sieges* (Cambridge: Cambridge University Press, 1994). As noted in Chapter 4 above, there may have been some slippage in Byzantine poliorcetic techniques, such as the abandonment of torsion-powered engines.

24 Linghu Defen, *Zhou shu* (Beijing: Zhonghua shuju, 1971), ch. 19, p. 304; *ZZTJ* 157, p. 4884.

25 *TD* 157, pp. 4031–2. For more examples of parallels between Li Jing's recommendations and the record of sixth-century Chinese warfare, see David A. Graff, "Li Jing's Antecedents: Continuity and Change in the Pragmatics of Medieval Chinese Warfare," *Early Medieval China* 13–14, part 1 (2007), pp. 81–97.

26 Hans Bielenstein, *The Restoration of the Han Dynasty*, vol. 2: *The Civil War* (Stockholm: Museum of Far Eastern Antiquities, 1959), pp. 203, 206, 216–17, 219, and 223 (quote).

27 Graham Webster, *The Roman Imperial Army of the First and Second Centuries A.D.* (New York: Funk & Wagnalls, 1969), pp. 30–1, 222, 224, and 225; Karen R. Dixon and Pat Southern, *The Roman Cavalry: From the First to the Third Century AD* (London: B.T. Batsford Ltd., 1992), p. 23; Elton, *Warfare in Roman Europe*, pp. 244, 247, and 251; Austin and Rankov, *Exploratio*, p. 9.

28 *Vegetius: Epitome of Military Science*, trans. N. P. Milner (Liverpool: Liverpool University Press, 1993), pp. 23–4 and 73; also see pp. 46, 69–70, 79, 93, and 94. Vegetius must have written his book some time between 383 and 450 CE. The argument for a date of composition in the 380s is presented by Milner in *Vegetius: Epitome of Military Science*, pp. xxv ff.

29 *Vegetius: Epitome of Military Science*, p. 90; also see pp. 49–50 and 107.

30 *Vegetius: Epitome of Military Science*, p. 108; cf. *Strategikon*, p. 83.

31 Eric McGeer, *Sowing the Dragon's Teeth: Byzantine Warfare in the Tenth Century* (Washington, DC: Dumbarton Oaks, 1995), p. 192.

32 Aineias the Tactician, *How to Survive Under Siege: A Historical Commentary, with Translation and Introduction*, trans. David Whitehead, second ed. (London: Bristol Classical Press, 2001), pp. 10–12.

33 Alphonse Dain, "Les Stratégistes byzantins," *Travaux et Mémoires* 2 (1967), p. 319.

34 Salvatore Cosentino, "The Syrianos's 'Strategikon': A Ninth Century Source?" *Bizantinistica: Rivista di studi bizantini e slavi*, n.s. 2 (2000), p. 262.

35 McGeer, *Sowing the Dragon's Teeth*, p. 281.

36 Dain, "Les Stratégistes byzantins," p. 356; McGeer, *Sowing the Dragon's Teeth*, p. 283. For a thorough examination of this aspect of the work, see John Haldon, *A Critical Commentary on the Taktika of Leo VI* (Washington, DC: Dumbarton Oaks, 2014).

37 Aineias, *How to Survive Under Siege*, pp. 78–9.

38 McGeer, *Sowing the Dragon's Teeth*, pp. 188 and 192.

39 Walter E. Kaegi, *Heraclius: Emperor of Byzantium* (Cambridge: Cambridge University Press, 2003), p. 130; also see p. 309 and *passim*. For Constantine Porphyrogenitus, see John F. Haldon (ed. and trans.), *Constantine Porphyrogenitus, Three Treatises on Imperial Military Expeditions* (Vienna: Verlag der Österreichischen Akademie der Wissenschaften, 1990), p. C-107.

40 Haldon, *Warfare, State and Society*, p. 276.
41 *SS* 34, p. 1017. The bibliographical monograph of the *Jiu Tangshu*, based on a cata-logue of the imperial library compiled in 721, lists only 45 works (in 289 *juan*) in the military section (*JTS* 47, pp. 2039–41). This is in part due to reclassification (books on strategic games, such as *weiqi*, are no longer classified as military works in the *Jiu Tang shu*), but many of the books in the Sui imperial library were surely lost in the chaos of the Sui–Tang transition (see, for example, *SS* 32, p. 908). The bibliographi-cal monograph of the *Xin Tangshu* lists sixty works by twenty-three authors in 319 *juan* (*XTS* 59, p. 1552).
42 Wei Zheng, *Qun shu zhi yao*, in *Lianyunyi congshu* (Rpt. Taipei: Yiwen yinshuguan, 1966).
43 Ouyang Xun, *Yiwen leiju* (Shanghai: Zhonghua shuju, 1965), ch. 59, pp. 1058–9, 1063, and 1064, and ch. 60, pp. 1082, 1088, and 1090–1; *TD* 148, 3784–6, and 3792; 149, pp. 3808 and 3810; and 159, p. 4075.
44 See Deng Zezong, *Li Jing bingfa jiben zhuyi* (Beijing: Jiefangjun chubanshe, 1990), pp. 2, 5, 16, and 31–2.
45 There has been an enormous amount of writing (and argument) concerning the dating of the early Chinese military texts. From Song to Qing times, quite a few scholars chal-lenged the authenticity of these books, arguing on philological grounds that they were forgeries dating from the period between Han and Tang; for examples of their reasoning, see the opinions on the *Liu tao* collected in Zhang Xincheng, *Weishu tongkao* (Shanghai: Commercial Press, 1954), pp. 793–6. With regard to *Sunzi bingfa*, *Liu tao*, and *Wei Liaozi*, these doubts were largely laid to rest by the discovery (in 1972) of materials very close to today's versions in an early Western Han tomb at Yinqueshan, near Linyi in Shandong (see Xu Di, "Lüe tan Linyi Yinqueshan Han mu chutu de gudai bingshu canjian," *Wenwu* 1974, no. 2, pp. 27–31). The ages of *Wuzi* and *Sima fa* have not been confirmed archaeologically, but most modern opinion holds that they, too, are of pre-Qin date; see Li Xunxiang, *Xian Qin de bingjia* (Taipei: National Taiwan University, 1991), pp. 11–12; Xu Baolin, *Zhongguo bingshu tonglan* (Beijing: Jiefangjun chubanshe, 1990), pp. 101 and 105; and Ralph D. Sawyer, *The Seven Military Classics of Ancient China* (Boulder, CO: Westview Press, 1993), pp. 115, 192, and 453–5, note 4. For the arguments that place *San lüe* in late Western Han, see Xu Baolin, p. 125, and Sawyer, pp. 283–4. Much ink has been spilled over the dating of *Sunzi bingfa*, with many schol-ars now assigning it to the fifth century BCE while others are more comfortable with a fourth-century date. For a summary of the various views, see Sawyer, pp. 150–1. More recently, E. Bruce Brooks has argued that the creation of the text was a gradual process that extended from *c.*345 BCE to *c.*272 BCE; see Victor Mair (trans.), *The Art of War: Sun Zi's Military Methods* (New York: Columbia University Press, 2007), pp. 67–8, note 56.
46 The *Sui shu* bibliography lists at least two and possibly as many as four editions of *Sunzi bingfa* (*SS* 34, p. 1012); its *Jiu Tangshu* counterpart has three editions, more than any other military text (*JTS* 47, p. 2039). The *Xin Tangshu* lists no less than seven separate commentaries on *Sunzi bingfa*, while its nearest competitor, *Wuzi*, has only two (*XTS* 59, pp. 1549–51). Also see Li Zhen, *Zhongguo junshi jiaoyu shi* (Taipei: Zhongyang wenwu gongying she, 1983), pp. 293 and 300. For an example of a general quoting Sunzi, see *ZZTJ* 198, p. 6228.
47 *Sunzi bingfa* was long thought to have been put into its present form by its earliest commentator, Cao Cao (155–220 CE). The text found in the Western Han tomb at Yinqueshan in 1972 is so close to the transmitted version, however, that Cao was evi-dently not a heavy-handed redactor. See Roger T. Ames, *Sun-tzu: The Art of Warfare* (New York: Ballantine Books, 1993), p. 270, and Sawyer, *Seven Military Classics*, pp. 422–3, note 11.
48 See Zhou Fengwu, "Dunhuang Tang xieben *Liu tao* canjuan jiaokanji," in *Diyijie guoji Tangdai xueshu huiyi lunwenji* (Taipei: Zhonghua minguo Tangdai xuezhe lianyihui, 1989), pp. 346–71.

49 For example, see Mark Edward Lewis, *Sanctioned Violence in Early China* (Albany: State University of New York Press, 1990), pp. 125, 130; and Liu Hongzhang, "*Liu tao chutan*," *Zhongguo zhexue shi yanjiu* 1985, no. 2 (April 1985), p. 53.

50 See Zhang Lie's comments in Cheng Liangshu (ed.), *Xu Weishu tongkao* (Taipei: Taiwan xuesheng shuju, 1984), p. 1597. The Song scholar Ye Shi saw parts of the *Liu tao* as an explication of some of the more abstruse concepts of *Sunzi bingfa* (see Zhang, *Weishu tongkao*, p. 793); a modern scholar, Liu Hongzhang, takes a similar view ("*Liu tao chutan*," p. 55). Also see Li Xunxiang, *Xian Qin de bingjia*, p. 223.

51 For a discussion of some of the similarities and differences in emphasis among the early military texts, see Li Xunxiang, *Xian Qin de bingjia*, pp. 154–5, 157–8, 160, 164–5, and 168.

52 James Legge, *The Chinese Classics*, vol. 5: *The Ch'un Ts'ew, with the Tso Chuen* (rpt. Taipei: Southern Materials Center, 1985), pp. 733 and 735. This passage would seem to lie behind the sixteen-character formula that Mao Zedong offered in his "Problems of Strategy in China's Revolutionary War" (1936), which borrows heavily from the *Zuo zhuan*; see *Selected Military Writings of Mao Tse-tung* (Beijing: Foreign Languages Press, 1967), p. 111. The "military" passages of the *Zuo zhuan* are conveniently excerpted in *Zuo shi bingfa qian shuo*, edited by Wang Zhiping and Wu Minxia (Beijing: Haichao chubanshe, 1992).

53 David McMullen, *State and Scholars in Tang China* (Cambridge: Cambridge University Press, 1988), p. 159; also see pp. 160 and 163.

54 For Li Shimin, see *CFYG* 454, p. 6b, and *ZZTJ* 189, p. 5915; for Li Jing, see *XTS* 93, p. 3811, and Li Zhen, *Zhongguo junshi jiaoyu shi*, p. 305.

55 *THY* 36, p. 667; *ZZTJ* 213, p. 6794. The *Zizhi tongjian* has the *Spring and Autumn Annals* (*Chun Qiu*) being presented instead of the *Zuo zhuan*; probably the two were presented together, as the latter was considered to be a commentary on the former. McMullen (*State and Scholars*, p. 79) points out that when the Tang histories praise military men for their mastery of Confucian texts, the specific book mentioned is always the *Zuo zhuan*.

56 This problem is addressed at length in David A. Graff, "Early T'ang Generalship and the Textual Tradition" (Ph.D. diss., Princeton University, 1995); see especially pp. 424–41 (for Li Shimin) and pp. 510–27 (for Li Jing).

57 For Wang Shichong, see Graff, "Early T'ang Generalship and the Textual Tradition," pp. 317–30. For Li Su, see Charles A. Peterson, "Regional Defense Against the Central Power: The Huai-hsi Campaign, 815–817," in Frank A. Kierman, Jr. and John King Fairbank (eds.), *Chinese Ways in Warfare* (Cambridge, MA: Harvard University Press, 1974), pp. 143–4.

58 Arthur F. Wright, *The Sui Dynasty* (New York: Alfred A. Knopf, 1978), p. 64.

59 *THY* 59, p. 1029; and Terrence Douglas O'Byrne, "Civil–Military Relations During the Middle T'ang: The Career of Kuo Tzu-i" (Ph.D. diss., University of Illinois at Urbana-Champaign, 1982), pp. 20–1, 22–5, and 27.

60 Wallace Johnson (trans.), *The Tang Code*, vol. 2: *Specific Articles* (Princeton, NJ: Princeton University Press, 1997), pp. 78–9 (Article 110). For Sui, see the biography of Wu Shihuo in *JTS* 58, pp. 2316–17.

61 For example, in 618 when Li Mi confronted Wang Shichong east of Luoyang, some of Li's generals demanded that he give battle on the grounds that "Military Methods" held that when outnumbering the enemy by a two-to-one ratio one should fight. This was a misquotation or distortion of Sunzi, who held that one should divide the enemy (or possibly, one's own army) when twice his strength, but one that was already attested in Han times. See *ZZTJ* 186, p. 5810; *SJ* 92, p. 2615; *The Art of War* (trans. Mair), ch. 3, p. 86; Guo Huaruo (ed.), *Shiyi jia zhu Sunzi* (Shanghai: Zhonghua shuju, 1962), pp. 42–3. Note, however, that one prominent authority has argued that the seeming misquotation is actually the authentic reading of the original *Sunzi* text; see Wu Jiulong (ed.), *Sunzi jiaoshi* (Beijing: Junshi kexue chubanshe, 1990), pp. 42–3.

62 Halsall, *Warfare and Society in the Barbarian West*, p. 145; also see Timothy Reuter, "Carolingian and Ottonian Warfare," in Maurice Keen, ed., *Medieval Warfare: A History* (Oxford: Oxford University Press, 1999), p. 19, and Nicholson, *Medieval Warfare*, p. 14. Bernard S. Bachrach has asserted the contrary, as in his "*Caballus et Caballarius* in Medieval Warfare," collected in *Warfare and Military Organization in Pre-Crusade Europe* (Aldershot, Hampshire: Ashgate, 2002), p. 186, but does not present a convincing case.

63 See Timothy S. Miller's introduction to *Peace and War in Byzantium: Essays in Honor of George T. Dennis, S.J.*, edited by Timothy S. Miller and John Nesbitt (Washington, DC: The Catholic University of America Press, 1995), pp. 5–8.

64 Sunzi's chapter 1, in *Shiyi jia zhu Sunzi*, p. 1, and *Sunzi jiaoshi*, p. 2. I have adopted Sawyer's translation with minor modification; see *The Seven Military Classics*, p. 157.

65 *Daodejing*, chapter 31; see *Tao Te Ching*, trans. D.C. Lau (Harmondsworth, UK: Penguin, 1985), p. 89; *Liu tao*, sec. 16 (*Bing dao*), in *Taigong Liu tao jin zhu jin yi*, trans. and ann. Xu Peigen, 2nd rev. ed. (Taipei: Taiwan Shangwu yinshuguan, 1986), p. 96; Zhao Rui, *Chang duan jing* (*c*.716 CE), in *Zhongguo bingshu jicheng*, vol. 2 (Beijing and Shenyang: Jiefangjun chubanshe and Liao-Shen shushe, 1988), p. 941.

66 "The Anonymous Byzantine Treatise on Strategy," in George T. Dennis (trans.), *Three Byzantine Military Treatises* (Washington, DC: Dumbarton Oaks, 1985), p. 21. This work is now thought to date from the ninth century CE.

67 For the Byzantines, see Edward N. Luttwak, *The Grand Strategy of the Byzantine Empire* (Cambridge, MA: The Belknap Press of Harvard University Press, 2009), pp. 5, 52, 55, 92–3, and 112 (however, Luttwak sees this as a relatively recent development that differentiated the Byzantines from the Romans). For a sense of the Chinese experience, see Yü Ying-shih's chapter on "Han Foreign Relations," in *The Cambridge History of China*, vol. 1: *The Ch'in and Han Empires, 221 B.C.-A.D. 220*, ed. Denis Twitchett and Michael Loewe (Cambridge: Cambridge University Press, 1986), pp. 377–462.

68 *Strategikon*, p. 88; also see p. 9 and pp. 79–80.

69 *Strategikon*, pp. 83 and 64.

70 *The Art of War* (trans. Mair), chapter 1, pp. 76–9; *Shiyi jia zhu Sunzi*, pp. 1–20.

71 *TD* 150, pp. 3841–2; also see *TD* 151, pp. 3862–3.

72 *Strategikon*, p. 65; also see p. 91. This material resonates well with several speeches that Procopius attributes to Belisarius and others; see his *History of the Wars*, trans. H. B. Dewing (London: William Heinemann Ltd., 1954), vol. 1, pp. 155, 165, and 421.

73 *Strategikon*, p. 23; *The Art of War* (trans. Mair), ch. 3, p. 85; *Shiyi jia zhu Sunzi*, p. 34.

74 Kaegi, *Some Thoughts on Byzantine Military Strategy*, p. 12.

75 Lisa Raphals, *Knowing Words: Wisdom and Cunning in the Classical Traditions of China and Greece* (Ithaca and London: Cornell University Press, 1992), pp. xi–xii.

76 Peter Krentz, "Deception in Archaic and Classical Greek Warfare," in Hans van Wees (ed.), *War and Violence in Ancient Greece* (London and Swansea: Duckworth and the Classical Press of Wales, 2000), pp. 183–99.

77 Hans van Wees, *Greek Warfare: Myths and Realities* (London: Gerald Duckworth & Co. Ltd., 2004), pp. 131 and 133.

78 Everett L. Wheeler, *Stratagem and the Vocabulary of Military Trickery* (Leiden: E.J. Brill, 1988), pp. 16, 24, 102, and 110.

79 *Strategikon*, pp. 80–3, 89.

80 *The Art of War* (trans. Mair), chapter 1, p. 78; *Shiyi jia zhu Sunzi*, p. 12.

81 Sawyer, *The Seven Military Classics of Ancient China*, p. 56; Chinese text in *Taigong Liu tao jin zhu jin yi*, pp. 88–90.

82 For a more detailed examination of this problem, see David A. Graff, "Narrative Maneuvers: The Representation of Battle in Tang Historical Writing," in Nicola Di Cosmo (ed.), *Military Culture in Imperial China* (Cambridge, MA: Harvard University Press 2009), pp. 141–64.

83 *XTS* 84, p. 3684. The original source for this anecdote is probably the now lost *Huguan lu*; see Sima Guang's comments in *ZZTJ* 186, p. 5811. As I discuss in detail in "Early T'ang Generalship and the Textual Tradition" (pp. 307–12) there are reasons for doubting the authenticity of this story.

84 Wheeler, *Stratagem and the Vocabulary of Military Trickery*, pp. x–xi.

85 *TD* 153, p. 3914. Also see Harro von Senger, *The Book of Stratagems* (New York: Viking Penguin, 1991), pp. 75–7; *The Art of War* (trans. Mair), chapter 6, pp. 96–7.

86 Polyaenus, *Stratagems of War*, trans. R. Shepherd (rpt. Chicago: Ares Publishers, 1974), p. 102.

87 Polyaenus, *Stratagems of War*, pp. 95–6.

88 Senger, *The Book of Stratagems*, pp. 33–7. The pithy four-character expression was not coined until the Ming dynasty.

89 *SJ* 65, pp. 2163–4, translated in Ssu-ma Ch'ien, *The Grand Scribe's Records*, ed. William H. Nienhauser, vol. 7: *The Memoirs of Pre-Han China* (Bloomington and Indianapolis: Indiana University Press, 1994), pp. 39–41.

90 *SJ* 65, p. 2164, translated in *The Grand Scribe's Records*, vol. 7, pp. 40–1.

91 *TD* 150, pp. 3840–1; *Aeneas Tacticus, Asclepiodotus, Onasander* (London: William Heinemann, 1923), p. 419; *Strategikon*, p. 81.

92 Frontinus also mentions an earlier Greek example of the same situation, which is repeated by Polyaenus. See Frontinus, *Stratagems*, pp. 21, 23; Polyaenus, *Stratagems of War*, p. 92.

93 *The Art of War* (trans. Mair), chapter 9, p. 110; *Shiyi jia zhu Sunzi*, p. 153.

94 *Aeneas Tacticus, Asclepiodotus, Onasander*, p. 463.

95 Frontinus, *Stratagems*, p. 129.

96 McGeer, *Sowing the Dragon's Teeth*, pp. 307–8. McGeer is speaking of the Byzantines and their opponents, but the general point can be applied to medieval Chinese armies as well.

97 *The Art of War* (trans. Mair), chapter 5, p. 94; *Shiyi jia zhu Sunzi*, p. 79.

98 *Strategikon*, p. 83; *The Art of War* (trans. Mair), chapter 11, pp. 117–18; *Shiyi jia zhu Sunzi*, p. 181–9.

99 *Strategikon*, pp. 107–8; *Three Treatises*, pp. 157–9; *The Art of War* (trans. Mair), chapter 7, p. 103. For Chinese text, *Shiyi jia zhu Sunzi*, pp. 119–31.

100 Polyaenus, *Stratagems of War*, p. 126; *The Art of War* (trans. Mair), chapter 6, p. 95; *Shiyi jia zhu Sunzi*, pp. 82–3; *TD* 154, pp. 3954–5; *TD* 158, pp. 4061–2.

101 *Aeneas Tacticus, Asclepiodotus, Onasander*, pp. 393–5 and 429.

102 *Li Weigong wang Jiangnan* (Taipei: Xin wenfeng chuban gongsi, 1990), 1.38.

103 *TD* 149, p. 3823; *The Art of War* (trans. Mair), chapter 11, p. 120; *Shiyi jia zhu Sunzi*, p. 195.

104 Harry Sidebottom, *Ancient Warfare: A Very Short Introduction* (Oxford: Oxford University Press, 2004), p. 78.

105 Polyaenus, *Stratagems of War*, p. 67; other examples can be found on pp. 59, 68–9, 180–1, and 331. Also see Frontinus, *Stratagems*, pp. 75–9.

106 *JS* 5, p. 131; and *JS* 63, p. 1707.

107 This episode can be found in *SS* 85, p. 1897, and *TD* 156, p. 4016. A more complex and probably later version is in *XTS* 85, p. 3692, and *ZZTJ* 186, p. 5809.

108 For the role of religion in the Byzantine military, see Paul Goubert, "Religion et superstitions dan l'armée byzantine à la fin du VIe siècle," *Orientalia Christiana Periodica* 13 (1947), pp. 495–500.

109 This story is in the *Shi ji* biography of Wu Qi, *SJ* 65, p. 2166. For an English translation, see *The Grand Scribe's Records*, vol. 7, p. 42.

110 *TD* 149, pp. 3819–20.

111 *TD* 149, p. 3820.

112 *Strategikon*, p. 70; also see p. 86.

113 *The Art of War* (trans. Mair), chapter 7, p. 104; *Shiyi jia zhu Sunzi*, pp. 128–31.

114 *TD* 159, p. 4087.
115 *Aeneas Tacticus, Asclepiodotus, Onasander*, p. 101.
116 Frontinus, *Stratagems*, pp. 165–9; the quotation about Caesar is from p. 167.
117 *Strategikon*, pp. 81 and 91; "The Anonymous Byzantine Treatise on Strategy," pp. 107 and 119, and "Skirmishing," p. 235, both in Dennis, *Three Byzantine Military Treatises*.
118 *The Art of War* (trans. Mair), chapter 11, pp. 119–20; *Shiyi jia zhu Sunzi*, p. 194.
119 *The Art of War* (trans. Mair), chapter 8, p. 105 (also see chapter 11, pp. 122, 124); *Shiyi jia zhu Sunzi*, pp. 133, 204–5, and 209.
120 Frank A. Kierman, Jr., "Phases and Modes of Combat in Early China," in Kierman and Fairbank, *Chinese Ways in Warfare*, especially pp. 56–62.
121 *ZZTJ* 157, pp. 4884–6; David A. Graff, *Medieval Chinese Warfare, 300–900* (London and New York: Routledge, 2002), p. 107.
122 This battle is described in *ZZTJ* 186, pp. 5810–11; *SS* 70, p. 1632, and *SS* 85, p. 1897; and in Graff, "Early T'ang Generalship and the Textual Tradition," pp. 289–317.
123 *ZZTJ* 177, p. 5532. Also see Chapter 3 above.
124 Polyaenus, *Stratagems of War*, p. 215 (with spelling modernized).
125 *Aeneas Tacticus, Asclepiodotus, Onasander*, pp. 475 and 477.
126 Geoffrey Greatrex, *Rome and Persia at War, 502–532* (Leeds: Francis Cairns, 1998), p. 110.
127 Theophylactus Simocatta, *The History of Theophylact Simocatta*, trans. Michael and Mary Whitby (Oxford: Clarendon Press, 1986), p. 49.

6   Contacts and influences

Between China and the Mediterranean world were over 4,000 miles of mountains, deserts, and sparsely populated grasslands. The Roman Empire and its Byzantine continuation never shared a contiguous land frontier with any Chinese territory. The intervening space was occupied by several long-established sedentary states (most notably Persia, under Sasanid rule from the third century CE to the Arab conquest of the mid-seventh century) and by pastoral, nomadic peoples such as the Türks, whose rulers dominated the steppelands of both eastern and western Eurasia at the beginning of the seventh century. Communications were tenuous and intermittent at best, and political contact between the two realms, Roman and Chinese, was extremely rare (if, indeed, it occurred at all). Yet some transmission of goods and knowledge did take place, even if the contacts were haphazard and heavily reliant upon a variety of intermediaries. Limited quantities of merchandise moved between east and west along the shifting networks of tracks that modern scholars have labeled the Silk Road, with Chinese silks appearing in the Roman world by the second century CE at the latest and Mediterranean glassware occasionally making its way to China where it was highly prized.[1] Ideas also moved along the trade routes. The spread of Buddhism from South Asia to China by way of the oases of Central Asia has been well studied and documented, and it has been suggested that, moving in another direction, Buddhist and other Indian practices influenced early Christian eremitism. Trade and proselytism operated not only overland, but also by sea. A network of oceanic trade routes linked Roman Egypt to India, and India to China via the Straits of Melaka and the South China Sea. When a man claiming to be a Roman ambassador arrived at the Later Han court in 166 CE, he came by way of Rinan (today's central Vietnam) in the far south of the Chinese empire.[2]

Historians today believe that he was more likely an enterprising Levantine merchant seeking entrée to the Chinese court than an authorized representative of the Emperor "Andun" (presumably either Antoninus Pius or his successor, Marcus Aurelius Antoninus).[3] In the centuries that followed, Chinese sources recorded the appearance of other Roman envoys and tribute-bearers. A Roman ambassador was reported at the Jin court in 285, and seven embassies from Byzantium are recorded during the Tang period, in 643, 667, 701, 711, 719 (twice), and 742.[4] In the absence of corroborating evidence from the Byzantine side, it is impossible to determine whether these were properly accredited emissaries or imposters.

Two of the envoys were monks (in 719 and 742), and one was a chieftain of the Tukhara (Tuhuoluo) state in the Oxus valley who claimed that he had been asked by the Byzantine emperor to present two lions and two antelopes to the Tang court. In 643, the tribute had included red glass among other items. China's rulers showed less interest in reaching out to make contact with Byzantium: in the early seventh century Emperor Yang of the Sui dynasty did send one ambassador to Constantinople, but he never succeeded in reaching his destination and there was no sequel.[5]

In the century before the founding of the Tang dynasty, Byzantine sources show an interest not in diplomatic contact with China but in access to that country's signature export, silk. The trade routes that brought Chinese silk to the Mediterranean world either passed through Sasanian territory or were dominated by Persian merchants, including the seaborne trade centered upon the Indian Ocean entrepôt of Taprobane (Ceylon), thus giving the Persians considerable economic leverage in their conflicts with Byzantium.[6] Around the middle of the sixth century, Emperor Justinian reportedly commissioned a group of monks (probably Nestorian Christians from Persia) to procure silkworm eggs from the land of "Serindia" (probably Sogdiana in Central Asia), with the result that the Byzantines were able to establish their own domestic silk industry.[7]

In the sixth and seventh centuries China and Byzantium were aware of one another's existence, but were generally rather vague (or simply wrong) about the details. The Chinese referred to the Roman Empire—or the portion of it that they were aware of—as Da Qin, with the notion that it was a sort of doppelganger of China beyond the Western Ocean, and brief accounts of this mysterious realm can be found in the chapters on foreign peoples in historical works such as the *Hou Han shu, Jin shu, Wei shu*, and *Tong dian*.[8] In Tang times, the Byzantine realm began to be called Fulin by the Chinese, a name thought to derive from its capital, Byzantium.[9] The *Jiu Tang shu*, completed in the 940s, contains a section on Fulin that incorporates much of the earlier Da Qin material.[10] It correctly locates the empire to the northwest of Persia and includes some reasonably accurate information about Constantinople, which we are told is a city built of stone with a population of more than 100,000 households. The sea is to city's south, and there is a great gate in the eastern wall more than twenty *zhang* (or about 200 feet) in height and completely covered with gold—recognizable as Constantinople's Golden Gate, which was in fact coated with bronze and probably closer to forty feet high.[11] An Arab siege of the city (perhaps that of the 670s) is also mentioned, and material is repeated from the Da Qin accounts to the effect that there is no "fixed" king, but rather one of the "worthies" is chosen and installed on the throne. This has a certain rough-and-ready accuracy with regard to the Byzantines' relative disregard for dynastic principles, but completely misses the violence that so often accompanied the transfer of power from one ruler to the next. The claim that emperors were removed and replaced when there were natural disasters is even less accurate (political and military disasters would have been closer to the mark), and some of the information provided—such as the story of the emperor's poison-detecting bird—may be dismissed as tall tales.

Byzantine sources have less to say about China, but the early seventh-century historian Theophylact Simocatta did devote a paragraph to the affairs of "Taugast," whose people "rear silkworms and excel in sericulture."[12] He relates that the country is divided by a river that once formed the boundary between two states, with the people wearing black clothing in one and red in the other, but during the reign of the Byzantine emperor Maurikios (582–602) the black coats crossed the river and conquered the whole empire. Theophylact's "Taugast" may be equated with Tagbach, the clan name of the Northern Wei rulers (and their Eastern and Western Wei successors in the sixth century), and the great sinologist Peter Boodberg has presented a convincing argument that the cross-river conquest refers not to the Sui dynasty's subjugation of the Chen state south of the Yangzi in 589, as might at first seem to be the case, but rather to Northern Zhou's conquest of Northern Qi across the Yellow River in 577. Boodberg adduces considerable evidence from Chinese sources that the colors black and red were associated with Northern Zhou and Northern Qi, respectively, and also notes that Theophylact's statement about the Taugast ruler having 700 female attendants is confirmed by material found in the Chinese dynastic histories. He concludes that the Byzantine historian presents "an amazingly accurate description of northern China at the close of the sixth century," but one acquired at second hand by way of the nomadic Türks, who were in contact with both Chinese states and with Byzantium, and dating from late 579 or early 580.[13]

Underlining the extent to which the Byzantines depended on intermediaries for their knowledge of China, Theophylact's account of the events in Taugast appears as a brief digression embedded within a more extensive narrative of Byzantine diplomatic relations with the Western Türks. In Chinese sources, the Türks first appear as metal-working vassals of the Rouran steppe empire, which dominated the pastoral peoples living to the north of China for most of the fifth century and the first half of the sixth century. In 552 the Türks, led by the brothers Bumin and Ishtemi, overthrew their Rouran masters and very quickly established their own dominance over the peoples of both the eastern and western steppes. For administrative convenience, the new Türk empire was soon divided into four regions: center, east, west, and western frontier. Political seniority belonged initially to the central ruler in the Altai and today's Mongolia, a role which fell to Bumin's son Muhan (r. 552–573), while the west was controlled by Muhan's uncle Ishtemi. During the early 580s, however, rivalries and infighting among the second-generation descendants of Bumin—and between them and Ishtemi's heir Tardu— resulted in a lasting division of the Türks into independent eastern and western qaghanates.[14]

The first recorded contact between the Türks and Byzantium occurred in 563, when a certain "Askel" (or Axijie), a lesser chieftain of the Western Türks, sent a mission to Constantinople. This demarche was followed by the more consequential visit of a second embassy in 568, this time dispatched by another, more powerful Türk leader (identified in the Byzantine sources as "Silziboulos") and led by a Sogdian merchant named Maniakh.[15] It seems that a major purpose of this mission was to open the direct trade of silk from the Türk empire to Byzantium, bypassing the Persian middleman, but ground was also found for strategic coop-eration against the Sasanian empire and other common foes (most notably the Avars, about whom more will be said later). The following year, when Maniakh returned to the Türks, he was accompanied by a Byzantine embassy led by the general Zemarchus, who brought another Türk ambassador back with him when he returned to Constantinople. Embassies continued to be exchanged on an almost annual basis over the next several years. Relations could be stormy, as in 576 when "Turxanth" (apparently a lesser ruler under Tardu) ordered an attack on a Byzantine city in the Crimea because of Byzantine dealings with the Avars, but the two empires did manage to cooperate effectively against the Persians from time to time. The high point of this cooperation came in 626 and 627, when the Western Türk qaghan Tong Yabghu sent forces that provided vital assistance to Herakleios during his operations against the Persians in the Caucasus region.[16]

The arrival of the Türks was only the latest iteration of a scenario that was already familiar to the Byzantines. When the Romans had first pushed their fron-tiers as far as the lower Danube and the edge of the Pontic steppe on the north side of the Black Sea, they encountered various groupings of Iranian nomads who had inhabited the region for centuries. Those who made the greatest impression on them were the militarily powerful Sarmatians and Alans, many of whom were eventually recruited into Roman military service. Beginning in the second half of the fourth century CE, these groups were defeated and subjugated by a new wave of pastoral nomads from the east, the Huns. After pushing various other peoples such as the Goths against the Roman frontiers on the Danube, the Huns came into direct contact with the empire in 395 when they raided across the Caucasus into northern Syria. In 408 the Huns themselves appeared along the Danube, raiding into Dacia and Thrace, and by 425 at the latest had established themselves in the Pannonian Basin west of the Carpathian Mountains (in today's Hungary).[17] Unified under the leadership of Attila, the Huns attacked along the Danube repeatedly between 441 and 447, taking the towns of Noviodunum, Viminacium, Naissus, Sirmium, and Ratiara and raiding almost as far as Constantinople itself; the emperor Theodosius II responded by building the Long Walls to screen the environs of the capital in southeastern Thrace.[18] Following the breakup of the Hun polity in the aftermath of Attila's death in 453, raids continued to be carried out by various steppe groupings including both Hun remnants and newcomers from the east, especially the various Oghuric tribes. The (probably) Turkic Bulgars raided Thrace in 493, Illyricum in 498, and Macedonia in 517, the Caucasian Huns attacked Armenia in 541, and the Kutrigurs joined with Bulgars and Slavs to raid the Balkans during the 550s.[19]

Hard on their heels came a new wave of invaders from the east, the most threat-ening since the onset of the Huns. These were the Avars, who first appeared on the Pontic steppe (in today's Ukraine) during the 550s and were in contact with the Byzantines on the Danube frontier by 558 or 559. In the course of their east-ward migration they subjugated many of the Kutrigurs and Bulgars and may have driven others ahead of them into imperial territories in the Balkans.[20] The emperor Justinian provided their *chagan* (or qaghan) Bayan with gifts and subsidies but

managed to avoid conceding any imperial territory. His successor, Justin II
(r. 565–574) terminated the subsidies, and in 567 the Avars moved northwest into
the Pannonian Basin at the invitation of Alboin, king of the Lombards, to assist
him in eliminating the Gepids, who had dominated the region since the collapse of
Attila's empire. The migration of the Lombards into northern Italy in 568 then left
the Avars in sole control of this small but fertile western outlier of the Eurasian
steppe. From their new base they began to wage war against the imperial territories in the Balkans, sending thousands of their vassal Kutrigurs to invade Dalmatia
in 568. After a serious defeat in 574, a new emperor, Tiberius, made peace by
agreeing to pay the Avars an annual subsidy of 80,000 gold pieces. For the next
few years the Avars actually assisted imperial operations against the Slav tribes,
but in 580 war erupted over control of the Byzantine-held city of Sirmium on the
Danube, which Bayan coveted as an addition to his new realm.[21] The city eventually fell in 582, and from then on conflict between the Avars and Byzantines was
almost incessant, with major invasions of imperial territory recorded in 583, 586,
588, 595, and 597.[22] Byzantine forces sometimes gained the upper hand and campaigned north of the Danube (as in 599–600), but the overthrow of Maurikios and
the outbreak of war with Persia left the Balkans largely unprotected against the
inroads of the Avars and their Slav allies. Probably in 619, they came very close to
capturing the emperor Herakleios outside the walls of Constantinople, and in the
summer of 626 they returned to besiege the city in coordination with the Persians.
The failure of this siege was followed by a rapid decline of Avar power, the defection of many of the Slavs, and internal turmoil in the form of a Bulgar revolt.
The Avars would continue to rule the Pannonian Basin until their destruction at
the hands of Charlemagne's Franks at the end of the eighth century, but, as one
historian has put it, "The kaghan's hand could no longer reach over the Sava."[23]

The Avars were followed by later waves of nomads. In the late seventh century, as a result of the breakup of the Western Türk empire, the Bulgars were
pushed westward by the Khazars and established a permanent lodgment in formerly Roman territory south of the Danube. Gradually mixing with their Slav
subjects and eventually converting to Orthodox Christianity, the Bulgars built
a strong sedentary state that would menace Constantinople for several hundred
years.[24] Later, the Pontic steppe would be traversed by the Magyars in the ninth
century, the Pechenegs beginning in the tenth century, and the Uzes (Oguz) and
Cumans in the eleventh century.[25] This pattern of westward motion was shaped by
both push and pull factors that have been succinctly described by Peter B. Golden,
a prominent authority on the early Turkic peoples:

> From the nomadic perspective, western Eurasia was ideal territory. Its pas-
> turages were extensive and excellent. It fronted on important sedentary
> cultures with which it could trade or raid as circumstances dictated. It was
> both spacious, providing room for maneuver and retreat that nomadic strata-
> gems required and sufficiently distant from the centers of military power of
> the sedentarist states to remove, for the most part, the fear of sustained attack
> from that quarter.[26]

Yet, "Western Eurasia was also the *terminus* to which the tattered remnants and fragments of Altaic nomads defeated in internecine or inter-nomadic struggles in Central or Inner Asia fled." For those "[d]riven westward by more powerful tribes and unable to break the barriers of the sedentary empires, the Ponto-Caspian steppes provided the final refuge."[27] Or perhaps the penultimate refuge, since the Huns, followed by the Avars and then the Magyars, all eventually crossed the Carpathian Mountains to shelter in the less extensive grasslands of the Pannonian Basin.

Very clearly, the Avars belong to the category of peoples driven westward by more powerful tribes. When the Türks first made diplomatic contact with Byzantium, they demanded the return of these runaway "slaves," and they would later retaliate against the empire for entering into treaty relations with the Avar qaghan.[28] And when the Avars departed the Pontic steppe for the Pannonian Basin in 567–568, it appears to have been more because of pressure from the Türks than opportunities beckoning from over the mountains to the west.

The question of the origin and identity of the Avars has occasioned much scholarly debate and disagreement. At one extreme is the view that the European Avars were the remnants of the East Asian Rouran who had been overthrown by the Türks and driven westward, and at the other extreme is the position that there was no relationship or connection whatsoever between the Avars and the Rouran. The evidence bearing on this question is scanty, ambiguous, and sometimes of questionable value. However, even a tentative answer is of considerable importance for this study, given the significance of the Avars as a possible vector for the transmission of technology and military techniques from East Asia to Europe.

The earliest substantive Byzantine account of the Avars is that provided by "Menander the Guardsman," a lawyer and historian active during the reign of Maurikios who wrote with imperial encouragement and apparently enjoyed access to government archives.[29] In Menander's *History*, the Avars are introduced as fugitive enemies of the victorious Türks. After "many wanderings" they arrived at the territory of the Alans in the North Caucasus and made contact with Byzantine officials:

> One Kandikh by name was chosen to be the first envoy from the Avars, and when he came to the palace he told the Emperor of the arrival of the greatest and most powerful of the tribes. The Avars were invincible and could easily crush and destroy all who stood in their path. The emperor should make an alliance with them and enjoy their efficient protection.[30]

When Justinian's ambassador Valentinus paid a return visit to the Avars, their qaghan, Bayan, was in the process of crushing various other steppe groupings, including the Onogurs, Zali, and Sabirs. Further information about the Avars was acquired indirectly, through diplomatic exchanges with the Türks after 568. When questioned by their Byzantine hosts, one group of envoys said that "about 20,000 Avars fled, while others stayed behind and adhered to the Turks."[31] Later, another Türk leader ("Turxanth" or "Turxanthus") declared to a Byzantine ambassador that the Avars, whom he called "Uarkhonitai," were slaves who had fled their masters the Türks:

When I wish it, the Uarkhonitai shall come to me as subjects of the Turks. If they so much as see my horsewhip sent to them, they will flee to the lower reaches of the earth. If they face me, they shall perish, as is proper, not by the sword but trampled under the hooves of our horses, like ants.

As recorded by Menander, the Byzantines were well aware of the Avars' fear of the Türks and were quick to exploit it for their own advantage.[32]

The next Byzantine historian to write about the Avars, Theophylact Simocatta, added a new wrinkle to the problem of Avar identity. After conquering the Hephthalites, an empire of nomadic origin centered on Bactria (today's Afghanistan), the Türks went on to enslave "the Avar nation."[33] Some remnants fled to Taugast (China) and Mucri (Korea), but those who arrived at the Danube claiming to be the Avars were actually imposters:

Then the [Türk] Chagan embarked on yet another enterprise, and subdued all the Ogur, which is one of the strongest tribes on account of its large population and its armed training for war. These make their habitations in the east, by the course of the river Til, which Turks are accustomed to call Melas. The earliest leaders of this nation were named Var and Chunni. Then, while the emperor Justinian was in possession of the royal power, a small section of these Var and Chunni fled from the ancestral tribe and settled in Europe. These named themselves Avars and glorified their leader with the appellation of Chagan. Let us declare, without departing the least from the truth, how the means of changing their name came to them. When the Barselt, Onogurs, Sabir, and other Hun nations in addition to these, saw that a section of those who were still Var and Chunni had fled to their regions, they plunged into extreme panic, since they suspected that the settlers were Avars. For this reason they honoured the fugitives with splendid gifts and supposed that they received from them security in exchange. Then, after the Var and Chunni saw the well-omened beginning to their flight, they appropriated the ambassadors' error and named themselves Avars: for among the Scythian nations that of the Avars is said to be the most adept tribe. In point of fact even up to our present times the Pseudo-Avars (for it is more correct to refer to them thus) are divided in their ancestry, some bearing the time-honoured name of Var while others are called Chunni.[34]

Theophylact's denial of a relationship between the European Avars (his "Pseudo-Avars") and the true Avars of Central and Eastern Asia has been accepted at face value by some scholars; S.A.M. Adshead, for one, takes "Avar" to be a prestigious preexisting tribal name that was apparently appropriated by these newcomers to the Western steppes for their own political advantage.[35] Theophylact provides a not inconsequential piece of evidence for those who would argue that there is no demonstrable connection between the Rouran and the European Avars, a position that has been taken by several prominent authorities.[36] Others have hedged their bets. For Samuel Szádeczky-Kardoss, it remains an open question whether we ought to consider the Juan-juan [Rouran] of Inner Asia or some nation of the Hephthalite Empire the ancestors of the later, Danubian Avars. Perhaps a combination of both these theories may cover the historical reality.[37]

A tentative case for connecting the Rouran of Eastern Asia with the later Avars, if not for identifying them as the one and the same, can be assembled from evidence presented by Edwin G. Pulleyblank, Károly Czeglédy, and Peter B. Golden—and even Theophylact himself. To begin with the name, Theophylact does not deny that the "true" Avars were the people known to China as the Rouran. On the contrary, what he says about them dovetails nicely with the Chinese sources: they were the "most adept" (or powerful) of the tribes, and in defeat their remnants fled to North China and Korea. Thus, even as he denies that Bayan's followers were real Avars, Theophylact may still be used to support the proposition that "Avar equals Rouran" at the nominal level. From the other end of Asia, early medieval Chinese sources place the origin of the Rouran among the Dong Hu or "Eastern Barbarians" who inhabited Manchuria in Han times.[38] Among the peoples classified as Dong Hu were the Wuhuan. And, according to Pulleyblank, Wuhuan is "a good transcription of *Awar according to the principles that apply in the Han period."[39] Golden notes that "Apar" appears in association with "Purum" (Rome) in the late seventh and early eighth century Eastern Türk runic inscriptions from Mongolia's Orkhon valley, suggesting that the Türks—who ought to have been in a position to know—did not necessarily share Theophylact's view of the European Avars as imposters.[40]

To this may be added certain practical objections to Theophylact's account. Is it really plausible that the tribes of the western steppe would have been fooled for very long, if it all, regarding the true identity of the "Pseudo-Avars"? Or that these "Var and Chunni" would have invited the enmity of the powerful and expansive Türks by masquerading as fugitive Rouran? Certainly, the Avars' fear of the Türks, and the latters' particularly intense hostility toward the former, would appear to be consistent with the interpretation that the Türks were not at all mistaken and the Avars (or at least their leadership core) were indeed a fugitive remnant of the Rouran empire.

Perhaps Theophylact was confused by Menander's earlier labeling of the European Avars as "Uarkhonitai," and seized upon the story of the "Var and Chunni" as an explanation for this apparent discrepancy in names.[41] Czeglédy's research has demonstrated, however, that the Var and Chunni were in fact closely associated with the Rouran. Uar (Avars) and Huns (Xiongnu), moving south from the Altai, established themselves in Bactria (today's Afghanistan) in the mid-fourth century CE, and were ruled by the Heftal or Hephthalite dynasty from about the mid-fifth century until 557, when the Hephthalites buckled under coordinated attacks from both the Sasanids and the Türks. Chinese sources, including the record of a Hephthalite embassy to the Northern Wei court in 457, make it clear that in the eyes of Wei elites the Hepthalites were descended from the Rouran.[42] Building on Czeglédy's work, Golden concludes that the Hephthalite state surely had some of the same ethnic components as the Rouran realm in Mongolia and the Altai and "was, in essence, the western wing of the Jou-Jan [Rouran] state."[43]

Whether the Avars came directly from the Rouran core area, from the Hephthalites in Central Asia, or from the core via the Hephthalite zone cannot be determined on the basis of available evidence. It is much more certain, however, that they were a mixed or composite group, with a possibly quite small elite of Rouran origin at the top. As we have already seen, the Avars broke and subjugated several other tribal groupings when they irrupted into the western steppe, and their movement across the Carpathians added significant numbers of Germans (Gepids) and Slavs to the mix. The creation of polyglot coalitions was the usual pattern of steppe politics, already seen in the case of the Huns.[44] Whether the Avar leader (the *chagan*, or qaghan) had a legitimate claim to the title held by the Rouran rulers in Mongolia is an open question, but it is worth noting that Baian was the only steppe chieftain to assert this title in the west prior to the arrival of the Türks. Its use is first attested around 265 CE among the proto-Mongol Xianbei (or Sarbi), whose origins could be traced to the Dong Hu.[45] This is perhaps further evidence that the Avar ruling group were also descended (via the Rouran) from the Dong Hu, and that they were a conduit for the relatively rapid transmission of ideas and techniques from East Asia to the western steppe. Rapid movements of nomadic peoples in significant numbers across great distances were certainly possible, as demonstrated by the case of the Torghuts (or Kalmyk) who migrated all the way from the Lower Volga to northern Xinjiang between January and July of 1771.[46]

Yet another reason for thinking that the leadership core of the European Avars was an element or remnant of the Rouran is the fact that the Avars are closely associated with the transmission westward of a number of items of military technology that had long been familiar in China and its adjacent steppe zone—but were unknown in the Mediterranean world, Europe, and the western steppe before the Avars' arrival in those parts. The *Strategikon* identifies many items of equipment used by the Byzantine armies around 600 CE as having been acquired from the Avars. These include "cavalry lances of the Avar type with leather thongs in the middle of the shaft and with pennons" and "round neck pieces of the Avar type made with linen fringes outside and wool inside." For the protection of the cavalry horses, "breast and neck covering such as the Avars use" were among the recommended options. The author of the *Strategikon* also recommends that the soldiers' clothing, "especially their tunics, whether made of linen, goat's hair, or rough wool, should be broad and full, cut according to the Avar pattern, so they can be fastened to cover the knees while riding and give a neat appearance." Even the tent provided to each squad of soldiers was, ideally, to be of the round and spacious Avar type, which was said to "combine practicality with good appearance."[47]

So extensive was the borrowing from this steppe people in the late sixth century that the *Strategikon*'s description of the panoply of the Avars, Türks, and other such "Scythian" peoples reads almost like a description of Byzantium's own cavalry forces:

They are armed with mail, swords, bows, and lances. In combat most of them attack doubly armed; lances slung over their shoulders and holding bows in their hands, they make use of both as need requires. Not only do they wear armor themselves, but in addition the horses of their illustrious men are covered in front with iron or felt. They give special attention to training in archery on horseback.[48]

There is reason to believe that quite a few other items of military equipment not specifically mentioned in the *Strategikon* may also have been introduced into Europe by the Avars. One such item is the "proto-saber" (or pallash), a long, straight, single-edged blade that has been found in Avar burials.[49] When the Byzantines began to adopt this weapon toward the end of the seventh century, they called it the *paramerion* and said that it was the same length as the earlier double-edged Byzantine sword, the *spathion*.[50]

Another element of Avar military equipment well attested from archaeological finds is lamellar armor, often accompanied by splint armor for the arms and lower legs. When the author of the *Strategikon* recommended horse armor of the Avar type, he may well have been referring to lamellar construction.[51] Although the Avar example did not produce an immediate transformation of the armor worn by Byzantine soldiers, it probably contributed to the increasing popularity of lamellar armor in southeastern Europe.[52]

Some authorities have also credited the Avars for the introduction of a variety of other items to Byzantium and Eastern Europe. These include an arrow guide or tube that permitted the shooting of darts or arrows otherwise too short for use with an ordinary bow, and the hourglass-shaped quiver in which arrows were kept with the arrowheads pointing upward.[53] They also include a new form of scabbard mounting (the so-called "P-form projection") and even the pennons or banneroles that were attached to lances.[54] It has been suggested that larger flags, too, may have owed something to the Avars. The flag attached vertically a flagpole, in contrast to the downward-hanging Roman vexillum, is thought to have been an early import from the steppes, initially taking the form of the *draco* borrowed by the Romans from the Sarmatians in the second century CE, consisting of "a hollow, open-mouthed dragon's head, to which was attached a long tube of material. A hole was cut in the underside of the dragon's mouth, through which a pole for carrying the standard was pushed."[55] The *draco* may have fallen out of use after the fourth century, to be reintroduced by later arrivals from the steppe such as the Avars and Magyars.[56] George Dennis has suggested that the transition to the more familiar flag form took place when a less expensive square of cloth was substituted for the dragon's head. Eventually the Byzantine battle flag (*bandon*) came to consist of a square or rectangular base to which streamers or tails were attached, and "it soon came to be borne sideways, as are our modern flags, with the streamers flying laterally, which is how the earliest illustrations depict the *bandon*."[57] Streamers were also a feature of Avar flags, as suggested by evidence dating from the middle of the seventh century.[58]

The important point is not simply that the Avar onslaught brought a package of steppe technologies to the West, but rather that this was also an East Asian package.

As may be recalled from the material presented in Chapter 3, lamellar armor had long been the dominant form for both man and horse in China, and the "proto-saber" or "pallash" is essentially the same weapon as the *dao* that had already seen centuries of use in the East. The Avar spearhead—described as "a blade which was narrow but which was also strong because of its rhomboid section and stiffening rib," all of which "made it suitable for fighting an armoured foe"—sounds generically similar (if not identical) to the Chinese *qiang*.[59] As we have seen, Chinese flags consisted of a square or rectangular base to which streamers were added, and the writings of Li Jing make it clear that the spears and lances of the Tang armies were decorated with pennons. Hourglass-shaped quivers and scabbards with P-form projections were used in northern China during the second half of the sixth century, at the same time the Avars were introducing them into Europe, and Chinese arrow tubes are well attested from the Tang period.[60]

For many if not all of these items it would be too simple to say that the Avars were carrying Chinese inventions to the West, for Chinese military technology had itself been greatly influenced by centuries of interaction with the world of the steppes. In general terms, the East Asian military package of the early medieval period may be understood as the product not of China or the steppe alone, but of the dynamic, ongoing interaction between the two. And nowhere is this more apparent than in the case of that signature item of early medieval East Asian military technology, the stirrup.

Although the earliest representations of stirrups on tomb figurines, from the early fourth century CE, come from southern China, almost all of the actual specimens thought to date from the fourth and fifth centuries have been found in northern China, Manchuria, and Korea; the oldest confidently datable pair of stirrups was unearthed from a 415 burial in southern Manchuria.[61] It should not be surprising that this new device appears to have first taken root in the interaction zone between the sedentary and nomadic worlds, and at a time when rulers of steppe origin were seizing power in northern China. Stirrups offered no obvious advantage to those who had been raised from early childhood to ride and fight from horseback without them, but were of great assistance to people from sedentary communities who were trying to emulate the skills of the nomads.[62] Early East Asian stirrups were typically oval in shape, made of wood, metal (usually iron), or metal over a wooden core, and had a rectangular handle at the top for attaching the strap. This type of stirrup was standard issue in East Asian armies by Sui and Tang times, and is clearly depicted in the relief carvings of his six warhorses that Li Shimin, the second Tang emperor, commissioned for his mortuary complex at Zhaoling (near today's Liquan, Shaanxi).[63]

Avar burials in Eastern Europe have yielded many stirrups of this type, while no stirrups of any sort have been found in the earlier Hun graves—or indeed in any earlier European context.[64] The stirrup first appears in the Byzantine historical record in the *Strategikon*, where it is called *skala* ("step" or "stair"). Although not specifically assigned an Avar provenance in that work, the stirrup is mentioned alongside other cavalry equipment that is clearly identified with the Avars.[65] Stirrups do not seem to have reached the Arabs and Persians until after the beginning of the great Islamic conquests in the 630s, and linguistic evidence suggests that they were known among the Arabs before they came to be adopted by the Persians.[66] All the available evidence, then, indicates that the Avars were the vector for the introduction of the East Asian stirrup into Europe, a thesis given its classic formulation by A.D.H. Bivar in 1955: "the cast-iron or bronze stirrup was perfected along the frontiers of China, and introduced to Europe by the single event of the Avar migration in the 6th century."[67]

Another, more specifically Chinese contribution to military technology that may have been carried westward by the Avars is the traction trebuchet. In contrast to the counterweighted trebuchet, which is first attested at the Byzantine siege of Zevgiminion in 1165, the traction trebuchet derived its motive force entirely from human muscle power.[68] Siege engines of this basic design, known as *pao* or *paoche*, had been used in China at least since the time of the Han dynasty, and probably even earlier. The device employed a lever made of one to ten flexible wooden rods between 5.6 and 8.4 meters in length, balanced on a transversal axle which was in turn mounted on a wooden frame. A leather pouch was attached at one end to hold the projectile, while the other end had 40–125 cords attached to it. The missile was launched when the crew (anywhere from forty men to 250 or more) hauled down on their cords in unison.[69] The missiles, preferably spherical stones, ranged from about one to sixty kilograms in weight, while the distances they could be thrown were highly variable. According to one authority, the best throwing distances usually ranged from seventy-five to 150 meters, depending on the weight of the projectile and the tactical purpose for which it was intended.[70] Trebuchets could be used for battering the walls of a besieged city and sweeping defending troops (and *their* trebuchets) off the ramparts; another important function was to hurl incendiary material in order to set fire to the town itself.[71] Trebuchets are mentioned very frequently in accounts of medieval Chinese sieges. The anti-Sui rebel leader Li Mi constructed 300 trebuchets (*jiangjun pao*) for his assault on Luoyang in 617.[72] Besieging the same city in 621, the Tang leader Li Shimin reportedly made use of huge trebuchets that could hurl thirty-kilogram stones as far as 137 meters.[73] Modern tests have produced less impressive results: the longest shot achieved in 1989 tests was 137 meters with a 1.9 kilogram stone, and in 1991 a crew of fourteen sent a 3.1 kilogram ball to a distance of 145 meters.[74] It would seem that not only the weight of the projectile, but also the size, training, and experience of the crew were important variables bearing on the effectiveness of this weapon.[75]

Since its first appearance in Sicily at the beginning of the fourth century BCE, Western artillery employed a very different sort of mechanism. The earliest devices used the tension of very large crossbows (also known in China) to project bolts and small stones, but these were soon joined by spring-powered torsion weapons (not attested in China) capable of hurling larger projectiles with greater force.[76] The waning years of the Roman Empire, however, saw a decline in artillery capabilities, though experts disagree over the particulars. Some argue that all torsion weapons had entirely disappeared by about 600 CE, while others believe that a relatively simple torsion catapult, the one-armed onager, continued in use for some time thereafter. Whatever its true extent, this regression is generally attributed to the decline of skill levels and resources in the age of the Germanic migrations and the fall of the Western empire.[77]

The earliest clear mention of the traction trebuchet in the Byzantine world is found in the *Miracles of St. Demetrius*, a religious text dating from about 620 that includes a description of the late sixth-century siege of Thessalonica by the Avars and their Slav allies. Its author, Bishop John, was an eyewitness of the siege. He describes the attackers using a variety of devices including iron rams and "tortoises" covered with hides. The rams were deployed against the gates, while the tortoises provided cover for men who attacked the foundations of the city wall with levers and axes. On the second day of the siege, Bishop John tells us, the attackers brought strange new weapons to bear:

> These were tetragonal and rested on broader bases, tapering to narrower extremities. Attached to them were thick cylinders, well clad in iron at the ends, and there were nailed to them timbers like the beams from a large house. These timbers had slings hung from the back side and from the front strong ropes, but which, pulling down and releasing the sling, they propel the stones up and high with a loud noise.[78]

These machines, which Bishop John calls *ballistrae*, were covered with boards on three sides to protect their operators, and we are told that the Avars built fifty of them on the spot to attack the eastern wall of the city.[79] It seems, however, that they were ineptly operated by inexperienced crews and did little damage to the city and its defenders.[80]

Before we conclude that it was the Avars who introduced the traction trebuchet to the West, however, there is some counterevidence that must be considered. In his *History*, completed in the late 620s, Theophylact Simocatta relates a story that a captured Roman soldier named Busas "taught the Avars to construct a sort of besieging machine, since they had as yet no knowledge of such implements," with his action leading immediately to their conquest of the city of Appiaria in the Danube delta (Moesia Inferior) in 587.[81] On the basis of this account, some historians have concluded that it was the Avars who acquired the trebuchet from the Byzantines and then used it against Thessalonica, some time after the Byzantines had acquired it through unknown and undocumented channels, perhaps by way of Persia.[82] Their position is also supported by the Greek word that Theophylact uses for the "besieging machine" betrayed by Busas: *helepolis*. In classical times this denoted a movable siege tower, but in Byzantine writings from the seventh-century onward it "almost invariably means a stone-throwing trebuchet."[83]

The problem is greatly complicated by the fact that Thessalonica was assailed repeatedly by the Avaro-Slavs in the late sixth and early seventh centuries, and our key source, the *Miracles of St. Demetrius*, does not provide a clear date for the particular siege in which the trebuchet makes its first appearance. The most likely candidates are 586 and 597. Unsurprisingly, the latter date is preferred by those who accept the Busas story, while scholars who are more receptive to the idea of an Avar role in the transmission of the trebuchet favor 586. A final resolution does not seem possible on the basis of the currently available evidence, but it is perhaps worth noting that Robin Cormack, a historian of Byzantine religious art with no apparent stake in the trebuchet debate, has quite confidently dated the siege in question to the week of September 22–29, 586.[84] If this is correct, attribution of Avar knowledge of the trebuchet to Busas becomes chronologically untenable.

Even if 597 were to be firmly established as the year in which the trebuchet was used against Thessalonica, however, Theophylact's account would still be problematic. As Stephen McCotter has pointed out, the Busas story raises more questions than it answers.[85] Why is its account of the siege device so vague, especially in contrast to the precise description left by Bishop John? How was it that the Avars were able to take so many Roman cities in the Balkans *before* 587? And if the trebuchet was already a part of the Byzantine armory, why was it such a complete novelty to the defenders of Thessalonica—not only to Bishop John, but presumably also to the military men in the city?[86] The Busas story also leaves the origin of the Byzantine trebuchet veiled in mystery. All the available evidence indicates that the trebuchet was not known in the Latin West until long after its arrival in Byzantium.[87] As of 550, there is no sign of the use of any siege machinery by the Slavs except for ladders.[88] The Arabs did not have the trebuchet until the second half of the seventh century, when its use is first definitely attested at the siege of Mecca in 683.[89] The Persians may have used trebuchets against Dara in the first decade of the seventh century and again at Jerusalem in 614, but there do not appear to be any clear instances that antedate the Avar siege of Thessalonica.[90] It is perhaps also worth noting that the Arabic word for trebuchet, *mandjanik*, is a loan word not from Persian but from the Greek *manganikon*, a technical term first used to describe Avar machines used against Constantinople in 626.[91] Did the Byzantines receive knowledge of the traction trebuchet directly from East Asia? Or did they invent it on their own without any such influence or assistance? In either case, the sources are silent. Almost in exasperation, one authority has concluded, "It is equally possible that the Avars (with their origins in Central Asia), the Byzantines, or the Persians could have been the first to learn and make use of this weapon in the western world."[92] Others, notably McCotter and Haldon, consider the Avar route the most likely; as McCotter puts it, "there is no good reason to doubt that the Avars may have brought it and the Byzantines copied it."[93]

The Byzantines' use of the trebuchet is also difficult to track and date. They may have employed it against a Persian fort near Akbas in 587, though they seem to have operated it rather inexpertly on that occasion, suggesting that the weapon was still new and unfamiliar.[94] Herakleios made use of a device identified as a *helepolis* during his siege of Tiflis in 627, and the *Strategikon* mentions "wagons carrying revolving ballistae at both ends."[95] Both have been interpreted as references to the trebuchet, though some would hold open the possibility that the device mentioned in the *Strategikon* is a more traditional weapon, the onager.[96] What is clear, however, is that the traction trebuchet spread quite rapidly among the peoples who encountered it. Although bolt-shooting tension machines would remain in use in many places, the trebuchet soon became the sole stone-throwing device across medieval Eurasia, superseding whatever torsion engines may have remained in the more technically sophisticated areas of the Mediterranean world and reigning unchallenged until the rise of gunpowder weapons at the end of the Middle Ages. The popularity of the trebuchet may be attributed not only to its capability of throwing heavier stones, but also to its simplicity of design, the relative ease with it could be constructed, dismantled, transported, and reassembled, and its lack of temperamental springs that could be built and maintained only by highly skilled experts.[97]

Although neither the role of the Avars in the diffusion of the traction trebuchet and many other items of military technology westward across Eurasia nor the connection between the European Avars and the East Asian Rouran can be established with certainty, the fit is nevertheless a good one. The theory of an East Asian origin for at least a key component of the Avar elite is congruent with the evidence for the arrival of East Asian technologies in western Eurasia in the last decades of the sixth century CE. The Rouran rose to power on the steppes around the beginning of the fifth century CE, at the same time the Tuoba Wei were in the process of extending their control over northern China from their base at Dai (today's Datong, Shanxi). Subjugating other nomadic peoples such as the Gaoche, the Rouran quickly created a steppe empire not just embracing today's Mongolia, but extending as far as northern Korea in the east and the Tarim Basin in the west. The character of the relationship between the Rouran and the Tuoba was nicely summarized by a prominent historian of Inner Asia, Denis Sinor: "Throughout their history the Juan-juan [Rouran] were locked in virtually unceasing combat with the Northern Wei dynasty of China (386–534)."[98] According to the dynastic history of the Northern Wei, major conflicts between the two occurred in 402, 406, 409–410, 424–425, 428–429, 438, 443, 449, 458, 464, 470, 492, and 522.[99] Throughout all of this, captives and defectors circulated between the two sides.[100] On one high-profile occasion in 520, when the Rouran qaghan Anagui was driven by a civil war within his own family to take temporary refuge at the Wei court at Luoyang, he and his followers were presented with bows and arrows, shields and sabers, lances with pennons, suits of armor for both men and horses, and sets of drums and horns.[101] These were quite practical gifts since the Rouran army, like that of Northern Wei, was organized around a core of heavy cavalry—as, indeed, were the forces of the European Avars and the Byzantines.[102]

To return to the question posed at the end of Chapter 5, the case of the Avars makes it clear that the similarity of Chinese and Byzantine military practice did indeed owe something to influences flowing across the Eurasian landmass, and the direction of this flow was, overwhelmingly, from east to west. It is also clear, however, that the flow—or at least the part of it that can be documented, however tentatively—involved material objects, especially weapons and other items of military equipment. As has often been observed, this is perhaps the quickest and easiest of all forms of cross-cultural diffusion. According to David Nicolle, who has written extensively about this phenomenon in medieval Eurasia,

The technology of warfare is an area in which cultures have readily copied their neighbours or rivals. The reasons are obvious. In war survival generally depends on success and so, throughout history, effective weapons or tactics have been widely copied. Only the most deep-rooted constraints, such as the availability of raw materials or certain fundamental sociological characteristics of the recipient culture, have been able to inhibit this kind of diffusion. Even non-essential military fashions, including clothing and the decoration of horse-harness, have moved remarkable ease across the most hostile frontiers. It remains a fact that imitation is the highest form of military compliment.[103]

In contrast to material products, ideas have crossed cultural boundaries "much more gradually and with much greater difficulty."[104] This applies not only to religions and philosophical systems, but also to more practical concepts, including military theories and instructions, which are often grounded in religious or philosophical assumptions and recorded in literary languages that are difficult for outsiders to penetrate. In any case, the early steppe peoples would not have been a promising vehicle for the diffusion of complicated, textually based knowledge; according to the Northern Wei dynastic history, the Rouran were illiterates whose leaders at first kept records of their troop numbers by piling up sheep turds as counters but eventually graduated to scratching simple marks onto pieces of wood.[105] Not surprisingly, there is no evidence of the transmission of Chinese military theories and texts to the West by way of the Avars, other steppe nomads, Silk Road caravans, or any other channel prior to the activities of the Jesuit missionaries in the seventeenth and eighteenth centuries.[106]

It would seem, then, that direct and indirect contacts between China and Byzantium had only a very limited role in shaping Byzantine military practice and no influence at all on the early Tang military. The final chapter of this book will examine the last and most promising explanation for the "Eurasian Way of War" shared by these early medieval empires: the long-term influence of the steppe nomads and their mode of warmaking on all of the sedentary states bordering the Eurasian steppeland.

Notes

1 For the silk trade, see Valerie Hansen, *The Silk Road: A New History* (New York: Oxford University Press, 2012), pp. 19–20. For Chinese importation of Roman glassware, see Albert E. Dien, *Six Dynasties Civilization* (New Haven and London: Yale University Press, 2007), pp. 288, 290, and 292–3.

2 Fan Ye, *Hou Han shu* (Shanghai: Zhonghua shuju, 1965), chapter 88, p. 2919–20, translated in John E. Hill, *Through the Jade Gate to Rome* (Charleston, SC: Booksurge, 2009), p. 27.

3 Hill, *Through the Jade Gate to Rome*, pp. 292–3; D.D. Leslie and K.H.J. Gardiner, *The Roman Empire in Chinese Sources*, Studi Orientali 15 (Rome: Bardi, 1996), pp. 14 and 155–8.

4 Qi Sihe, *Zhongguo he Baizhanting diguo de guanxi* (Shanghai: Shanghai renmin chubanshe, 1956), pp. 10, 13, and 15; *JTS* 198, pp. 5314–15; *TD* 193, pp. 5265–6; *THY* 99, pp. 1778–9; *JS* 97, pp. 2544–5; *WS* 102, pp. 2275–6; *CFYG* 970 and 971. Also see Leslie and Gardiner, *The Roman Empire in Chinese Sources*, pp. 82 and 159–60.

5 Qi Sihe, *Zhongguo he Baizhanting diguo de guanxi*, p. 13. There is no record that any Chinese embassy ever reached the Roman Empire; Leslie and Gardiner, *The Roman Empire in Chinese Sources*, p. 161.

6 George Ostrogorsky, *History of the Byzantine State*, trans. Joan Hussey, rev. ed. (New Brunswick, NJ: Rutgers University Press, 1969), p. 74; James Howard-Johnston, "The Two Great Powers in Late Antiquity: A Comparison," in Averil Cameron (ed.), *The Byzantine and Early Islamic Near East*, vol. 3: *States, Resources and Armies* (Princeton, NJ: The Darwin Press, 1995), pp. 204–5.

7 Procopius, *History of the Wars*, trans. H.B. Dewing (London: William Heinemann Ltd., 1954), vol. 5, pp. 227–31 [Book VIII, chapter xvii, 1–8]; Geoffrey Greatrex and Samuel N.C. Lieu (ed. and comp.), *The Roman Eastern Frontier and the Persian Wars*, Part 2: *AD 363–630, A Narrative Sourcebook* (London and New York: Routledge, 2002), p. 129.

8 Translations of the relevant passages from these works can be found in Leslie and Gardiner, *The Roman Empire in Chinese Sources*.

9 Edwin G. Pulleyblank, "The Roman Empire as Known to Han China," *Journal of the American Oriental Society* 119.1 (1999), pp. 71–9.

10 *JTS* 198, pp. 5313–15; also see the comments in Qi Sihe, *Zhongguo he Baizhanting diguo de guanxi*, pp. 11 and 14–16.

11 For the actual height of the Golden Gate, see Cyril Mango, "The Triumphal Way of Constantinople and the Golden Gate," *Dumbarton Oaks Papers* 54 (2000), p. 186, http://www.doaks.org/resources/publications/dumbarton-oaks-papers/dop54/dp54ch9. pdf (accessed September 29, 2014).

12 Peter A. Boodberg, "Marginalia to the Histories of the Northern Dynasties," *Harvard Journal of Asiatic Studies* 3 (1938), pp. 222–4. Theophylact was born into the "Graeco-Egyptian administrative class" *c.*585–590 and pursued a career as a lawyer and imperial judge; his *History* was probably completed in the late 620s. See Michael Whitby, *The Emperor Maurice and His Historian: Theophylact Simocatta on Persian and Balkan Warfare* (Oxford: Clarendon Press, 1988), pp. 28–32 and 50. The passage on Taugast can be found in *The History of Theophylact Simocatta*, trans. Michael and Mary Whitby (Oxford: The Clarendon Press, 1986), pp. 191–2.

13 Boodberg, "Marginalia to the Histories of the Northern Dynasties," pp. 223–43; the quotation is from page 243.

14 These complex maneuverings, which saw a grandson of Bumin displace Tardu from his position in the West, are summarized in Denis Sinor, "The Establishment and Dissolution of the Türk Empire," in *The Cambridge History of Early Inner Asia* (Cambridge: Cambridge University Press, 1990), pp. 305–7.

15 The diplomatic exchanges between the Türks and the Byzantines are described in *The History of Menander the Guardsman*, trans. R.C. Blockley (Liverpool: Francis Cairns, 1985), pp. 111–17 and 171–5, summarized in Sinor, "Establishment and Dissolution of the Türk Empire," pp. 301–5. Sinor rejects the usual identification of Silziboulos with Ishtemi.

16 Walter E. Kaegi, *Heraclius: Emperor of Byzantium* (Cambridge: Cambridge University Press, 2003), pp. 142–4, 158, and 190; James Howard-Johnston, "Heraclius' Persian Campaigns and the Revival of the East Roman Empire, 622–630," *War in History* 6.1 (January 1999), pp. 17–25 and 40–1.

17 Peter Heather, "The Huns and the End of the Roman Empire in Western Europe," *English Historical Review* 110 (1995), pp. 8 and 14–17.

18 Whitby, *The Emperor Maurice and His Historian*, p. 68; J. Otto Maenchen-Helfen, *The World of the Huns: Studies in Their History and Culture*, ed. Max Knight (Berkeley and Los Angeles: University of California Press, 1973), pp. 116–17; Fergus Millar, *A Greek Roman Empire: Power and Belief under Theodosius II (408–450)* (Berkeley and Los Angeles: University of California Press, 2006), pp. 80–1.

19 Warren Treadgold, *A History of the Byzantine State and Society* (Stanford, CA: Stanford University Press, 1997), pp. 165–6, 169, 172, 192, 195, 208, and 213. Also see Peter B. Golden, *An Introduction to the History of the Turkic Peoples: Ethnogenesis and State-Formation in the Medieval and Early Modern Eurasia and the Middle East* (Wiesbaden: Otto Harrassowitz, 1992), pp. 92–3.

20 Golden, *Introduction to the History of the Turkic Peoples*, pp. 100–1 and 103–4.
21 Samuel Szádeczky-Kardoss, "The Avars," in Denis Sinor (ed.), *The Cambridge History of Early Inner Asia* (Cambridge: Cambridge University Press, 1990), pp. 207–10.
22 Whitby, *The Emperor Maurice and His Historian*, p. 171.
23 Szádeczky-Kardoss, "The Avars," p. 214.
24 Mark Whittow, *The Making of Orthodox Byzantium, 600–1025* (Basingstoke, Hampshire: Macmillan, 1996), pp. 270 ff.; Treadgold, *A History of the Byzantine State and Society*, pp. 328, 343, and 366; Golden, *An Introduction to the History of the Turkic Peoples*, pp. 244–8; and Florin Curta, *Southeastern Europe in the Middle Ages, 500–1250* (Cambridge: Cambridge University Press, 2006), pp. 77–90.
25 Ostrogorsky, *History of the Byzantine State*, pp. 256, 277, 334, 343, 360–1, and 377–8; Treadgold, *A History of the Byzantine State and Society*, pp. 481, 493, 495, 586–7, 593, 600, 617, and 630; Golden, *An Introduction to the History of the Turkic Peoples*, pp. 262, 265, 268–70, 277, and 280.
26 Golden *An Introduction to the History of the Turkic Peoples*, p. 85.
27 Golden, *An Introduction to the History of the Turkic Peoples*, pp. 85–6 (emphasis in original).
28 Whitby, *The Emperor Maurice and His Historian*, p. 85.
29 *History of Menander the Guardsman*, pp. 1–2 and 18.
30 *History of Menander the Guardsman*, p. 49.
31 *History of Menander the Guardsman*, p. 117.
32 *History of Menander the Guardsman*, pp. 175 (quotation), 223–5.
33 *History of Theophylact Simocatta*, p. 188.
34 *History of Theophylact Simocatta*, pp. 189–90.
35 S.A.M. Adshead, *T'ang China: The Rise of the East in World History* (Basingstoke, Hampshire: Palgrave Macmillan, 2004), p. 37.
36 Most notably Walter Pohl, *Die Awaren: Ein Steppenvolk in Mitteleuropa, 567–822 n.Chr.* (Munich: Verlag C.H. Beck, 1989), but also see Arnulf Kollautz and Hisayuki Miyakawa, *Geschichte und Kultur eines völkerwanderungszeitlichen Nomadenvolkes* (Klagenfurt: Geschichtsverein f. Kärnten, 1970), as well as Curta, *Southeastern Europe in the Middle Ages*, pp. 612.
37 Szádeczky-Kardoss, "The Avars," p. 207.
38 *WS* 130, p. 2289.
39 E. G. Pulleyblank, "The Chinese and Their Neighbors in Prehistoric and Early Historic Times," in David N. Keightley (ed.), *The Origins of Chinese Civilization* (Berkeley and Los Angeles: University of California Press, 1983), p. 453. Pulleyblank goes on to say,

> Though the Juan-juan [Rouran] are not connected with the Wu-huan in Chinese sources, they were undoubtedly proto-Mongol in language, and their ruling group may well have come from the Wu-huan fraction of the Eastern Hu. In this case, both the "true Avars" and the "Pseudo-Avars" may have been entitled to the name.

40 Golden *An Introduction to the History of the Turkic Peoples*, p. 76. He acknowledges, however, that this "is an extremely tangled problem."
41 See Whitby's comment in *History of Theophylact Simocatta*, p. 189, note 39.
42 K. Czeglédy, "From East to West: The Age of Nomadic Migrations in Eurasia," *Archivum Eurasiae Medii Aevi* 3 (1983), pp. 33–4, 75, 77, 96–7, 100–1, and 106.
43 Golden, *An Introduction to the History of the Turkic Peoples*, p. 79. Czeglédy is more cautious:

> In summary, we can state that in the final analysis the Avars were undoubtedly composed of the same two ethnic components, the *Uar* and the *Khünni*, as the Hephthalites. The direct Juan-juan [Rouran] origin of the Avars can be

convincingly demonstrated from the Chinese sources. But, in actuality, the *Uar* and the *Khünni* tribal groupings of the Hephthalites separated from the Juan-juan already in the fourth century and, according to our sources, were not in contact with the Avars either. Thus, although some data could perhaps be inter-preted as saying that in 557 it was the Hephthalite Uar-Huns who migrated to Europe and hence would be identical with the Avars, neither the written sources nor the archaeological data can serve as an adequate basis for such a conclusion.

("From East to West," p. 120)

44 Czeglédy, "From East to West," pp. 88–9; Golden, *An Introduction to the History of the Turkic Peoples*, pp. 110–11.
45 Golden, *An Introduction to the History of the Turkic Peoples*, p. 71.
46 The Torghuts' exodus from Russian to Qing rule is described in Peter C. Perdue, *China Marches West: The Qing Conquest of Central Eurasia* (Cambridge, MA: The Belknap Press of Harvard University Press, 2005), pp. 292–9. They had to fight both the elements and hostile Kazakhs along the way, and of the approximately 150,000 people who began the journey only 70,000 reached the Qing border.
47 George T. Dennis (trans.), *Maurice's Strategikon: Handbook of Byzantine Military Strategy* (Philadelphia: University of Pennsylvania Press, 1984), pp. 12–13. Also see the discussion in John Haldon, *Warfare, State and Society in the Byzantine World, 565–1204* (London: UCL Press, 1999), pp. 129–30.
48 *Strategikon*, p. 116. Also see Ann Hyland, *The Medieval Warhorse: From Byzantium to the Crusades* (Stroud, Gloucestershire: Alan Sutton, 1994), pp. 27 and 31.
49 Michael Gorelik, "Arms and Armour in South-Eastern Europe in the Second Half of the First Millennium AD," in David Nicolle (ed.), *A Companion to Medieval Arms and Armour* (Woodbridge, Suffolk: The Boydell Press, 2002), p. 129; David Nicolle, "Byzantine and Islamic Arms and Armour: Evidence for Mutual Influence," in David Nicolle, *Warriors and Their Weapons around the Time of the Crusades: Relationships between Byzantium, the West and the Islamic World* (Aldershot, Hampshire: Ashgate, 2002), pp. 303–4; and É. Somlósi, "Restoration of the Csolnok Avar Iron Sword," *Acta Archaeologica Academiae Scientiarum Hungaricae* 40 (1988), 207–10.
50 John Haldon, "Some Aspects of Early Byzantine Arms and Armour," in David Nicolle (ed.), *A Companion to Medieval Arms and Armour*, p. 73; J. F. Haldon, "Some Aspects of Byzantine Military Technology from the Sixth to the Tenth Centuries," *Byzantine and Modern Greek Studies* 1 (1975), p. 31. The curved saber was a somewhat later development variously attributed to the Avars, Khazars, and Magyars. See Gorelik, "Arms and Armour in South-Eastern Europe," p. 129.
51 Haldon, "Some Aspects of Byzantine Military Technology from the Sixth to the Tenth Centuries," pp. 15, 22, and 25; Gorelik, "Arms and Armour in South-Eastern Europe," p. 130; Michael J. Decker, *The Byzantine Art of War* (Yardley, PA: Westholme Publishing, 2013), pp. 112–13.
52 Haldon, "Some Aspects of Early Byzantine Arms and Armour," pp. 66 and 70; Helmut Nickel, "The Mutual Influence of Europe and Asia in the Field of Arms and Armour," in Nicolle (ed.), *A Companion to Medieval Arms and Armour*, p. 110.
53 For the arrow guide, see Haldon, "Some Aspects of Early Byzantine Arms and Armour," p. 78, and David Nishimura, "Crossbows, Arrow Guides, and the *Solenarion*," *Byzantion* 58 (1988), p. 425 and *passim*. For the quiver, see Gorelik, "Arms and Armour in South-Eastern Europe," p. 129; Markus Mode, "Art and Ideology at Taq-I Bustan: The Armoured Equestrian," in Markus Mode and Jürgen Tubach (eds.), *Arms and Armour as Indicators of Cultural Transfer: The Steppes and the Ancient World from Hellenistic Times to the Early Middle Ages* (Wiesbaden: Dr. Ludwig Reichert Verlag, 2006), p. 394; and Jon Coulston, "Arms and Armour of the Late Roman Army," in Nicolle (ed.), *A Companion to Medieval Arms and Armour*, pp. 14–15.

54 For scabbard mountings, see Valentina I. Raspopova, "Sogdian Arms and Armour in the Period of the Great Migrations," in Mode and Tubach (eds.), *Arms and Armour as Indicators of Cultural Transfer*, p. 80, and Helmut Nickel, "The Mutual Influence of Europe and Asia," in Nicolle (ed.), *A Companion to Medieval Arms and Armour*, p. 119. For the bannerole, see J.C. Coulston, "Roman, Parthian and Sassanid Tactical Developments," in Philip Freeman and David Kennedy (eds.), *The Defence of the Roman and Byzantine East: Proceedings of a Colloquium Held at the University of Sheffield in April 1986* (British Institute of Archaeology at Ankara, 1986), p. 66, and Hyland, *The Medieval Warhorse*, p. 31.

55 Pat Southern and Karen Ramsey Dixon, *The Late Roman Army* (New Haven and London: Yale University Press, 1996), p. 126. Also see Nickel, "The Mutual Influence of Europe and Asia," p. 118.

56 Coulston, "Arms and Armour of the Late Roman Army," p. 24.

57 George T. Dennis, "Byzantine Battle Flags," *Byzantinische Forschungen* 8 (1982), p. 53.

58 Nickel, "The Mutual Influence of Europe and Asia," p. 118.

59 Gorelik, "Arms and Armour in South-Eastern Europe," p. 130.

60 The best representation of an hourglass quiver is on one of the relief carvings from Tang Taizong's mid-seventh-century mortuary complex at Zhaoling. The carving, now in the collection of the University of Pennsylvania Museum of Archaeology and Anthropology, depicts an officer named Qiu Xinggong removing an arrow from the chest of Taizong's charger Saluzi ("Autumn Dew"), an episode that occurred during a battle near Luoyang in 621. See the Penn Museum's web site, http://www.penn.museum/ collections/object/167942 (accessed June 23, 2014). A modern artist's interpretation of Qiu Xinggong can be seen in Chris Peers and Michael Perry, *Imperial Chinese Armies (2), 590–1260 AD* (London: Osprey, 1996), plate B. For P-form projections, see Raspopova, "Sogdian Arms and Armour," p. 80. For arrow tubes, see Joseph Needham and Robin D.S. Yates, *Science and Civilisation in China*, vol. 5, part 6: *Military Technology: Missiles and Sieges* (Cambridge: Cambridge University Press, 1994), pp. 166–7.

61 Albert E. Dien, "The Stirrup and Its Effect on Chinese Military History," *Ars Orientalis* 16 (1986), pp. 33–5.

62 Mary Aiken Littauer, "Early Stirrups," *Antiquity* 55 (1981), pp. 104–5; H.G. Creel, "The Role of the Horse in Chinese History," *American Historical Review* 70.3 (April 1965), pp. 670–1; John W. Eadie, "The Development of Roman Mailed Cavalry," *Journal of Roman Studies* 57 (1967), pp. 162–3; Coulston, "Roman, Parthian and Sassanid Tactical Developments," p. 61.

63 Good photos of the carvings of two of Li Shimin's chargers can be found at the web site of the University of Pennsylvania Museum of Archaeology and Anthropology: http://www.penn.museum/collections/object/167942 and http://www.penn.museum/ collections/object/239945 (accessed June 23, 2014). For more information about the Zhaoling necropolis in general and the "six steeds" in particular, see Cheng Yufeng, "Tangdai Zhaoling liu jun shike shi kao," *Gu jin tan*, No. 184 (September 1980), pp. 14–16; Yan Zhenwei, "Zhaoling: Tangdai wenwu yicun de yi zuo baoku," *Renwen zazhi* 1980, No. 4, pp. 77–81; and Li Xuezhi, "Tang Taizong Zhaoling liu jun shike jianjie," *Dalu zazhi* 16.3 (February 15, 1958), pp. 5 and 30. For sketches of early East Asian stirrups, see Littauer, "Early Stirrups," pp. 102–3.

64 A.D.H. Bivar, "The Stirrup and Its Origins," *Oriental Art*, n.s., 1.2 (Summer 1955), pp. 62–3; Maenchen-Helfen, *The World of the Huns*, p. 206; Littauer, "Early Stirrups," p. 104; Hyland, *The Medieval Warhorse*, p. 11.

65 *Strategikon*, p. 13. Also see John Haldon, *The Byzantine Wars* (Stroud, Gloucestershire: Tempus, 2001), p. 45.

66 Hugh Kennedy, *The Armies of the Caliphs: Military and Society in the Early Islamic State* (London and New York: Routledge, 2001), pp. 171–3. Sadly, the lower part of the Sasanian armored equestrian figure at Taq-i Bustan (Iran) is too badly damaged to

determine whether it was originally equipped with stirrups, and the authorities disagree. Bivar maintains "it is obvious from the attitude of the legs that stirrups are not being used," whereas Markus Mode extrapolates their existence from the presence of other items of Turkish origin. See Bivar, "The Stirrup and Its Origins," p. 61, and Markus Mode, "Art and Ideology at Taq-i Bustan," p. 402.

67 Bivar, "The Stirrup and Its Origins," p. 65.
68 For the counterweight trebuchet, see Kelly DeVries and Robert Douglas Smith, *Medieval Military Technology*, 2nd edition (Toronto: University of Toronto Press, 2012), pp. 126–7.
69 This is based on the detailed description of trebuchet design and operation in Sergej Aleksandrovič Školjar, "L'Artillerie de jet a l'époque Sung," *Études Sung*, Series 1: History and Institutions, vol. 1 (1970), pp. 124–29. Školjar describes the workings of a Song engine, but points out that the fundamentals of its design were already in place by Tang times (p. 124). There is nothing in the *Tong dian*'s description of a *paoche* (*TD* 160, p. 4110) that is incompatible with Školjar.
70 Školjar, "L'Artillerie de jet," p. 134, and also pp. 126 and 135. For a collection of figures on ranges and throw weights, see Needham and Yates, *Science and Civilisation in China*, vol. 5, part 6, pp. 216–17 (table 4).
71 Školjar, "L'Artillerie de jet," p. 139; Herbert Franke, "The Siege and Defense of Cities in Medieval China," in Frank A. Kierman, Jr. and John K. Fairbank (eds.), *Chinese Ways in Warfare* (Cambridge, MA: Harvard University Press, 1974), p. 169.
72 *XTS* 84, p. 3680.
73 *ZZTJ* 188, p. 5905; Joseph Needham, "China's Trebuchets, Manned and Counterweighted," in Bert S. Hall and Delno C. West (eds.), *On Pre-Modern Technology and Science, A Volume of Studies in Honor of Lynn White, Jr.* (Malibu, CA: Undena Publications, 1976), p. 109.
74 W.T.S. Tarner, "The Traction Trebuchet: A Reconstruction of an Early Medieval Siege Engine," *Technology and Culture* 36.1 (January 1995), pp. 161–2.
75 DeVries and Smith, *Medieval Military Technology*, p. 126.
76 E. W. Marsden, *Greek and Roman Artillery: Historical Development* (Oxford: Oxford University Press, 1969).
77 Tarner, "The Traction Trebuchet," pp. 139–40 and 142; DeVries and Smith, *Medieval Military Technology*, pp. 122–3; Paul E. Chevedden, "Artillery in Late Antiquity: Prelude to the Middle Ages," in Ivy A. Corfis and Michael Wolfe (eds.), *The Medieval City under Siege* (Woodbridge: The Boydell Press, 1995), p. 164; Peter Purton, *A History of the Early Medieval Siege, c. 450–1220* (Woodbridge, UK: The Boydell Press, 2009), pp. 9, 11, and 24.
78 The *Miracula of St. Demetrius*, quoted in Speros Vryonis, Jr., "The Evolution of Slavic Society and the Slavic Invasions in Greece: The First Major Slavic Attack on Thessaloniki, A.D. 597," *Hesperia* 50 (1981), p. 384.
79 Vryonis, "The Evolution of Slavic Society," p. 384.
80 Purton, *A History of the Early Medieval Siege*, p. 30.
81 *The History of Theophylact Simocatta*, p. 66; Vryonis, "The Evolution of Slavic Society," pp. 387–8; Whitby, *The Emperor Maurice and His Historian*, p. 50.
82 Vryonis, "The Evolution of Slavic Society," pp. 385 and 388–9; George T. Dennis, "Byzantine Heavy Artillery: The Helepolis," *Greek, Roman, and Byzantine Studies* 39 (1998), pp. 99–115; Bernard S. Bachrach, *Early Carolingian Warfare: Prelude to Empire* (Philadelphia: University of Pennsylvania Press, 2001), pp. 114–15.
83 Dennis, "Byzantine Heavy Artillery," pp. 101 and 103.
84 Robin Cormack, *Writing in Gold: Byzantine Society and Its Icons* (London: George Philip, 1985), p. 66.
85 Stephen McCotter, "Byzantines, Avars and the Introduction of the Trebuchet" (2003), paper posted at the *De Re Militari* web site: http://web.archive.org/web/20110720012051/http://www.deremilitari.org/resources/articles/mcotter1.htm (accessed May 7, 2013). Most of the objections that follow were raised by McCotter.

86 Purton, *A History of the Early Medieval Siege*, p. 32.
87 Carroll M. Gilmor, "The Introduction of the Traction Trebuchet into the Latin West," *Viator* 12 (1981), pp. 1–8. The use of the traction trebuchet is not clearly attested until the siege of Lisbon in 1147, but may have been used as early as the ninth century.
88 Vryonis, "The Evolution of Slavic Society," pp. 386–7.
89 Donald R. Hill, "Trebuchets," *Viator* 4 (1973), pp. 100–2.
90 Dennis, "Byzantine Heavy Artillery," p. 104; McCotter, "Byzantines, Avars and the Introduction of the Trebuchet."
91 McCotter, "Byzantines, Avars and the Introduction of the Trebuchet."
92 Purton, *A History of the Early Medieval Siege*, p. 33.
93 McCotter, "Byzantines, Avars and the Introduction of the Trebuchet," note 11. For Haldon's views, see *The Byzantine Wars*, p. 49, and *Warfare, State and Society*, p. 136.
94 McCotter, "Byzantines, Avars and the Introduction of the Trebuchet."
95 Walter E. Kaegi, *Heraclius: Emperor of Byzantium* (Cambridge: Cambridge University Press, 2003), p. 144; Purton, *A History of the Early Medieval Siege*, pp. 31–2; *Strategikon*, p. 139.
96 Dennis, "Byzantine Heavy Artillery," pp. 99–100; Purton, *A History of the Early Medieval Siege*, p. 24.
97 Purton, *A History of the Medieval Siege*, pp. 565–7; Chevedden, "Artillery in Late Antiquity," p. 164.
98 Denis Sinor, "The Establishment and Dissolution of the Türk Empire," in *The Cambridge History of Early Inner Asia* (Cambridge: Cambridge University Press, 1990), p. 293.
99 *WS* 103, pp. 2291–302.
100 See, for example, *WS* 103, p. 2295.
101 *WS* 103, p. 2300.
102 For the Rouran heavy cavalry, see Wang Yuanchao, "Tang chao jiaji juzhuang shuailuo yu qing qibing xingqi zhi yuanyin," *Lishi yanjiu* 1996, no. 4, p. 50. For the Avars, see Michael J. Decker, *The Byzantine Art of War* (Yardley, PA: Westholme Publishing, 2013), pp. 168–9; and Gorelik, "Arms and Armour in South-Eastern Europe," p. 130.
103 David Nicolle, "Byzantine and Islamic Arms and Armour," p. 299. Also see Nicolle's "Medieval Warfare: The Unfriendly Interface," *Journal of Military History* 63 (1999), p. 580, and Haldon, "Some Aspects of Early Byzantine Arms and Armour," p. 67.
104 Jerry H. Bentley, *Old World Encounters: Cross-Cultural Contacts and Exchanges in Pre-Modern Times* (New York: Oxford University Press, 1993), p. 19.
105 *WS* 103, p. 2290.
106 For the Jesuits' transmission of *Sunzi bingfa* to Europe in the eighteenth century, see Samuel B. Griffith (trans.), *Sun Tzu: The Art of War* (Oxford: Oxford University Press, 1963), pp. 179–81.

7   The shadow of the steppe

By the beginning of the seventh century CE, both China and the Mediterranean world had already experienced many centuries of contact with the pastoral nomads of the Eurasian grasslands. Humans on the steppes and elsewhere had probably begun to experiment with horseback riding as early as 4000 BCE, but it was only around the end of the second millennium BCE that the combination of equestrian skills and mounted archery that became central to the nomads' way of life first appeared on the grasslands north of the Black Sea and the Caspian Sea.[1] According to Nicola Di Cosmo,

> "true" early pastoral nomads, that is, pastoralists moving with their herds according to a fixed seasonal cycle, appear only in the late Bronze and early Iron Age, a phenomenon that brought about a great expansion across Central Eurasia of mounted warlike nomads.[2]

The "classic nomadic steppe culture" marked by weapons, horse gear, and objects decorated with animal motifs first appeared on the steppes adjacent to northern China during the sixth century BCE, and the presence of mounted nomads is clearly attested in Chinese textual sources by fourth century BCE at the latest.[3] Accounts of the nomads written by Greek and Chinese authors mention essentially the same set of key characteristics. The great Han historian Sima Qian, writing around the end of the first century BCE, described the dominant steppe people of his time, the Xiongnu, in the following terms:

> The animals they raise consist mainly of horses, cows, and sheep, but include such rare beasts as camels, asses, mules, and the wild horses known as *taotu* and *tuoji*. They move about in search of water and pasture and have no walled cities or fixed dwellings, nor do they engage in any kind of agriculture. Their lands, however, are divided into regions under the control of various leaders. They have no writing, and even promises and agreements are only verbal. The little boys start out by learning to ride sheep and shoot birds and rats with a bow and arrow, and when they get a little older they shoot foxes and hares, which are used for food. Thus all the young men are able to use a bow and act as armed cavalry in time of war. It is their custom to herd their flocks in times

of peace and make their living by hunting, but in periods of crisis they take up arms and go off on plundering and marauding expeditions. This seems to be their inborn nature. For long-range weapons they use bows and arrows, and swords and spears at close range. If the battle is going well for them they will advance, but if not, they will retreat, for they do not consider it a disgrace to run away. Their only concern is self-advantage, and they know nothing of propriety or righteousness.[4]

The mid-fifth century BCE Greek historian Herodotus also commented on the mobile way of life of the Scythians who roamed the Pontic steppe north of the Black Sea, noting their lack of fixed dwellings, their reliance on herds of live-stock for their livelihood, and their use of mounted archery in war. Although Herodotus did not make quite the same moral judgments as Sima Qian, he did call the Scythians "the most uncivilized nations in the world."[5]

The military skills of the nomads were of particular interest to observers from sedentary civilizations. Not only were groups such as the Xiongnu and Scythians able to shower their opponents from horseback with rapid, accurate barrages of arrows in battle, but as forces composed entirely of cavalry they also enjoyed an impressive strategic mobility that enabled them to ride circles around the infantry-based armies of sedentary states. This mobility was enhanced by a logistical system that allowed the nomads to travel wherever there was grass and water while avoiding the burden of a supply train: each warrior brought along a number of extra horses; the horses ate the grass, and the men slaughtered and ate the horses as necessary.[6] When pressed by more powerful armies the nomads could exploit their superior mobility to avoid contact with their enemy entirely, a strategy that, according to Herodotus, completely frustrated the Persian king Darius' invasion of Scythia in 511 BCE.[7]

The extensive, pastoral lifestyle of the nomads, requiring the dispersal of small encampment groups across vast expanses of pastureland, meant that their popula-tions were almost always less numerous than those of their sedentary neighbors. Until the early twentieth century, for example, the population of the Mongolian steppe is believed to have held stable at no more than one million persons, a number that was probably fixed by the limit of the ecological carrying capacity of the grass-lands under conditions of extensive pastoralism and one that stood in stark contrast to the populations of 50–60 million people recorded in the Han and Tang empires at their height.[8] The same way of life that kept populations small, however, also ensured that almost every able-bodied adult male possessed certain rudimentary military skills. Horsemanship and archery, the mainstays of warfare as practiced by the steppe peoples, were also the essential skills of everyday life in a pastoral econ-omy where the main business of herding was frequently supplemented by hunting.[9] As a result, all the able-bodied men of a tribe could, and did, serve as soldiers when the need arose, allowing the nomads to "hit above their weight" and put armies into the field that were often roughly equal in size to those of their sedentary opponents.

Geography dictated that the Chinese came into earlier and more intimate contact with the steppe dwellers than did the peoples of the ancient Mediterranean world.

For the Greeks, the Scythians were an exotic, distant people dwelling beyond the Danube River, far to the north and east of the civilized world. The only such people that the inhabitants of classical Athens were likely to come into contact with were not raiders or invaders but the so-called "Scythian archers," a municipal police force composed of Scythians and other foreigners, and when Herodotus wrote of the military exploits of the nomads, it was Persians they were fighting, not Greeks.[10] In Warring States China, in contrast, the major kingdoms of Yan, Zhao, and Qin directly abutted the grasslands of Inner Mongolia and southwestern Manchuria roamed by the Dong Hu and other nomadic peoples. By the fourth century BCE at the latest, conflict with the nomads had become a fact of life for the sedentary states of northern China.

Over time, Chinese rulers developed a variety of means for coping with the threat. Among the earliest of these was an asymmetrical approach that played to China's strengths in engineering, social organization, and human numbers: the construction of "long walls" of pounded earth to obstruct the southward movements of the nomads and hold them at a distance. Such fortifications were built in what is now Inner Mongolia by the states of Yan and Zhao around 300 BCE.[11] Another, more symmetric approach was to imitate the effective tactics and techniques of the nomads. Near the end of the fourth century BCE, King Wuling of Zhao ordered at least some of his soldiers to trade their long robes for trousers and learn how to fight from horseback as mounted archers, an event that is often taken to mark the first real use of cavalry in Chinese warfare. According to the Western Han compilation *Stratagems of the Warring States* (*Zhanguo ce*), King Wuling's new model army went on to drive the Hu nomads out of an extensive tract of grasslands along the Zhao frontier.[12] Early in the Western Han dynasty, the prominent statesman Chao Cuo laid out the relative strengths and weaknesses of the Han and Xiongnu forces for his master, Emperor Wen. The advantages of the Chinese lay in their ability to deploy disciplined formations of armored infantry and bring long-range crossbows to bear on the enemy, but they were still unable to equal the nomads in mounted archery. To make up for this weakness, Chao Cuo urged the emperor to recruit surrendered steppe tribes into the Han army.[13]

Additional security policies practiced during the Western Han period included more wall-building and the famous system of "harmonious kinship" (*heqin*), whereby young women designated as imperial "princesses" and material goods such as grain and silk were sent to the leader of the Xiongnu confederation in the hope of converting him to Chinese ways—or at least moderating his aggressiveness. When Emperor Wu abandoned the early Han policies and took the offensive against the Xiongnu after 133 BCE, powerful cavalry forces that included mounted archers became an essential ingredient of military success, and—following the course earlier recommended by Chao Cuo—many fighting men of steppe or frontier origin were enrolled in the Han forces.[14] The inclusion of steppe warriors and tribal cavalry continued under the Eastern Han in the first and second centuries CE, and beyond into the Three Kingdoms, Wei, and Jin. Cao Cao, the greatest warlord of the Three Kingdoms period, incorporated large numbers of surrendered Wuhuan tribesmen into his army after his victory at White Wolf Mountain in 207, and under his leadership they acquired a reputation as the best cavalry in all of China.[15] Faced with the need to fill the ranks of their armies with high-quality troops and to replenish the declining population of the northern provinces, Chinese leaders continued to accept the submission of steppe peoples along the frontier. The Western Jin government, for example, received the surrender of 29,300 Xiongnu in 284, more than 100,000 in 286, and another 11,500 in 287.[16]

The early fourth century saw a string of rebellions against the Western Jin by the Xiongnu and other steppe peoples who had been settled within the empire, with the result that they ruled North China under a series of often ephemeral and unstable "imperial" regimes for more than 250 years. During this time the original Xiongnu leadership was supplanted by more recent arrivals from the steppe, including the Murong Xianbei who established states in Hebei and Shandong and the Tuoba Xianbei who expanded from an original base in the Dai region of northern Shanxi to bring all of the north under the sway of their Northern Wei empire, a political structure that was more substantial and less ephemeral than any of the other "Northern Dynasties." During these centuries the Chinese living in the north became well acquainted with their non-Han rulers. A great deal of cultural exchange and intermarriage occurred, giving rise to a mixed-blood elite that was well versed in both the martial skills of the steppe and the literary culture of the Chinese world. Out of this milieu emerged the ruling houses of the Sui dynasty (the Yang family) and the Tang dynasty (the Li family, which had marriage ties to the Yang). Both had their roots in the Xianbei elite of Northern Wei, and in such diverse traits as marriage patterns, language use, and fashions in clothing they continued to show signs of their North Asian heritage.[17] And they also inherited the martial traditions of the steppe. The first Tang emperor, Li Yuan, was an excellent horseman and archer, as was his second son and eventual successor, Li Shimin, who claimed to have personally slain more than a thousand men in battle.[18] To choose only one example, in an engagement fought to the east of Luoyang in 621, Li Shimin led his cavalry in a raid on the enemy's camp and felled a number of the opposing horsemen with his arrows.[19] Not only were the Tang founders men of non-Han descent who had the warrior culture of the steppe in their blood, as it were, but they also had direct experience of confronting the nomadic Türks along the northern frontier. In 615, Emperor Yang of the Sui dynasty had sent Li Yuan to serve as regional pacification commissioner (*anfu dashi*) at Taiyuan in today's Shanxi, an assignment that put him athwart one of the main invasion routes favored by the Türks and required him to give serious thought to the nomads' way of war and the best means of dealing with it. His solution was to select 2,000 of his cavalrymen who were able to shoot from horseback and train them to fight in the same fashion as the Türks:

> Their food, drink, and lodgings were the same as those of the Türks. They followed the grass and water, and placed outposts at a distance. Whenever they encountered Türk scouts, they behaved as if no one was watching and galloped around shooting and hunting, so as to flaunt their awesome martiality. . . . When they encountered the Türks suddenly, the bravest and

keenest were organized as a separate unit and ordered to maintain their cohesion in order to watch for their opportunity. Whenever the Türks saw [Li Yuan's] troops, they always said that because of their behavior they suspected that they belonged to their own tribe.[20]

A small contingent of Türks participated in Li Yuan's campaign to seize the Sui western capital (Daxingcheng, soon to be renamed Chang'an) in the autumn of 617, and steppe warriors and their techniques continued to play a prominent role in Tang military operations after the Li family had consolidated their control over China. Li Jing's surprise attack on the Eastern Türk Illig qaghan's encampment at Iron Mountain in 630, the episode that opened this book, was spearheaded by 200 mounted archers.[21] And once the Eastern Türks had submitted to Tang Taizong (Li Shimin), he put them to work fighting against other enemies of the empire. Many Tang expeditionary armies of the mid-to-late seventh century included a strong steppe component, especially when those armies were fielded against foes who were themselves nomads. In 646, for example, the Chinese general Li Shiji led 20,000 Tiele cavalry to attack the Xueyantuo, and in 651 some 30,000 Han Chinese soldiers and 50,000 Uighur cavalry were mobilized to attack the Western Türk Shaboluo qaghan.[22] In early Tang times, the steppe warriors and their tools, techniques, and tactics were already an integral part of Chinese warfare.[23]

During their rise to imperial mastery over the Mediterranean lands and much of Western Europe, the Romans—like the Greeks before them—had little military contact with the nomads of the Eurasian steppe. The battle of Carrhae, where a typical Roman army consisting mainly of heavy infantry was effectively annihilated by the fast-moving horse archers of the Parthians in northern Mesopotamia in 53 BCE, was an almost unique event that occurred far from the center of Roman power and prompted no changes in weaponry, tactics, or military organization.[24] Imperial expansion, however, eventually brought the Romans into significant and prolonged contact with steppe ways of warfare. As Simon James has observed,

> Rome was in direct contact with "Iranian cavalry peoples," and other societies heavily influenced by them, along a vast stretch of her frontiers, from the Hungarian Plain to the Syrian Desert, via the long borders of Dacia to the shores of the Black Sea and the fringes of the Caucasus, and via Armenia to the Euphrates Basin and Palmyra.[25]

Apart from the Parthians themselves, who controlled Persia and Mesopotamia, the most important of these "Iranian cavalry peoples" were the Alans and Sarmatians, whose range extended from the lower Danube frontier across the Pontic steppe to the North Caucasus. Although not without horse archers of their own, the Alans and Sarmatians were best known for their armored cavalry equipped with long lances. During the second century CE, they had a palpable influence on the Roman military. There was a gradual increase in the numbers of the Roman cavalry, especially in the East, and the adoption by cavalry units of the streaming banners (*draco*) of the Sarmatians and in some cases also their long lance, the *kontos*.[26]

This was not just the result of learning from the barbarians, but also involved bringing some of the barbarians into the imperial ranks. In 175 CE, for example, 8,000 Sarmatians from Pannonia were sent to serve with the Roman forces in Gaul.[27] The incorporation of steppe equipment and personnel was paralleled by the adoption of at least some elements of steppe tactics. In his *Ars Tactica*, written around 136 CE, the Roman governor of Cappadocia (and historian of Alexander the Great) Flavius Arrianus Xenophon noted that his ruler, Hadrian, had already called for the Roman cavalry to practice the feigned retreats of the Sarmatians and the maneuvers of the Parthian and Armenian horse archers.[28]

Contact with the Parthians along the Euphrates frontier provided another vector for steppe influences on the Roman military. It was here that the Romans first acquired the thumb ring, associated with the "Mongolian release" used by the mounted archers of the Eurasian steppes. The new technique, which used a thumb lock rather than the fingers to draw and release the arrow, eventually superseded the earlier "Mediterranean release" and was standard in Roman archery by the sixth century CE.[29] Hostile encounters along the same frontier, especially after the Sasanids replaced the Parthians as the rulers of Persia in the first half of the third century CE, stimulated an increase in Rome's heavy cavalry forces, the *catafractii* and *clibanarii*, as a symmetrical response to the Sasanian reliance on such armored horsemen.[30] Under the Principate cavalry had been rather sparse in the Roman army, with only 120 horsemen assigned to each legion (though the army also included a few *alae* of auxiliary cavalry). By the time the *Notitia Dignitatum* was compiled around 395 CE, however, there were fourteen units of heavy cavalry stationed in the East and only four in the West, a clear indication that the buildup in mounted forces was a response to pressures along the empire's eastern frontiers.[31] The increase was real, even though it took place gradually over time and did not see cavalry supplant infantry as the main force of the Roman army in the East.[32]

The next wave of adaptation was triggered by the arrival of the Huns near the end of fourth century CE. In contrast to the Parthians, the Sasanian Persians, and even the Sarmatians (many of whom appear to have followed a rather settled way of life), the Huns were true nomads when they made their first appearance on the western steppes.[33] There is good reason to doubt that those who migrated into the Pannonian Basin in the early fifth century could have continued to practice extensive pastoral nomadism in this more limited geographical niche, but this does not mean that all of them would have immediately abandoned the equestrian skills, mounted archery, and light cavalry tactics that had served them so well for many generations on the open grasslands—an observation that also applies to the Avars who followed them into the same region more than a hundred years later.[34] The Romans found the Huns (and later, the Avars), to be formidable opponents because of their mobility and archery. The Huns were the first to bring to the West an improved version of the composite bow, probably developed to counter the heavy armor worn by peoples such as the Sarmatians. The ends (or ears) of the bow were lengthened, stiffened, and set at a sharply recurved angle to the main part of the bow:

In effect, these alterations act to "shorten" the bow, creating a higher initial draw weight prior to the strings lifting off the limbs as they are pulled back. This, in turn, increases overall energy storage allowing the weapon to propel a heavier arrow more efficiently.[35]

This type of bow was soon adopted by the Romans,[36] but training men to use it effectively was a more complicated proposition. Although the Roman army had long included units of horse archers,[37] the challenge from the Huns put a new premium on this military skill that was so rare among sedentary populations and so difficult to learn. As in the earlier case of the Sarmatians, an obvious solution was to recruit some of the steppe warriors into the Roman military. There were Huns fighting for the emperor Theodosius I as early as 388, and Hunnic units continued to be found in the Roman army on through the fifth century and well into the sixth.[38] Unsurprisingly, these troops appear to have been mostly or entirely archers.[39] And they proved highly effective. During an encounter in 409 between a band of Goths and a regiment of 300 Huns in Roman service, the superior archery of the latter reportedly produced the lopsided casualty totals of 1,100 for the Goths and only seventeen for the "Romans."[40] A letter to the Roman military commander in Libya written just a year or two later by a local bishop makes it clear that, in the view of the inhabitants, a group of only forty Hun soldiers (Unnigardae) had been playing a key role in guarding the Libyan frontier against raids from the desert.[41] More than a century after this, Procopius could still report that the Huns were the best archers in the army of Belisarius.[42]

This prolonged contact with the Huns, whether as enemies, allies, or comrades in arms, is also thought to have produced an improvement in the equestrian skills, archery, and tactical finesse of the majority, non-Hun elements of the late Roman army.[43] By the 520s and 530s, Roman archery was highly effective and elements of the cavalry were proficient in steppe maneuvers such as the feigned flight.[44] The observation of Vegetius that the Roman cavalry benefited from "the example of the Goths, and the Alans and the Huns" has been echoed by modern authorities who hold that the Romans' success in coping with the Avars was due largely to their earlier experience of learning from the Huns.[45]

The same adaptive pressures felt by the Romans and Chinese were also experienced, to varying degrees, by all the other sedentary societies bordering the Eurasian steppes. The earliest and perhaps deepest adjustments were made by the Persians and other settled Iranian peoples, many of whom lived in contact or interspersed with nomads across a vast extent of land in (to use today's terms) northeastern Iran, Afghanistan, Turkmenistan, Uzbekistan, and Tajikistan. The founder of the Achaemenid Persian empire, Cyrus the Great, was killed in battle against a steppe people, the Massagetae, in 530 BCE. Persian armies came to include a powerful cavalry component, including mounted archers, and northeastern Iran was probably the first sedentary region to make use of armored cavalry as a counter to the nomad threat.[46] Under the Sasanians, heavy cavalry formed the core of the army; in the mid-sixth century, each cavalryman is said to have been equipped with horse-armour, a hauberk, a breastplate, greaves, a sword, a spear, a circular shield, a mace strapped to his belt, an axe, and a quiver holding two bows with strings and 30 arrows.[47]

The Greek historian Herodian, writing in the middle of the third century CE, presented the skills of the Persians as little different from those of the nomads:

> They use the bow and the horse in war, as the Romans do, but the barbarians are reared with these from childhood, and live by hunting; they never lay aside their quivers or dismount from their horses, but employ them constantly for war and the chase.[48]

Such perceptions notwithstanding, the Sasanian heavy cavalry relied more on "shock" action than on archery in battle. But just as the Romans and Chinese did, the Sasanians also supplemented their native forces with mounted archers recruited from the steppes. In the late sixth century, for example, a Persian army campaigning in the Transcaucasus was assisted by 12,000 Sabir Huns.[49] During the wars of the sixth and seventh centuries, Sasanian armies frequently employed the steppe tactic of feigned flight against their Roman opponents, and when pursuing fleeing Romans the Persians would advance cautiously in order to avoid falling into such traps themselves.[50]

   Although it falls outside the chronological framework of this study, the military experience of the Russian principalities can be fit into the same adaptive pattern. The emerging East Slav states dominated by the originally Scandinavian Rus were in contact with steppe powers from their very beginning in the eighth century CE— first the semi-nomadic Khazars and then, after the defeat of the Khazars in the tenth century, the fully nomadic Pechenegs (or Patzinaks).[51] The princes of Kiev and the other Russian cities built their armies around the elite cavalrymen of the *druzhina*, who were well trained and equipped with sword, spear, helmet, cuirass, and shield, and relied primarily on "shock" action in battle.[52] When the Pechenegs were displaced by a new wave of nomads, the Kipchaks (also known as Polovtsy to the Russians and Cumans in the Latin West), in the eleventh century, the Russian princes began to recruit large numbers of Pechenegs (now called Karakalpaks or Chernye Klobuky) into their own armies. These steppe warriors fought mainly as bow-armed light cavalry; they "were the match of the Polovtsy in steppe warfare as mounted archers and were precious sources of intelligence, as well as serving as border guards and scouts."[53] There must have been considerable exchange of military knowledge between the Turkic nomads and the sedentary Russians, and there was certainly plenty of mingling at the elite level—by the late twelfth century, some of the Russian princes were seven-eighths Turkic.[54] The gradual process culminated with the impact of the Mongol onslaught in the thirteenth century. According to a recent general survey of Russia's military history, "Russian styles of warfare, shaped by hundreds of years of fighting against nomads, were crystallized by Mongol influence. Russian city-states went to war as bow-armed light cavalry armies, like the nomads they fought and the Tatars who ruled them."[55]

In all of the sedentary societies in contact with the steppe, we can discern the same basic pattern. Sedentary rulers strengthened their cavalry forces, recruited nomadic warriors from the steppe,[56] and adopted many of the weapons, tactics, and techniques of steppe warfare. By their very nature, however, sedentary powers were incapable of pursuing a purely symmetric strategy of emulating the steppe powers. Because of their settled, agricultural upbringing, most of their people never had an opportunity to acquire the characteristic martial skills of the nomads; those who did had to be taught slowly and laboriously, and rarely—if ever—attained the same level of proficiency as the steppe dwellers. It is a telling feature that both the late Roman military author Vegetius and a late eighth-century Chinese encyclopedia recommend the use of artificial expedients to teach soldiers to ride horses. Vegetius calls for the use of wooden horses to train recruits how to mount and dismount,[57] while Du You's *Tong dian* offers the following:

> On the two sides of each encampment, set up twelve earthen horses (*tu ma*) of the same size as ordinary horses, and equip them with saddles. Order the soldiers to put on their helmets and armor, carry their bowcases and quivers of arrows, wear sabers and swords at their waists, and grasp lances and shields, and then mount and dismount from both left and right, so as to facilitate proficiency in these actions.[58]

Earlier, in 702, a similar provision calling for villages to set up dummy horses of wood and earth and practice "riding" during the agricultural slack season was included in an edict issued by the Empress Wu Zetian.[59] The nomads, of course, had no need for such artificial measures, and would no doubt have regarded them with contempt and derision.

Another factor that prevented sedentary states from competing with steppe powers on an equal footing was that they were simply unable to produce enough horses. This was a serious problem for China in particular. The horse had always been a rather marginal animal in China's agrarian economy, and in the interior of the country horses were raised in only a few areas such as Huainan, Fujian, and aboriginal areas in Lingnan and Hunan—but many of the horses from the far south were too small and frail to carry the weight of an armored soldier.[60] This made China's rulers heavily dependent on the extensive grasslands along the empire's northern steppe margin. As the Tang state extended its control over the rich pastures of Hexi and Longyou, its herds grew accordingly. Beginning with 3,000 horses inherited from the Sui and 2,000 more procured from the Türks, the early Tang emperors managed to increase their horse herds to a peak of 706,000 animals during the Linde period (*c*.665), before Tibetan raiding reduced the number to perhaps 200,000 by the Yifeng period (676–679). After further ups and downs, the herds counted 325,700 horses in 754, on the eve of the An Lushan Rebellion.[61] Several modern Chinese historians have argued that there was a direct correlation between the military power of the Tang court and the number of horses at its disposal. When the empire had large numbers of horses, it dominated the steppe, but after the An Lushan Rebellion the loss of the pastures in the northwest to the Tibetans condemned the once mighty Tang to a permanent condition of weakness and military inferiority.[62]

Even with very large numbers of horses and skilled equestrians to ride them, however, no sedentary state could afford to rely entirely on its cavalry forces. Walled cities and other fortified positions could only be defended—and attacked— by foot soldiers. Naval forces had to be maintained in order to protect coastlines and rivers from both hostile fleets and everyday piracy. And when campaigns were fought in mountainous, forested, or swampy terrain that was not suitable to cavalry action, strong, well-trained infantry forces were a necessity. The sedentary state had no choice but to devote a significant portion of its resources to build up forces other than cavalry. Thus, we see that the early Tang military establishment was composed mostly of infantry, even at a time when the most serious threats to the empire's security came from the northern steppes.[63] The army that Emperor Yang of the Sui dynasty had led against Koguryŏ in 612 included many more foot soldiers then horsemen.[64] And around 600 CE, when the *Strategikon* was written and the Avar influence was at its peak, the Byzantine army still included a very substantial infantry component.[65]

Given these realities, sedentary states necessarily had to pursue asymmetric approaches to countering the nomads. These approaches often sought to leverage the superior material resources and technology of sedentary populations. Although it may well have originated among the steppe dwellers themselves, the use of heavily armored cavalry eventually enabled Iranian regimes such as those of the Parthians and Sasanians to bring sedentary advantages (superior metallurgy and blacksmithing; larger, grain-fed horses) to bear against a poorer and less technologically sophisticated nomadic foe.[66] The early Chinese crossbow with its intricate bronze trigger mechanism is another case in point. And fortifications were built everywhere sedentary states confronted steppe opponents. The Qin and Han practice of building "long walls" was continued by later dynasties such as Northern Wei, Northern Qi, and Sui. The Roman emperor Theodosius II built his own long wall across Thrace from the Black Sea to the Aegean in order to keep the Huns away from Constantinople and its immediate hinterland.[67] The Sasanians fortified key strategic chokepoints on the steppe approaches, and somewhat later, from the eighth century CE, the oasis of Bukhara built its own long wall.[68] And in the tenth, eleventh, and twelfth centuries the Russians would erect "lines of earthen walls and forts" to impede the Pechenegs and Polovtsy.[69] Here again, the labor power, organization, and engineering skills of sedentary populations were brought to bear against the nomads in asymmetric fashion.

Yet another sort of asymmetric approach involved adjusting one's tactics and techniques of war so as to counter or frustrate the usual tactics of the nomads. The many devices that have been detailed in Chapters 3 and 4, including highly articulated, multiple-echelon formations for battle, the strict control of pursuits, the division of armies into *cursores* and *defensores* (or their equivalents), the attention to long-range reconnaissance and the establishment of distant outposts, and the elaborate precautions for the security of the army both in camp and on the march can all be understood in this context. They are well suited for dealing with the peculiar strengths of the nomads, above all their extreme tactical mobility, which made feigned flights, ambushes, sudden reversals, and surprise attacks into routine occurrences that had to be guarded against at all times lest a single moment of laxity should lead directly to disaster. To a very great extent, the similarity between the *Strategikon* and the "Military Methods" of Li Jing can be traced to their expectation that they will be confronting the same sort of opponent.

The author of the *Strategikon* is quite clear about who he considers to be the most likely opponents of the Romano-Byzantine military around the end of the sixth century, and he devotes one of the twelve major sections of his work (Book XI) to describing the fighting methods of each of these peoples and the best means of countering them. Four broad groups are introduced: the Persians, the Scythians (who are identified more specifically as "the Avars, Turks, and others whose way of life resembles that of the Hunnish peoples"), the "light-haired peoples" (further identified as "the Franks, Lombards, and others like them"), and the "Slavs, Antes, and the like."[70] The "Scythians" and Slavs receive the greatest attention, while the Arabs are not mentioned at all—an odd omission that suggests the work was likely based on direct experience of campaigning against the Avars and their Slav allies in the Balkans rather than against Persians and Arabs on the Euphrates frontier. Whether as Scythians or as Avars, the nomads are also invoked repeatedly in sections of the *Strategikon* apart from Book XI.[71] Clearly, knowledge of the steppe peoples' way of war and how to deal with it was of great importance to the author of the *Strategikon*.

The practice of writing about the military peculiarities of foreign peoples, a genre known to the Byzantines as *ethnika*, was considerably less developed among the Chinese.[72] In what remains of his "Military Methods," Li Jing never once mentions his assumed opponents by name. Quite apart from his own command experience against the Türks and the Tuyuhun, however, there are a number of hints scattered through the text that he, too, was thinking about how to confront the steppe dwellers in their own environment. These include his expectation that most of the soldiers of the expeditionary army will ride horses, even if many them are supposed to dismount for combat, and his recommendation that patrols and fire beacons be extended as far away as sixty miles from the army, a provision that would have been difficult to implement and probably also unnecessary in areas with more constrictive, blocking terrain and greater population density.[73] His attention to pasture and water, with particular concern about ensuring that water sources are not fouled or otherwise rendered unusable in areas where water is scarce, is also consistent with steppe campaigning.[74] As for the enemy, Li Jing observes that they are prone to make use of surprise attacks, night attacks, ambushes, and feigned flight.[75] In addition, they appear to be accomplished horse rustlers: "Should the deranged enemy steal horses, they must flee as is their custom."[76] In the passages on fire beacons and long-range scouts, approaching enemies are identified as "riders" (*ji* 騎) who are more than just ordinary horsemen: the army's most distant scouts must always be mounted on good horses or they will be taken by the enemy.[77] Although some parts of Li Jing's "Military Methods" are written in a florid, archaizing style that harks back to the ancient military classics and the intra-Chinese warfare of the Warring States period, his more practical, direct, and matter-of-fact passages seem to assume that the Tang expeditionary army will be campaigning against nomads on the open steppe.

The *Strategikon*'s section on the Türks, Avars, and other "Scythians" opens with a series of general observations about the nomads' social and political organization, way of life, and behavioral traits, much of which Chinese authors reaching as far back as Sima Qian would surely have agreed with. Readers are told that these steppe peoples are inured to hardships such as heat and cold, and are harshly governed by their despotic rulers. They are also "treacherous, foul, faithless" and "possessed by an insatiate desire for riches. They scorn their oath, do not observe agreements, and are not satisfied by gifts."[78] These well-worn tropes are then followed by more specific observations regarding the military practices of the nomads. Their large herds of horses and emphasis on mounted archery are noted, along with their attention to sentries and scouting in order to avoid surprise (although they are unwilling to fortify their encampments in the manner of civilized peoples such as the Romans and the Persians). When deploying for battle, they form

> several units of irregular size, all joined closely together to give the appearance of one long battle line. Separate from their main formation, they have an additional force which they can send out to ambush a careless adversary or hold in reserve to aid a hard-pressed section.[79]

Mirroring the approach favored by the Byzantines (and the Chinese), the nomads "prefer to prevail over their enemies not so much by force as by deceit, surprise attacks, and cutting off supplies."[80] When and if the application of force against force does become necessary, their preference is for "battles fought at long range, ambushes, encircling their adversaries, simulated retreats and sudden returns, and wedge-shaped formations, that is, in scattered groups." In contrast to civilized peoples, when the battle is won they do not leave a way out and follow the fleeing enemy at a safe distance, but rather "they do not let up at all until they have achieved the complete destruction of their enemies, and they employ every means to this end."[81]

The author of the *Strategikon* then goes on to note the particular vulnerabilities of the "Scythians." Because they travel with large herds of horses, they can be hurt by a shortage of fodder. In battle, they are reluctant—or even entirely unable—to fight dismounted. Since they prefer to fight in scattered groups, at a distance, and with ranged weapons, "a cavalry force should advance against them in a dense, unbroken mass to engage them in hand-to-hand fighting." They are also vulnerable to night attacks, "with part of our force maintaining its formation while the other lies in ambush." Another, perhaps more serious weakness is political rather than tactical:

> They are seriously hurt by defections and desertions. They are very fickle, avaricious and, composed of so many tribes as they are, they have no sense

of kinship or unity with one another. If a few begin to desert and are well received, many more will follow.[82]

When preparing for battle against steppe opponents, the Byzantine commander is advised to take a number of precautions. Scouts are to be kept "on the alert, stationed at regular intervals." In the event that the battle goes badly, the army should have ample supplies on hand and a good defensive position or refuge identified beforehand. The army should be drawn up with the infantry in the front line, cavalry to the rear, "and a numerous and capable force on the flanks." If possible, the battle line should be formed in an area without any obstructing terrain such as woods or hollows that "might serve as a screen for enemy ambushes," and scouts should be positioned in all directions from the formation. Even better would be a deployment in front of an unfordable river or other impassible obstacle in order to rule out surprise attacks on the army's rear. Great caution is to be exercised even in the event of apparent success:

> If the battle turns out well, do not be hasty in pursuing the enemy or behave carelessly. For this nation does not, as do the others, give up the struggle when worsted in the first battle. But until their strength gives out, they try all sorts of ways to assail their enemies.

Hence, when the assault troops pursue the enemy, they "should not get more than three or four bowshots away from the formation of defenders, nor should they become carried away in the charge."[83]

With its emphasis on scouting to avoid ambushes or other surprises, deployment in multiple echelons, security of the flanks and rear, and controlled pursuit, this advice reads like a summary or précis of many recommendations offered repeatedly and at greater length elsewhere in the *Strategikon*, giving the distinct impression that the book as a whole was shaped primarily by contact with steppe armies, and by the pressing need to counter their fluid, flexible, and resilient tactics. This pressure had been building for a long time, as we have seen, but the onslaught of first the Huns and then the Avars ratcheted it up quite a few notches. As John Haldon has pointed out, the division of the Byzantine battle formation into several lines or echelons—as seen in the *Strategikon*— appears to be the result of recent Avar pressures and influences.[84] The author of the *Strategikon* explicitly attributes such formations to the Turks and Avars, who "do not draw themselves up in one battle line only, as do the Romans and Persians, staking the fate of tens of thousand of horsemen on a single throw." Instead, "they form two, sometimes even three lines, distributing the units in depth, especially when their troops are numerous, and they can easily undertake any sort of action."[85] He goes on to note that troops formed in a single line tend to get broken up and disordered during a pursuit, thus becoming vulnerable to the sudden counterattacks practiced by the "Scythians." The way to avoid this is to form two lines, with the second line serving as a support.[86]

Although not framed as a discussion of steppe tactics and how to counter them, the surviving portions of Li Jing's "Military Methods" make many recommendations that are quite similar to those we find in the *Strategikon*. Li Jing makes it clear that whether the army is in camp, on the march, or deploying for battle, scouts are to keep watch in all directions and at a considerable distance. He does not, like the author of the *Strategikon*, advise the general to choose a battlefield with no places for the enemy to hide, but he does recommend that such possible hiding places should be thoroughly scouted and searched:

> all within one hundred *li* must be reconnoitered [to make sure it is] clear and quiet. Otherwise, when the soldiers have been led half way through or are making camp on the eve of battle, concealed troops may rise from ambush and cause damage to the army.[87]

Like his Byzantine counterpart, Li Jing seems concerned to create a refuge or fallback position:

> If the camp is not secure and there is no precipitous ground to rely upon, each division on a proportional basis pulls out one or two companies to serve as support companies tasked to harden the fortifications of the camp.[88]

Although he does not call for backing up the battle line against impassible terrain, he makes just such a recommendation for the army's camp—the presumptive base from which it will move forward into battle.[89] And like the Byzantine author, he calls for a deployment in multiple echelons with foot soldiers in front and cavalry positioned to their rear and toward the flanks. When the enemy comes in close, Li Jing appears to envision something like the *Strategikon*'s attack "in a dense, unbroken mass to engage them in hand-to-hand fighting":

> Should the infantry be pushed back by the enemy, the assault troops, maneu- ver troops, and cavalry go forward to meet the enemy with a spirited attack; the infantry must fall back and reform to assist the troops in front. Should the assault troops, maneuver troops, and cavalry be repulsed by the enemy, the spearhead and other companies must advance together to attack vigorously. If the enemy fall back, the maneuver troops and the cavalry may not exploit over a distance. Only after it has been learned through careful examination that the enemy are panicked and in disorder are they permitted to mount their horses to pursue and exploit. The support companies may not move on their own initiative.[90]

This passage also reveals two additional parallels with the Byzantine material: pursuit is to be very carefully controlled, and there is a division of labor between the troops engaged in combat or pursuit and those whose task is to remain in for- mation to provide a secure base or fallback position on battlefield (comparable to the Byzantine tactical division between *cursores* and *defensores*). Both of these would have served as effective countermeasures against the feigned flights and sudden counterattacks that were the military stock in trade of the steppe peoples.

Moving beyond the writings of Li Jing, the Tang dynastic histories provide further confirmation that Chinese and Byzantine military men had developed very much the same repertoire of techniques for dealing with the nomads. When confronting steppe armies, Chinese generals sometimes practiced a "scorched earth" policy in the most literal sense to deprive the enemy of pasture for their horses – targeting one of the key weaknesses identified in the *Strategikon*. In 641, when the northern frontier was threatened by the nomadic Xueyantuo, Li Shimin ordered his field commander to burn off the grass cover north of the "long walls" (*chang cheng*) in order to force the enemy to retreat. Nearly a century later, in 727, Tang forces were still using much the same tactic, this time against the Tibetans.[91] The seasonal pattern of steppe warfare was also well understood by both the Chinese and the Byzantines. The *Strategikon* notes that the best time to attack nomads is in February and March "when their horses are in wretched condition after suffering through the winter," and the Chinese traditionally favored the same season for their campaigns onto the steppe—when the nomads' horses were thin and weak and had not had a chance to fatten on the spring grass. It was precisely at this juncture, in late winter and very early spring, that Li Jing had launched his decisive blow against the Eastern Türks in 630.[92] The ground for the Tang general's success had already been prepared by his emperor's exploitation of yet another of the weaknesses identified in the *Strategikon*, the fissiparous nature of steppe politics. The Eastern Türk qaghan Illig was vulnerable because Tang Taizong (Li Shimin) had earlier driven a wedge between him and his nephew the Tuli qaghan, leading eventually to the latter's defection to the Tang with a large following in 628.[93] And when Li Jing carried out his final attack against Illig's camp at Iron Mountain, his approach was cloaked by heavy mist and had probably been planned as a night attack—just as recommended by the *Strategikon*.[94]

Having long been in contact and armed confrontation with the pastoral peoples of the Eurasian steppes, both the Chinese and the Romano-Byzantines would appear to have learned much from their opponents and hit upon essentially the same set of countermeasures for coping with the military challenge posed by the nomads. The objection may again be raised, however, that many if not all of these methods of coping were not really new but had been known and practiced by sedentary armies against one another long before the steppe challenge came to the fore. As we have already seen in Chapter 5, a cautious attitude toward military operations is very pronounced in both the ancient Chinese and Greco-Roman literature on the art of war. Many specific measures, including secure, well-guarded camps, long-range scouting, and flank security while the army is on the march may be considered universal "best practices" that were adopted by the well-organized armies of both East and West in ancient times. Even quite specific devices that were considered the signature tactics of the Eurasian nomads, such as the ambush and the feigned flight, had a pedigree in sedentary civilizations that reached back long before horse-riding pastoralists arrived on the scene. Perhaps as early as the fifth century BCE, Sunzi urged his readers not to "pursue feigned retreats." Even earlier, during the "Spring and Autumn" period (722–479 BCE) when chariots dominated the battlefields of northern China, the feigned retreat was already a familiar tactic. The *Zuo zhuan* contains a story about one Cao Gui, a man of Lu who offered advice to his duke during a battle fought against the neighboring state of Qi in 683 BCE:

> The duke was about to order the drums to beat an advance, when Gui said, "Not yet." After the men of Qi had advanced three times with their drums beating, he said, "Now is the time." The army of Qi received a severe defeat, but when the duke was about dash after them, Gui again said, "Not yet." He then got down and examined the tracks left by their chariot wheels, remounted, got on the front bar, and looked after the flying enemy. After this he said, "Pursue," which the duke did. When the victory had been secured, the duke asked Gui the reasons of what he had done. "In fighting," was the reply, "all depends on the courageous spirit. When the drums first beat, that excites the spirit. A second advance occasions a diminution of the spirit; and with a third, it is exhausted. With our spirit at the highest pitch we fell on them with their spirit exhausted; and so we conquered them. But it is difficult to fathom a great state – I was afraid there might be an ambuscade. I looked therefore at the traces of their wheels, and found them all confused; I looked after their flags, and they were drooping – then I gave the order to pursue them."[95]

The feigned flight was also well known in the classical Mediterranean world. Onasander, a Greek author of the first century CE, had this to say on the subject:

> It is sometimes a useful stratagem for an army facing the enemy to retire gradually, as if struck by fear, or to about-face and make a retreat similar to a flight but in order, and then, suddenly turning, to attack their pursuers. For sometimes the enemy, delighted by the belief that their opponents are fleeing, break ranks and rush forward, leaping ahead of one another. There is no danger in turning to attack these men; and those who have for some time been pursuing, terrified by the very unexpectedness of this bold stand, immediately take to flight.[96]

In the mid-fourth century BCE another Greek military writer, Aineias "the Tactician," had recommended that troops be sent out of a besieged city to skirmish and then lure the enemy to attack through a gate left open; on the other side of the gate, the attackers would fall into a previously prepared ditch where they could easily be killed by the defenders.[97] Further examples could be added, but these few are surely sufficient to establish the point.

Just because a tactic is attested, however, we should not assume that it was widely used or easy to execute. The feigned flight was a particularly tricky maneuver insofar as simulated panic could quickly degenerate into the real thing when soldiers exposed their vulnerable backs to the enemy. To pull off the maneuver successfully, with less harm to themselves than to the enemy, soldiers had to be well trained, tightly disciplined, and highly motivated. With their relatively limited mobility and need to maintain rigid formations for mutual protection, foot soldiers found the feigned flight especially challenging. Once engaged in rapid and disorderly retrograde motion, it could not have been easy for them to halt and turn on their pursuers. When infantry were able to make the feigned flight work, it often involved what was effectively a real flight by a decoy unit, whose retreat lured the enemy into a position where, already disordered, they could be surprised by a second detachment concealed in ambush. This is the fate that befell the Sui general Zhang Xutuo in the autumn of 616 when he confronted the rebel leaders Zhai Rang and Li Mi south of the Yellow River, an episode that has already been described in Chapter 3.[98]

Despite their apparently greater speed, the horse-drawn chariots of ancient China also had serious limitations that made successful feigned-flight gambits rather difficult. As Ralph Sawyer, one of the foremost authorities on early Chinese military history, has pointed out, "Chariot operations were . . . known to be severely impeded on any but ideal terrain unbroken by woods, furrows, cultivation, irrigation ditches, shrubbery, and other obstacles."[99] Chariots were fragile contraptions that broke down easily, and they were especially vulnerable in marshes, quagmires, and waterlogged fields. The *Zuo zhuan*, our best source for the sixth, seventh, and eighth centuries BCE, includes several accounts of war chariots getting stuck in the mud on the battlefield. Even without the added disadvantage of unfavorable terrain, an episode from 714 BCE related in the *Zuo zhuan* suggests that "chariots normally proceeded so slowly that they became vulnerable to being outflanked by infantry."[100]

It was only with the advent of cavalry—especially light cavalry of the steppe variety characterized by speed, flexibility, and a somewhat decentralized tactical organization— that maneuvers such as the feigned flight could be executed with greater ease and significantly less risk. The threat such cavalry posed to slower moving, less agile armies was transformative, as old practices such as scouting, reconnaissance, and security took on new and enhanced importance. More than ever before, doing these things well became a matter of life and death. On the Chinese side, the change can be seen by comparing the ancient military classics with the early seventh-century "Military Methods" of Li Jing. In all of the "Seven Military Classics" (or, more to the point, in the six of them that are truly ancient) there is only one clear reference to scouting, found in the *Liu tao*, a work traditionally attributed to the eleventh-century BCE statesman Qi Taigong but actually dating mostly from the late Warring States (and probably also incorporating some material from the Western Han period). In response to a question from the Zhou founder King Wu about how to respond to a difficult military situation, the Taigong is made to offer the following advice:

Now the rule for commanding an army is always to first dispatch scouts far forward so that when you are two hundred *li* from the enemy, you will already know their location. If the strategic configuration of the terrain is not advantageous, then use the Martial Attack chariots to form a mobile rampart and advance. Also establish two rear guard armies to the rear—the further one hundred *li* away, the nearer fifty *li* away. Thus when there is a sudden alarm or an urgent situation, both front and rear will know about it, and the Three Armies will always be able to complete [their deployment into] a solid formation, never suffering any destruction or harm.[101]

This is good advice, and something similar was probably indeed practiced by the armies of the Warring States, Qin, and Han. It is, however, the only mention of scouting in a rather long book,[102] and it pales in comparison with the lavish, redundant, and even obsessive attention devoted to such matters in the much shorter remnants of Li Jing's "Military Methods," with its long-range cavalry scouts, roving patrols, beacon stations, and listening posts all described in very considerable detail. Li Jing's obsession is the reflection of a sea change in Chinese warfare that had taken place between the third century BCE and his own time, a change driven above all by the speed and power of the dominant military paradigm of the age, the mounted archer of the Eurasian steppe.

Notes

1 I follow the evidence and arguments presented in Robert Drews, *Early Riders: The Beginnings of Mounted Warfare in Asia and Europe* (London and New York: Routledge, 2004), pp. 48, 54, 62–3, 66, 68–9, and 99–100. Nicola Di Cosmo has also concluded that

> the transition to actual pastoral nomadism as practiced by horseback riders was probably not completed until the beginning of the first millennium B.C., and the first Scythian mounted archers appear on the scene only in the tenth or ninth century B.C.
>
> (Di Cosmo, *Ancient China and Its Enemies: The Rise of Nomadic Power in East Asian History* (Cambridge: Cambridge University Press, 2002), p. 27)

2 Di Cosmo, *Ancient China and Its Enemies*, p. 31.
3 Di Cosmo, *Ancient China and Its Enemies*, pp. 57–8.
4 Sima Qian, *Records of the Grand Historian: Han Dynasty II*, trans. Burton Watson, rev. ed. (Hong Kong and New York: Columbia University Press, 1993), p. 129. For Chinese text, see *SJ* 110, p. 2879.
5 Herodotus, *The Histories*, trans. Aubrey de Sélincourt (Harmondsworth, UK: Penguin, 1972), p. 286.
6 More detailed discussions of steppe logistics can be found in David A. Graff, "Early T'ang Generalship and the Textual Tradition" (Ph.D. diss., Princeton University, 1995), pp. 126–9, and John Masson Smith, Jr., "Ayn Jālūt: Mamlūk Success or Mongol Failure?" *Harvard Journal of Asiatic Studies* 44.2 (December 1984), pp. 331–9.
7 Herodotus, *The Histories*, pp. 310–17.
8 Rhoads Murphey, "An Ecological History of Central Asian Nomadism," in Gary Seaman (ed.), *Ecology and Empire: Nomads in the Cultural Evolution of the Old World* (Los Angeles: Ethnographics/USC, Center for Visual Anthropology, University of Southern California, 1989), p. 43.
9 Thomas J. Barfield, *The Perilous Frontier: Nomadic Empires and China* (Oxford: Basil Blackwell, 1990), p. 221.
10 Elizabeth Baughman, "Scythian Archers," in C.W. Blackwell (ed.), *Dēmos: The Classical Athenian Democracy* (A. Mahoney and R. Scaife, edd., *The Stoa: A consortium for*

electronic publication in the humanities [www.stoa.org]), edition of January 30, 2003, http://www.stoa.org/projects/demos/article_scythian_archers?page=all&greekEncod ing=, (accessed October 1, 2014).

11 Arthur Waldron, *The Great Wall of China: From History to Myth* (Cambridge: Cambridge University Press, 1990), pp. 13, 15.

12 J.I. Crump, Jr. (trans.), *Chan-Kuo Ts'e*, rev. ed. (Ann Arbor, MI: Center for Chinese Studies, University of Michigan, 1996), pp. 288–98.

13 *HS* 49, pp. 2278–83, translated in Joseph Needham and Robin D.S. Yates, *Science and Civilisation in China*, vol. 5, part 6: *Military Technology: Missiles and Sieges* (Cambridge: Cambridge University Press, 1994), pp. 124–5.

14 Mark Edward Lewis, "The Han Abolition of Universal Military Service," in Hans van de Ven (ed.), *Warfare in Chinese History* (Leiden: Brill, 2000), p. 48 and *passim*.

15 Rafe de Crespigny, *Northern Frontier: The Policies and Strategy of the Later Han Empire* (Canberra: Faculty of Asian Studies, Australian National University, 1984), p. 415.

16 Ni Jinsheng, "Wu Hu luan Hua qianye de Zhongguo jingji," *Shi huo banyuekan* 1.7 (March 1, 1935), p. 39.

17 For details, see Sanping Chen, *Multicultural China in the Early Middle Ages* (Philadelphia: University of Pennsylvania Press, 2012), especially pp. 3–38.

18 For Li Yuan, see Howard J. Wechsler, *Mirror to the Son of Heaven: Wei Cheng at the Court of T'ang T'ai-tsung* (New Haven and London: Yale University Press, 1974), p. 16. For Li Shimin's claim to have killed "a thousand or more" men in battle, see *QTW* 4, p. 25a.

19 *ZZTJ* 189, p. 5910, and the discussion in David A. Graff, "Li Shimin and the Representation of Military Leadership in Medieval China," in Rosemarie Diest (ed.), *Knight and Samurai: Actions and Images of Elite Warriors in Europe and East Asia*, Göppinger Arbeiten zur Germanistik no. 707 (Göppingen: Kümmerle Verlag, 2003), pp. 155–67.

20 Wen Daya, *Da Tang chuang ye qi ju zhu* (Shanghai: Shanghai Guji chubanshe, 1983), p. 2. A much less detailed version can be found in *ZZTJ* 183, p. 5717, where it is placed at the end of 616.

21 *XTS* 111, p. 4137.

22 *ZZTJ* 198, p. 6237 and *ZZTJ* 199, pp. 6274–5; *JTS* 199B, p. 5348.

23 For a specialized study of the steppe influence on early Tang strategic culture, see Jonathan Karam Skaff, "Tang Military Culture and Its Inner Asian Influences," in Nicola Di Cosmo (ed.), *Military Culture in Imperial China* (Cambridge, MA: Harvard University Press, 2009), pp. 165–91.

24 For an account of the campaign and battle of Carrhae, see Ehsan Yarshater (ed.), *The Cambridge History of Iran*, vol. 3(1): *The Seleucid, Parthian, and Sasanian Periods* (Cambridge: Cambridge University Press, 1983), pp. 48–56.

25 Simon James, "The Impact of Steppe Peoples and the Partho-Sassanian World on the Development of Roman Military Equipment and Dress, 1st to 3rd Centuries AD," in Markus Mode and Jürgen Tubach (eds.), *Arms and Armour as Indicators of Cultural Transfer: The Steppes and the Ancient World from Hellenistic Times to the Early Middle Ages* (Wiesbaden: Dr. Ludwig Reichert Verlag, 2006), p. 372.

26 Jon Coulston, "Arms and Armour of the Late Roman Army," in David Nicolle (ed.), *A Companion to Medieval Arms and Armour* (Woodbridge, Suffolk: The Boydell Press, 2002), p. 7; Pat Southern and Karen Ramsey Dixon, *The Late Roman Army* (New Haven and London: Yale University Press, 1996), p. 126; James, "The Impact of Steppe Peoples," pp. 364–5.

27 Helmut Nickel, "The Mutual Influence of Europe and Asia in the Field of Arms and Armour," in David Nicolle (ed.), *A Companion to Medieval Arms and Armour* (Woodbridge, Suffolk: The Boydell Press, 2002), p. 108. Also see Graham Webster, *The Roman Imperial Army* (New York: Funk & Wagnalls, 1969), pp. 152–3.

28 Ann Hyland, *Training the Roman Cavalry; from Arrian's Ars Tactica* (Stroud, Gloucestershire: Alan Sutton, 1993), pp. 3–5 and 77.

29 Ann Hyland, *The Medieval Warhorse: From Byzantium to the Crusades* (Stroud, Gloucestershire: Alan Sutton, 1994), p. 21; James, "The Impact of Steppe Peoples," p. 368; J.C. Coulston, "Roman, Parthian and Sassanid Tactical Developments," in Philip Freeman and David Kennedy (eds.), *The Defence of the Roman and Byzantine East: Proceedings of a Colloquium Held at the University of Sheffield in April 1986*, part 1 (British Institute of Archaeology at Ankara, 1986), p. 67.

30 John Haldon, *The Byzantine Wars* (Stroud, Gloucestershire: Tempus, 2001), p. 26. For the distinction between *catafractii* and *clibanarii*, which is still not entirely clear, see Karen R. Dixon and Pat Southern, *The Roman Cavalry: From the First to the Third Centuries AD* (London: B.T. Batsford Ltd., 1992), p. 76; John W. Eadie, "The Development of Roman Mailed Cavalry," *Journal of Roman Studies* 57 (1967), 169–70; and Coulston, "Arms and Armour of the Late Roman Army," p. 11.

31 Coulston, "Arms and Armour of the Late Roman Army," p. 12.

32 John Haldon, "Some Aspects of Early Byzantine Arms and Armour," in David Nicolle (ed.), *A Companion to Medieval Arms and Armour* (Woodbridge, UK: The Boydell Press, 2002), pp. 67–8; Warren Treadgold, *Byzantium and Its Army, 284–1081* (Stanford, CA: Stanford University Press, 1995), p. 93.

33 Hugh Elton, *Warfare in Roman Europe, AD 350–425* (Oxford: Clarendon Press, 1996), pp. 24–7.

34 Refer to the arguments offered in Rudi Paul Lindner, "Nomadism, Horses and Huns," *Past and Present*, no. 92 (August 1981), pp. 3–19, and the responses in Harry Sidebottom, *Ancient Warfare: A Very Short Introduction* (Oxford: Oxford University Press, 2004), pp. 79–81, and Elton, *Warfare in Roman Europe*, pp. 27–9.

35 Christopher A. Bergman and Edward McEwen, "Sinew-Reinforced and Composite Bows: Technology, Function, and Social Implications," in Heidi Knecht (ed.), *Projectile Technology* (New York and London: Plenum Press, 1997), p. 153. Also see Edward McEwen et al., "Early Bow Design and Construction," *Scientific American*, vol. 264, no. 6 (June 1991), p. 82, and Edward N. Luttwak, *The Grand Strategy of the Byzantine Empire* (Cambridge, MA: The Belknap Press of Harvard University Press, 2009), p. 22.

36 Haldon, "Some Aspects of Early Byzantine Arms and Armour," p. 78.

37 Hyland, *Training the Roman Cavalry*, p. 162; Coulston, "Arms and Armour of the Late Roman Army," p. 5.

38 J. Otto Maenchen-Helfen, *The World of the Huns: Studies in Their History and Culture* (Berkeley and Los Angeles: University of California Press, 1973), pp. 10, 44–6, 48–9, 76–7, 168, and 255–8; Geoffrey Greatrex, *Rome and Persia at War, 502–532* (Leeds: Francis Cairns, 1998), pp. 31 and 173.

39 Elton, *Warfare in Roman Europe*, pp. 68 and 94.

40 Elton, *Warfare in Roman Europe*, p. 253.

41 Fergus Millar, *A Greek Roman Empire: Power and Belief under Theodosius II (408–450)* (Berkeley and Los Angeles: University of California Press, 2006), p. 60.

42 Maenchen-Helfen, *The World of the Huns*, p. 221. More than half a century later, the author of the *Strategikon* reserves a special role for foreign troops, presumably of steppe origin: "Foreign contingents, if stationed by themselves, should be drawn up according to their own customs. It is advantageous to employ them as assault and ambush troops." *Strategikon*, p. 28.

43 Coulston, "Arms and Armour of the Late Roman Army," pp. 6–7 and 17–18; Haldon, *The Byzantine Wars*, pp. 26–7 and 83; Hyland, *The Medieval Warhorse*, p. 21.

44 Greatrex, *Rome and Persia at War*, pp. 39, 177, 188, and 209.

45 J.F. Haldon, "Some Aspects of Byzantine Military Technology from the Sixth to the Tenth Centuries," *Byzantine and Modern Greek Studies* 1 (1975), p. 12; and Luttwak, *The Grand Strategy of the Byzantine Empire*, pp. 58–9. For Vegetius, see *Vegetius:*

Epitome of Military Science, trans. N.P. Milner (Liverpool: Liverpool University Press, 1993), p. 18.

46 Eadie, "The Development of Roman Mailed Cavalry," 162–5; Kaveh Farrokh, *Shadows in the Desert: Ancient Persia at War* (Oxford: Osprey Publishing, 2007), pp. 56–7. For an extensive examination of cavalry in the Achaemenid Persian army, see Christopher Tuplin, "All the King's Horse: In Search of Achaemenid Persian Cavalry," in Garrett G. Fagan and Matthew Trundle (eds.), *New Perspectives on Ancient Warfare* (Leiden: Brill, 2010), pp. 100–82.

47 Greatrex, *Rome and Persia at War*, pp. 53–4.

48 Michael H. Dodgeon and Samuel N. C. Lieu, *The Roman Eastern Frontier and the Persian Wars (AD 226–363): A Documentary History* (London and New York: Routledge, 1991), p. 24.

49 Greatrex, *Rome and Persia at War*, pp. 54, 55, 58, and 186.

50 Greatrex, *Rome and Persia at War*, p. 188; Geoffrey Greatrex and Samuel N.C. Lieu (eds.), *The Roman Eastern Frontier and the Persian Wars*, Part II: *A.D. 363–630, a narrative sourcebook* (London and New York: Routledge, 2002), pp. 87 and 206; Procopius, *History of the Wars*, trans. H.B. Dewing (London: William Heinemann Ltd., 1954), vol. 1, p. 487.

51 Charles J. Halperin, *Russia and the Golden Horde: The Mongol Impact on Medieval Russian History* (Bloomington: Indiana University Press, 1987), pp. 10–11.

52 George Vernadsky, *Kievan Russia* (New Haven: Yale University Press, 1976), pp. 192–3.

53 Halperin, *Russia and the Golden Horde*, p. 13.

54 Halperin, *Russia and the Golden Horde*, p. 18.

55 David R. Stone, *A Military History of Russia: From Ivan the Terrible to the War in Chechnya* (Westport, CT: Praeger Security International, 2006), p. 4.

56 "All of the major and minor states on the periphery of the steppe had military forces of Eurasian nomadic origin." Peter B. Golden, "War and Warfare in the Pre-Činggisid Western Steppes of Eurasia," in Nicola Di Cosmo (ed.), *Warfare in Inner Asian History, 500–1800* (Leiden: Brill, 2002), p. 157.

57 *Vegetius: Epitome of Military Science*, p. 17.

58 *TD* 149, p. 3818.

59 *CFYG* 639, p. 4b. One modern historian observes that this "shows how seriously the government needed skilled military personnel, and how little it understood how to train them." Terrence Douglas O'Byrne, "Civil–Military Relations During the Middle T'ang: The Career of Kuo Tzu-i" (Ph.D. diss, University of Illinois at Urbana-Champaign, 1982), p. 20. Other Western scholars have also made unkind comments about the "hippological incompetence" of the Chinese farmer; see Paul J. Smith, *Taxing Heaven's Storehouse: Horses, Bureaucrats, and the Destruction of the Sichuan Tea Industry, 1074–1224* (Cambridge, MA: Council on East Asian Studies, Harvard University, 1991), pp. 259 and 294–5, and H.G. Creel, "The Role of the Horse in Chinese History," *American Historical Review* 70.3 (April 1965), pp. 670–1.

60 Smith, *Taxing Heaven's Storehouse*, pp. 20–1; also see Ma Junmin and Wang Shiping, *Tangdai mazheng* (Taipei: Wunan tushu chuban gongsi, 1995), p. 95.

61 *XTS* 50, pp. 1337–8; *ZZTJ* 202, p. 6401, and 212, p. 6767; Song Changlian, "Tangdai de mazheng," *Dalu zazhi* 29.1–2 (July 15 and 31, 1964), pp. 29–30 and 61–2.

62 Chen Yinke, "Lun Tangdai zhi fanjiang yu fubing," in *Chen Yinke xiansheng wen shi lunji* (Hong Kong: Wenwen chubanshe, 1972), vol. 2, p. 32; Li Shutong, "Tangdai zhi junshi yu ma," in idem, *Tang shi yanjiu* (Taipei: Taiwan Commercial Press, 1979), p. 241 ff.; Fu Lecheng, "Huihe ma yu Shuofang bing," in idem, *Han-Tang shi lunji* (Taipei: Lianjing, 1977), pp. 313–14; Ma Junmin and Wang Shiping, *Tangdai mazheng*, p. 5.

63 Graff, "Early T'ang Generalship and the Textual Tradition," pp. 170–2.

64 The infantry to cavalry ratio was at least 2:1, and possibly as high as 4:1. See *SS* 8, pp. 161–2; *ZZTJ* 181, pp. 5659–60; and Asami Naoichirō, "Yōdai no dai ichi ji Kōkuri enseigun: sono kibo to heishu," *Tōyōshi kenkyū* 44.1 (June 1985), p. 27.

65 John Haldon, *Warfare, State and Society in the Byzantine World, 565–1204* (London: UCL Press, 1999), pp. 196–7.

66 William H. McNeill, *The Rise of the West: A History of the Human Community* (rpt. Chicago: University of Chicago Press, 1991), p. 393; Farrokh, *Shadows in the Desert*, pp. 56–7, 131–2, and 231.

67 Michael Whitby, *The Emperor Maurice and His Historian: Theophylact Simocatta on Persian and Balkan Warfare* (Oxford: Clarendon Press, 1988), p. 68.

68 Early Central Asian fortifications are the focus of Sören Stark's current research and forthcoming book; see his page at the web site of New York University's Institute for the Study of the Ancient World (ISAW), http://isaw.nyu.edu/research/long-walls (accessed October 1, 2014).

69 Halperin, *Russia and the Golden Horde*, p. 16.

70 George T. Dennis (trans.), *Maurice's Strategikon: Handbook of Byzantine Military Strategy* (Philadelphia: University of Pennsylvania Press, 1984), pp. 113–26.

71 See, for example, *Strategikon*, pp. 23–4, 62, 95, and 167.

72 For the Byzantine *ethnika*, see John E. Wiita, "The *Ethnika* in Byzantine Military Treatises" (Ph.D. dissertation, University of Minnesota, 1977). Although some Chinese works, such as the memorials of the Former Han statesman Chao Cuo, devote some attention to the tactics of foreign peoples, the most influential of all Chinese military writings, the "Seven Military Classics," are silent on this point—probably because most are focused entirely on the Warring States *problematique* of conflict with other Sinic states.

73 See *TD* 157, p. 4029–30; these passages are also discussed in Chapter 4.

74 *TD* 149, p. 3822; *TD* 157, p. 4041.

75 *TD* 157, p. 4024: "The general rule is that enemy troops like to make surprise attacks on us." Also see *TD* 150, p. 3840; *TD* 157, pp. 4027 and 4034.

76 *TD* 149, p. 3822.

77 *TD* 157, pp. 4029–30.

78 *Strategikon*, p. 116.

79 *Strategikon*, p. 117.

80 *Strategikon*, p. 116.

81 *Strategikon*, p. 117.

82 All of the material quoted in this paragraph can be found in *Strategikon*, pp. 117–18.

83 All of the material quoted in this paragraph can be found in *Strategikon*, p. 118.

84 Haldon, *Warfare, State and Society*, p. 208.

85 *Strategikon*, p. 23.

86 *Strategikon*, p. 24.

87 *TD* 157, p. 4034.

88 *TD* 157, p. 4034.

89 *TD* 157, p. 4025.

90 *TD* 157, pp. 4033–4.

91 *ZZTJ* 196, p. 6171, and *ZZTJ* 213, pp. 6776–7. The nomads employed the same techniques against the Chinese and probably each other as well. In 635, for example, the Tuyuhun burned the prairie grass behind them as they retreated in order to prevent the Tang cavalry from pursuing (*XTS* 221A, p. 6225), eliciting the following comment from Tang officers: "The horses are without grass, tired and thin; we can't go in deep" (*ZZTJ* 194, p. 6111).

92 *Strategikon*, p. 65; David A. Graff, "Strategy and Contingency in the Tang Defeat of the Eastern Turks, 629–630," in Nicola Di Cosmo (ed.), *Warfare in Inner Asian History (500–1800)* (Leiden: Brill, 2002), pp. 50–4. Also see David Curtis Wright, "Nomadic Power, Sedentary Security, and the Crossbow," *Acta Orientalia* 58.1 (2005), p. 17. The horses of sedentary armies, fed on stored fodder and even grain, were much better prepared for campaigns in the late winter or early spring.

93 For Li Shimin's cultivation of the Tuli qaghan and sowing dissension among the Türks, see Wang Zhenping, *Tang China in Multi-Polar Asia: A History of Diplomacy and War* (Honolulu: University of Hawai'i Press, 2013), pp. 25–6 and 32.

94 Graff, "Strategy and Contingency," 53–4; *Strategikon*, p. 118.

95 Duke Zhuang, tenth year, in James Legge (trans.), *The Chinese Classics*, vol. 5: *The Ch'un Ts'ew with the Tso Chuen* (rpt. Taipei: Southern Materials Center, 1985), p. 86. Spelling and punctuation modernized.

96 *Aeneas Tacticus, Asclepiodotus, Onasander* (London: William Heinemann, 1923), pp. 457–9.

97 Aineias the Tactician, *How to Survive Under Siege: A Historical Commentary, with Translation and Introduction*, trans. David Whitehead, 2nd ed. (London: Bristol Classical Press, 2001), p. 95.

98 *ZZTJ* 183, p. 5711; variant accounts of the same battle can be found in *SS* 71, p. 1647, and *TD* 152, p. 3889. For translation, see Chapter 3 above (at note 136).

99 Ralph D. Sawyer, *Ancient Chinese Warfare* (New York: Basic Books, 2011), p. 382.

100 Sawyer, *Ancient Chinese Warfare*, p. 383; also see pp. 375–7 and 379.

101 Ralph D. Sawyer, *The Seven Military Classics of Ancient China* (Boulder, CO: Westview Press, 1993), p. 86. Chinese text in Xu Peigen (ann. and trans.), *Taigong Liu tao jin zhu jin yi*, 2nd rev. ed. (Taipei: Taiwan Shangwu yinshuguan, 1986), p. 163.

102 Skeptical readers who cannot access the Chinese military classics in the original language and do not have the time to read them in translation should at least examine the subject index to Sawyer's translation of *The Seven Military Classics* (pp. 549–68), which is quite revealing. Setting aside the one mention of scouting, the terms "reconnaissance," "patrols," and "sentries" do not appear, and references to "security" all refer to national security writ large rather the mundane details of maintaining the security of one's forces in camp and on the march.

8   Conclusion

This book has emphasized the similarity of Chinese and Byzantine military methods in the years around 600 CE, while giving relatively little attention to their many differences. I have noted in passing that the Chinese empire of the early Tang was significantly larger than the Eastern Roman Empire of Maurikios and his successors, and disposed of greater resources, and suggested that this difference may have made Byzantine generals even more cautious than their Chinese counterparts, and less open to the idea of throwing their troops into desperate situations in order to compel them to do their utmost—as recommended by classical military writings in both China and the ancient Mediterranean world. I have pointed out that China depended far less on naval power than Byzantium did and then, because this is an area of difference rather than similarity, devoted no further attention to it. A third field of divergence that I have scarcely mentioned at all, but one that deserves very serious consideration because it made the experience of service in the armies of these two empires so very different, is an obvious one: religion.

From the reign of Theodosius I (r. 379–395) onward, Orthodox Christianity was the state religion of the Eastern Roman Empire. With the exception of discrete contingents of foreign troops (such as Huns), by the time the *Strategikon* was written almost all of the empire's soldiers were Christians and the religious character of the army was reflected in a host of concrete institutional arrangements and procedures.[1] Armies in the field were usually accompanied by priests, who conducted religious services on a regular basis and, according to the *Strategikon*, led prayers before battle:

> All, led by the priests, the general, and the other officers, should recite the "Kyrie eleison" (Lord have mercy) for some time in unison. Then, in hopes of success, each meros should shout the "Nobiscum Deus" (God is with us) three times as it marches out of camp.[2]

According to some military manuals, soldiers were expected to attend religious services twice daily.[3] The *Strategikon* begins by invoking the guidance of the Holy Trinity, and goes on to offer the following advice to the army's commander:

> First, we urge upon the general that his most important concern be the love of God and justice; building on these, he should strive to win the favor of God,

without which it is impossible to carry out any plan, however well devised it may seem, or to overcome any enemy, however weak he may be thought. For all things are ruled by the providence of God, a providence which extends even to the birds and the fishes.[4]

Early Tang armies certainly had their own share of military rituals with a religious character. Before an expeditionary army marched forth from the capital, sacrifices were supposed to be made at the altar of earth (*she*) and at the imperial ancestral temple (*tai miao*). If the emperor intended to lead the campaign in person, he would perform these ceremonies himself and would also make an offering to the Lord-on-High (*Shang Di*). During the course of a campaign, the army's commanders would also be expected to make offerings to the divinities of the lands through which they passed, including the gods of mountains and rivers. An eighth-century Chinese military encyclopedia, the *Taibai yinjing*, even has the texts of sample prayers including one directed to the god of horses, a very sensible proposition in the context of medieval warfare. And a parallel to the triumphs of ancient Rome (still carried out in a Christianized form in Byzantium) could also be found in the Chinese world: the successful completion of a major military campaign was supposed to be marked by a great victory parade (*kaixuan*) and the presentation of captives, severed heads, and other spoils of war at the south entrance of the imperial ancestral temple, which was also the site of the ceremonial drinking (*yinzhi*) and recording of merit (*cexun*).[5] At a much more basic level, as we have seen, there were also official rites of sacrifice and burial for fallen soldiers.

These public rituals, both great and small, were of course only one facet of a quite complicated religious scene. Followers of all of China's great religious traditions— including Buddhism, Daoism, and a great variety of shamanistic local folk beliefs—could be found among the rank and file of Sui and Tang armies. The Sui rulers had actively promoted Buddhism as a unifying force for their empire, while the Tang founders, claiming descent from the ancient sage Laozi, favored Daoism. And, as we have seen in Chapter 5, clever generals were more than willing to exploit local folk beliefs to raise the morale of their troops. In contrast to the situation in the Byzantine armies, however, there was no single common faith in the Chinese military to bind soldiers together and motivate them to fight for a shared sacred cause. In what survives of his "Military Methods," Li Jing seems to regard popular religious beliefs as a disruptive and even potentially subversive influence rather than a positive force, and there is nothing in the corpus of Chinese military writings, both ancient and medieval, that remotely resembles the *Strategikon*'s advice that the general should make it a priority to win the favor of God.[6]

The religious element also looms large in Byzantium's grand strategy and sense of imperial purpose. Although authorities generally agree that the Byzantines did not have a concept of holy war comparable to that of their Muslim opponents (or the Latin Crusaders), the centrality of their Christian identity meant that almost all of their wars, both defensive and offensive, could easily be viewed through a religious lens and justified as necessary means to ensure the survival of the

Orthodox state and people.[7] Religious faith rarely provided the Byzantines with a positive motive for going to war, but it did serve as an important resource in the repeated conflicts that seemed to be thrust upon them. In an extensive recent study of Byzantine grand strategy, Edward Luttwak identifies diplomacy, bribery, and alliance-building—rather than direct appeals to military force—as the hallmark of the Byzantine approach that took shape during the two centuries between the onslaught of the Huns and the time of Herakleios:

> To wear out their own forces, chiefly of expensive cavalry, in order to utterly destroy the immediate enemy would only open the way for the next wave of invaders. The genius of Byzantine grand strategy was to turn the very multiplicity of enemies to advantage, by employing diplomacy, deception, payoffs, and religious conversion to induce them to fight one another instead of fighting the empire. Only their firm self-image as the only defenders of the only true faith preserved their moral equilibrium. In the Byzantine scheme of things, military strength was subordinated to diplomacy instead of the other way around, and used mostly to contain, punish, or intimidate rather than to attack or defend in full force.[8]

Grand strategy, like culture, is a widely used term that is sometimes not very carefully defined—and one that is often defined in rather different ways. For Luttwak, "grand strategy is simply the *level* at which knowledge and persuasion, or in modern terms intelligence and diplomacy, interact with military strength to determine outcomes in a world of other states, with their own 'grand strategies.'"[9] For another prominent historian who has written about grand strategy, Geoffrey Parker, it "may be defined as the decisions of a given state about its overall security – the threats it perceives, the ways it confronts them, and the steps it takes to match ends and means."[10] Yet another variant has been offered by Alastair Iain Johnston, for whom grand strategy involves "definitions of the enemy, of the threat environment, and of . . . preferred ways of responding to this environment."[11] Whatever else it may be, grand strategy is certainly about identifying (and prioritizing) threats (and opportunities), and deciding what means to use in response to them.

For the Byzantines, the main threat was usually whatever tribe or state was exerting the greatest pressure against the empire's territory; opportunities for expansion (or more accurately, the recovery of lost territories) were few and far between, and the preferred means usually involved some combination of diplomacy and bribery rather than the maximal application of force, which was seen as both risky and expensive. All of these methods, including the time-honored technique of "using barbarians to control barbarians," were well known to Chinese statesmen. Yet the Sui and Tang dynasties seem to have resorted to large-scale, offensive military campaigns more easily and frequently than the Byzantine rulers of the late sixth and early seventh centuries. Obvious examples from the Sui include the conquest of southern China in 589 and Emperor Yang's repeated campaigns against Koguryŏ beginning in 612, as well as lesser campaigns such as the invasion of Linyi (the central part of today's Vietnam) in 605, and cases from the early Tang are also quite numerous. From the reign of Taizong, we have the campaign against the Eastern Türks in 629–630, the subjugation of the Tuyuhun of the northwest in 634–635, the conquest of oasis-states such as Gaochang (640) and Kucha (648), and the invasion of Koguryŏ in 645, and from the reign of his successor Gaozong, we have further offensives by both land and sea against the states of the Korean Peninsula, long-range expeditions against the Western Türks, and campaigns against the Tibetans. Although the Chinese were well versed in risk avoidance and the use of all sorts of wiles at the tactical and operational levels, their approach to strategy during this period tended to be quite aggressive and was often on a very large scale.

The difference between Chinese and Byzantine grand strategy may not, however, have been as great as it first appears. As we have already seen (in Chapter 2), the Chinese empire of Sui and early Tang times was favored with a much larger population, more extensive resources, and greater strategic depth than its Byzantine counterpart. Losses could be made up more easily, and miscalculations were less likely to spiral downward into complete disaster. This is not to say that disasters did not occur, the collapse of the Sui empire in the wake of its repeated assaults on Koguryŏ being a prime example—but one that required the pig-headed persistence of Emperor Yang launching new campaigns in 613 and 614 after the failure of his original effort in 612. When the material balance was in their favor, Byzantine rulers, too, could adopt the strategic offensive, as with Justinian's campaigns to recover North Africa and Italy in the sixth century and, much later, the recovery of southeastern Anatolia and parts of Syria in the tenth century and the destruction of the Bulgarian state in the early eleventh century. A considerable amount of risk-taking was also seen in Herakleios' long-range offensive campaigns into the Sasanian heartland in the 620s, though these may be understood as a desperate response to a terrible situation, with Constantinople under siege and many of the empire's most productive provinces overrun by the Persians. Nevertheless, much of the difference between Chinese and Byzantine behavior may be attributed to their varying capabilities rather than to fundamentally different strategic orientations. Both empires seem to have been happy to recover lost territories when the opportunity beckoned and the risk did not appear to be too great.

Similarly, the religious aspect of Byzantine warfare, though it surely made the subjective experience and understanding of war qualitatively different from what was known in China, does not seem to have produced much difference in actual military practice. This book has demonstrated the broad similarity of Chinese and Byzantine military tactics and techniques in the early seventh century. The similarities are not limited to equipment, weapons, and troop types, but extend to battlefield formations, march organization, camp security, scouting, patrols, reconnaissance, discipline (no breaking ranks in battle, especially to plunder), controlled pursuit, and a generally cautious approach to the inherent risks of battle. These findings directly challenge the notion of opposing Western and "Oriental" ways of war promoted by scholars such as John Keegan and Victor Davis Hanson. With its well-drilled and disciplined foot soldiers deployed in formation and advancing into close combat against an enemy to their front, the Tang expeditionary army described by Li Jing is far too "Western" to fit into this crude schema. The Byzantine army of the *Strategikon*, meanwhile, with its heavy reliance on archery and cavalry, its trickiness, standoffishness, and cautious approach to battle, appears too "Oriental" to ever qualify as Western. It is not that two sides have traded positions, but rather that they share a broad middle ground that may be called "the Eurasian Way of War."

The common ground shared by China and Byzantium in the early seventh century cannot be attributed to a shared cultural inheritance. It also owes little, if anything, to the diffusion of ideas, tools, and techniques from each of these empires to the other. It surely owes something to universal military best practices (such as reconnaissance and security) and to long traditions of record keeping, lesson learning, and rational thinking about war in both societies. Above all, however, it reflects the long-term influence of Eurasian steppe peoples on the military practices of both China and Byzantium, an influence that had both symmetrical aspects (imitation of the nomads' strengths in cavalry and archery) and asymmetrical aspects (in the form of a variety of countermeasures). As we have seen, most of the common characteristics shared by the Chinese and Byzantine militaries were either borrowed directly from the steppe warriors or of obvious utility in countering their preferred tactics. These include, most obviously, the deployment of an army on the battlefield in multiple echelons with both *cursores* and *defensores* (or their equivalents), the control and limitation of pursuits, careful attention to long-range scouting, and an almost obsessive concern for the security of the army, both in camp and on the march.

This evidence not only challenges the specific construct of a distinctive "Western Way of War", but also calls into question the broader notion of long-term, culturally based ways of war that are strongly resistant to change over time. Instead, it suggests that military systems and practices are much more flexible, that they are forever "works in progress" shaped by current needs, recent experiences, and changing conditions. For approximately 2,000 years, all of the sedentary societies that came into close and prolonged contact with the nomads of the Eurasian steppes found it necessary to adapt and adjust in order to cope effectively with the threat from what was, over much of the Old World, the dominant military paradigm.[12] They recruited "barbarians" into their armies, copied their weaponry, equipment, and tactics, and adopted countermeasures ranging from wall building to the sophisticated tactical methods described by Li Jing and the author of the *Strategikon*.[13]

This story is just one example of a widespread, even universal phenomenon. Long before the period treated in this book, the use of the war chariot spread across much of Eurasia in a similar wave of imitation. Just a few decades after the era of Li Jing and Maurikios, in the second half of the seventh century, Japan's Yamato rulers—apparently spurred on by the fear of a Tang invasion—reorganized both their government and their military institutions along Chinese lines.[14] Approximately 1,000 years further on, military tools, techniques, and best practices—including repeated improvements of gunpowder weaponry (better cannon, flintlock muskets, the socket bayonet)—were spread around the Western world by the ongoing competition of the various European states. And then, during the nineteenth century especially, the military package developed in Europe was imitated first in part and then *in toto* by powers ranging from the Ottoman Empire to the Sikhs in India to late Qing China and Meiji Japan. As of the early twenty-first century, the armed forces of all of the world's approximately 200 states are organized, without significant exception, according to a Western pattern.

This is not, however, to propose a crude technological determinism in place of cultural determinism. Adaptation to new threats and new conditions is not necessarily a matter of imitation; it may just as easily be a matter of innovation involving the use of asymmetric countermeasures, and may rely on organization and ideas more than on hardware. Although they disagree on a number of points, the studies by William H. McNeill and Kenneth Chase on the spread and use of firearms in Eurasia in the early modern period concur with regard to the basic point that a technological cause (gunpowder) did not produce the same political, military, and social results everywhere it was introduced.[15] Different local conditions led to different outcomes. As Chase points out, sedentary armies that seldom if ever had to fight against steppe nomads (such as those of Western Europe and Japan) developed massed infantry firepower, while those in closer contact with the steppe (such as the Ottomans, Mughals, and Ming Chinese) tended to use firearms more sparingly and in concert with wagon laagers. Moving forward to the nineteenth century, not all non-Western successes against European powers were gained by acquiring the weaponry of the colonizers and copying their methods. The West African leader Samori Touré held the off the French from the early 1870s to the late 1890s—in part by acquiring modern rifles, and in part by employing guerrilla tactics and avoiding large-scale engagements.[16] And during the twentieth century, of course, the use of guerrilla tactics in asymmetric conflicts against materially and technologically superior opponents became the hallmark of anticolonial struggles and liberation movements ranging from China and Vietnam to Latin America and Africa.

In all of these examples, and in the Chinese and Byzantine cases examined at length in this book, the common denominator is not technology transfer but rather adaptation in response to changing conditions and new military needs. The evidence presented in these pages suggests that, in war at least, we are not the prisoners of fixed cultural heritages. To borrow the "old Arab proverb" once quoted by Marc Bloch, "Men resemble their times more than they do their fathers."[17]

Notes

1 A. D. Lee, *War in Late Antiquity: A Social History* (Malden, MA: Blackwell Publishing, 2007), pp. 188–9; Michael McCormick, *Eternal Victory: Triumphal Rulership in Late Antiquity, Byzantium, and the Early Medieval West* (Cambridge: Cambridge University Press, 1986), pp. 245–9; Paul Goubert, "Religion et superstitions dans l'armée byzantine à la fin du VIe siècle," *Orientalia Christiana Periodica* 13 (1947), 495–500.

2 George T. Dennis (trans.), *Maurice's Strategikon: Handbook of Byzantine Military Strategy* (Philadelphia: University of Pennsylvania Press, 1984), pp. 33–4; also see John Haldon, *Warfare, State and Society in the Byzantine World, 565–1204* (London: UCL Press, 1999), p. 24.

IN WAR, WE ARE NOT THE PRISONERS OF FIXED CULTURAL HERITAGES

3 Tia M. Kolbaba, "Fighting for Christianity: Holy War in the Byzantine Empire," *Byzantion* 68 (1998), p. 206.
4 *Strategikon*, p. 9.
5 This borrows from the more complete discussion of Sui and Tang military ritual in David A. Graff, "Dou Jiande's Dilemma: Logistics, Strategy, and State-Formation in Seventh-Century China," in Hans van de Ven (ed.), *Warfare in Chinese History* (Leiden: Brill, 2000), pp. 98–102. For Byzantine triumphs, see McCormick, *Eternal Victory*, pp. 6 and 79, and the material presented on pp. 80–130. For the texts of prayers, see Li Quan, *Taibai yinjing*, chapter 7, sections 73–78, in *Zhongguo bingshu jicheng*, vol. 2 (Beijing and Shenyang: Jiefangjun chubanshe and Liao-Shen shushe, 1988), pp. 601–9.
6 Li Jing:

> If one speaks of Dao or Buddha, or prays to ghosts and spirits, or performs divination with yin and yang, or spreads false talk of auspicious and inauspicious omens, thereby shaking the morale of the masses, execute him and those who run back and forth to carry on conversations with him.
>
> (*TD* 149, p. 3823)

7 Haldon, *Warfare, State and Society*, pp. 23 and 32, and George T. Dennis, "Defenders of the Christian People: Holy War in Byzantium," in Angeliki E. Laiou and Roy P. Mottahedeh (eds.), *The Crusades from the Perspective of Byzantium and the Muslim World* (Washington, DC: Dumbarton Oaks, 2001), pp. 31–9. For a rare dissenting opinion, see Kolbaba, "Fighting for Christianity," especially pp. 209–10.
8 Edward N. Luttwak, *The Grand Strategy of the Byzantine Empire* (Cambridge, MA: The Belknap Press of Harvard University Press, 2009), p. 415.
9 Luttwak, *The Grand Strategy of the Byzantine Empire*, p. 409. Also see the same author's *Strategy: The Logic of War and Peace* (Cambridge, MA: The Belknap Press of Harvard University Press, 1987), pp. 179–80.
10 Geoffrey Parker, *The Grand Strategy of Philip II* (New Haven and London: Yale University Press, 1998), p. 1.
11 Alastair Iain Johnston, *Cultural Realism: Strategic Culture and Grand Strategy in Chinese History* (Princeton, NJ: Princeton University Press, 1995), p. 36, note 2.
12 Gerard Chaliand, *Nomadic Empires: From Mongolia to the Danube*, trans. A.M. Berrett (New Brunswick, NJ: Transaction Publishers, 2004), p. 2.
13 As Andre Gunder Frank rather blandly put it,

> The fact that Central Asians were . . . victorious suggests that they had developed something of value in a competitive world. Their more sedentary neighbors also developed technology and social organization in response to their relations with Central Asians and, of course, with each other.
>
> (*The Centrality of Central Asia* (Amsterdam: VU University Press, 1992), p. 13)

For the recruitment of steppe warriors by sedentary states, see Peter B. Golden, "War and Warfare in the Pre-Činggisid Western Steppes of Eurasia," in Nicola Di Cosmo (ed.), *Warfare in Inner Asian History, 500–1800* (Leiden: Brill, 2002), p. 157.
14 Bruce L. Batten, "Foreign Threat and Domestic Reforms: The Emergence of the *Ritsuryō* State," *Monumenta Nipponica* 41.2 (Summer 1986), pp. 199–219.
15 William H. McNeill, *The Age of Gunpowder Empires, 1450–1800* (Washington, DC: American Historical Association, 1989); Kenneth Chase, *Firearms: A Global History to 1700* (Cambridge: Cambridge University Press, 2003).
16 Daniel R. Headrick, *The Tools of Empire: Technology and European Imperialism in the Nineteenth Century* (New York: Oxford University Press, 1981), p. 119.
17 Marc Bloch, *The Historian's Craft*, trans. Peter Putnam (New York: Alfred A. Knopf, 1953), p. 35.

Bibliography

Traditional Chinese works

CFYG Wang Qinruo 王欽若. *Cefu yuangui* 冊府元龜. Taipei: Taiwan Zhonghua shuju, 1967.
HS Ban Gu 班固. *Han shu* 漢書. Beijing: Zhonghua shuju, 1962.
JS Fang Xuanling 房玄齡. *Jin shu* 晉書. Beijing: Zhonghua shuju, 1974.
JTS Liu Xu 劉昫. *Jiu Tang shu* 舊唐書. Beijing: Zhonghua shuju, 1975.
QTW *Quan Tang wen* 全唐文. Taipei: Jingwei shuju, 1965.
SJ Sima Qian 司馬遷. *Shi ji* 史記. Beijing: Zhonghua shuju, 1959.
SS Wei Zheng 魏徵. *Sui shu* 隋書. Beijing: Zhonghua shuju, 1973.
TD Du You 杜佑. *Tong dian* 通典. Beijing: Zhonghua shuju, 1988.
THY Wang Pu 王溥. *Tang hui yao* 唐會要. Beijing: Zhonghua shuju, 1990.
TLD Li Linfu 李林甫. *Tang liu dian* 唐六典. Beijing: Zhonghua shuju, 1992.
WS Wei Shou 魏收. *Wei shu* 魏書. Beijing: Zhonghua shuju, 1974.
XTS Ouyang Xiu 歐陽修 and Song Qi 宋祁. *Xin Tang shu* 新唐書. Beijing: Zhonghua shuju, 1975.
ZZTJ Sima Guang 司馬光. *Zizhi tongjian* 資治通鑒. Beijing: Guji chubanshe, 1956.

The Art of War: Sun Zi's Military Methods. Translated by Victor H. Mair. New York: Columbia University Press, 2007.
Chan-kuo Ts'e. Translated by J.I. Crump, Jr. Revised edition. Ann Arbor, MI: Center for Chinese Studies, The University of Michigan, 1996.
Chao Gongwu 晁公武. *Jun zhai du shu zhi* 郡齋讀書志. Rpt. of Qing edn. of Wang Xianqian 王先謙. Taipei: Guangwen shuju, 1967.
The Chinese Classics, vol. 5: *The Ch'un Ts'ew, with the Tso Chuen*. Translated by James Legge. Rpt. Taipei: Southern Materials Center, 1985.
Fan Ye 范曄. *Hou Han shu* 後漢書. Shanghai: Zhonghua shuju, 1965.
Leslie, D.D. and K.H.J. Gardiner. *The Roman Empire in Chinese Sources*. Studi Orientali 15. Rome: Bardi, 1996.
Li Jing bingfa jiben zhuyi 李靖兵法輯本註譯. Translated and annotated by Deng Zezong 鄧澤宗. Beijing: Jiefangjun chubanshe, 1990.
Li Quan 李筌. *Taibai yinjing* 太白陰經. In *Zhongguo bingshu jicheng* 中國兵書集成, vol. 2. Beijing and Shenyang: Jiefangjun chubanshe and Liao-Shen shushe, 1988.
Li Weigong wang Jiangnan 李衛公望江南. Edited by Rao Zongyi 饒宗頤. Taipei: Xin wenfeng chuban gongsi, 1990.
Linghu Defen 令狐德棻. *Zhou shu* 周書. Beijing: Zhonghua shuju, 1971.

Liu Junwen 劉俊文. *Tang lü shuyi qian jie* 唐律疏議淺解. Beijing: Zhonghua shuju, 1996. 2 vols.

Loewe, Michael. *Records of Han Administration*. London: Cambridge University Press, 1967. 2 vols.

Ouyang Xun 歐陽詢. *Yiwen leiju* 藝文類聚. Shanghai: Zhonghua shuju, 1965.

The Seven Military Classics of Ancient China. Translated by Ralph D. Sawyer. Boulder, CO: Westview Press, 1993.

Shiyi jia zhu Sunzi 十一家註孫子. Edited by Guo Huaruo 郭化若. Shanghai: Zhonghua shuju, 1962.

Sima Qian. *Records of the Grand Historian: Han Dynasty II*. Translated by Burton Watson. Revised edition. Hong Kong and New York: Columbia University Press, 1993.

Sima Qian. *The Grand Scribe's Records*, vol. 7: *The Memoirs of Pre-Han China*. Edited by William H. Nienhauser. Bloomington and Indianapolis: Indiana University Press, 1994.

Sun-Tzu: The Art of War. Translated by Samuel B. Griffith. Oxford: Oxford University Press, 1963.

Sun-Tzu: The Art of Warfare. Translated by Roger T. Ames. New York: Ballantine Books, 1993.

Sunzi jiaoshi 孫子校釋. Edited by Wu Jiulong 吳九龍, Yang Bing'an, Wu Rusong, Mu Zhichao, and Huang Pumin. Beijing: Junshi kexue chubanshe, 1990.

Taigong Liu tao jin zhu jin yi 太公六韜今註今譯. Translated and annotated by Xu Peigen 徐培根. Second revised edition. Taipei: Taiwan Shangwu yinshuguan, 1986.

The Tang Code, vol. 2: *Specific Articles*. Translated by Wallace Johnson. Princeton, NJ: Princeton University Press, 1997.

Tang Taizong Li Weigong wendui jin zhu jin yi 唐太宗李衛公問對今註今譯. Translated and annotated by Zeng Zhen 曾振. Third edition. Taipei: Taiwan Shangwu yinshuguan, 1981.

Tao Te Ching. Translated by D.C. Lau. Harmondsworth, UK: Penguin, 1985.

Trombert, Éric (with the collaboration of Ikeda On and Zhang Guangda). *Les manuscrits chinois de Koutcha: Fonds Pelliot de la Bibliothèque Nationale de France*. Paris: Insitut des Hautes Études Chinoises du Collège de France, 2000.

Wang Ju 王琚. *She jing* 射經. In *Zhongguo bingshu jicheng* 中國兵書集成, vol. 2. Beijing and Shenyang: Jiefangjun chubanshe and Liao-Shen shushe, 1988.

Wang Yaochen 王堯臣. *Chongwen zongmu* 崇文總目. Taipei: Taiwan shangwu yinshuguan, 1965.

Wang Zongyi 汪宗沂. *Li Weigong bingfa jiben* 李衛公兵法輯本. In *Jianxi cunshe congkan* 漸西村舍叢刊. Facsimile rpt. in *Zhongguo bingshu jicheng* 中國兵書集成, vol. 2. Beijing and Shenyang: Jiefangjun chubanshe and Liao-Shen shushe, 1988.

Wei Zheng 魏徵. *Qun shu zhi yao* 群書治要. In *Lianyunyi congshu* 蓮筠簃叢書. Rpt. Taipei: Yiwen yinshuguan, 1966.

Wen Daya 溫大雅. *Da Tang chuang ye qi ju zhu* 大唐創業起居注. Shanghai: Shanghai guji chubanshe, 1983.

Wu Jing 吳競. *Zhenguan zhengyao* 貞觀政要. Taipei: Hongye shuju, 1990.

Yao Silian 姚思廉. *Liang shu* 梁書. Beijing: Zhonghua shuju, 1973.

Zeng Gongliang 曾公亮. *Wujing zongyao* 武經總要. In *Zhongguo bingshu jicheng* 中國兵書集成, vols. 3–5. Beijing and Shenyang: Jiefangjun chubanshe and Liao-Shen shushe, 1988.

Zhao Rui 趙蕤. *Chang duan jing* 長短經. In *Zhongguo bingshu jicheng* 中國兵書集成, vol. 2. Beijing and Shenyang: Jiefangjun chubanshe and Liao-Shen shushe, 1988.

Zuo shi bingfa qian shuo 左氏兵法淺說. Edited by Wang Zhiping 王志平 and Wu Minxia 吳敏霞. Beijing: Haichao chubanshe, 1992.

Greek, Roman, and Byzantine works

Aeneas Tacticus, Asclepiodotus, Onasander. London: William Heinemann, 1923.

Aineias the Tactician. *How to Survive Under Siege: A Historical Commentary, with Translation and Introduction.* Translated by David Whitehead. Second edition. London: Bristol Classical Press, 2001.

Constantine Porphyrogenitus, Three Treatises on Imperial Military Expeditions. Edited and translated by John F. Haldon. Vienna: Verlag der Österreichischen Akademie der Wissenschaften, 1990.

Dodgeon, Michael H. and Samuel N.C. Lieu. *The Roman Eastern Frontier and the Persian Wars (AD 226–363): A Documentary History.* London and New York: Routledge, 1991.

Fink, Robert O. *Roman Military Records on Papyrus.* Philological Monographs of the American Philological Association, No. 26. Cleveland, OH: Case Western Reserve University, 1971.

Frontinus, Sextus Julius. *The Stratagems and The Aqueducts of Rome.* Translated by Charles E. Bennett. 1925. Rpt. London: William Heinemann Ltd., 1980.

Greatrex, Geoffrey and Samuel N.C. Lieu. *The Roman Eastern Frontier and the Persian Wars,* Part 2: *AD 363–630, A narrative sourcebook.* London and New York: Routledge, 2002.

The History of Menander the Guardsman. Translated by R.C. Blockley. ARCA 17. Liverpool: Francis Cairns, 1985.

Herodotus. *The Histories.* Translated by Aubrey de Sélincourt. Harmondsworth, UK: Penguin, 1972.

Maurice's Strategikon: Handbook of Byzantine Military Strategy. Translated by George T. Dennis. Philadelphia: University of Pennsylvania Press, 1984.

McGeer, Eric. *Sowing the Dragon's Teeth: Byzantine Warfare in the Tenth Century.* Dumbarton Oaks Studies 33. Washington, DC: Dumbarton Oaks Research Library and Collection, 1995.

Polyaenus. *Stratagems of War.* Translated by R. Shepherd. Rpt. Chicago: Ares Publishers, 1974.

Procopius. *History of the Wars.* Translated by H.B. Dewing. Loeb Classical Library. London: William Heinemann Ltd., 1954.

Siegecraft: Two Tenth-Century Instructional Manuals by "Heron of Byzantium." Translated by Denis F. Sullivan. Dumbarton Oaks Studies 36. Washington, DC: Dumbarton Oaks Research Library and Collection, 2000.

Simocatta, Theophylactus. *The History of Theophylact Simocatta.* Translated by Michael and Mary Whitby. Oxford: Clarendon Press, 1986.

The Taktika of Leo VI. Translated by George T. Dennis. Washington, DC: Dumbarton Oaks, 2010.

Three Byzantine Military Treatises. Translated by George T. Dennis. Washington, DC: Dumbarton Oaks, 1985.

Vegetius: Epitome of Military Science. Translated by N.P. Milner. Liverpool: Liverpool University Press, 1993.

Selected literature

Adshead, S.A.M. *T'ang China: The Rise of the East in World History.* Basingstoke, Hampshire: Palgrave Macmillan, 2004.

Ahrweiler, Hélène. "L'organisation des campagnes militaires à Byzance." In *War, Technology and Society in the Middle East.* Edited by V.J. Parry and M.E. Yapp, 89–96. London: Oxford University Press, 1975.

Aoyama Sadao 青山定雄. *Tō Sō jidai no kōtsū to chishi chizu no kenkyū* 唐宋時代の交通と地誌地圖の研究. Tokyo: Yoshikawa kōbunkan, 1963.

Asami Naoichirō 淺見直一郎. "Yōdai no dai ichi ji Kokuri enseigun: sono kibo to heishu" 煬帝の第一次高句麗遠征軍：その規模と兵種. *Tōyōshi kenkyū* 44.1 (June 1985), 23–44.

Austin, N.J.E. and N.B. Rankov. *Exploratio: Military and Political Intelligence in the Roman World from the Second Punic War to the Battle of Adrianople*. London and New York: Routledge, 1995.

Bachrach, Bernard S. *Early Carolingian Warfare: Prelude to Empire*. Philadelphia: University of Pennsylvania Press, 2001.

Bachrach, Bernard S. "*Caballus* and *Caballarius* in Medieval Warfare." 1988. In *Warfare and Military Organization in Pre-Crusade Europe*, II/173–II/211. Variorum Collected Studies. Aldershot, Hampshire: Ashgate. 2002.

Barfield, Thomas J. *The Perilous Frontier: Nomadic Empires and China*. Oxford: Basil Blackwell, 1990.

Batten, Bruce L. "Foreign Threat and Domestic Reforms: The Emergence of the *Ritsuryō* State." *Monumenta Nipponica* 41.2 (Summer 1986), 199–219.

Baughman, Elizabeth. "Scythian Archers." In *Dēmos: The Classical Athenian Democracy*. Edited by C.W. Blackwell (A. Mahoney and R. Scaife, edd., *The Stoa: A consortium for electronic publication in the humanities* [www.stoa.org]), edition of January 30, 2003, http://www.stoa.org/projects/demos/article_scythian_archers?page=all&greekEncoding=, (accessed October 1, 2014).

Beeler, John. *Warfare in Feudal Europe, 730–1200*. Ithaca and London: Cornell University Press, 1971.

Benn, Charles. *Daily Life in Traditional China: The Tang Dynasty*. Westport, CT: Greenwood Press, 2002.

Bentley, Jerry H. *Old World Encounters: Cross-Cultural Contacts and Exchanges in Pre-Modern Times*. New York: Oxford University Press, 1993.

Bergman, Christopher A. and Edward McEwen. "Sinew-Reinforced and Composite Bows: Technology, Function, and Social Implications." In *Projectile Technology*. Edited by Heidi Knecht, 143–60. Interdisciplinary Contributions to Archaeology. New York and London: Plenum Press, 1997.

Bielenstein, Hans. *The Restoration of the Han Dynasty*, vol. 2: *The Civil War*. In *Bulletin of the Museum of Far Eastern Antiquities* (Stockholm), 31 (1959), 1–287.

Bivar, A.D.H. "The Stirrup and Its Origins." *Oriental Art*, n.s., 1.2 (Summer 1955), 61–5.

Bivar, A.D.H. "Cavalry Equipment and Tactics on the Euphrates Frontier." *Dumbarton Oaks Papers* 26 (1972), 271–91.

Black, Jeremy. *Rethinking Military History*. London and New York: Routledge, 2004.

Bloch, Marc. *The Historian's Craft*. Translated by Peter Putnam. New York: Alfred A. Knopf, 1953.

Boodberg, Peter A. "The Art of War in Ancient China: A Study Based upon the Dialogues of Li Duke of Wei." Ph.D. dissertation, University of California, 1930.

Boodberg, Peter A. "Marginalia to the Histories of the Northern Dynasties." *Harvard Journal of Asiatic Studies* 3 (1938), 223–53.

Bray, Francesca and Joseph Needham. *Science and Civilisation in China*, vol. 6, part 2: *Agriculture*. Cambridge: Cambridge University Press, 1984.

Burne, Alfred H. *Battlefields of England*. London: Methuen and Co., 1950.

Carrié, Jean-Michel and Sylvain Janniard. "L'armée romaine tardive dans quelques travaux récents: 1re Partie, L'institution militaire et les modes de combat." *L'Antiquité Tardive* 8 (2000), 321–41.

Cen Zhongmian 岑仲勉. *Fubing zhidu yanjiu* 府兵制度研究. Shanghai: Renmin chubanshe, 1957.

Cen Zhongmian. *Sui Tang shi* 隋唐史. Beijing: Gaodeng jiaoyu chubanshe, 1957.

Chaliand, Gerard. *Nomadic Empires: From Mongolia to the Danube.* Translated by A. M. Berrett. New Brunswick, NJ: Transaction Publishers, 2004.

Chase, Kenneth. *Firearms: A Global History to 1700.* Cambridge: Cambridge University Press, 2003.

Chen Qinglong 陳慶隆. "Tujue xizu de bingqi" 突厥系族的兵器. *Dalu zazhi* 68.5 (May 15, 1984), 234–8.

Chen, Sanping. *Multicultural China in the Early Middle Ages.* Philadelphia: University of Pennsylvania Press, 2012.

Chen Yinke 陳寅恪. "Lun Tangdai zhi fanjiang yu fubing" 論唐代之蕃將與府兵. In *Chen Yinke xiansheng wen shi lunji*陳寅恪先生文史論集, vol. 2, 27–40. Hong Kong: Wenwen chubanshe, 1972.

Cheng Liangshu 鄭良樹, ed. *Xu Weishu tongkao* 續偽書通考. Taipei: Taiwan xuesheng shuju, 1984.

Cheng Yufeng 程玉鳳. "Tangdai Zhaoling liu jun shike shi kao" 唐代昭陵六駿石刻史考. *Gu jin tan*, No. 184 (September 1980), 14–16.

Chevedden, Paul E. "Artillery in Late Antiquity: Prelude to the Middle Ages." In *The Medieval City under Siege.* Edited by Ivy A. Corfis and Michael Wolfe, 131–73. Woodbridge, UK: The Boydell Press, 1995.

Citino, Robert M. *The German Way of War: From the Thirty Years' War to the Third Reich.* Lawrence: University Press of Kansas, 2005.

Clark, Colin and Margaret Haswell. *The Economics of Subsistence Agriculture.* Fourth edition. London: Macmillan and St. Martin's Press, 1970.

Cohen, Eliot A. *Citizens and Soldiers: The Dilemmas of Military Service.* Ithaca and London: Cornell University Press, 1985.

Cormack, Robin. *Writing in Gold: Byzantine Society and Its Icons.* London: George Philip, 1985.

Cosentino, Salvatore. "The Syrianos' Strategikon: A Ninth Century Source?" *Bizantinistica: Rivista di studi bizantini e slavi*, n.s. 2 (2000), 243–80.

Coulston, J.C. "Roman, Parthian and Sassanid Tactical Developments." In *The Defence of the Roman and Byzantine East: Proceedings of a Colloquium Held at the University of Sheffield in April 1986.* Edited by Philip Freeman and David Kennedy, Part I, 59–75. British Institute of Archaeology at Ankara Monograph No. 8; BAR International Series 297 (i). N.p.: British Institute of Archaeology at Ankara, 1986.

Coulston, Jon. "Arms and Armour of the Late Roman Army." In *A Companion to Medieval Arms and Armour.* Edited by David Nicolle, 3–24. Woodbridge, UK: The Boydell Press, 2002.

Creel, H.G. "The Role of the Horse in Chinese History." *American Historical Review* 70.3 (April 1965), 647–72.

Crosby, Alfred W. *Throwing Fire: Projectile Technology Through History.* Cambridge: Cambridge University Press, 2002.

Curta, Florin. *Southeastern Europe in the Middle Ages, 500–1250.* Cambridge: Cambridge University Press, 2006.

Czeglédy, K. "From East to West: The Age of Nomadic Migrations in Eurasia." *Archivum Eurasiae Medii Aevi* 3 (1983), 25–125.

Dain, Alphonse. "Les Stratégistes byzantins." *Travaux et mémoires* 2 (1967), 317–92.

Darkó, Eugène. "Influences Touraniennes sur l'évolution de l'art militaire des Grecs, des Romains et des Byzantins." *Byzantion* 12 (1937), 119–47.

Decker, Michael J. *The Byzantine Art of War.* Yardley, PA: Westholme Publishing, 2013.

De Crespigny, Rafe. *Northern Frontier: The Policies and Strategy of the Later Han Empire.* Canberra: Faculty of Asian Studies, Australian National University, 1984.

Demiéville, Paul. *Le Concile de Lhasa: Une controverse sur le quiétisme entre Bouddhistes de l'Inde et de la Chine au VIIIe siècle de l'ère chrétienne.* 1952. Rpt. Paris: Collège de France, Institut des Hautes Études Chinoises, 1987.

Dennis, George T. "Flies, Mice and the Byzantine Crossbow." *Byzantine and Modern Greek Studies* 7 (1981), 1–5.

Dennis, George T. "Byzantine Battle Flags." *Byzantinische Forschungen* 8 (1982), 51–9.

Dennis, George T. "Byzantine Heavy Artillery: The Helepolis." *Greek, Roman, and Byzantine Studies* 39 (1998), 99–115.

Dennis, George T. "Defenders of the Christian People: Holy War in Byzantium." In *The Crusades from the Perspective of Byzantium and the Muslim World.* Edited by Angeliki E. Laiou and Roy P. Mottahedeh, 31–9. Washington, DC: Dumbarton Oaks, 2001.

DeVries, Kelly and Robert Douglas Smith. *Medieval Military Technology.* Second edition. Toronto: University of Toronto Press, 2012.

Di Cosmo, Nicola. *Ancient China and Its Enemies: The Rise of Nomadic Power in East Asian History.* Cambridge: Cambridge University Press, 2002.

Dien, Albert E. "A Study of Early Chinese Armor." *Artibus Asiae* 43 (1982), 5–66.

Dien, Albert E. "The Stirrup and Its Effect on Chinese Military History." *Ars Orientalis* 16 (1986), 33–56.

Dien, Albert E. *Six Dynasties Civilization.* New Haven and London: Yale University Press, 2007.

Dixon, Karen R. and Pat Southern. *The Roman Cavalry: From the First to the Third Century AD.* London: B.T. Batsford Ltd., 1992.

Drews, Robert. *Early Riders: The Beginnings of Mounted Warfare in Asia and Europe.* London and New York: Routledge, 2004.

Eadie, John W. "The Development of Roman Mailed Cavalry." *Journal of Roman Studies* 57 (1967), 161–73.

Elton, Hugh. *Warfare in Roman Europe, AD 350–425.* Oxford: Clarendon Press, 1996.

Engels, Donald W. *Alexander the Great and the Logistics of the Macedonian Army.* Berkeley and Los Angeles: University of California Press, 1978.

Farrokh, Kaveh. *Shadows in the Desert: Ancient Persia at War.* Oxford: Osprey Publishing, 2007.

Feng, Huiyun. *Chinese Strategic Culture and Foreign Policy Decision-Making: Confucianism, Leadership and War.* London and New York: Routledge, 2007.

Foley, Vernard, George Palmer, and Werner Soedel. "The Crossbow." *Scientific American* 252.1 (January 1985), 104–10.

Fotiou, A. "Recruitment Shortages in Sixth-Century Byzantium." *Byzantion* 58 (1988), 65–77.

Frank, Andre Gunder. *The Centrality of Central Asia.* Amsterdam: VU University Press, 1992.

Franke, Herbert. "The Siege and Defense of Towns in Medieval China." In *Chinese Ways in Warfare.* Edited by Frank A. Kierman, Jr. and John K. Fairbank, 151–201. Cambridge, MA: Harvard University Press, 1974.

Friday, Karl F. *Samurai, Warfare and the State in Early Medieval Japan.* Warfare and History. New York and London: Routledge, 2004.

Fu Lecheng 傅樂成. "Huihe ma yu Shuofang bing" 迴紇馬與朔方兵. In *Han-Tang shi lunji* 漢唐史論集, 305–17. Taipei: Lianjing, 1977.

Fuller, J.F.C. *The Foundations of the Science of War*. London: Hutchinson and Co., 1926.

Geertz, Clifford. *The Interpretation of Cultures*. New York: Basic Books, 1973.

Gillingham, John. "'Up with Orthodoxy!' In Defense of Vegetian Warfare." *Journal of Medieval Military History* 2 (2004), 149–58.

Gilmor, Carroll M. "The Introduction of the Traction Trebuchet into the Latin West." *Viator* 12 (1981), 1–8.

Golden, Peter B. *An Introduction to the History of the Turkic Peoples: Ethnogenesis and State Formation in Medieval and Early Modern Eurasia and the Middle East*. Turcologica, Band 9. Wiesbaden: Otto Harrassowitz, 1992.

Golden, Peter B. "War and Warfare in the Pre-Činggisid Western Steppes of Eurasia." In *Warfare in Inner Asian History, 500–1800*. Edited by Nicola Di Cosmo, 105–72. Leiden: Brill, 2002.

Gorelik, Michael. "Arms and Armour in South-Eastern Europe in the Second Half of the First Millennium AD." In *A Companion to Medieval Arms and Armour*. Edited by David Nicolle, 127–47. Woodbridge, Suffolk: The Boydell Press, 2002.

Goubert, Paul. "Religion et superstitions dan l'armée byzantine à la fin du VIe siècle." *Orientalia Christiana Periodica* 13 (1947), 495–500.

Graff, David A. "The Battle of Huo-i." *Asia Major*, 3rd Series, 5.1 (1992), 33–54.

Graff, David A. "Early T'ang Generalship and the Textual Tradition." Ph.D. dissertation, Princeton University, 1995.

Graff, David A. "Dou Jiande's Dilemma: Logistics, Strategy, and State-Formation in Seventh-Century China." In *Warfare in Chinese History*. Edited by Hans van de Ven, 75–105. Leiden: Brill, 2000.

Graff, David A. *Medieval Chinese Warfare, 300–900*. Warfare and History. London and New York: Routledge, 2002.

Graff, David A. "Strategy and Contingency in the Tang Defeat of the Eastern Turks, 629–630." In *Warfare in Inner Asian History (500–1800)*. Edited by Nicola Di Cosmo, 33–71. Handbook of Oriental Studies, section 8, vol. 6. Leiden: Brill, 2002.

Graff, David A. "Li Shimin and the Representation of Military Leadership in Medieval China." In *Knight and Samurai: Actions and Images of Elite Warriors in Europe and East Asia*. Edited by Rosemarie Deist, 155–67. Göppinger Arbeiten zur Germanistik, Nr. 707. Göppingen: Kümmerle Verlag, 2003.

Graff, David A. "Li Jing's Antecedents: Continuity and Change in the Pragmatics of Medieval Chinese Warfare." *Early Medieval China* vols. 13–14, part 1 (2007), 81–97.

Graff, David A. "Narrative Maneuvers: The Representation of Battle in Tang Historical Writing." In *Military Culture in Imperial China*. Edited by Nicola Di Cosmo, 141–64. Cambridge, MA: Harvard University Press, 2009.

Greatrex, Geoffrey. *Rome and Persia at War, 502–532*. Leeds: Francis Cairns, 1998.

Grenier, John. *The First Way of War: American War Making on the Frontier, 1607–1814*. Cambridge: Cambridge University Press, 2005.

Gu Jiguang 谷霽光. *Fubing zhidu kaoshi* 府兵制度考釋. Shanghai: Shanghai renmin chubanshe, 1962. Rpt. Taipei: Hongwenguan chubanshe, 1985.

Gu Yiqing 古怡青. *Tangdai fubing zhidu xingshuai yanjiu: cong weishi fudan tanqi* 唐代府兵制度興衰研究: 從衛士負擔談起. Taipei: Xin wenfeng chuban youxian gongsi, 2002.

Guo Dehe 郭德河. *Gudai bingqi* 古代兵器. Beijing: Zhongguo da baike quanshu chubanshe, 2006.

Guo Rugui 郭汝瑰. *Binglei* 兵壘. 1991. Vol. 6 of *Zhongguo junshi shi* 中國軍事史. 8 vols. Beijing: Jiefangjun chubanshe, 1983–1991.

Haldon, John. *Warfare, State and Society in the Byzantine World, 565–1204*. Warfare and History. London: UCL Press, 1999.

Haldon, John. *The Byzantine Wars*. Stroud, Gloucestershire: Tempus, 2001.

Haldon, John. "Some Aspects of Early Byzantine Arms and Armour." In *A Companion to Medieval Arms and Armour*. Edited by David Nicolle, 65–79. Woodbridge, UK: The Boydell Press, 2002.

Haldon, John. *Byzantium at War, AD 600–1453*. Rpt. New York and London: Routledge, 2003.

Haldon, John. "Roads and Communications in the Byzantine Empire: Wagons, Horses, and Supplies." In *Logistics in the Age of the Crusades: Proceedings of a Workshop Held at the Centre for Medieval Studies, University of Sydney, 30 September to 4 October 2002*. Edited by John H. Pryor, 131–58. Aldershot, Hampshire: Ashgate, 2006.

Haldon, John, Andrew Lacey and Colin Hewes. "'Greek Fire' Revisited: Recent and Current Research." In *Byzantine Style, Religion and Civilization: In Honour of Sir Steven Runciman*, 290–325. Cambridge: Cambridge University Press, 2006.

Haldon, John. *A Critical Commentary on the Taktika of Leo VI*. Washington, DC: Dumbarton Oaks, 2014.

Haldon, John F. "Solenarion – The Byzantine Crossbow?" *Historical Journal of the University of Birmingham* 12 (1970), 155–7.

Haldon, John F. "Some Aspects of Byzantine Military Technology from the Sixth to the Tenth Centuries." *Byzantine and Modern Greek Studies* 1 (1975), 11–47.

Hall, Bert S. "Crossbows and Crosswords." *Isis* 64 (1973), 527–33.

Halperin, Charles J. *Russia and the Golden Horde: The Mongol Impact on Medieval Russian History*. Bloomington: Indiana University Press, 1987.

Halsall, Guy. *Warfare and Society in the Barbarian West, 450–900*. Warfare and History. London and New York: Routledge, 2003.

Hamaguchi Shigekuni 濱口重國. "Fuhei seido yori shin heisei e" 府兵制度より新兵制 へ *Shigaku zasshi* 41 (1930).

Handel, Michael I. *Masters of War: Classical Strategic Thought*. Second, revised edition. London: Frank Cass, 1996.

Hansen, Valerie. *The Silk Road: A New History*. New York: Oxford University Press, 2012.

Hanson, Victor Davis. *The Western Way of War: Infantry Battle in Classical Greece*. New York: Oxford University Press, 1990 (Originally published by Knopf in 1989).

Hanson, Victor Davis. "Hoplite Battle as Ancient Greek Warfare: When, Where, and Why?" In *War and Violence in Ancient Greece*. Edited by Hans van Wees, 201–32. London and Swansea: Duckworth and The Classical Press of Wales, 2000.

Hanson, Victor Davis. *Carnage and Culture: Landmark Battles in the Rise of Western Power*. New York: Random House, 2001.

Harrison, Richard W. *The Russian Way of War: Operational Art, 1904–1940*. Lawrence: University Press of Kansas, 2001.

Headrick, Daniel R. *The Tools of Empire: Technology and European Imperialism in the Nineteenth Century*. New York: Oxford University Press, 1981.

Heather, Peter. "The Huns and the End of the Roman Empire in Western Europe." *English Historical Review* 110 (1995), 4–41.

Herzog, Chaim, and Mordechai Gichon. *Battles of the Bible*. Toronto: Stoddart Publishing Company, 1997.

Heuser, Beatrice. *The Evolution of Strategy: Thinking War from Antiquity to the Present*. Cambridge: Cambridge University Press, 2010.

Hibino Takeo 日比野丈夫. "Tōdai Ho-shō-fu bunsho no kenkyū" 唐代蒲昌府文書の研究. *Tōhō gakuhō* 33 (1963), 267–314.

Hill, Donald R. "Trebuchets." *Viator* 4 (1973), 99–116.

Hill, John E. *Through the Jade Gate to Rome.* Charleston, SC: Booksurge, 2009.

Howard-Johnston, James. "The Two Great Powers in Late Antiquity: A Comparison." In *The Byzantine and Early Islamic Near East,* vol. 3: *States, Resources and Armies.* Edited by Averil Cameron, 157–226. Studies in Late Antiquity and Early Islam, 1. Princeton, NJ: The Darwin Press, 1995.

Howard-Johnston, James. "Heraclius' Persian Campaigns and the Revival of the East Roman Empire, 622–630." *War in History* 6.1 (January 1999), 1–44.

Huang K'uan-ch'ung 黃寬重. "Songdai cheng guo de fangyu sheshi ji cailiao" 宋代城郭的防禦設施及材料. *Dalu zazhi* 81.2 (August 25, 1990), 1–2.

Hyland, Ann. *Training the Roman Cavalry: From Arrian's Ars Tactica.* Stroud, Gloucestershire: Alan Sutton, 1993.

Hyland, Ann. *The Medieval Warhorse: From Byzantium to the Crusades.* Stroud, Gloucestershire: Alan Sutton, 1994.

James, Simon. "The Impact of Steppe Peoples and the Partho-Sasanian World on the Development of Roman Military Equipment and Dress, 1st to 3rd Centuries AD." In *Arms and Armour as Indicators of Cultural Transfer: The Steppes and the Ancient World from Hellenistic Times to the Early Middle Ages.* Edited by Markus Mode and Jürgen Tubach in cooperation with G. Sophia Vashalomidze, 357–92. Nomaden und Sesshafte, Band 4. Wiesbaden: Dr. Ludwig Reichert Verlag, 2006.

Jamieson, John Charles. "The *Samguk Sagi* and the Unification Wars." Ph.D. dissertation, University of California at Berkeley, 1969.

Johnston, Alastair Iain. *Cultural Realism: Strategic Culture and Grand Strategy in Chinese History.* Princeton, NJ: Princeton University Press, 1995.

Jones, A.H.M. *The Later Roman Empire, 284–602: A Social, Economic, and Administrative Survey.* Norman: University of Oklahoma Press, 1964. 2 vols.

Jullien, François. *A Treatise on Efficacy: Between Western and Chinese Thinking.* Translated by Janet Lloyd. Honolulu: University of Hawai'i Press, 2004.

Kaegi, Walter E. *Byzantium and the Early Islamic Conquests.* Cambridge: Cambridge University Press, 1992.

Kaegi, Walter E. "Byzantine Logistics: Problems and Perspectives." In *Feeding Mars: Logistics in Western Warfare from the Middle Ages to the Present.* Edited by John A. Lynn, 39–55. Boulder, CO: Westview Press, 1993.

Kaegi, Walter E. *Heraclius: Emperor of Byzantium.* Cambridge: Cambridge University Press, 2003.

Kaegi, Walter Emil. *Byzantine Military Unrest, 471–843: An Interpretation.* Amsterdam: Hakkert, 1981.

Kaegi, Walter Emil Jr. *Some Thoughts on Byzantine Military Strategy.* Brookline, MA: Hellenic College Press, 1983.

Kang Le 康樂. *Tangdai qianqi de bianfang* 唐代前期的邊防. Taipei: National Taiwan University, 1979.

Keegan, John. *The Mask of Command.* New York: Viking, 1987.

Keegan, John. *A History of Warfare.* New York: Alfred A. Knopf, 1993.

Kegasawa Yasunori 氣賀澤保規. *Fuheisei no kenkyū* 府兵制度の研究. Tokyo: Dohosha, 1999.

Kennedy, Hugh. *The Armies of the Caliphs: Military and Society in the Early Islamic State.* London and New York: Routledge, 2001.

Kierman, Frank A. Jr. "Phases and Modes of Combat in Early China." In *Chinese Ways in Warfare*. Edited by Frank A. Kierman. Jr. and John K. Fairbank, 27–66. Cambridge, MA: Harvard University Press, 1974.

Kern, Paul Bentley. *Ancient Siege Warfare*. Bloomington and Indianapolis: Indiana University Press, 1999.

Kikuchi Hideo 菊池英夫. "Tōdai heibo no seikaku to meishō to ni tsuite" 唐代兵募の性格と名稱戶について. *Shien* 67–8 (May 1956), 75–98.

Kikuchi Hideo. "Setsudoshisei kakuritsu izen ni okeru gun seido no tenkai" 節度使制確立以前における"軍"制度の展開. *Tōyō gakuhō* 44.2 (September 1961), 54–88.

Kikuchi Hideo. "Tō setsushōfu no bunpu mondai ni kansuru ichi kaishaku" 唐折衝府の分布問題に關する一解釋. *Tōyōshi kenkyū* 27.2 (September 1968), 1–37.

Kolbaba, Tia M. "Fighting for Christianity: Holy War in the Byzantine Empire." *Byzantion* 68 (1998), 194–221.

Kollautz, Arnulf and Hisayuki Miyakawa. *Geschichte und Kultur eines völkerwanderungszeitlichen Nomadenvolkes*. Klagenfurt: Geschichtsverein f. Kärnten, 1970. 2 vols.

Krentz, Peter. "Deception in Archaic and Classical Greek Warfare." In *War and Violence in Ancient Greece*. Edited by Hans van Wees, 167–200. London and Swansea: Duckworth and The Classical Press of Wales, 2000.

Lai, Swee Fo. "The Military and Defense System under the T'ang Dynasty." Ph.D. dissertation, Princeton University, 1986.

Lee, A.D. *War in Late Antiquity: A Social History*. Malden, MA: Blackwell Publishing, 2007.

Lei Jiaji 雷家驥. *Li Jing* 李靖. Zhanluejia congshu 戰略家叢書. Yonghe, Taiwan: Lianming wenhua youxian gongsi, 1980.

Lewis, Mark Edward. *Sanctioned Violence in Early China*. Albany: SUNY Press, 1990.

Lewis, Mark Edward. "The Han Abolition of Universal Military Service." In *Warfare in Chinese History*. Edited by Hans van de Ven, 33–76. Leiden: Brill, 2000.

Lewis, Mark Edward. *The Early Chinese Empires: Qin and Han*. Cambridge, MA: The Belknap Press of Harvard University Press, 2007.

Leyser, Karl. "Early Medieval Warfare." In *The Battle of Maldon: Fiction and Fact*. Edited by Janet Cooper, 87–108. London: The Hambledon Press, 1993.

Li Jinxiu 李錦繡. "Modao yu da Tang diguo de junshi" 陌刀與大唐帝國的軍事. In *Tangdai zhidu shi lue lun gao* 唐代制度史略論稿, 295–308. Beijing: Zhongguo zhengfa daxue chubanshe, 1998.

Li Shutong 李樹桐. "Tangdai zhi junshi yu ma" 唐代之軍事與馬. In *Tang shi yanjiu* 唐史研究. Taipei: Taiwan Commercial Press, 1979, 231–76.

Li Xuezhi 李學智. "Tang Taizong Zhaoling liu jun shike jianjie" 唐太宗昭陵六駿石刻簡介. *Dalu zazhi* 16.3 (February 15, 1958), 5, 30.

Li Xunxiang 李訓詳. *Xian Qin de bingjia* 先秦的兵家. Taipei: National Taiwan University, 1991.

Li Zhen 李震. *Zhongguo junshi jiaoyu shi* 中國軍事教育史. Taipei: Zhongyang wenwu gongying she, 1983.

Liddell Hart, B.H. "The Concentrated Essence of War." *Infantry Journal* 27 (1930), 607–8.

Lindner, Rudi Paul. "Nomadism, Horses and Huns." *Past and Present*, No. 92 (August 1981), 3–19.

Littauer, Mary Aiken. "Early Stirrups." *Antiquity* 55 (1981), 99–105.

Little, Lester K., ed. *Plague and the End of Late Antiquity: The Pandemic of 541–750*. New York: Cambridge University Press, 2007.

Liu Hongzhang 劉宏章. "*Liu tao* chutan" 六韜初探. *Zhongguo zhexue shi yanjiu* 1985, No. 2 (April 1985), 48–56.

Loewe, Michael. "The Campaigns of Han Wu-ti." In *Chinese Ways in Warfare*. Edited by Frank A. Kierman, Jr. and John K. Fairbank, 67–122. Cambridge, MA: Harvard University Press, 1974.

Lorge, Peter A. *Chinese Martial Arts: From Antiquity to the Twenty-first Century*. New York: Cambridge University Press, 2012.

Luttwak, Edward N. *Strategy: The Logic of War and Peace*. Cambridge, MA: The Belknap Press of Harvard University Press, 1987.

Luttwak, Edward N. *The Grand Strategy of the Byzantine Empire*. Cambridge, MA: The Belknap Press of Harvard University Press, 2009.

Lynn, John A. *Battle: A History of Combat and Culture*. Boulder, CO: Westview Press, 2003.

Ma Junmin 馬俊民 and Wang Shiping 王世平. *Tangdai mazheng* 唐代馬政. Taipei: Wunan tushu chuban gongsi, 1995.

MacMullen, Ramsay. *Soldier and Civilian in the Later Roman Empire*. Cambridge, MA: Harvard University Press, 1963.

McCormick, Michael. *Eternal Victory: Triumphal Rulership in Late Antiquity, Byzantium, and the Early Medieval West*. Cambridge: Cambridge University Press, 1986.

McCotter, Stephen. "Byzantines, Avars and the Introduction of the Trebuchet." 2003. Paper posted at the *De Re Militari* web site: http://web.archive.org/web/20110720012051/ http://www.deremilitari.org/resources/articles/mcotter1.htm (accessed May 7, 2013).

McEwen, Edward, Robert L. Miller, and Christopher A. Bergman. "Early Bow Design and Construction." *Scientific American* 264.6 (June 1991), 76–82.

McGeer, Eric. "Byzantine Siege Warfare in Theory and Practice." In *The Medieval City under Siege*. Edited by Ivy A. Corfis and Michael Wolfe, 123–9. Woodbridge, UK: The Boydell Press, 1995.

McGeer, Eric. *Sowing the Dragon's Teeth: Byzantine Warfare in the Tenth Century*. Washington, DC: Dumbarton Oaks, 1995.

McLeod, Wallace. "The Range of the Ancient Bow." *Phoenix: The Journal of the Classical Association of Canada* 19 (1965), 1–14.

McMullen, David. *State and Scholars in T'ang China*. Cambridge: Cambridge University Press, 1988.

McNeill, William H. *The Age of Gunpowder Empires, 1450–1800*. Washington, DC: American Historical Association, 1989.

McNeill, William H. *The Rise of the West: A History of the Human Community*. Rpt. Chicago: University of Chicago Press, 1991.

McNeill, William H. *Keeping Together in Time: Dance and Drill in Human History*. Cambridge, MA: Harvard University Press, 1995.

Maenchen-Helfen, J. Otto. *The World of the Huns: Studies in Their History and Culture*. Edited by Max Knight. Berkeley and Los Angeles: University of California Press, 1973.

Mango, Cyril. "The Triumphal Way of Constantinople and the Golden Gate." *Dumbarton Oaks Papers* 54 (2000). http://www.doaks.org/resources/publications/dumbarton-oaks-papers/dop54/dp54ch9.pdf (accessed September 29, 2014).

Marsden, E.W. *Greek and Roman Artillery: Historical Development*. Oxford: Oxford University Press, 1969.

Millar, Fergus. *A Greek Roman Empire: Power and Belief under Theodosius II (408–450)*. Berkeley and Los Angeles: University of California Press, 2006.

Miller, Timothy S. and John Nesbitt, eds. *Peace and War in Byzantium: Essays in Honor of George T. Dennis, S.J.* Washington, DC: The Catholic University of America Press, 1995.

Mode, Markus. "Art and Ideology at Taq-i Bustan: The Armoured Equestrian." In *Arms and Armour as Indicators of Cultural Transfer: The Steppes and the Ancient World from Hellenistic Times to the Early Middle Ages*. Edited by Markus Mode and Jürgen Tubach in cooperation with G. Sophia Vashalomidze, 393–413. Nomaden und Sesshafte, Band 4. Wiesbaden: Dr. Ludwig Reichert Verlag, 2006.

Morillo, Stephen. "Battle Seeking: The Contexts and Limits of Vegetian Strategy." *Journal of Medieval Military History* 1 (2002), 21–41.

Morris, Ian. *War! What Is It Good For? – Conflict and the Progress of Civilization from Primates to Robots*. New York: Farrar, Straus and Giroux, 2014.

Murphey, Rhoads. "An Ecological History of Central Asian Nomadism." In *Ecology and Empire: Nomads in the Cultural Evolution of the Old World*. Edited by Gary Seaman, 41–58. Los Angeles: Ethnographics/USC, Center for Visual Anthropology, University of Southern California, 1989.

Myasnikova, A.V. *Handbook of Food Products: Grain and Its Products*. Translated by S. Nemchonok. Jerusalem: Israel Program for Scientific Translations, 1969.

Needham, Joseph. *The Development of Iron and Steel Technology in China*. Second Biennial Dickinson Memorial Lecture to the Newcomen Society, 1956. London: The Newcomen Society, 1958.

Needham, Joseph. *Science and Civilisation in China*, vol. 4: *Physics and Physical Technology*, part 2: *Mechanical Engineering*. Cambridge: Cambridge University Press, 1965.

Needham, Joseph. "China's Trebuchets, Manned and Counterweighted." In *On Pre-Modern Technology and Science, A Volume of Studies in Honor of Lynn White, Jr.* Edited by Bert S. Hall and Delno C. West, 107–45. Published under the auspices of the Center for Medieval and Renaissance Studies, University of California, Los Angeles. Malibu, CA: Undena Publications, 1976.

Needham, Joseph, and Robin D.S. Yates. *Science and Civilisation in China*, vol. 5: *Chemistry and Chemical Technology*, part 6: *Military Technology: Missiles and Sieges*. Cambridge: Cambridge University Press, 1994.

Ni Jinsheng 倪今生. "Wu Hu luan Hua qianye de Zhongguo jingji" 五胡亂華前夜的中國經濟. *Shi huo banyuekan* 1.7 (March 1, 1935), 38–49.

Nicholson, Helen. *Medieval Warfare: Theory and Practice of War in Europe, 300–1500*. Basingstoke, Hampshire: Palgrave Macmillan, 2004.

Nickel, Helmut. "The Mutual Influence of Europe and Asia in the Field of Arms and Armour." In *A Companion to Medieval Arms and Armour*. Edited by David Nicolle, 107–25. Woodbridge, Suffolk: The Boydell Press, 2002.

Nicolle, David. "Medieval Warfare: The Unfriendly Interface." *The Journal of Military History* 63 (1999), 579–99.

Nicolle, David. "Byzantine and Islamic Arms and Armour: Evidence for Mutual Influence." *Graeco-Arabic* IV (1991), 299–325. Rpt. in David Nicolle, *Warriors and their Weapons around the Time of the Crusades: Relationships between Byzantium, the West and the Islamic World*. Variorum Collected Studies Series. Aldershot, Hampshire: Ashgate, 2002.

Niida Noboru 仁井田陞. *Tōryō shūi* 唐令拾遺. Tokyo: Tōhō bunka gakuin Tōkyō kenkyūjo, 1933.

Nishimura, David. "Crossbow, Arrow Guides, and the *Solenarion*." *Byzantion* 58 (1988), 422–35.

Nolan, L.E. *Cavalry: Its History and Tactics*. Second edition. London: Thomas Bosworth, 1854.

Nunome Chōfū 布目潮渢. "Tōdai eji banjo no futan" 唐代衛士番上の負擔. In *Yamamoto hakushi kanreki kinen tōyōshi ronsō* 山本博士還暦記念東洋史論叢. Tokyo: Yamakawa shuppansha, 1972.

O'Byrne, Terrence Douglas. "Civil–Military Relations During the Middle T'ang: The Career of Kuo Tzu-i." Ph.D. dissertation, University of Illinois at Urbana-Champaign, 1982.

Ostrogorsky, George. *History of the Byzantine State.* Translated by Joan Hussey. Revised edition. New Brunswick, NJ: Rutgers University Press, 1969.

Otagi Hajime 愛宕元. "Tōdai shū ken jōkaku no kibo to kōzō" 唐代州城郭の規模と構造. In *Di yi jie guoji Tangdai xueshu huiyi lunwenji* 第一屆國際唐代學術會議論文 集, 648–82. Taipei: Zhonghua minguo Tangdai xuezhe lianyihui, 1989.

Parker, Geoffrey, ed. *The Cambridge Illustrated History of Warfare.* Cambridge: Cambridge University Press, 1995.

Parker, Geoffrey. *The Grand Strategy of Philip II.* New Haven and London: Yale University Press, 1998.

Paterson, W.F. "The Archers of Islam." *Journal of the Economic and Social History of the Orient* 9 (1966), 69–87.

Payne-Gallwey, Ralph. *A Treatise on the Construction, Power and Management of Turkish and Other Oriental Bows of Mediaeval and Later Times.* London: Longmans, Green, and Co., 1907.

Peers, Chris and Michael Perry. *Imperial Chinese Armies (2), 590–1260 AD.* London: Osprey, 1996.

Peng Guangqian and Yao Youzhi, eds. *The Science of Military Strategy.* Beijing: Military Science Publishing House, 2005.

Perdue, Peter C. *China Marches West: The Qing Conquest of Central Eurasia.* Cambridge, MA: The Belknap Press of Harvard University Press, 2005.

Peterson, Charles. "The Autonomy of the Northeastern Provinces in the Period Following the An Lu-shan Rebellion." Ph.D. dissertation, University of Washington, 1966.

Peterson, Charles A. "Regional Defense Against the Central Power: The Huai-hsi Campaign, 815–817." In *Chinese Ways in Warfare.* Edited by Frank A. Kierman, Jr. and John K. Fairbank, 123–50. Cambridge, MA: Harvard University Press, 1974.

Pohl, Walter. *Die Awaren: Ein Steppenvolk in Mitteleuropa, 567–822 n.Chr.* Munich: Verlag C.H. Beck, 1989.

Pope, Saxton T. "A Study of Bows and Arrows." *University of California Publications in American Archaeology and Ethnology* 13.9 (August 10, 1923), 329–414.

Porter, Patrick. *Military Orientalism: Eastern War Through Western Eyes.* New York: Columbia University Press, 2009.

Pryor, John H. and Elizabeth M. Jeffreys. *The Age of the Dromon: The Byzantine Navy ca 500–1204.* Leiden and Boston: Brill, 2006.

Pulleyblank, Edwin G. *The Background of the Rebellion of An Lu-shan.* London: Oxford University Press, 1955.

Pulleyblank, Edwin G. "Registration of Population in China in the Sui and T'ang Periods." *Journal of the Economic and Social History of the Orient* 4 (1961), 289–301.

Pulleyblank, E.G. "The Chinese and Their Neighbors in Prehistoric and Early Historic Times." In *The Origins of Chinese Civilization.* Edited by David N. Keightley, 411–66. Berkeley and Los Angeles: University of California Press, 1983.

Pulleyblank, Edwin G. "The Roman Empire as Known to Han China." *Journal of the American Oriental Society* 119.1 (1999), 1–79.

Purton, Peter. *A History of the Early Medieval Siege, c. 450–1220.* Woodbridge, UK: The Boydell Press, 2009.

Qi Sihe 齊思和. *Zhongguo he Baizhanting diguo de guanxi* 中國和拜占廷帝國的關係. Shanghai: Shanghai renmin chubanshe, 1956.

Rance, Philip. "Narses and the Battle of Taginae (Busta Gallorum) 552: Procopius and Sixth-Century Warfare." *Historia* 54 (2005), 424–72.

Raphals, Lisa. *Knowing Words: Wisdom and Cunning in the Classical Traditions of China and Greece*. Ithaca and London: Cornell University Press, 1992.

Raspopova, Valentina I. "Sogdian Arms and Armour in the Period of the Great Migrations." In *Arms and Armour as Indicators of Cultural Transfer: The Steppes and the Ancient World from Hellenistic Times to the Early Middle Ages*. Edited by Markus Mode and Jürgen Tubach in cooperation with G. Sophia Vashalomidze, 79–95. Nomaden und Sesshafte, Band 4. Wiesbaden: Dr. Ludwig Reichert Verlag, 2006.

Reuter, Timothy. "Carolingian and Ottonian Warfare." In *Medieval Warfare: A History*. Edited by Maurice Keen, 13–35. Oxford: Oxford University Press, 1999.

Robinson, H. Russell. *Oriental Armour*. London: Herbert Jenkins, 1967.

Rogers, Clifford J. "The Vegetian 'Science of Warfare' in the Middle Ages." *Journal of Medieval Military History* 1 (2002), 1–19.

Roland, Alex. "Secrecy, Technology, and War: Greek Fire and the Defense of Byzantium, 678–1204." *Technology and Culture* 33.4 (October 1992), 655–79.

Sawyer, Ralph D. *The Tao of Deception: Unorthodox Warfare in Historic and Modern China*. New York: Basic Books, 2007.

Sawyer, Ralph D. *Ancient Chinese Warfare*. New York: Basic Books, 2011.

Scheidel, Walter, ed. *Rome and China: Comparative Perspectives on Ancient World Empires*. New York: Oxford University Press, 2009.

Scobell, Andrew. *China's Use of Military Force: Beyond the Great Wall and the Long March*. Cambridge: Cambridge University Press, 2003.

Selby, Stephen. *Chinese Archery*. Hong Kong: Hong Kong University Press, 2000.

Selected Military Writings of Mao Tse-tung. Beijing: Foreign Languages Press, 1967.

Senger, Harro von. *The Book of Stratagems*. New York: Viking Penguin, 1991.

Sidebottom, Harry. *Ancient Warfare: A Very Short Introduction*. Oxford: Oxford University Press, 2004.

Sinor, Denis. "Horse and Pasture in Inner Asian History." *Oriens Extremus* 19 (1972), 171–84.

Sinor, Denis. "The Establishment and Dissolution of the Türk Empire." In *The Cambridge History of Early Inner Asia*, 285–316. Cambridge: Cambridge University Press, 1990.

Skaff, Jonathan Karam. "Tang Military Culture and Its Inner Asian Influences." In *Military Culture in Imperial China*. Edited by Nicola Di Cosmo, 165–91. Cambridge, MA: Harvard University Press, 2009.

Skaff, Jonathan Karam. *Sui–Tang China and Its Turko-Mongol Neighbors: Culture, Power, and Connections, 580–800*. New York: Oxford University Press, 2012.

Školjar, Sergej Aleksandrovič. "L'Artillerie de jet a l'époque Sung." *Études Sung*, Series 1: History and Institutions, vol. 1 (1970), 119–42.

Smith, John Masson Jr. "Äyn Jālūt: Mamlūk Success or Mongol Failure?" *Harvard Journal of Asiatic Studies* 44.2 (December 1984), 307–45.

Smith, Paul J. *Taxing Heaven's Storehouse: Horses, Bureaucrats, and the Destruction of the Sichuan Tea Industry, 1074–1224*. Cambridge, MA: Council on East Asian Studies, Harvard University, 1991.

Somers, Robert M. "Time, Space, and Structure in the Consolidation of the T'ang Dynasty (A.D. 617–700)." *Journal of Asian Studies* 45.5 (November 1986), 971–94.

Somlósi, É. "Restoration of the Csolnok Avar Iron Sword." *Acta Archaeologica Academiae Scientiarum Hungaricae* 40 (1988), 207–10.

Sondhaus, Lawrence. *Strategic Culture and Ways of War*. London and New York: Routledge, 2006.

Song Changlian 宋常廉. "Tangdai de mazheng" 唐代的馬政. *Dalu zazhi* 29.1–2 (July 15 and 31, 1964), 29–30, 61–2.

Southern, Pat, and Karen Ramsey Dixon. *The Late Roman Army*. New Haven and London: Yale University Press, 1996.

Stone, David R. *A Military History of Russia: From Ivan the Terrible to the War in Chechnya*. Westport, CT: Praeger Security International, 2006.

Sullivan, Denis. "Tenth Century Byzantine Offensive Siege Warfare: Instructional Prescriptions and Historical Practice." In *Byzantium at War (9th-12th Century)*. Edited by N. Oikonomidès, 179–200. Athens: Institute of Byzantine Research, 1997. Rpt. in John Haldon, *Byzantine Warfare, 497–518*. Aldershot, Hampshire: Ashgate, 2007.

Sun Jimin 孫繼民. *Tangdai xingjun zhidu yanjiu* 唐代行軍制度研究. Wen shi zhe daxi 文史哲大系, 87. Taipei: Wenjin chubanshe, 1995.

Sun Jimin. *Dunhuang Tulufan suo chu Tangdai junshi wenshu chutan* 敦煌吐魯番所出唐代軍事文書初探. Tang Research Foundation Studies. Beijing: Zhongguo shehui kexue chubanshe, 2000.

Swann, Nancy Lee. *Food and Money in Ancient China*. Princeton, NJ: Princeton University Press, 1950.

Szádeczky-Kardoss, Samuel. "The Avars." In *The Cambridge History of Early Inner Asia*. Edited by Denis Sinor, 206–28. Cambridge: Cambridge University Press, 1990.

Tang Geng'ou 唐耕耦. "Tangdai qianqi de bingmu" 唐代前期的兵募. *Lishi yanjiu* 1981, no. 4, 159–72.

Tang Zhangru 唐長孺. *Tangshu bingzhi jianzheng* 唐書兵志箋正. Beijing: Kexue chubanshe, 1957.

Tarner, W.T.S. "The Traction Trebuchet: A Reconstruction of an Early Medieval Siege Engine." *Technology and Culture* 36.1 (January 1995), 136–67.

Tekin, Talat. *A Grammar of Orkhon Turkic*. Bloomington: Indiana University, 1968.

Treadgold, Warren. *Byzantium and Its Army, 284–1081*. Stanford, CA: Stanford University Press, 1995.

Treadgold, Warren. *A History of the Byzantine State and Society*. Stanford, CA: Stanford University Press, 1997.

Tuplin, Christopher. "All the King's Horse: In Search of Achaemenid Persian Cavalry." In *New Perspectives on Ancient Warfare*. Edited by Garrett G. Fagan and Matthew Trundle, 100–82. Leiden: Brill, 2010.

Turney-High, Harry Holbert. *Primitive War: Its Practice and Concepts*. Second edition. Columbia: University of South Carolina Press, 1991.

Twitchett, D.C. *Financial Administration Under the T'ang Dynasty*. Cambridge: Cambridge University Press, 1970.

Twitchett, Denis. *The Writing of Official History Under the T'ang*. Cambridge: Cambridge University Press, 1992.

Van Creveld, Martin. *Supplying War: Logistics from Wallenstein to Patton*. Cambridge: Cambridge University Press, 1977.

Van Creveld, Martin. *Command in War*. Cambridge, MA: Harvard University Press, 1985.

Van Creveld, Martin. *Technology and War: From 2000 BC to the Present*. Revised edition. New York: The Free Press, 1991.

Verbruggen, J.F. *The Art of Warfare in Western Europe during the Middle Ages*. Amsterdam and New York: North-Holland Publishing Company, 1977.

Vernadsky, George. *Kievan Russia*. New Haven: Yale University Press, 1976.

Vryonis, Speros Jr. "The Evolution of Slavic Society and the Slavic Invasions in Greece: The Major Slavic Attack on Thessaloniki, A.D. 597." *Hesperia* 50 (1981), 378–90.

Waldron, Arthur. *The Great Wall of China: From History to Myth*. Cambridge: Cambridge University Press, 1990.

Wales, H.G. Quaritch. *Ancient South-East Asian Warfare*. London: Bernard Quaritch, 1952.

Wallacker, Benjamin E. "Studies in Medieval Chinese Siegecraft: The Siege of Yü-pi, A.D. 546." *Journal of Asian Studies* 28.4 (August 1969), 789–802.

Wallacker, Benjamin E. "Studies in Medieval Chinese Siegecraft: The Siege of Fengtian, A.D. 783." *Journal of Asian History* 33.2 (1999), 184–93.

Wang Yongxing 王永興. *Tangdai qianqi xibei junshi yanjiu* 唐代前期西北軍事研究. Beijing: Zhongguo shehui kexue chubanshe, 1994.

Wang Yuanchao 王援朝. "Tang chao jiaji juzhuang shuailuo, yu qing qibing xingqi zhi yuanyin" 唐初甲騎具裝衰落, 與輕騎兵興起之原因. *Lishi yanjiu* 1996, No. 4, 50–8.

Wang Zhenping. *Tang China in Multi-Polar Asia: A History of Diplomacy and War*. Honolulu: University of Hawai'i Press, 2013.

Webster, Graham. *The Roman Imperial Army of the First and Second Centuries A.D.* New York: Funk & Wagnalls, 1969.

Wechsler, Howard J. *Mirror to the Son of Heaven: Wei Cheng at the Court of T'ang T'ai-tsung*. New Haven and London: Yale University Press, 1974.

Wees, Hans van. "The Development of the Hoplite Phalanx: Iconography and Reality in the Seventh Century." In *War and Violence in Ancient Greece*, 125–66. London and Swansea: Duckworth and The Classical Press of Wales, 2000.

Wees, Hans van. *Greek Warfare: Myths and Realities*. London: Gerald Duckworth & Co. Ltd., 2004.

Wei Zhenfu 韋鎮福 et al. *Bingqi* 兵器. 1983. Vol. 1 of *Zhongguo junshi shi* 中國軍事史, edited by Guo Rugui 郭汝瑰 et al. 8 vols. Beijing: Jiefangjun chubanshe, 1983–91.

Weigley, Russell F. *The American Way of War: A History of United States Military Strategy and Policy*. Bloomington: Indiana University Press, 1973.

Weng Junxiong 翁俊雄. *Tang chu zhengqu yu renkou* 唐初政區與人口. Beijing: Beijing shifan xueyuan chubanshe, 1990.

Wheeler, Everett L. *Stratagem and the Vocabulary of Military Trickery*. Leiden: E.J. Brill, 1988.

Whitby, Michael. *The Emperor Maurice and His Historian: Theophylact Simocatta on Persian and Balkan Warfare*. Oxford: Clarendon Press, 1988.

Whitby, Michael. "Recruitment in Roman Armies from Justinian to Heraclius (*ca.* 565–615)." In *The Byzantine and Early Islamic Near East*, vol. 3: *States, Resources and Armies*. Edited by Averil Cameron, 61–124. Studies in Late Antiquity and Early Islam, 1. Princeton, NJ: The Darwin Press, 1995.

Whittow, Mark. *The Making of Orthodox Byzantium, 600–1025*. Basingstoke, Hampshire: Macmillan, 1996.

Wiita, John E. "The *Ethnika* in Byzantine Military Treatises." Ph.D. dissertation, University of Minnesota, 1977.

Wilbur, C. Martin. "The History of the Crossbow." *Annual Report, 1936*, 427–38. Washington, DC: Smithsonian Institution, 1937.

Worley, Leslie J. *Hippeis: The Cavalry of Ancient Greece*. Boulder, CO: Westview Press, 1994.

Wright, Arthur F. *The Sui Dynasty*. New York: Alfred A. Knopf, 1978.

Wright, David Curtis. "Nomadic Power, Sedentary Security, and the Crossbow." *Acta Orientalia* 58.1 (2005), 15–31.

Wu Chengluo 吳承洛. *Zhongguo du liang heng shi* 中國度量衡史. Shanghai: Shangwu yinshuguan, 1957.

Xu Baolin 許保林. *Zhongguo bingshu tonglan* 中國兵書通覽. Beijing: Jiefangjun chubanshe, 1990.

Xu Di 許荻. "Lüe tan Linyi Yinqueshan Han mu chutu de gudai bingshu canjian" 略談臨沂銀雀山出土的古代兵書殘簡. *Wenwu* 1974, No. 2, 27–31.

Yan Zhenwei 閻振維. "Zhaoling: Tangdai wenwu yicun de yi zuo baoku" 昭陵：唐代文物遺存的一座寶庫. *Renwen zazhi* 1980, No. 4, 77–81.

Yang Hong 楊泓. *Zhongguo gu bingqi luncong* 中國古兵器論叢. Second edition. Beijing: Wenwu chubanshe, 1985.

Yang Hong. *Gudai bingqi shihua* 古代兵器史話. Shanghai: Shanghai kexue jishu chubanshe, 1988.

Yang Hong, ed. *Weapons in Ancient China*. Translated by Zhang Lijing. Rego Park, NY: Science Press, 1992.

Yang Kuan 楊寬. *Zhongguo gudai ye tie jishu fazhan shi* 中國古代冶鐵技術發展史. Shanghai: Shanghai Renmin chubanshe, 1982.

Yarshater, Ehsan, ed. *The Cambridge History of Iran*, vol. 3(1): *The Seleucid, Parthian, and Sasanian Periods*. Cambridge: Cambridge University Press, 1983.

Yü Ying-shih. "Han Foreign Relations." In *The Cambridge History of China*, vol. 1: *The Ch'in and Han Empires, 221 B.C.–A.D. 220*, edited by Denis Twitchett and Michael Loewe, 377–462. Cambridge: Cambridge University Press, 1986.

Zhang Guogang 張國剛. "Tangdai jianjun zhidu kaolun" 唐代監軍制度考論. *Zhongguo shi yanjiu* 1981, No. 2, 120–32.

Zhang Guogang. *Tangdai zhengzhi zhidu yanjiu lunji* 唐代政治制度研究論集. Taipei: Wenjin chubanshe, 1994.

Zhang Qun 張群. *Tangdai fanjiang yanjiu* 唐代蕃將研究. Taipei: Lianjing, 1986.

Zhang Rongfang 張榮芳. "Tangdai zhongyang de wuqi guanzhi cuoshi" 唐代中央的武器管制措施. In *Di er jie guoji Tangdai xueshu huiyi lunwenji* 第二屆國際唐代學術會議論文集, vol. 2, 1351–66. Taipei: Wenjin chubanshe, 1993.

Zhang Xincheng 張心澂. *Weishu tongkao* 偽書通考. Shanghai: Shangwu yinshuguan, 1954.

Zhou Fengwu 周鳳五. "Dunhuang Tang xieben *Liu tao* canjuan jiaokanji" 敦煌唐寫本六韜殘卷校勘記. In *Diyijie guoji Tangdai xueshu huiyi lunwenji* 第一屆國際唐代學術會議論文集, 346–71. Taipei: Zhonghua minguo Tangdai xuezhe lianyihui, 1989.

Zhou Wei 周緯. *Zhongguo bingqi shigao* 中國兵器史稿. Taipei: Mingwen shuju, 1981.

Zhou Xibao 周錫保. *Zhongguo gudai fushi shi* 中國古代服飾史. Beijing: Zhongguo xiju chubanshe, 1984.

Index

Made in the USA
Columbia, SC
04 May 2021